Advance praise for *New Sincerity*

"For well over a decade, my conversations with Adam Kelly have made a vibrant addition to my writing life, both strengthening my awareness of my literary context and helping me to define—and even understand—what I'm trying to do."
—**Jennifer Egan**, author of *The Candy House*

"Adam Kelly is one of the liveliest and most exciting thinkers around."
—**Paul Murray**, author of *The Bee Sting*

"Kelly is a major voice in the scholarly conversation on contemporary US fiction. This book is both a lucid summary and a brilliant further development of his important arguments about New Sincerity aesthetics."
—**Lee Konstantinou**, University of Maryland, College Park

"*New Sincerity* is a blockbuster, the deepest account we have of the complex ethical orientation of a whole generation of US writers to neoliberal capitalism. Kelly ably revivifies the literary period immediately preceding our own in all its conflicted glory."
—**Mark McGurl**, Stanford University

"*New Sincerity* provides a compelling framework for understanding millennial American literature. Kelly traces a generation's commitment to sincerity in its fiction and culture, while revealing its failures to wholly escape the market values and dictates it contests."
—**Ralph Clare**, Boise State University

"This groundbreaking book is riveting to read, philosophically sophisticated, and politically insightful. Equally sensitive to the historical and the aesthetic, the economic and the existential, Kelly sets a new standard for the expressive power of literary criticism."
—**Martin Hägglund**, Yale University

New Sincerity

Post 45 Loren Glass and Kate Marshall, Editors
Post•45 Group, Editorial Committee

New Sincerity
American Fiction in
the Neoliberal Age

Adam Kelly

Stanford University Press
Stanford, California

Stanford University Press
Stanford, California

© 2024 by Adam Kelly. All rights reserved.

No part of this book may be reproduced or transmitted in any form or by any means, electronic or mechanical, including photocopying and recording, or in any information storage or retrieval system, without the prior written permission of Stanford University Press.

Printed in the United States of America on acid-free, archival-quality paper.

Library of Congress Cataloging-in-Publication Data
Names: Kelly, Adam, author.
Title: New sincerity : American fiction in the neoliberal age / Adam Kelly.
Other titles: Post 45.
Description: Stanford, California : Stanford University Press, 2024. | Series: Post·45 | Includes bibliographical references and index.
Identifiers: LCCN 2024003585 (print) | LCCN 2024003586 (ebook) | ISBN 9781503640269 (cloth) | ISBN 9781503640696 (paperback) | ISBN 9781503640702 (ebook)
Subjects: LCSH: American fiction—20th century—History and criticism. | American fiction—21st century—History and criticism. | Sincerity in literature.
Classification: LCC PS374.S55 K45 2024 (print) | LCC PS374.S55 (ebook) | DDC 813/.54091—dc23/eng/20240402
LC record available at https://lccn.loc.gov/2024003585
LC ebook record available at https://lccn.loc.gov/2024003586

Cover design: Jason Anscomb
Typeset by Newgen in Minion Pro 10/15

For Ríona, sincerely

Table of Contents

Acknowledgments ix

Introduction 1

1. Achieving the Art of Sincerity 43
2. New Economy, New Sincerity 88
3. Gendered Histories and Novel Genres 128
4. Freedom Struggle, Class Struggle, Sincerity Struggle 167
5. Seeing Like a Neoliberal 208
6. The Politics of Sincerity and the Sincerity of Politics 247

Conclusion: Sincerity in Common 291

Notes 297

Index 353

Acknowledgments

NEW SINCERITY **EMERGED AND COALESCED** over a decade and a half, and countless friends and colleagues have contributed to this book's making, vanishingly few of whom I can mention here. The earliest iteration of these ideas appeared in the first essay collection on David Foster Wallace, ushered into the world in 2010 by the dynamic duo of David Hering and Matt Bucher. That essay was published while I was completing my doctoral studies at University College Dublin, where I had the good fortune to work with John Brannigan and Ron Callan. Galvanized by the essay's reception, my initial attempt to pitch the larger project as a coherent entity took me to Harvard University under the generous mentorship of Werner Sollors, a two-year period during which my experience greatly widened and my thinking progressed apace. Thanks go especially to the members of the American Literature Colloquium for companionship and feedback, as well as to the inspiring students I taught in spring 2013 in a seminar on the generation of writers featured in this book. I also want to acknowledge the role played by the Irish Research Council in funding my research during much of this early period of my career.

There followed seven happy years teaching at the University of York, where so many colleagues enabled my growth as a reader and critic that it would be invidious to begin listing names lest I leave people out. I want, nevertheless, to acknowledge in particular the mentorship of Derek Attridge and the role played during this period by my five PhD students—Lola Boorman, Adam Bristow-Smith, Evan Lower, Joe Rollins, and Daniel South—with whom

I had exciting conversations about their work that deeply informed my own. I would also like to offer thanks to those who invited me to speak on the themes of the book at universities in the UK and elsewhere, and to those who edited the various essays from the project that appeared during these years. In 2020 I returned to Ireland and to UCD, and continue to be grateful to students and colleagues who contribute to the exciting research culture that surrounds and inspires me.

Since the late 2000s I have been a regular attendee at the American Thought and Culture Group, founded by the late, great intellectual historians Richard King and Michael O'Brien. The biannual meetings of this group have done more to shape me as a scholar than any other activity during the period of writing this book. Also influential on my development has been the Post45 UK research network that I co-founded in 2015 with Will Norman. Many of the chapters that follow were first tried out at the annual meetings of the group, with the final versions shaped by the feedback I received.

When it comes to feedback, I am most directly indebted to those who read parts of the manuscript as it was coming together. Those who read whole chapters, often more than one, include Tim Groenland, Lee Konstantinou, Günter Leypoldt, and Will Norman. Lola Boorman read drafts of almost every chapter; Martin Hägglund read at least one version of them all. Among these names are some of my most valued interlocutors and friends in academia, and I am grateful to all of them.

Thanks to the Post•45 series editors Kate Marshall and Loren Glass, and to the team at Stanford University Press who smoothed the book's journey through production, including Erica Wetter, Emily Smith, Caroline McKusick, and Jennifer Gordon. I owe substantial gratitude to the two anonymous reviewers of my manuscript, both for writing such positive reports and for offering helpful advice that enabled me to refine the book into its ultimate form. Thanks too to Barry McCrea for reminding me that this was the way to go, and to the National University of Ireland for assistance with the index.

I want lastly to thank family members for their support, including my mother Anne and father Liam, my sister Fiona and brother Mark, and my in-laws Marie and Noel. This book, already long in gestation, would have taken even longer had Marie and Noel not opened their home to our family during the pandemic lockdowns, tending to our small children so that their parents could work. They have continued to offer invaluable support since that time, and I am deeply in their debt. Those aforementioned children—Léana, Cillian, and Ruairí—are of course much more than an obstacle to productivity, having become a big part of why I do any of this in the first place. The person with whom I share them, along with so much else, is Ríona Nic Congáil, and it is to her that I dedicate this book.

New Sincerity

INTRODUCTION

Sincerely Yours

Early in the hybrid 2006 work *What Is the What*, the Sudanese narrator Achak Deng, bound and gagged by an African American couple while they rob his Atlanta apartment, imagines telling his captors about the event that brought him to the United States. "The broad strokes of the story of the civil war in Sudan," he silently informs them, "a story perpetuated by us Lost Boys, in the interest of drama and expediency, tells that one day we were sitting in our villages bathing in the river and grinding grain and the next the Arabs were raiding us, killing and looting and enslaving."[1] Deng takes as his task to expand on and complicate this "broad strokes" story, detailing the tensions that existed before the war, its onset in "increments" (57), its various underreported horrors, and his own experiences as a refugee in Sudan, Ethiopia, Kenya, and finally the US. Much of the power of *What Is the What* derives from the palpable authenticity of Deng's first-person testimony as a child of war, and particularly the painful way his innocent and instinctive trust in other people is consistently betrayed by their insincere and often brutal actions. At the same time, his testimony short-circuits assumptions about its unmediated authenticity through regular reflections on how it has been shaped by the requirements of a potential readership, by Deng's anticipation of how his story will be received and put to work. This we can already see in his allusion to the fact that the "broad strokes" version of his story has been "perpetuated by us Lost Boys, in the interest of drama and expediency." "Survivors tell the stories the sympathetic want," he observes elsewhere, "and that means making them as shocking as possible. My own story includes enough small embellishments that I cannot criticize the accounts of others" (21). In acknowledging that he is instrumentalizing the authenticity of his testimonial account, using it as a strategic means to achieve certain ends, Deng knows that he does not thereby render it inauthentic. Rather, *What Is the What* is here reminding its reader that the struggle to tell the truth in public cannot be separated from the ends that truth will be put to, and a foreknowledge of those ends necessarily imbues the telling with a level of calculation from the beginning. This specter of calculation, in turn, serves to raise questions less about the authentic truth of the tale than about the sincerity of the teller.

Choosing to embrace rather than shy away from this structuring dilemma, *What Is the What* presses the issue of sincerity in two further ways. The first is by implicitly contrasting the figure of a *readership*—that collective addressee, recipient of the "broad strokes" story, whose generic expectations must be met and manipulated in order to gain their attention and support—with the figure of a *reader*, imagined as an individual person more open and responsive to morally complicating elements in the stories they encounter. This reader, prefigured throughout the book in Deng's silent monologues to individuals he encounters in the narrative present, comes fully into view in the concluding chapter. As Deng talks about moving on from the robbery and begins to envisage a future, his closing lines take the form of direct address:

> I speak to these people, and I speak to you because I cannot help it. It gives me strength, almost unbelievable strength, to know that you are there. I covet your eyes, your ears, the collapsible space between us. How blessed are we to have each other? I am alive and you are alive so we must fill the air with our words.... All the while I will know that you are there. How can I pretend that you do not exist? It would be almost as impossible as you pretending that I do not exist. (535)

The "you" here is ambiguously singular and plural, so that the book concludes by bringing together the previously distinguished figures of readership and reader. In so doing, Deng's address mobilizes all the pathos associated with an ideal of sincerity defined, in the words of its most famous theorist Lionel Trilling, as "a congruence between avowal and actual feeling."[2] For Trilling, sincerity names a state or activity wherein being true to oneself does not serve as its own end but as a means of being true to others, an activity in which "the moral end in view implies a public end in view."[3] Developing this conception of sincerity, the book you are reading argues that, as a fundamentally social practice, sincerity is not only other-directed but depends for its very possibility on acknowledgment by another, acknowledgment that is in significant part an act of trust. As Deng recognizes in his closing words, it is trust in sincerity that enables sincerity to come into being, for the speaker as much as for their listener(s).

And yet, in a pattern we will likewise see repeated throughout *New Sincerity*, a second specter haunts Achak Deng's culminating vision of sincere and trusting communion between speaker and listener, writer and reader. This is the specter of the ghostwriter, in this case the author Dave Eggers. For readers familiar with any of Eggers's first three books—his best-selling memoir *A Heartbreaking Work of Staggering Genius* (2000), first novel *You Shall Know Our Velocity* (2002), and story collection *How We Are Hungry* (2004)—the invocatory conclusion of *What Is the What* should ring familiar bells. The second-person address, collapsing space between writer and reader, stress on collective strength and existential plenitude, urgent present-tense interrogatives: these are the defining elements of Eggers's early writing, the characteristic features of its most heightened moments. The recapitulation of this authorial style at the finale of *What Is the What* offers a closing reminder that we are here encountering not the actual words of the real-life Achak Deng, but a version of his autobiography fictionalized by Eggers. The latter is therefore writing not in his own voice (as in *A Heartbreaking Work*), nor in the voice of a character whose experience closely resembles his own (as in *Velocity* and most of his stories), but in the voice of a real-life African refugee reimagined as a literary character. Moreover, while Eggers was careful when promoting the book to outline its collective origins in his detailed interviews with Deng (a process confirmed in Deng's preface to the text), when the paperback edition appeared, it featured only the title *What Is the What* and Eggers's name on the cover and spine, with *The Autobiography of Valentino Achak Deng*, the book's original subtitle, relegated to the inside flyleaf.[4]

When the issue is put this way, it is tempting to summon some contemporary epithets: on the face of it, shouldn't we be suspicious of Eggers's approach to Deng's story? Doesn't it constitute an act, however well intentioned, of cultural appropriation? Yet at the time of the book's publication, this was not the response of its reviewers.[5] Comparing the overwhelmingly positive reception of *What Is the What* to the outrage that so often greeted earlier attempts by white American authors to write in a black African voice, Elizabeth Twitchell marveled in a 2011 article that "Eggers's project of ventriloquizing the suffering of another—and African suffering at that—was not only tolerated but praised as a profoundly moral undertaking."[6] This led Twitchell to frame a historical question: "What confluence of events has made it ethically possible for an American writer to fictionalize African trauma?"[7] Her answer—that Eggers's text successfully navigated the stalemate in 1990s theory between "the moral obligation to empathize with distant and dissimilar persons, and a skepticism about the morality of empathic identification itself"—has since been joined by a host of other critical responses, many of which offer nuanced considerations of how *What Is the What* draws on and departs from the twentieth-century tradition of human rights literature.[8]

In the present book I set out both to amplify Twitchell's historical question—by attending to the material as well as discursive conditions that underpin contemporary literary authorship—and to answer that question in a different way, drawing on the intersection between the two key phrases in my title: "New Sincerity" and "the Neoliberal Age." *What Is the What*, I argue, could receive such a glowing reception because it was published at the very moment when both of these dynamics in American culture were at their zenith—which is also to say, at the moment they began their decline. I will later explain what I mean by this claim in the case of neoliberalism, the decline of which has been the subject of some debate. But for now it makes sense to begin with New Sincerity, since this is the central label under which I bring together the writers examined in this book.

These writers are all born within a fifteen-year window between 1957 (Helen DeWitt) and 1972 (Benjamin Kunkel). I refer to them collectively as post-boomers, born at the tail end of, and in the period directly after, the postwar US baby boom that began in the early to mid-1940s and peaked in the late 1950s.[9] Having been no more than children during the 1960s, the historical experience of this post-boomer generation is defined by belatedness vis-à-vis the radical emancipatory politics, egalitarian social movements, and experimental artistic impulses that marked the earlier period. Coming to intellectual maturity in the last two decades of the century—a period retrospectively dubbed the "age of fracture" and "the unwinding"—this cohort began writing and publishing in a very different economic and political climate, one steeped in Reaganomics, the Washington Consensus, and the rise (and rise) of global multinational capitalism.[10] The US literary academy, where virtually all budding authors now spend several years and many their entire careers, witnessed a number of significant developments: new paradigms for literary study were generated through the influence of European, particularly French, thinkers; the mainstream American canon fragmented and diversified under pressure from social change, feeding into the so-called culture wars; and the creative writing program continued its ascent from one authorship route among others to a near-obligatory professional rite of passage.[11] In the media sphere, "the late age of print" was heralded by the coming of the World Wide Web, a radically new technological form that supplemented the challenges to the printed word mounted by cinema and television earlier in the century.[12] And in the cultural sphere, something called "postmodern irony" was taken to define the spirit of the age, tying together everything from consumerism and identity to politics and art.[13]

In addressing the early to midcareer fiction of this post-boomer generation—running from David Foster Wallace's first story collection published on the cusp of the 1990s in my opening chapter, to a set of novels from the mid-2000s by Susan Choi, Dana Spiotta, and Benjamin Kunkel in my final chapter—*New Sincerity* aims not only to offer a generational portrait, but also to delineate a central development in American literary fiction in the nearly two decades from 1989 to 2008. This was a period defined in political-economic terms by "normative neoliberalism" and "capitalist realism," by an atmosphere in which "the horizons of political hope had been delimited to a single political-economic system," and "capitalism seamlessly occupies the horizon of the thinkable."[14] In Chapter One I date the beginning of this period to the fall of the Berlin Wall and Francis Fukuyama's now notorious argument that the end of the Cold War marked the "End of History." I argue that the concluding text in Wallace's *Girl with Curious Hair*, the novella *Westward the Course of Empire Takes Its Way*, addresses this moment of historical transition by conceiving it as necessitating a moment of aesthetic transition, from exhausted paradigms of postmodernist metafiction and minimalism to something else. Over subsequent chapters, I explore how this something else—literary New Sincerity—coalesces through the work of Wallace and his peers into a dominant generational aesthetic, one that to this day continues to retain a serious influence on the themes and forms of contemporary writing. This stylistic and thematic longevity can be seen in the work of younger novelists such as Ben Lerner, Sheila Heti, Ottessa Moshfegh, and Charles Yu, as well as across an array of fictions published since the 2000s by the authors featured in this book—for instance, Dana Spiotta's *Stone Arabia* (2011), George Saunders's *Tenth of December* (2013), Susan Choi's *Trust Exercise* (2019), and Jennifer Egan's *The Candy House* (2022).

Despite its sustained presence in American fiction, however, my argument is that the highpoint of New Sincerity as a literary paradigm had been reached by the mid-2000s, and therefore the story I tell ends at this juncture. Rather than the suddenness of the global financial crisis that closed the period of normative neoliberalism in economic terms, the material and ideological changes that on my conception heralded the close of this literary period arrived more gradually around the mid-2000s, with the coming of social media, the crystallization of identity categories as the vehicle for both political organization and market segmentation, the waning of American unipolar hegemony, and the shift in the publishing world to the "Age of Amazon." According to Mark McGurl, this latter age is defined from an author's point of view by "the reader as customer, a quasi-deity around whose needs—assuming you want to earn money from your writing—your creative labor must revolve."[15] Not coincidentally, it is around this time that we witness the widely noted "genre turn" in contemporary literary fiction, the prominence of which has much to do with technological and economic shifts, but the aesthetic ground for which was laid by the prior moment of literary New Sincerity.[16] Building on the work of McGurl and others, I propose that the New Sincerity moment occupies the period between the dominance of literary postmodernism in the 1970s and 80s and the genre turn of the mid-2000s. Literary New Sincerity therefore displays elements of both postmodernist metafiction and genre aesthetics; but unlike postmodernism and the genre turn, both of which are usually identified primarily in formal terms, literary New Sincerity has at its core a question of sensibility or ethos. Indeed, it is driven in part by a questioning of the formalist project itself, not only in aesthetic but in ethical terms.

In the next section I nevertheless begin by exploring New Sincerity writing on formal grounds, establishing a set of general characteristics that lay the foundation for the case studies pursued in my chapters. The section that follows addresses the nature and history of sincerity itself, tracking a fascination with the relationship between literature and sincerity back to midcentury American liberalism's vision of literary history, which culminated in Trilling's *Sincerity and Authenticity*. I then consider why it makes sense to speak, as my title does, of a *new* sincerity. By retracing the origins of my project, I connect the literary aesthetics at the heart of this book to broader cultural engagements with sincerity in and around 2000. In the final sections I move to address the other key term in my subtitle, "neoliberalism," offering a genealogy of neoliberal sincerity and asking whether the fictions explored in this book stake out a complicit or resistant position to it. The Introduction concludes with a summary of the chapters, which progress through a series of nine central authors—most of them named above—as well as a set of key themes: art, economy, gender, race, class, and politics, each made central in one chapter but at play in them all. Through this approach, *New Sincerity* aims not only to analyze a key strand of literature in the period of normative neoliberalism: by looking back from the perspective of the present, it also assesses what lessons that literature holds for where we stand today.

Sincerely Novel

What are the formal coordinates of literary New Sincerity? The answer is complicated by the fact that a distinguishing feature of this writing is its revival of what Andrew Hoberek has dubbed "intentional bad form," where "bad form in the aesthetic sense merges with bad form in the social sense to connote sincerity: in the process of speaking from one's deepest self, one cannot bother with, or is indeed actively hindered by the artificiality of, the canons of good form."[17] As I explain in Chapter One, rather than an aesthetics of self-expression, this turn to bad form among post-boomer writers is better understood along Hegelian lines as an attempt to reconstitute the artwork in dialogical terms, as (in Robert Pippin's paraphrase of Hegel) a "subject-subject relation, not some sort of subject-object relation."[18] As Pippin outlines, the achievement of a sincere "subject-subject relation" in art is perennially threatened, on the one hand, by the danger of the artist's "submission to a collective subjectivity," and, on the other, by "an attempt by the artist to dominate or overwhelm the artwork's audience."[19] This either/or opposition neatly indexes the twin polarities of genre fiction on the one side—where the artist internalizes the preferences of the market in their formal choices—and postmodernist metafiction on the other, where "mastery" over the reader is often taken to constitute a key aesthetic principle.[20] For the writers examined in this study, both these polarities are depicted as aesthetically and ethically threatening, with a healthier relationship to the reader and the market imagined to lie somewhere between them.

But if postmodernism and genre fiction crowd literary New Sincerity from either end of its moment of prominence, then retreading the boards of modernist autonomy does not offer a satisfactory way out of this formal-historical bind. In a 1996 essay favorably comparing the fiction of Fyodor Dostoevsky to "our own lit's thematic poverty," Wallace typifies the New Sincerity reaction to the legacy of modernism:

> The good old modernists, among their other accomplishments, elevated aesthetics to the level of ethics—maybe even metaphysics—and Serious Novels after Joyce tend to be valued and studied mainly for their formal ingenuity. Such is the modernist legacy that we now presume as a matter of course that "serious" literature will be aesthetically distanced from real lived life.[21]

"Real lived life" is understood to be what the reader wants from fiction, and it is incumbent on authors to cast aside elitist pretensions and meet their reader halfway.[22] In *Sincerity and Authenticity*, Trilling had cited formulations by Joyce, Eliot, and Gide to support his claim that the modernists' aesthetics of impersonality—the artist as aloof genius, as *persona* rather than person—meant that "the criterion of sincerity, the calculation of the degree of congruence between feeling and avowal, is not pertinent to the judgement of their work."[23] For Trilling, modernism represented the culmination of "two centuries of aesthetic theory and artistic practice which have been less and less willing to take account of the habitual preferences of the audience."[24] Wallace implicitly agrees and argues instead for a mode of literature that takes those preferences into account, so that, as he put it, "The reader feels like someone is talking to him rather than striking a number of poses."[25]

As Wallace's paeans to Dostoevsky and Tolstoy suggest, the novel of the nineteenth century would seem to offer a more promising light to guide the way through the formal and ethical thicket of the millennial moment.

Indeed, Hoberek identifies "intentional bad form" in millennial-era fiction with a return to the nineteenth century and earlier, "to the form of the novel in place before even the rules of realism were fully formulated."[26] Yet as I explain in my reading of Jennifer Egan's *Look at Me* (2001) in Chapter Three, returning to the pre-modernist novel is not the balm it might initially promise to be. This is the case because the modernist critique of realism still has purchase—one cannot wish away the innovations of the twentieth century, and the twinned discoveries about human subjectivity and literary form that it witnessed—and also because in the millennial moment, as Egan's novel shows, a return to that earlier brand of realism can be made to serve the same purpose as genre fiction, flattering the reader's sentiments to commercial ends.[27] Whatever route one takes, in other words, the problem of aesthetic insincerity inevitably rears its ugly head. As Wallace's *Westward the Course of Empire Takes Its Way* articulated in its knotty and convoluted way at the outset of the period of normative neoliberalism, the literary search for sincerity among his generation is not only a *response* to the contemporary economic, political, and cultural landscape, but also a *symptom* of the norms and pressures of that landscape. Fundamentally, it is in this unstable gap between symptom and response that literary New Sincerity finds its home. As I will identify more fully when I deal with neoliberalism later in this Introduction, it is the struggle with material complicity that gives this writing its aesthetic, ethical, and political energy.

In formal terms, much of that energy resides in narrative voice. A colloquial mode of address characterizes not only obvious cases like Wallace's third-person *Infinite Jest* (1996) or Eggers's first-person *A Heartbreaking Work*, but also less attention-grabbing examples such as the elusive narrator of Colson Whitehead's *The Intuitionist* (1999) or the unstable third/first person in the opening chapter of Egan's *The Keep* (2006). As each of these instances makes clear, the question of voice brings with it the question of narrative perspective, and New Sincerity writers employ sudden alterations in perspective to create many of their most distinctive aesthetic effects. In particular, a shift from first-person or third-person narration into second-person address frequently characterizes climactic moments in this body of literature, making evident in a heightened and punctual way the basic orientation toward dialogue that underpins New Sincerity writing more generally. At the same time, the voice that speaks in these climactic moments, while evoking the pathos of direct address, is often more difficult to situate than it might initially seem. Deng's direct address to the reader at the conclusion of *What Is the What* is typical here, in that it is haunted by Eggers as ghostwriter, by the book's production of what Twitchell calls "a third voice" out of the author's real-life dialogue with Deng.[28] While the cross-racial element in this example is somewhat unusual, we will see that forms of ghostwriting are otherwise common across New Sincerity texts, from the filmmaker James Incandenza's inhabitation of Don Gately's mind and language in *Infinite Jest*, to the journalist Irene Maitlock's penning of the fashion model Charlotte Swenson's blog in *Look at Me*, to the way brand names haunt the mind of the "nomenclature consultant" in Whitehead's *Apex Hides the Hurt* (2006), to the multiple ghosts that inhabit the fiction of George Saunders.

As we can already glean from the example of *What Is the What*, these ghosts in the machine of writing make palpable the contradictions that exist around authorial sincerity. While, at least in the modern age, those contradictions can never be fully absent from the scene of writing, they nonetheless have a specific material force in the neoliberal moment. As Deborah Brandt records in her book *The Rise of Writing*, with the coming of the knowledge economy from the 1970s and the digital age from the 1990s, "For perhaps the first time in the history of mass literacy, writing seems to be eclipsing reading as the literate experience of consequence."[29] And writing possesses a contrasting cultural heritage to reading, being "connected not to citizenship but to work," belonging to "the transactional sphere," with its value "captured largely for private enterprise, trade and artisanship."[30] As Brandt notes, this utilitarian, capitalist conception of writing—so different to the historically dominant understanding of reading as a pathway to citizenship, worship, and personal autonomy—is underscored by the law of the land:

> According to the Supreme Court, people do not really write at work as citizens or free beings but rather as willingly enlisted corporate voices. . . . They are not individually responsible for what they are paid to say. Consequently, they don't really mean what they say. In fact, according to the Court, people who write for pay can't really mean what they say. Their speech rights are corrupted and, hence, inoperable. From this perspective, writing starts to look a lot less romantic, and a lot more feudal.[31]

It is against this legal and economic background that we can begin to understand all writing (for pay) as a kind of ghostwriting, where individuals find themselves voicing and being voiced by larger entities. But Brandt also observes that ghostwriting in its more restricted sense—"writing something for which someone else will take authorship credit"—is also on the rise in the digital age in a way that "simultaneously relies upon and erodes conceptions of authorship that have shaped literacy practices over time."[32] I would add that it is not only *literacy* practices but *literary* practices that are affected by such deep-rooted material changes. In neoliberal culture, meaning what you say as an artist would seem to require distinguishing yourself from those who write only for pay, who must perforce inhabit the role of ghosts in the commercial machine. Yet as we will explore below, neoliberalism's insistence on an economic view of everyday life heightens the contradictions faced by literary writers who want to distinguish aesthetic concerns from market requirements.

Throughout this book, I read New Sincerity texts as attempts to mediate these contradictions in writerly sincerity under neoliberalism—if not to resolve those contradictions then at least to draw them close to the center of the work, to make them a concern for the reader as well as the writer. The direct invocation of a reader becomes a crucial element in this process, and explains why, as Zadie Smith puts it in her introduction to a collection of post-boomer fiction, these texts "seem to be attempting to make something happen *off* the page, *outside* words, a curious thing for a piece of writing to want to do."[33] What happens off the page, outside words, depends upon the invocation and response of another; this other to whom I respond, and whose response I await, is for New Sincerity writers the actual reader of their text. It is striking how many novels of this period conclude with the kind of direct address we see at the end of *What Is the What*, such as when Joshua Ferris's *Then We Came to the End* (2007)—to cite an example not treated elsewhere in this book—breaks with its first-person-plural narrative voice only in its closing line: "We were the only two left. Just the two of us, you and me."[34] In their punctual effect, these concluding words recall the classic example of direct address in nineteenth-century fiction: *Jane Eyre*'s "Reader, I married him." The realist novel's rhetoric of sincerity is thus being summoned by Ferris, but with a twist. In place of what Garrett Stewart identifies as the Brontë sentence's "collaborative motivation . . . of second, first, and third person in an independent transitive—and transactional—grammar," the ending of *Then We Came to the End* gives us second, first, and first-person plural combining to displace the transactional quality of the "we" (which heretofore in the novel has referred to a group of advertising colleagues connected by their precarious work situation) with an invocation of community that seems to put the narrator-writer and the reader into direct relationship with one another.[35]

The cultural contexts of the two phrases are also worth comparing. Of "Reader, I married him," Stewart remarks that "there is a reader in attendance, rhetorically hailed or otherwise."[36] Yet while Stewart considers this "the only existential ground possible for a fictional text," the assumption that there will inevitably be a reader in attendance for a fictional utterance should also be regarded historically, as redolent of the novel in its most confident time and place: the middle of the British nineteenth century, when an eager and rapidly growing reading public had few other forms of entertainment competing for their attention. By contrast, Ferris's implicit acknowledgment that there is neither a "me" nor a "we" without a reading "you," while superficially similar, has—like the "fractious" first-person plural of his novel more generally—a more precarious edge.[37] In an early twenty-first-century America swamped by competing draws on a potential reader's time—not to mention a general crisis of literacy, with rates "stagnant" since the 1980s[38]—the presumption that "readers would be many and writers would be few," and thus that there will always be an empirical reader to ground every literary text, can be made with far less certainty.[39]

Against this background, rhetorical gestures toward sincerity, which are also gestures toward community and "a public end in view," take on a double temporal character in New Sincerity texts.[40] On the one hand, such gestures reach back to the heyday of the novel, transmitting palpable nostalgia for the kind of cultural centrality that literature could once claim. On the other hand, such gestures possess an open-ended, futural quality, hoping to bring into being the reader (and readership) that can no longer be taken for granted. In each text featured in *New Sincerity*, this doubleness plays out with a different tonality—sometimes anxious and passive-aggressive, sometimes smooth and inviting, sometimes puzzled and questioning—but the general effect is to diminish the gap between narrator and writer, a gap that literary modernism had done so much to widen at the beginning of the last century. This is why I referred above to the "me" of Ferris's closing line as a "narrator-writer," since the culminating moments in New Sincerity texts like *Then We Came to the End* often read as efforts to break through the fictional mask. And yet they are not that, not quite; it is not so much that these authors are interested in having sincerity break with fiction in these moments, as that they are interested in performing a kind of sincerity that inheres *only in fiction*. Which is not to say a purer kind of sincerity, just a distinctive one. The cultivation of this contemporary form of aesthetic sincerity is one of the things, indeed, that might be said to be *new* about literary New Sincerity, as this book aims to show.

I hope the account thus far has begun to make persuasive my choice of literary New Sincerity as a term to describe the work of this generation of American writers. But what was sincerity before it was new? And how did it become new? A journey back in literary and intellectual history will help us to address these questions over the next two sections.

Sincerely Liberal

In a scene midway through William Gaddis's 1955 novel *The Recognitions*, the struggling and immature playwright Otto, trying in vain to seduce his ethereal poet friend Esmé, catches up with her on a New York City street and proclaims his undying love. "You know I'm sincere," he pleads, "I've always been sincere with you." Esmé hears him out, turns to him wearily, and responds flatly. "Sincerity," she tells him, "becomes the honesty of people who cannot be honest with themselves."[41]

Although Lionel Trilling may or may not have read *The Recognitions*—which was not exactly a smash hit upon its release—it is precisely the opposition Esmé draws here between sincerity with others and honesty with oneself that lies at the heart of Trilling's 1972 study in the history of ideas, *Sincerity and Authenticity*. At the outset of the book, based on his Charles Eliot Norton lectures at Harvard, Trilling defines sincerity as "a congruence between avowal and actual feeling" and traces its emergence in "the moral life of Europe" to the advent of Renaissance humanism.[42] He cites *Hamlet* as a central text, placing particular emphasis on Polonius's famous advice to Laertes as the latter prepares to depart for Paris:

> This above all: to thine own self be true
> And it doth follow, as the night the day
> Thou canst not then be false to any man.

For Trilling, the otherwise corrupt Polonius here experiences "a moment of self-transcendence, of grace, of truth" (3). His words are to be taken seriously, and crucial to their import is that truth to one's own self should be understood not as an end but as a means of ensuring truth to others.

Trilling goes on to claim—via readings of Molière, Rousseau, Goethe, Hegel, Wordsworth, and Austen, among others—that this public-oriented ideal of sincerity would become "a salient, perhaps a definitive, characteristic of Western culture for some four hundred years" (6). But by the twentieth century it had gone into sharp decline, superseded by the ideal of authenticity, which conceives truth to the self as an end and not simply as a means. Of Polonius's three lines of counsel, only the first now remains: "To thine own self be true." The goal of authenticity is self-integrity rather than other-directed communication; authenticity rejects the playing of roles, and it is precisely the public orientation underlying sincerity—which emerged in an early modern period dominated by the theater—that makes the notion suspect to the new anti-social temperament. Drawing on Jean-Paul Sartre's critique of sincerity as bad faith, Trilling outlines the modern dialectic between sincerity and authenticity as follows:

> Society requires of us that we present ourselves as being sincere, and the most efficacious way of satisfying this demand is to see to it that we really are sincere, that we actually are what we want our community to know we are. In short, we play the role of being ourselves, we sincerely act the part of the sincere person, with the result that a judgement may be passed upon our sincerity that it is not authentic. (10–11)

This, in essence, is Esmé's judgment on Otto's declaration of love in *The Recognitions*: he may indeed be as sincere as he says he is, but his sincerity is not authentic, and is no replacement for the honesty with oneself that authenticity names. Authenticity denotes, in Trilling's summary, "a more strenuous moral experience than 'sincerity' does, a more exigent conception of the self and of what being true to it consists in, a wider reference to the universe and man's place in it, and a less acceptant and genial view of the social circumstances of life" (11). And Gaddis's novel—an emblematic late modernist artwork—could not be less genial in its portrayal of midcentury American society and those who inhabit it, making constant analogies between forgery in the art world and the forgery of the self that is everywhere prevalent in social life.

Of course, Gaddis and Trilling were far from alone among intellectuals and writers of their time in drawing attention to the cultural importance of sincerity and authenticity in the postwar United States. The questions that Gaddis was probing in *The Recognitions* received more accessible treatment in novels including *The Catcher in the Rye* (1951), *On the Road* (1957), *Revolutionary Road* (1961), and *The Moviegoer* (1961). Social scientists such as David Riesman, C. Wright Mills, Erving Goffman, and William Whyte explored notions of sincerity, authenticity, and performance in theorizing the lives of the increasingly bureaucratized middle class of the midcentury era.[43] In *Sincerity and Authenticity*, Trilling was thus employing concepts with a certain zeitgeist quality, and the author of *The Liberal Imagination* (1950) was doing so at least in part to defend the liberalism—now aligned with a commitment to sincerity—that he viewed as under threat from the authenticity-obsessed radical movements of the 1960s.[44]

In employing literature as the primary ground for his historical exploration of sincerity, Trilling's study was part of a stream of similar work in this period on both sides of the Atlantic. Beginning in the early 1960s, a range of philosophers and critics wrote on the connection between sincerity and literary aesthetics; following the publication of *Sincerity and Authenticity*, the last work in this wave of sincerity studies was Leon Guilhamet's 1974 treatise on eighteenth-century poetry, *The Sincere Ideal*.[45] By the mid-1970s, however, the literary and cultural landscape had changed. "Theory" had arrived in the US academy, and scholars were now busy deconstructing the humanist conceptions of the self and literary expression that underlay the work of virtually all the midcentury writers, critics, and sociologists I have just named.[46]

Across the decades that followed, concomitant with the neoliberal turn in politics and economy, both sincerity and authenticity suffered setbacks as normative cultural ideals. There are many ways to tell this story, but one of the most generative is offered by Amanda Anderson's *The Way We Argue Now* (2005), which maps Trilling's opposition onto a newer distinction between "proceduralism"—which she associates with the political and social theory of John Rawls and Jurgen Habermas in the 1970s and 1980s—and "poststructuralism," which became familiar over the same period through the influence of French thinkers such as Jacques Derrida and Michel Foucault. "Proceduralism constitutes an extension of the sincerity paradigm," Anderson contends, "while poststructuralism remains the inheritor of the authenticity paradigm."[47] Nevertheless, both terms in this new polarity can be understood to subordinate the focus on the deep self and the relation between self and other that characterized both sides of Trilling's sincerity/authenticity dichotomy. Proceduralism achieves this subordination through its focus on universalist norms and systems, whether legal or discursive; poststructuralism by its emphasis on difference, and its philosophical commitment to the priority of language, or what Derrida would term "general writing." Anderson, who wants to argue the case for a proceduralist approach in literary and cultural studies, sees proceduralism as "a dialectical overcoming of the sincerity/authenticity problematic."[48] She downplays, however, the extent to which poststructuralism marks the same dialectical overcoming from a different direction. It may well be true that poststructuralism inherits the authenticity mantle, in that it "looks beneath or beyond the surface of convention to access meaningful funds of human experience," but poststructuralism can also be understood to undermine all claims to authenticity, any positing of an origin point from which truth flows.[49]

The classic deconstruction of the notion of an origin was offered by Derrida in "Structure, Sign and Play in the Discourse of the Human Sciences," delivered at a 1966 conference at Johns Hopkins University that is often cited (ironically enough) as the origin point of Theory's rise to hegemony in the US academy.[50] But the poststructuralist dismantling of the sincerity/authenticity paradigm is perhaps best exemplified by the debate between Derrida and Paul de Man concerning Jean-Jacques Rousseau, the central figure in many influential accounts of the transition from the sincerity ideal to the modern age of authenticity.[51] In his breakthrough work *Of Grammatology* (1967), Derrida had proposed that Rousseau's repeated attempts, most notably in the *Confessions*, to ground the authenticity of self-presence in the experience of hearing oneself speak, would always end up depending on the disavowed and inauthentic "supplement" of writing.[52] In a review of the book, de Man praised Derrida's reading while nonetheless taking him to task for failing to go beyond the traditional privileging in Rousseau criticism of "the relations the subject sustains with himself in the interiority of consciousness."[53] In distinguishing between what Rousseau *wants* to say and what he *does* say, "Derrida goes very far in attributing to Rousseau a systematic and verified knowledge of the duplicity of his own discourse," but he does not go far enough.[54] In a later essay, de Man casts Derrida's inability to appreciate fully the self-reflexivity of Rousseau's writing as an unwillingness to acknowledge its *literary* quality—and by "literary" he designates "any text that implicitly or explicitly signifies its own rhetorical mode and prefigures its own misunderstanding as the correlative of its rhetorical nature."[55] This conception of literary writing as fully self-conscious rhetoric—which one could argue Derrida in fact shares (the question being whether he considers Rousseau to qualify as literature in this sense)—enables de Man to position self-consciousness in an unusual place. "It follows from the rhetorical nature of literary language that the cognitive function resides in the language and not in the subject," he concludes: "The question as to whether the author himself is or is not blinded is to some extent irrelevant; it can only be asked heuristically, as a means to accede to the true question: whether his language is or is not blind to its own statement."[56]

From the vantage point of deconstruction, it therefore makes little sense to talk about sincerity as a relevant literary category: to (mis)appropriate Trilling's terms, even in a work like the *Confessions* it is *language* doing the "avowing" and "feeling," rather than Rousseau himself. But de Man's position also implies, as he notes above, that all reading is inevitably misreading. In an important sense, then, the reader's intervention is just as "irrelevant" for de Man as the author's conception of what they are doing. The only agent that really matters is language, and even history itself becomes a construct of language's grammatology. The ethical problems with this position have been picked over many times, with the scandal concerning de Man's posthumously published wartime writings casting an unavoidably dark shadow on the more radical conclusions of his deconstructive practice.[57] But from our vantage point, we can glimpse in the Derrida–de Man picture of literature another spur for those direct invocations of the reader that litter New Sincerity texts. These rhetorical gestures mark an aesthetic response not only to the historical and material factors explored above and below, but also to the conclusions set out in some of the most radical Theory of the preceding age, which placed writer and reader in a thoroughly subordinate position to the language of the text.

Those radical conclusions were resisted by liberal attempts in the 2000s to revive Trilling's categories, including Anderson's *The Way We Argue Now* and Bernard Williams's influential *Truth and Truthfulness* (2002), wherein "Sincerity" (capitalized in his text) is conceived as one of "the two basic virtues of truth."[58] Indeed, Anderson and Williams's contributions formed part of a twenty-first-century revival in "sincerity studies," after almost three decades of scholarly neglect.[59] In a 2010 essay surveying this expanding field of scholarship, Angela Esterhammer highlighted some differences between the earlier wave of interest in the relationship between sincerity and literature during the 1960s and 1970s, and the more recent revival. Noting that the majority of scholarship in both waves had been anchored in the context of literary Romanticism, Esterhammer positions Wordsworth, "the first poet to cultivate sincerity as a poetic value," as the presiding figure for the earlier wave, while identifying Byron, who "interprets sincerity as a code or convention," as the model for sincerity's more recent revival.[60] It is part of the argument of this book that literary New Sincerity bridges these two positions, combining the cultivation of sincerity as a poetic value with an awareness of sincerity as a convention. This literary combination is better described, however, as a dialectic, which it is the task of the next section to explore.

Sincerely New

The New Sincerity dialectic can be glimpsed in theoretical formation throughout the early essays of David Foster Wallace, which provide a running commentary on the commitments of his emerging literary practice in the late 1980s and early 1990s. Having produced a debut novel in *The Broom of the System* (1987) that he would later describe as "a conversation between Wittgenstein and Derrida,"[61] Wallace's first significant critical essay, published the following year, advocated for the relevance of continental philosophy and literary theory—"such aliens as Husserl, Heidegger, Bakhtin, Lacan, Barthes, Poulet, Gadamer, de Man"—to the concerns of the contemporary writer.[62] Wallace opined that writers could not ignore the insight that "the idea that literary language is any kind of neutral medium" had been shown by Theory to be an ideological delusion.[63] Three years later, in a pithy overview of debates around the "death of the author," Wallace reaffirmed that the writer must take seriously the idea that literary language is "not a tool but an environment," albeit he now downplayed his alignment with the poststructuralist view, presenting himself as one of those "civilians who know in our gut that writing is an act of communication between one human being and another."[64]

This treatment of his generation's response to Theory would reach its most potent expression in 1993's "E Unibus Pluram: Television and U.S. Fiction," which has become the ur-text for tracing the turn to sincerity among postboomer writers. An attack on the commodification of ironic modes of audience address in contemporary television and advertising, and on American fiction's lack of critical response to this development, "E Unibus Pluram" culminates with a clarion call for a new generation of literary "*anti*-rebels" who would eschew postmodern irony in favor of "single-entendre principles," and thus risk appearing "too sincere. Clearly repressed. Backward, quaint, naïve, anachronistic."[65] Initially published alongside an equally striking interview with Larry McCaffery, Wallace's essay has had a major impact on both the writing of his contemporaries and how that writing has been received by critics. As Jason Gladstone and Daniel Worden would later note—making the initial claim in 2011 and repeating it in 2016—"E Unibus Pluram" has wielded "predictive, or, perhaps, programmatic power" for contemporary American culture.[66] Wallace's appeal for "a shift away from 'ironic watching' and toward the embrace of 'single entendre principles'" had now become observable "almost everywhere."[67]

The renown that has attached itself to Wallace's statements about irony and sincerity can make the problem of creating new literary art after postmodernism appear to involve little more than a shift in an author's ethos or attitude: say what you mean and mean what you say, Wallace seems to imply, and everything else will follow. As I am not the first to point out, however, this relatively straightforward nonfiction message contrasts with the highly wrought technical complexity of Wallace's fiction. Taking their cue from the stress in "E Unibus Pluram" on the problem of irony—as well as its felt prevalence in the cultural air of the American 1990s—critics have addressed this complexity primarily through the lens of that term, and a cottage industry of Wallace criticism has emerged on the subject of how, as one early critic put it, the author's fiction turns "irony back on itself."[68] The most sophisticated reading of this kind is offered by Lee Konstantinou, who devotes more than half his book on irony in postwar American fiction to the "postirony" he takes to characterize the writing of Wallace, Eggers, Egan, Alex Shakar, and other authors of their cohort and era. As Konstantinou acknowledges, "postirony" and "New Sincerity" share obvious kinship as cultural monikers, but he distinguishes them with a claim of priority, arguing that "postironic belief must precede the ethics of New Sincerity."[69] Addressing a version of my ideas published in earlier articles that contributed to the writing of the present book, Konstantinou contends that "Kelly's account does not address the specific threat these writers see in irony."[70] "Why, after all, would sincerity be the aspired state one might want to attain if one was concerned about irony?" he wonders. "Why not commitment, or passion, or emotion, or decision?"[71]

My claim, however, is that irony is just one name—and perhaps not the best one—for the set of material, ideological, and aesthetic conditions that the post-boomer generation of writers are concerned with in their millennial-era fiction. These conditions—which I have outlined in brief above and will return to throughout the book—drive the central questions raised in and by this writing, all of which could be described as having to do not only with sincerity but precisely with "commitment, or passion, or emotion, or decision." These questions include: in a neoliberal culture that validates self-interest above all other ends, how does one prioritize what Trilling calls the "public end in view"? If one takes into account the preferences of the reader, as Wallace suggests one should, how does one know one is not doing so in the way advertising does, anticipating the response of the receiver for commercial ends? How, in other words, does one establish one's own sincerity in an era of neoliberal branding? Can sincerity itself become a brand? Is sincerity always valuable (morally, politically, economically)? Moreover, how does one address this set of questions in literature without the risk of outward performance trumping inner conviction? How does one establish "a congruence between avowal and actual feeling"—Trilling's definition of sincerity again—if one cannot be sure about the status of one's "actual feeling" because one is always anticipating the response of others, and performing for them? When one's writing might simply be a kind of ghostwriting, determined by the economic character of language in the present, or even by the conglomerate character of literary publishing, can one ever know what one truly believes or means to say?[72]

These are moral and epistemological questions, but they are primarily addressed by the writers featured in *New Sincerity* as questions of literary form. For this reason, throughout the book I mainly refer to literary New Sincerity as an *aesthetic*, although I also want to acknowledge that aspects of this aesthetic can helpfully be grasped through related notions such as *sensibility* and *structure of feeling*. These two terms, in their canonical definitions by Susan Sontag and Raymond Williams, share an emphasis on a collectively experienced affectivity that has not yet hardened into a system or idea. "The sensibility of an era is not only its most decisive, but also its most perishable, aspect," writes Sontag; it is "almost, but not quite, ineffable."[73] For Williams, meanwhile, a structure of feeling names emerging cultural meanings and values that "do not have to await definition, classification, or rationalization before they exert palpable pressures."[74] Both notions capture something of the ephemeral quality of the affects that New Sincerity writers aim to evoke, particularly through their defining use of ambiguously situated second-person address. Yet both Sontag and Williams were writing long before the coming of the internet, and it is a rare sensibility or structure of feeling that these days is not immediately turned into a *discourse* via that medium.

So it was that by the mid-2000s there existed online manifestos explicitly naming New Sincerity (however mock-sincerely) as a cultural movement, such as poet Anthony Robinson's "A Few Notes from a New Sincerist" or radio host Jesse Thorn's "Manifesto for the New Sincerity."[75] In her 2017 study *Sincerity After Communism*, Ellen Rutten offers a remarkably thorough overview of this New Sincerity discourse. Despite her central focus on Russia, Rutten covers a wide range of uses of "New Sincerity" in the American context, piecing together a narrative that begins with conversations about Austin rock bands in the mid-1980s, continues through Wallace's essays and fiction in the 1990s, and then explodes across popular culture and the internet after 9/11. The granular details of this narrative are certainly of interest, but for our purposes Rutten's general summary will serve:

> Visions of a new sincerity have circulated increasingly in discussions of novel trends in music, literature, film, new media, and the visual arts. By the early 2000s, genres that rely on discourses of personal confession and sincerity began to hold sway—whether the talk show, the weblog, the memoir, or

autobiography; and toward the late 2000s, sincerity gained the renewed attention of leading philosophers and cultural and political theorists.[76]

When I first found myself writing about literary New Sincerity in the summer of 2009, it was partly in response to this broadly circulating cultural discourse, and partly in response to the specific reception of Wallace's work, a notable aspect of which, as we have seen, had been the persistent foregrounding of questions of irony and sincerity. That initial essay, "David Foster Wallace and the New Sincerity in American Fiction," was driven by two questions, framed in its opening paragraph. The first—"in terms of literary and intellectual history, what does this attribution of sincerity to Wallace mean?"—is one I have begun to answer in this section and the last.[77] The second question inspired much of my subsequent thinking and writing on the topic: "is there something fundamentally new about Wallace's sincerity, a re-working of the concept as a complex and radical response to contemporary conditions?"[78] Were we talking about the revival of an old kind of sincerity, or was there something about Wallace's brand of sincerity that was genuinely novel? Can there even *be* a new kind of sincerity? Although the weight of my initial argument was towards the claim that yes, there could be a qualitatively new kind of sincerity, I still prevaricated somewhat on the question. This is evident in the essay's closing sentence, which describes Wallace's fiction as grappling with "the possibility of a reconceived, and renewed, sincerity."[79] Reconceived, and renewed. Which was it? Was New Sincerity simply the renewal of sincerity—in response to postmodern irony, perhaps, or to the commodification of authenticity, or the manipulations of advertising, or political apathy, or social hypocrisy—or was it a substantial reconceiving of what had gone before?[80]

We find something of this same ambiguity when we look to the work of other scholars who have explored contemporary modes of sincerity in and out of American fiction. Those whose stress falls on the revival of older forms of sincerity as a response to the ironies and inauthenticities of postmodern culture include Liesbeth Korthals Altes, A. D. Jameson, Jonathan D. Fitzgerald, Ruth Barton Palmer, and Allard den Dulk.[81] Others, particularly those interested in the legacy of Theory and the affordances of new media, are more emphatic that the kind of sincerity that does—or should—characterize contemporary culture needs to involve "a new theorization of the concept."[82]

Summarizing this second strand, and referring to two essays published in 1993—film scholar Jim Collins's "Genericity in the 90s" and Wallace's "E Unibus Pluram"—Rutten notes that "Collins and Wallace were early advocates of a conceptual link that several cultural commentators would defend in the 2000s: the nexus between changing mediascapes and a radically transformed, new notion of sincerity."[83]

My approach in this book is not to resolve this debate between new and old sincerity in the terms set out above, but to transfer the opposition onto the terrain of a more pragmatic distinction between fictional and nonfictional contexts, understood as constituted by different writerly norms and conditions. In the case of Wallace, for instance, although the sentiments expressed in "E Unibus Pluram" make the author sound like a wannabe Wordsworth, his fiction—as we shall see in Chapter One—is closer in spirit to Byron in its ironic awareness of its own artificiality and inability to attain a pure sincerity, while adding a further layer of self-consciousness concerning the material conditions underpinning contemporary literary expression. As Wallace scholars have understood for a long time, the very form of his writing is part of the problem the author is trying to solve. *New Sincerity* argues that the same is true for all the post-boomer writers addressed in this study. In this sense, literary New Sincerity does not mark a rejection of poststructuralist ideas about language so much as an attempt to work through their implications in the service of something ethically traditional but aesthetically novel.[84] But this working through is occurring in a distinctive political and economic context, which the remainder of this Introduction will explore.

Sincerely Neoliberal

Mr. Pivner, estranged father of Otto in *The Recognitions*, is a figure of bathos and pathos. He spends his days reading newspaper advertisements and listening to radio commercials, which haunt his thoughts with the promise that following the latest self-help trends will enable him to overcome the smallness and dissatisfactions of his life. He is particularly under the sway of one book, which he peruses as he prepares "to meet his son, to win him as a friend, and influence him as a person."[85] The almost ten pages of *The Recognitions* devoted to satirizing Dale Carnegie's 1936 bestseller *How To Win Friends and Influence People* provide a microcosm of Gaddis's book-long lament for the high philosophical and existential values that he sees being corrupted by the venal commercial culture of postwar America. Quoting Carnegie directly, Gaddis especially targets the way his book, for all that its title suggests a stance of open manipulation, nevertheless foregrounds tropes of sincerity in order to win the confidence of gullible readers like Mr. Pivner:

> He had taken this most worn of his books from the shelf because it inspired in him what he believed to be confidence. As he read there (underscored), "Let me repeat: the principles taught in this book will work only when they come from the heart. I am not advocating a bag of tricks. I am talking about a new way of life."[86]

Gaddis locates the origins of Carnegie's "new way of life" in the American transcendentalists—especially Henry David Thoreau—whose values of sincerity, self-reliance, and self-making had morphed in the twentieth century into a cult of self-improvement in the service of self-selling. But this self-selling was not exactly selling out—the role played by sincerity in Carnegie's worldview could not be so easily dismissed or diminished. "I am talking about a real smile," Mr. Pivner reads in *How to Win Friends*, "a heart-warming smile, a smile that comes from within, the kind of smile that will bring a good price in the market place."[87]

On the face of it, "a smile that comes from within" would seem to signify a contradictory set of social and moral values to "the kind of smile that will bring a good price in the market place." And yet it is precisely the intertwining of these values in postwar America that Gaddis was exploring—and in this, again, he was far from alone. In *The Power Elite*, published the year after *The Recognitions*, the sociologist C. Wright Mills likewise pinpointed the importance of sincerity to the self-perception of midcentury American business culture, as evidenced by books like Carnegie's:

> The American literature of practical inspiration—which carries the great fetish of success—has undergone a significant shift in its advice about "what it takes to succeed." The sober, personal virtues of will power and honesty, of high-mindedness and the constitutional inability to say "yes" to The Easy Road of women, tobacco, and wine—this later nineteenth-century image has given way to "the most important single factor, the effective personality," which "commands attention by charm," and "radiates self-confidence." In this

"new way of life," one must smile often and be a good listener, talk in terms of the other man's interests and make the other feel important—and one must do all this *sincerely*. Personal relations, in short, have become part of "public relations," a sacrifice of selfhood on a personality market, to the sole end of individual success in the corporate way of life.[88]

In Trilling's terms, we have here a model of sincerity without any pretensions to authenticity. Rather than join the anti-social cult of the authentic self that Trilling finds so threatening among 1960s radicals, Mills's "elite careerist" sacrifices his self to the terms of the market.[89] He acts sincerely toward others while instrumentalizing that sincerity in the service of a success that is always and only to be measured financially. As Gaddis writes of *How to Win Friends*, "It left no doubt but that money may be expected to accrue as testimonial to the only friendships worth the having, and, eventually, the only ones possible."[90]

While Mr. Pivner might aspire to be an "elite careerist," however, he more closely resembles a character type made famous by another midcentury sociologist. In *The Lonely Crowd* (1950), David Riesman argues that the "inner-directed personality"—characteristic of an industrial era that emphasizes "technical competence," familial authority, and the "sober, personal virtues" referred to by Mills—is giving way in American culture to the "other-directed personality." Emerging out of a post-industrial society that stresses "social competence"—the manipulation of people rather than things—other-directedness is characterized by responsiveness not to traditional authority but to peer behavior and media messaging.[91] "The other-directed person wants to be loved rather than esteemed," writes Riesman, and this dependence on the opinion of others results in "no clear core of self"—or, in Trilling's gloss, "scarcely a self at all, but rather, a reiterated impersonation."[92]

And yet, as Erving Goffman would argue in *The Presentation of Self in Everyday Life* (1956), impersonation and sincerity were not necessarily mutually exclusive. For Goffman, the term *sincere* could be used "for individuals who believed in the impression fostered by their own performance."[93] Still, if there is nothing but performance—if the most that can be achieved is "Belief in the Part One Is Playing," as the subtitle of Goffman's opening chapter has it—then some more fundamental model of sincerity as truth to oneself and others seems to have gone missing. Riesman acknowledges this in his discussion of the increasing importance of sincerity in what midcentury audiences look for in artistic performance. "The source of criteria for judgment has shifted from the content of the performance and its goodness or badness, aesthetically speaking, to the personality of the performer," he observes, warning that

> it is obviously most difficult to judge sincerity. While the audience which uses the term sincerity thinks that it is escaping, in its tolerant mood, from the difficulty of judging skills, it is actually moving into a domain of considerably greater complexity. Just because such a premium is put on sincerity, a premium is put on faking it.[94]

In these influential works written at the height of midcentury American liberalism, when FDR's New Deal underpinned an economy in which state intervention and market regulation were seen not only as legitimate but necessary, Riesman, Mills, Goffman, and Gaddis could nonetheless see the writing on the capitalist wall. They worried about the effects of market values on the American individual as society and economy shifted from production to consumption. Those anxieties were filtered through a concern that the meaning of sincerity was changing: not, as Trilling worried, in the direction of an exacting or Dionysian authenticity; rather, in the direction of accommodation with market values bearing no relation to the authentic truth of being. Most fundamentally, these liberals worried that in the "personality market" and beyond it, no one would any longer know whether they were really being sincere in the traditional sense, whether there were "actual feelings" underlying the things they avowed.

Could sincerity be saved, and if so, how? One answer comes from a perhaps unexpected source. At the same time as the self-identified liberals named above were writing their anxious and authoritative masterworks of social science, another set of thinkers, marginalized in the midcentury but to become regnant by the century's end, were claiming the mantle of "liberalism" for a different, far more market-friendly set of beliefs. We now refer to these thinkers—among them Milton Friedman, Gary Becker, James Buchanan, and Friedrich von Hayek—as *neoliberals*, and they have recently become among the most revered and reviled thinkers of the twentieth century.[95] Amid all the scholarship on these individuals, their ideas, their institutions, and their influence on the post-1960s world, what has often gone underappreciated is the moral philosophy that underpinned their cheerleading for the "free market." Trilling's definition of sincerity—"a congruence between avowal and actual feeling"—makes it a question of the relationship between thought and speech. But one might view sincerity in a different way, as having to do not with a congruence between avowal and *feeling* but with a congruence between avowal and *action*. The key test of sincerity then becomes the willingness to act on what one professes to believe.

If neoliberals hold a view of sincerity, it is something like this, but operating in reverse: it is through action that the subject discovers what they sincerely believe. And the key sphere of action for neoliberals is the market. This is an arena in which what economists rather mildly call "revealed preference" can apparently tell us more about the moral beliefs of citizens than something as limited and unsatisfactory as casting one's vote at the ballot box. As the Austrian godfather of neoliberalism Friedrich von Hayek put it in his 1944 treatise *The Road to Serfdom*:

> The periodical election of representatives, to which the moral choice of the individual tends to be more and more reduced, is not an occasion on which his moral values are tested or where he has constantly to reassert and prove the order of his values and to testify to the sincerity of his profession by the sacrifice of those of his values he rates lower to those he puts higher.[96]

The logical outcome of this view is that sincerity as the congruence of avowal and action is discovered through market choice; sincerity does not preexist the sphere of the market. Or if it does, it does so in an unproven state, as a congruence between avowal and feeling that is to all intents and purposes meaningless (and valueless) without being tested. "Freedom to order our own conduct in the sphere where material circumstances force a choice upon us, and the responsibility for the arrangement of our own life according to our own conscience," Hayek writes, "is the air in which alone moral sense grows and in which moral values are daily re-created in the free decision of the individual."[97] One commentator glosses Hayek's position thus: "By imposing this drama of choice, the economy becomes a theater of self-disclosure, the stage upon which we discover and reveal our ultimate ends."[98]

So if sincerity as the congruence of avowal and feeling—a principle that powers the liberal imagination, in Trilling's terms—is vulnerable on one side to the "purer" ideal of authenticity as the truth of feeling, then on the other side it is vulnerable to another kind of purity: the test of action through the making of choices under circumstances of constraint. While we might associate the first kind of challenge, as Trilling does, with the (New) Left, the second challenge stems—as its articulation by Hayek would suggest—from the (New) Right.[99] In each case the danger is that the center cannot hold, that the fragile balances involved in the moral ideal of sincerity will be destroyed. To the extent that those fragile balances underpinned the structure of feeling of postwar liberalism, this is exactly what happened in the post-1960s period: the liberal subject was attacked from both Left and Right, from a position emphasizing authenticity as personal autonomy on the one hand, and from a position that saw the market as the true test of moral action on the other. It was the way these two apparently opposed attacks overlapped with one another that set the scene for the neoliberal turn in politics, economy, society, and subjectivity.

This is another story that has by now been told in many ways, and I will return to it most fully in Chapter Six, when I consider revisionist accounts of the politics of the 1960s in recent fiction and scholarship. But for now we can zero in on one influential account of the historical shift from liberalism to neoliberalism: Michel Feher's 2009 article "Self-Appreciation; or the Aspirations of Human Capital." Building on the foundational work undertaken by Foucault in his 1979 lectures on neoliberalism—later published as *The Birth of Biopolitics*—Feher argues that the notion of *human capital* has come to replace the conception of the free laborer on which liberal capitalism was premised. In liberal theory, the free laborer enters the realm of the market to exchange their labor power for a wage, but much of their life exists outside this realm in the sphere of reproduction, where market values do not hold sway. "The sphere of reproduction," Feher explains, "is one that values selfless giving (whether in one's relation to God or to one's neighbor), exalts people's unconditional ties (with their family, with their nation, and with humanity), and justifies the social services required for the physical and psychological upkeep of individuals, to prepare them for their entry into the market."[100] Moving between the market and this non-market realm, the free laborer of liberal capitalism is "a split being," divided between "a subjectivity that is inalienable and a labor power that is to be rented out," between "spiritual aspirations and the pursuit of material interests" (29). So long as this division persists, the free laborer cannot be equated with their labor power; rather, they exist in a relation of "possessive individualism" to that labor power (34). This is crucial to the dignity of the subject under liberalism, which "can legitimately claim to be a humanism, for it never confuses what we are with what we own and therefore never treats us as commodities that can be appropriated" (23).

The key claim that underpins *neoliberalism* is that the separation between the spheres of production and reproduction, and thus the "split being" of the free laborer, can be overcome through the concept of human capital. Developed in the 1960s by University of Chicago economists Theodore Schultz and Gary Becker, the concept was initially restricted to the educational context, referring to skills an individual could acquire by investing in pedagogy and training.[101] Soon, however, human capital would expand its scope considerably, coming to refer not to one aspect of a person's life, but to every aspect. "The things that I inherit, the things that happen to me, and the things I do all contribute to the maintenance or the deterioration of my human capital," writes Feher. "More radically put, my human capital is me, as a set of skills and capabilities that is modified by all that affects me and all that I effect" (26). This view places the subject beyond the liberal terrain of possessive individualism, because while the free laborer owns their labor power, "neoliberal subjects do not exactly own their human capital; they invest in it" (34).

This view also entails the "de-proletarianization" of the wage-earning subject, who becomes an entrepreneur of himself (in Foucault's formulation) or an investor in himself (in Feher's), a producer as much as a worker or consumer.[102] All behavior now comes under the remit of production, meaning that there is no longer a separate sphere of reproduction, and so "domains such as health, education, culture, and the like" shift from a realm external to the market to "instead become sectors of the valorizing of the self (understood as capital)" (33). While many critics have lamented this colonization of the lifeworld by economic self-interest, Feher (like Foucault before him) uncovers a kind of utopianism in the neoliberal worldview.[103] "What was at stake for Schultz, Becker, and their associates," he argues, "was to challenge the alleged heterogeneity between the aspirations of the authentic self and the kind of optimizing calculations required by the business world" (33). The point was not only to make people more like firms but also to imagine firms as more like people.[104]

Here is where the overlap between the Left and Right critiques of liberalism starts to emerge. Toward the end of his essay, Feher spends time laying out a summary of the New Left's three-fold critique of the subject of liberal capitalism. This critique combined an attack on the Freudian notion of desire as a symptom of lack; a reinterpretation of disinterested love and selfless giving as ideologies that enable the subject to be governed; and a rejection of economic self-interest as a handmaiden to capitalist exploitation and state socialist subjection.[105] While this threefold critique clearly aimed at the radical emancipation of contemporary subjects, one of its main effects—most notoriously in the case of Foucault's much-debated dalliance with neoliberalism—was to muddy the distinctions between Left and Right.[106] As Feher summarizes:

> Neoliberal and "radical" critiques of the liberal condition clearly came from opposite political corners and harbored antagonistic aspirations. At the same time, however, they not only developed during the same period, and out of an equally acute allergy to the hegemony of the Keynesian welfare state, but also centered their critical perspective on the subjective formation that liberal governmentality presupposes, targets, and seeks to reproduce. Indeed, for both neoliberal and radical critics of the 1960s and 1970s, the relationship that individuals establish with themselves—how they care about and take care of themselves—emerged as the privileged framework for political reflection. (37)

Far from rejecting social concerns, neoliberals and radicals came to see those concerns playing out at the level of personal autonomy. Care for others would now be conjoined with and premised upon care of the self. By dissolving—from different directions—the distinction between the realms of production and reproduction, both neoliberals and radicals espoused the idea that "the personal is (the) political," that self-appreciation is the basis for all action. "The contest for the definition of the conditions under which we may appreciate ourselves is politically decisive," Feher therefore concludes, lamenting that over recent decades it is only neoliberalism that "has imposed its definition of what self-appreciation entails" (37, 38).[107]

For Feher—and this is where he is distinctive—the radical project of the New Left should be reawakened not by repudiating the notion of human capital, but by co-opting it. The idea of the free laborer was indeed an ideological ruse, as Marx had argued. Granted formal equality with their employer and imagined as free to exchange their labor power at its proper value in the market, the free laborer—unlike the peasant they replaced in the transition from feudalism to capitalism—was in reality coerced into entering the market by their loss of ownership of the means of production and subsistence. Yet rather than repudiate the notion of the free laborer, the mainstream Left in the industrial era embraced that category with a view to establishing a labor movement that could build resistance from within the system, gaining rights and retaining a greater share of surplus value for laborers as a class. Comparing Marx's analysis to Foucault's reflections on early feminism, Feher finds in both thinkers "a call to accept and inhabit a certain mode of subjection in order to redirect it or turn it against its instigators" (22). This is the same route he now counsels with respect to neoliberalism, which can only be overcome by embracing the notion of human capital at its heart. For Feher, the point is not to go *back* but to go *through*. He counsels today's activists "to explore the possibility of defying neoliberalism from *within*—that is, by embracing the very condition that its discourses and practices delineate" (21).

As a political prescription, I cannot say that I am fully persuaded by the merits of this indubitably creative response to the neoliberal condition.[108] But as a description of the practice of literary New Sincerity, Feher's idea of working to defy neoliberalism from within functions surprisingly well. Returning now to our home ground of post-boomer fiction, I want to connect the discussion of human capital above with the formal observations I made about literary New Sincerity in earlier sections. In particular, I want to revisit once more this body of literature's reflections on writing and reading in the neoliberal age.

Sincerely Ours

In his recent *Liberalism and American Literature in the Clinton Era*, Ryan Brooks—addressing many of the same authors I do, and in dialogue, like Konstantinou, with my work on New Sincerity—agrees on the importance of the human capital paradigm for reading post-boomer writing in the age of normative neoliberalism. Acknowledging that "these writers embrace the logic of 'human capital,' the neoliberal discourse that transforms the free market from a structure made possible by the antagonism between workers and capitalists to a structure in which *everyone* is a capitalist, an 'entrepreneur of the self,'"

Brooks's structuralist Marxist approach leads him to be critical of this move, calling it "the means by which left-leaning writers negotiate the neoliberal turn—a version of, rather than an alternative to, this new consensus."[109] My countering contention is that while post-boomer writers do indeed embrace (or at least engage) the logic of human capital, they do so in order to expose its workings and to articulate anxiety about how it operates in its current neoliberal form, with a view (often inchoate) to overcoming that form. While Brooks implies that we should resist the human capital paradigm by going *back*, in other words, I argue that New Sincerity writers are seeking, in the dialectical manner suggested by Feher, a way *through*. And while Brooks suggests that these writers' fictional texts "celebrate socially conscious values like empathy, sincerity, and respect for 'internal experience,'" I maintain that these texts are not celebratory but ambivalent, and that it is precisely their literary qualities—including their distance from argumentation and celebration, and their self-consciousness about language and literary expression in a neoliberal economy—that enables them to turn this ambivalence into aesthetic form.[110]

A good way to explore this aesthetics of ambivalence is via consideration of the figure of the gift. Many post-boomer writers have praised Lewis Hyde's 1983 book *The Gift* as a model for artistic practice, no doubt attracted to the way Hyde's text describes the act of imaginative creativity as a thoroughly sincere one, wherein "the future artist finds himself or herself moved by a work of art, and, through that experience, comes to labor in the service of art until he can profess his own gifts."[111] Significantly, Hyde distinguishes the term "labor" from the term "work": while work is something "we do by the hour" and "if possible, we do it for money," labor contributes to the act of creation for its own sake.[112] This distinction preserves a space for artistic purity to exist in an otherwise commodified culture; as Konstantinou has noted, Hyde "seeks to articulate the conditions of compatibility of capitalism and the gift economy for the individual artist. He defends the claim that the gift might endure—even thrive—despite the ubiquity of the calculating disposition that dominates contemporary life."[113] Even as he protects a space for art as gift, however, Hyde does not ignore the necessary claims of the market where the artist sells their "work." The real lesson of *The Gift*, according to Konstantinou, can thus be summarized as follows: "Make your art in the gift-sphere, but when entering the marketplace, you had better find a good agent."[114]

Yet if these divisions between labor and work, the gift-sphere and the market, and the sincere artist and the wily agent all seem designed to preserve the gift as a purely positive force, then the insights of recent scholarship on the creative economy cast doubt on the viability of this model. As Sarah Brouillette among others has argued, the artist figure can in fact be understood as the ideal neoliberal subject, the "profitable, pervasive, regulated symbol of autonomy from routine," an example of how you should do what you love and love what you do, sincerely working to produce your wares for a capitalist market that is indifferent to use value except as an indirect route to keeping labor costs down.[115] "Hyde's account of the gift participates in the idealizing discourses of the 'artist-author,'" Konstantinou observes, and as such *The Gift*'s imagined division between sincere gift-giving creator and wily market-traversing agent—a division internalized in the consciousness of the laboring artist—turns out to be unsatisfactory, because the creator side of the dichotomy cannot escape the taint of neoliberal interpellation, throwing into doubt the meaning of their sincerity in the contemporary socioeconomic context.[116]

With this critique in mind, the praise for *The Gift* among post-boomer writers would seem to constitute a kind of wish fulfillment, a way of retaining some undialectically pure image of the artist in a world of neoliberal commodification.[117] Yet while throughout Hyde's text the gift is understood to be something inherently positive and even transformative, and while their public commentary on the book would seem to align many post-boomer writers with this view, their fiction suggests a more complicated, more double-edged conception of the gift. For a start, it is a conception much less sanguine about the separation of work (and pay) from the labor of creation. In an essay on Wallace's 1999 collection *Brief Interviews with Hideous Men*, Zadie Smith remarks that "in these stories, the act of giving is in crisis; the logic of the market seeps into every aspect of life."[118] Notably, the "giver" in Wallace's stories is often an artist who is presented as more interested in self-appreciation, both psychic and economic, than in the aesthetic integrity of their work.

This kind of compromised artist figure is not unique to Wallace, but appears regularly across New Sincerity texts, from Eggers's narrator-entrepreneur in *A Heartbreaking Work* to Egan's creative-writer-cum-social-media-guru in *Look at Me*, from Whitehead's intuitive branding consultant in *Apex Hides the Hurt* to DeWitt's genius salesman in *Lightning Rods* (2011).

Through their fictions, New Sincerity writers tell a more anxious story than Hyde's artistic alibi would imply, a story in which the cross-contamination of love and money becomes the inescapable condition of writing in a neoliberal age. If literary New Sincerity is sincere about anything, we might say, it is this cross-contamination, this basic threat to a pure sincerity, in life and art.[119] But the dialectical move on which literary New Sincerity is premised involves a deconstruction of these two poles—the pure and the contaminated—so that the former is no longer the positively valued term. And it is here that the final piece of the puzzle, the reader, becomes crucial. The reader is the figure via whom purity and autonomy can be questioned, and contamination can be rethought as something not to be resisted but embraced.

It is the insights of poststructuralism that allow us to see contamination not as an inherently negative trope, but as a necessary condition for existence. "Contamination is not a privation or a lack of purity," writes Martin Hägglund in his account of Derrida's work,

> It is the originary possibility for anything to be. Thus, a pure gift is not impossible because it is contaminated by our selfish intentions or by the constraints of economic exchange; it is impossible because a gift must be contaminated in order to be a gift.[120]

In literary New Sincerity, the writer articulates a desire for contamination—"the very desire for a gift is a desire for contamination"—by invoking a reader who can acknowledge and even co-produce the gift of writing.[121] The key split in the authorial consciousness dramatized in these texts is therefore not between artist and agent—as Hyde and Konstantinou suggest—but between writer and reader. The reader becomes the internalized figure that contaminates the pure autonomy of the writer, an autonomy that has come to serve an ideological function under neoliberal capitalism.[122] Though I am describing it somewhat abstractly, on the page this plays out in highly affective ways, with the undecidability of the gift—its haunting by debt and indebtedness—contributing to the fraught psychodynamics of the writer-reader relationship staged in New Sincerity fiction. The reader is consistently imagined in these texts to represent a future beyond what the writer can anticipate, and thus to offer the only possible relief from solipsistic self-consciousness and pure autonomy. But this relief is also a risk. In becoming the internalized figure of historical change beyond the enclosing neoliberal horizon, the reader figures the chance but also the threat of a future that can negate the self-appreciation of the writer.

Chapter Two will offer a concrete account of the undecidability of the gift in the context of neoliberal political economy. For now, we can say that literary New Sincerity represents not an unwitting symptom but an ambivalent struggle to register and respond to a set of dilemmas historically specific to neoliberalism: the shift from the free laborer to the human capital paradigm; the worry that supposedly disinterested liberal values and feelings can be reduced to calculations of interest; the recasting of purity as ideology; and the interpellation of the gift-giving, labor-loving artist as ideal neoliberal subject. In other words, this literature is self-conscious not only about its own complicity with neoliberal logic, but also about the difficulty of diluting that complicity by reverting to a division within the authorial self whereby the autonomous creator could be walled off from the canny literary agent. This is a literature, we might go as far as to say, that endeavors to read its own political and sociological unconscious, to uncover the historical entanglements that underpin and enable the act of apparently free creation.[123] Directly invoking the figure of the reader—including the prominence in heightened moments of second-person address—then becomes a way to suggest the foundational priority of the other's perspective, a way to reverse engineer the formulation of sincerity that Trilling finds in Polonius ("To thine own self be true / And it doth follow . . . Thou canst not then be false to any man") by aiming instead to be true to others as a *means* to discover the truth about oneself. But where Trilling emphasizes the realm of psychology, I argue that something more than psychological ambivalence is at work in this writing. What literary New Sincerity most tellingly exposes, on my reading, is a structuring tension between the liberal emphasis on individual intention and conscience on the one hand, and the Marxist and Bourdieusian accounts of determining class interest on the other.[124]

While a picture of late-twentieth-century American fiction writers as a class—more specifically, a fraction of the professional-managerial class—will only come fully into view in the second half of this book, it is worth briefly drawing out here the differences between my account of the response by New Sincerity writers to complicity with neoliberalism, and Linda Hutcheon's influential account of postmodernist fiction as "complicitous critique." For Hutcheon, acknowledging complicity is a radical stance, working out from a hegemonic cultural discourse to find its aporias and edges: "postmodernism does not pretend to operate outside the system, for it knows it cannot; it therefore overtly acknowledges its complicity, only to work covertly to subvert the system's values from within."[125] Yet despite her acknowledgment of literature's embeddedness within the capitalist system, Hutcheon's conception of complicity remains primarily linguistic rather than materialist, and on her account fiction writers remain free to invoke questions of complicity from an implicitly autonomous aesthetic space. For New Sincerity writers, by contrast, complicity is not only linguistic but a feature of the writer's economic embeddedness in neoliberal culture, often filtered through particular developments in the publishing industry even before the arrival of the "Age of Amazon."[126] This embeddedness registers in the fiction, often on an allegorical level, as a greater sincerity about positionality vis-à-vis the intensification of market ideology over the neoliberal period. Facing this intensification, New Sincerity writers are much less confident than Hutcheon's postmodernists that they can get beyond complicity to critique. Acknowledging complicity is no longer such a radical move: it is only the first step in the articulation of a positive politics, an articulation that—as I explore in Chapter Six—is itself a notably difficult task under neoliberal hegemony.

In this climate, too, any move from irony to "postirony" cannot simply be a question of changing one's conscious ethos. It must also involve acknowledging—and increasingly so as our historical distance from Wallace's "E Unibus Pluram" becomes ever greater—that such a move can function as its own kind of branding exercise. The term "New Sincerity" (capitals and all), though not my own, is intended in this book to capture succinctly these writers' self-awareness about branding, and to indicate that, especially in a media-saturated age, sincerity can always resemble insincerity, with the difference not a question of knowledge but of trust and even faith. If, as Brian McHale has claimed, modernism is characterized by an epistemological dominant and postmodernism by an ontological dominant, then the equivalent dominant in New Sincerity writing is the ethical.[127] Contemporary sincerity privileges ethical questions by performing the confusions that divide the writer's self and that complicate old notions of inner truth and wholeness that underpin sincerity and authenticity as Trilling defines them. Yet this also is an ethics deeply informed by politics and economics, and by a self-conscious acknowledgment of complicity that goes beyond that found in earlier literary movements and moments.[128] If such self-consciousness is no longer a route to freedom, as the postmodernists hoped or assumed, then the ambivalent turn to the reader in literary New Sincerity should be read dialectically, as expressive of a historical impasse.

It would thus be a mistake to assume that the role of the reader *imagined* by the texts studied in the following pages is coextensive with the role of *actual* readers of those texts. The reader's role as imagined in literary New Sincerity is not necessarily a liberatory one; it is simply the necessary corollary of the vertiginous but impotent self-consciousness that attends the writing of neoliberal-era fiction, a fiction that structurally requires an other to relieve it of its burdens. How the actual reader responds to a New Sincerity text is a different matter to how that text imagines its reader. In this book I do propose a critical role for the reader of New Sincerity texts, one that works to establish the historical and theoretical distance from neoliberal norms that the texts themselves find so hard to imagine. This imaginative difficulty is figured not only in direct appeals to the reader for dialogue and decision—"So decide," the famous closing imperative of Wallace's story "Octet," being perhaps the signature such appeal—but also in the common motif of evacuating conscious intention from the subject who acts.[129]

I explore this negation of conscious intention most thoroughly in Chapter Five, in a consideration of the dramatized escape from consciousness that concludes many of George Saunders's stories. But this escape—like the escapes from consciousness that structure, in varying ways, the imaginaries of novels like Egan's *Look at Me*, Eggers's *You Shall Know Our Velocity*, Kunkel's *Indecision*, and Whitehead's *Apex Hides the Hurt*—should not be taken as a positive recommendation or prescription for action in a neoliberal world. Gestures such as these in literary New Sincerity must instead be read both critically—as informed by skepticism of earlier (modernist and postmodernist) solutions offered through an emphasis on individual (self-) consciousness—and dialectically, as an admission of uncertainty about "actual feeling" and actual solutions, as a symptom of the imaginative limits imposed by the dominance of normative neoliberalism and the "End of History." In this way, literary New

Sincerity frames the outlines of a political project, albeit one not fully articulated but waiting to be taken up, as Zadie Smith has it, "off the page, outside words." In the Conclusion to this book, I offer some brief thoughts on how this project has developed in American fiction after 2008. But it seems fair to say that it remains a political project that is, as the title of this section has it, *sincerely ours*.

Chapter Outline

In *New Sincerity*, six chapters develop the themes set out above in what I hope are fresh and stimulating ways. Chapter One continues the core discussion begun in this Introduction by asking how an art of sincerity might be achieved under neoliberal conditions. Taking David Foster Wallace's *Westward the Course of Empire Takes Its Way* (1989) and *Infinite Jest* (1996) as case studies, the chapter pursues a Hegelian reading that looks to artworks to articulate the conditions of intelligibility for contemporary social life. The opening section reads *Westward* as an aesthetic response to Fukuyama's "End of History" and offers a paradigmatic account of how New Sincerity texts address their reader, which serves as a reference point for the remainder of the book. The chapter then moves to *Infinite Jest* and explores the Hegelian dimensions of Wallace's world-building, including the continuum he depicts between neoliberalism and fascism, and the way in which the tragic story of Hal Incandenza exemplifies the sincerity crisis of neoliberal life. This reading of Hal prepares the way for an analysis of the films of his father James Incandenza, which I argue should be considered through the generous reading offered them by Joelle van Dyne, Wallace's surrogate for the ideal reader he imagines for his own fiction. I then consider the story of *Infinite Jest*'s hero, Don Gately, alongside the novel's invocation of Alcoholics Anonymous as a paradoxical model of sincerity and freedom. The chapter concludes by analyzing Wallace's singular style and reflecting on why literary fiction provides the primary ground for the expression of New Sincerity aesthetics in the neoliberal moment.

If Chapter One addresses that moment in primarily cultural and philosophical terms, Chapter Two focuses on the economic underpinnings of New Sincerity writing in the era of the so-called New Economy. The idealism of Wallace's Hegelian aesthetics is supplemented and modified by this chapter's materialist reading of Dave Eggers's early work, namely his first two books:

A Heartbreaking Work of Staggering Genius (2000) and *You Shall Know Our Velocity* (2002). The opening section introduces the rhetoric of the New Economy and connects Eggers's memoir to that discursive milieu through its "sincerity of credit," while also laying out its resistance through a counterlogic I call the "sincerity of debt." After outlining the centrality of credit and debt to the neoliberal economy as problems of time and space, the chapter moves to examine how neoliberal capitalism's "temporal fix" is embedded in the formal qualities of *A Heartbreaking Work*. The "spatial fix" is then mobilized as a lens through which to read *Velocity*, linking its narrator's ethical anxieties to a financial system inextricable from global inequality and American imperialism. The final section turns to the psychodynamics of the "sincerity fix" in Eggers's relation to his reader, connecting the ambivalences in this textual relation to the economic conditions that underpin his writing. These are the pages of *New Sincerity* that focus most thoroughly on the dialectical character of the writer-reader relationship in literary New Sincerity, contextualizing that relationship as one shaped by, and responsive to, the material pressures of neoliberal economy.

Wallace and Eggers are the literary figures most often associated with the New Sincerity paradigm, which has led some critics to characterize the paradigm itself as the preserve of privileged white males. Chapter Three begins the process of correcting that vision, exploring Jennifer Egan's first two novels, *The Invisible Circus* (1994) and *Look at Me* (2001), as feminist reworkings of the themes and formal innovations examined in the opening chapters. This chapter takes up two distinct but related topics: the relationship between sincerity and the history of the novel, and the role played by gender in that relationship. The first section reads *The Invisible Circus* as a formally realist but thematically postmodernist Bildungsroman, concerned with the problem of its protagonist's sincerity at the dawn of the neoliberal era but lacking a metafictional framework that might reflect on deeper questions of literary sincerity. The chapter then offers an overview of the relationship between sincerity and the modern novel from *Robinson Crusoe* to *Gravity's Rainbow*, highlighting the innovative ways that *Look at Me* engages the canon of eighteenth- and nineteenth-century fiction. Further sections examine the uncanny role played by gothic and postmodernist intertexts in *Look at Me*, with a particular focus on the way its visual themes intersect with the problem of female visibility.

Drawing on Nancy Armstrong's influential argument that the rise of the novel testifies to the fact that "the modern individual was first and foremost a woman," the chapter concludes by considering the question of whether the paradigmatic subject of literary New Sincerity could likewise be said to be a woman. Egan's response to neoliberal image culture sits at the heart of this chapter, as does the question of literary New Sincerity as both a resistance to branding and itself a brand.

The issue of branding is likewise central to Chapter Four, which takes up questions of race and class that have remained implicit over the book's first half. The chapter addresses three of Colson Whitehead's early novels—*The Intuitionist* (1999), *Apex Hides the Hurt* (2006), and *Sag Harbor* (2009)—to consider the role played by sincerity in the African American literary tradition, in particular its relationship to that tradition's key trope of "signifying." It begins with Whitehead's signifying on Du Bois's "double consciousness" in *Sag Harbor*, a reading that opens onto the debate in contemporary African American literary studies about the relative importance of race and class under neoliberal conditions. This is followed by a reading of *The Intuitionist* as exploring African American complicity with, and resistance to, technological and capitalist modernity, and as an allegory for the challenges posed by the black writer's newly mainstream position within the neoliberal culture industry. Considering the significance of black individual success and its relationship to racial "uplift," the chapter then turns to *Apex Hides the Hurt* to frame an analysis of discourses of human capital in racial capitalism. A comparison with Zora Neale Hurston's *Their Eyes Were Watching God* opens onto an account of the role played by "freedom" across Whitehead's early fiction, and the ironic rather than sincere ways he tends to invoke the term. Summarizing the themes of complicity, uplift, and double consciousness, the chapter concludes by reading Whitehead's early novels as expressing the problem raised for the artist by growing African American political, economic, and cultural power—"black faces in high places"—across the post–Civil Rights decades, culminating in the "postracial" presidency of Barack Obama.

With the first four chapters addressing the milieu of the professional-managerial class, Chapter Five shifts the focus to the stories of working-class characters, while considering how capitalist restructuring has impacted class distinctions and affects. Moving from the single-author focus of the earlier chapters, this chapter twins Helen DeWitt and George Saunders as writers who address the intersections of sincerity, shame, and what I dub *seeing like a neoliberal*. I read the title story of Saunders's *Pastoralia* (2000) as a depiction of the changed status of the working-class subject under neoliberalism, now imagined as an investor and possessor of human capital while suffering increasingly oppressive and precarious working conditions. *Pastoralia*'s closing story, "The Falls," allows us to track how this ideological and material shift in class relations occurred, and to connect Saunders's emphasis on revision as the "hard work" of the writer to his own class trajectory. The chapter then turns from Saunders's depiction of neoliberalism's losers, who fail to make the adjustment from liberal to neoliberal values, to the archetype who represents the winner in the neoliberal imaginary: the entrepreneur. Addressing Joe, the protagonist of Helen DeWitt's *Lightning Rods* (published 2011, though written in the late 1990s) as a figure of neoliberal sincerity, I also read DeWitt's second novel as an allegory of the altered position of experimental fiction in the contemporary publishing industry. The final section then takes public statements by DeWitt and Saunders following David Foster Wallace's death as a springboard for considering the ambivalence toward capitalism among New Sincerity writers. The chapter ends by arguing that class consciousness is displaced in this writing by an imagined escape from consciousness altogether and suggests that such an escape should be read dialectically, as a symptom of the predominance of capitalist realism during this period.

Chapter Six represents a necessary final step in the book's argument by moving from the political implications of literary New Sincerity to the explicit topic of political resistance, as featured in novels concerned with the liberation movements of the 1960s and their legacy over later decades. The chapter looks to three novels that grapple with the question of political sincerity, against a background of recent revisionist scholarship that ties the values of the New Left surprisingly closely to those of the rising neoliberal Right. The opening section employs a 2014 essay by Jedediah Purdy to consider the political character of the 1989–2008 period and to frame the chapter's central question: *what does it mean to oppose sincerely a system from which one comparatively benefits?* The next two sections read Susan Choi's *American Woman* (2003) as reflecting on the sincerity of political activism mediated through speech, action, the body, and writing, and as historicizing the intersecting rise of identity politics and the neoliberal marketplace. The chapter then turns to Dana Spiotta's *Eat the Document* (2006) to explore problems of responsibility, intention, and the symbolic resonances of political action across time, all of which bear on the question of political sincerity in the millennial moment. The final sections address Benjamin Kunkel's *Indecision* (2005) as a self-conscious exploration of the possibility of committing, in the early twenty-first century, to democratic socialism, especially when one is a privileged white male who benefits from the system one ostensibly opposes.

The choice of literary texts and sequence of chapters in *New Sincerity* are intended to take the reader on a broadly chronological journey through the period of normative neoliberalism, beginning in the late 1980s and ending in the mid-2000s, with certain chapters (especially Two, Four, and Six) reaching back to tell the story of neoliberalism's emergence in the mid-to-late twentieth century. But as my chapter descriptions should indicate, the book's structure is also designed to develop an internal dialectic whereby each chapter speaks back to the chapters prior, reframing what has gone before. So the (Hegelian) emphasis on art in Chapter One is revised from the (Marxist) viewpoint of economy in Chapter Two, while in Chapter Three the implicitly male framing of the story of literary New Sincerity is countered by a feminist retelling of that story. Chapter Four then turns to a major writer of color to shine a light on the whiteness of the opening three chapters, while Chapter Five reframes the argument from the viewpoint of working-class rather than middle-class characters. Chapter Six turns to novels engaging directly with political activism, thereby moving past the implicit quality of the political in the first five chapters. My Conclusion first examines the revival of left-liberal and socialist little magazines in the United States in the 2000s, before arguing that in the literature of the post-2008 period, with the eclipse of normative neoliberalism, the model of sincerity traced across the chapters of this book has been transformed.

Achieving the Art of Sincerity

Westward to the End of History

In July 1989 the political scientist Francis Fukuyama published "The End of History?" in the American foreign policy magazine *The National Interest*. This was four months before the fall of the Berlin Wall and the beginning of the end of the Cold War, but Fukuyama was already looking beyond those events to the world that was coming into being in their wake. Professing to offer a "conceptual framework for distinguishing between what is essential and what is contingent or accidental in world history," Fukuyama proposed that what was essential in world history as the twentieth century drew to a close was an "unabashed victory of economic and political liberalism," which also represented "the triumph of the West, of the Western *idea*."[1] Anticipating the coming collapse of Soviet communism and observing "the ineluctable spread of consumerist Western culture" (3)—what would later be called globalization—Fukuyama argued that it was not simply the Cold War or a particular period of history that was coming to a close. History itself was ending, in that we had now reached "the end point of mankind's ideological evolution and the universalization of Western liberal democracy as the final form of human government" (4). Hegel had been right, Marx had been wrong: the final stage of history, embodied in the victory and unipolar hegemony of the United States, would be liberalism and capitalism rather than socialism and communism.

"The End of History?" is often remembered as an unfettered trumpeting of American power and values, an interpretation abetted by its author's links to the RAND Corporation and the fact that he would soon enter the employment of the US State Department. Nevertheless, Fukuyama's essay is more ambivalent regarding history's termination than these institutional affiliations would suggest. "We might summarize the content of the universal homogenous state," he writes, "as liberal democracy in the political sphere combined with easy access to VCRs and stereos in the economic" (8). This tart observation already hints that the triumph of capitalism and consumerism will come at a spiritual cost, and in his final paragraph Fukuyama undertakes a striking tonal about-turn, lamenting that "the end of history will be a very sad time" (18). Shorn of ideological struggle, of "the willingness to risk one's life for a purely abstract goal," Western man will now be reduced to "economic calculation, the endless solving of technical problems, environmental concerns, and the satisfaction of sophisticated consumer demands." Paraphrasing what he takes to be Hegel's prediction that "in the post-historical period there will be neither art nor philosophy," Fukuyama turns the optimism of Hegel's vision on its head. He envisages only the coming prospect of "centuries of boredom," set amid "the perpetual caretaking of the museum of human history" (18).

The month after "The End of History?" appeared, David Foster Wallace—whose debut novel *The Broom of the System* had received positive attention but who was still, at age twenty-seven, a relative newcomer on the American literary scene—published his first collection of short fiction, *Girl with Curious Hair*. Most of the stories had appeared in small journals and magazines in prior years, the main exception being the collection's closing novella, *Westward the Course of Empire Takes Its Way*. At 143 pages, taking up nearly two fifths of the book, *Westward* constituted its author's first substantial artistic statement of intent, a direct response to the literary aesthetics of his postmodern predecessors. Moreover, as its mock-heroic title indicates, Wallace's novella framed this aesthetic response within the emerging set of historical conditions that would both excite and trouble Fukuyama, namely the global victory of American power and its vision of consumerist democratic rule, in perpetuity.[2] Written against the background of neoliberal capitalism's ascent to political and cultural dominance in the United States and elsewhere, *Westward* contains many characteristic elements of what would become identifiable as the New Sincerity aesthetic. Yet it combines those elements in a manner that is clearly formative, somehow both overly condensed and overly diffuse.

The basic narrative haltingly follows three characters on a journey to a town in Illinois called Collision, where they will take part in "the scheduled

Reunion of everyone who has ever been in a McDonald's commercial."[3] Two of the travelers, Mark Nechtr and Drew-Lynn Eberhardt, are members of a creative writing workshop taught in Baltimore by Professor Ambrose, an obvious stand-in for Wallace's own metaphorical teacher, John Barth.[4] Barth's "Lost in the Funhouse," attributed to Ambrose and described by Wallace's narrator as "American metafiction's most famous story" (237), provides both an epigraph to *Westward*—"For whom is the Funhouse fun?"—and the inspiration within the plot for the plan to build a series of "mirrored discotheque franchises" (240) across American marketing territories. Funhouse 1 will be opened at the McDonald's Reunion party in Collision, with the architect behind the whole event being J. D. Steelritter, whose advertising firm controls "the image and perception of McDonald's franchise empire" (246). Steelritter's origin story as the child of a Midwestern rose farm is twinned with a religiously inflected recounting of the birth of market capitalism in the region: "The area was substantially transfigured. Misery, guilt and charity became prosperity, redemption, market" (258). Yet despite going onto great financial success, Steelritter presents in *Westward* as a sad figure, a man for whom "life just goes on, emptily, sadly, with always direction but never center" (240). Frying and chewing the roses that once lent beauty to his childhood surroundings, and haunted throughout the story by the phrase "*For Whom*," Steelritter intuits the lack of purpose that Fukuyama identified at the End of History, when consumerist hegemony has replaced ideological struggle and contestation, but to no heroic end. Aiming both to address his own ennui and "to turn millennial boredom around" (340), Steelritter conceives his McDonald's Reunion as "a party to end all parties" (235), "a Reunion to end all reunions" (267). The event will short-circuit the boredom of the end of history with an eschatological orgy of consumer desire, bringing history to its apotheosis in a more conclusive way:

> And that, as they say, will be that. No one will ever leave the rose farm's Reunion. The revelation of What They Want will be on them; and, in that revelation of Desire, they will Possess. They will all Pay the Price—without persuasion. It's J.D.'s swan song. No more need for J.D. Steelritter Advertising or its helmsman's genius. Life, the truth, will be its own commercial. Advertising will have finally arrived at the death that's been its object all along. And, in Death, it will of course become Life. The last commercial. (310)[5]

Yet *Westward* never takes us as far as the Reunion and this negation and sublation of history's end. The novella's coterie of characters, traveling together in a car to Collision, never arrive there. Instead, Wallace's story morphs into a digressive, self-reflexive, and at times confusing meditation upon the kind of art that might redeem the nihilism of Steelritter's vision. The brand of art associated with Ambrose—postmodernist metafiction—is ruled out early as a redemptive possibility. In selling his Funhouse concept, Ambrose has become "a client and entrepreneur" of Steelritter Advertising (239), his work now indistinguishable from commercial entertainment, his instrumentalist ethos enabling him to teach his students "*how* but not *why* to write fiction" (237, my emphasis). This literal selling out only confirms Steelritter's belief that literature and advertising, both concerned with the manipulation of desire for market ends, are fundamentally inseparable: "Stories are basically like ad campaigns, no?" (330). Likewise excluded from redemptive consideration is the aesthetic that Wallace's narrator refers to as "New Realism," a popular minimalist style of the 1980s that "diverges, in its slowness, from the really real only in its extreme economy" (267). This play on "economy" serves to twin New Realism with metafiction as two sides of the same capitalist coin. Despite their association with the creative writing program, both literary styles are divorced from the traditional ideals of modernist aesthetics, which placed faith in the autonomy of the work of art, its opposition to market values, and its unrepeatable and unprogrammable singularity.[6]

The stage seems set for a revitalization of these ideals through a new kind of art. Yet it is hard not to notice that the narrative voice throughout *Westward* seems caught up with the same economic logic it wants to disavow, often invoking the very co-implication of storytelling and advertising that Steelritter embraces and Ambrose self-servingly ignores. "I am *acutely* aware that our time together is valuable. Honest" (235), the narrator assures us early on, while regularly finding it necessary to remind his reader that "the narrative bought and paid for and now under time-consuming scrutiny is *not* in fact a barely-there window onto a different and truly diverting world" (265). But while it seems inclined to combine metafiction and realism, despite ruling out the redemptive possibilities of either, *Westward* nonetheless professes to have as its mission to answer the questions "why" and "*For Whom*," to construct a Funhouse that provides not superficial entertainment or empty experimentation but real shelter and nourishment, a house for the reader to reside in. And the novella concludes with a story-within-the-story that seems intended to model this redemptive kind of art.

This story—which is in fact mostly the paraphrase of a story rather than its direct reproduction—represents the sole work that Mark Nechtr, the protagonist who "desires, some distant, hard-earned day, to write something that stabs you in the heart" (332), will ever manage to submit to Professor Ambrose's writing workshop. It tells of an archer-turned-prisoner named Dave, convicted of the murder of his girlfriend even though in reality she has used his archer's arrow to commit suicide in his presence. In prison, Dave's cellmate Mark is a grotesque and hardened criminal, "horror embodied" (361). He repeatedly beats and rapes Dave before escaping one night with the threat that, if Dave betrays knowledge of his whereabouts, Mark will have him brutalized and killed by the remaining inmates. Despite keeping quiet, Dave is in fact regularly beaten to within an inch of his life before the prison warden—played by 1970s television star Jack Lord—tries to persuade him that his only chance to save himself is to inform on Mark. To support his argument, Lord employs language redolent of the economic logic that pervades *Westward*:

> The price of life in the penal system is low, because the Facility is overstocked with lives, lives that wear only numbers, lives without honor or value or end. There is no demand for them. The market's invisible hand hefts a finger, damning the guilty to an existence of utter freedom, freedom to choke and starve, alone in a riot. (367)

The neoliberal lexicon is fully on display here: price, numbers, value, demand, market, freedom. Lord makes clear to Dave that his life is "simultaneously worthless and valuable" (367): worthless as an end in itself, valuable only as the exchange value of one hundred cigarettes. Dave is living at the End of History, the time and space of Fukuyama's "economic calculation" and "satisfaction of sophisticated consumer demands." The only freedom he has in this context is freedom of access to the market. Lord's logic is thus ironclad: in exchange for his life, Dave must sell his information, the only thing he owns. There is no alternative.

Except that Dave, to the consternation of the prison warden, refuses to tell. He does what Fukuyama would claim had become impossible, displaying a "willingness to risk one's life for a purely abstract goal." This goal or end he calls "honor," and it is in the name of honor that he remains silent: "He's had time to think, and he's no idiot, and he's been able to come up with just one thing. They can't take your honor. Only that can be only given" (369). Jack Lord is distinctly unimpressed by this reasoning: "This weak kid's own life worth less to him than some *idea?*" (369). Pushed to explain further, Dave's response begins to articulate a deep complication at the heart of Wallace's emerging aesthetic project. Where he had seemed only now to rely on an opposition between honor and the market, Dave goes on to deconstruct that opposition:

> The supine murderer would sincerely like to make the erect peace officer understand. It is no matter, this *To Whom* the debt is owed. Dave's just too fucking selfish to do it. . . . O Mr. Lord, but the fact that he *does not rat*: this is his self's coin, value constant against every curve's wave-like surge. Dave covets, values, hoards, and will not spend his honor. He'll not trade. (369–370)

Rather than present his silence as selflessness on behalf of another, or in service of a moral principle, Dave imagines that silence as selfishness on behalf of himself. Rather than refuse Lord's language of the market and the circulation of value, he reiterates that language: debt, coin, value, curve, covet, hoard, spend, trade. Despite the turn to honor, therefore, the economic logic that dominates Wallace's novella is not obviously challenged by Dave's reading of his own action. It is unclear what the alternative being presented really amounts to.

But the scenario also invites another reading. In the choice Dave faces between honor and life, the story invokes the specter of Hegel, and specifically the philosopher's dialectic of *Herrschaft und Knechtschaft*, of lord (or Lord) and bondsman.[7] In Hegel's narrative, told in the most famous section of *The Phenomenology of Spirit*, the battle for recognition between two primordial self-consciousnesses is resolved only when one submits to the other by choosing survival over honor, thereby becoming the bondsman to the other's lord. Importantly, the story told in *Westward* offers something like the inverse of Hegel's narrative, in that the one who chooses honor over life becomes—at least in material terms—not the master but the slave.[8] This suggests that honor will fail to be materially rewarded in the neoliberal context inhabited by Dave. Honor is a notion with feudal resonances, and Hegel's story of lord and bondsman is among other things a reflection on feudalism.[9] Thus when Fukuyama conceives of honor as a lost ideal for which one might risk one's life, he is invoking a feudal logic that the historical advent of capitalism places under erasure.[10] Neoliberal ideology completes this erasure by making all notions of honor unintelligible as anything other than a version of economic self-interest. Dave's characterization of honor as self-interest might therefore be explicable in neoliberal terms, except that—and this is the major complication in Wallace's scenario—this brand of selfishness can lead only to literal selflessness through the loss of Dave's life, thus confirming the insight that "selflessness is, of course, horror embodied" (368).

The source of this insight is Professor Ambrose, whose comments on Mark Nechtr's story for his workshop class are interspersed throughout the summary of the story (paralleling how the outer narrative of *Westward* suffers regular interruption by the novella's narrator). Ambrose objects to the twist in the tale rendered by Mark. Up to this point, he claims, the dialogue between Lord and Dave has been "handled with a deftness that earns our approval, a lengthy economy born of a precision that promises Payoff" (368). But the payoff that Dave's selflessness is, at a higher level, a form of selfishness, which is, at a still higher level, a form of selflessness, does not convince. Employing the same economic rhetoric used by Dave and Jack Lord, Ambrose advises Nechtr to undertake "some very simple cost-benefit analyses" (360) to address the story's "technical fuck-ups" (368). In particular, Ambrose opines, Dave's noble assertions seem inconsistent with his portrayal as a weak character: "That shit with Jack Lord: that was just words. Could a weak person *act* so?" (370). Can Dave's actions back up his statements? Even Nechtr, the story's author, doesn't appear able to answer this question. "Well and understandably Mark wants to know, too," we are told. "Does the archer who's guilty of his lover rat? Doesn't he, Mark Nechtr, have to know, if he's going to make it up?" (370).

Seen through the Hegelian lens that the reader of *Westward* is being invited to adopt, the answer to this last question—does the author of the story have to know its outcome?—is *no*. In Mark's quandary about how Dave will act, the story is bringing together three modes of expressing intention: the speaking of words, the carrying out of an action, and the creation of a work of art. As Robert Pippin explains, Hegel saw these modes as analogous to one another, because in each case the animating "inner" intention can only be understood retroactively through the "outer" words, deed, or work, and then only in a context of broader communal recognition.[11] What I intend to say, do, or make is inextricable from the social interpretation of my words, deed, or work. Unless that social interpretation can be entirely predicted in advance, a gap or uncertainty will remain in the connection between intention and deed; from this Hegelian standpoint, a successful artwork achieves a special status "as the achievement of a speculative identity of inner and outer."[12] Indeed art, in Hegel's modernity, becomes the model for what a realized intention looks like, so that "the externalization of our ideas about ourselves in artworks is essential, not merely exemplifying."[13]

This powerful new historical role for art, conceived by Hegel with the help of his predecessors in the German Idealist tradition, most notably Kant, prepared the ground for a shift in the arts away from a primary concern with beauty—the imitation of natural or classical models—toward an overriding concern with meaning.[14] In *Westward*, the roses fried and chewed by J. D. Steelritter represent beauty's exhaustion at the coalface of capitalist commodification. This in turn raises the question of what Wallace's own art is doing if it is not aiming for beauty. One answer, rooted in Mark Nechtr's story about Dave, is that Wallace's art is aiming to uphold honor, to exemplify sincere moral purpose in a world that denies such a possibility, whether in action or in art.[15] But as with Nechtr's hobby of archery, the aim can only be judged successful if the target is hit. The proof is in the aesthetic execution, and the execution can only be judged *ex post facto*. The stakes of this judgment are high: according to Pippin, one of the key innovations of Kant's *Critique of Judgment* was that it "suggested that the deepest issue in the Idealist tradition—the problem of 'the Absolute' (neither subject nor object)—could be addressed, rendered in some way intelligible, *only* aesthetically."[16] *Westward* thus calls for an interpretation and judgment from its reader of the kind that can be rendered only in response to a work of art.

The animating question of literary New Sincerity thus lies embedded in the flagrant allegory that is Mark's story about Dave. Can sincere action be taken, and sincere art be created, under historical conditions anathema to both ethical conduct and artistic practice, when corporate capitalism and neoliberal ideology have rendered moral and aesthetic ends increasingly inseparable from economic ones? The difficulty of answering this question is deepened by the way it is raised in Wallace's text. As I've noted, Mark Nechtr's story-within-the-story is given to us not directly but in a form that is "extremely uneven, moving between a third-person retelling of the content and context of Mark's story, and an apparently unmediated telling of the story itself."[17] We get the action of the story and some of its dialogue, as well as the reactions of Ambrose and members of his writing workshop, which includes the narrator of *Westward*. What we are deprived access to is the story's *form*, a necessity for judging its aesthetic success. Moreover, as the final pages of *Westward* shift from Mark's story back to the outer frame of the journey to Collision, this confusion of registers comes to inflect the narrative voice, with the very idea of a single narrator becoming unstable as the novella reaches its concluding lines:

> Just a tad too long? Lovesick! *Mark'd!* I have hidden exactly nothing. So trust me: we will arrive. Cross my heart. Stick a needle. To tell the truth, we might already be there. . . . See this thing. See inside what spins without purchase. Close your eye. Absolutely no salesman will call. Relax. Lie back. I want nothing from you. Relax. Lie back. . . . Jesus, Sweets, *listen*. Hear it? It's a love song. For whom? You are loved. (372–373)

Describing *Westward* as a "drama of transformed perception" for its narrator, Jeffrey Severs sees this ending as a rejection of the "commodity terms" that have dominated the novella to this point.[18] Not only is this an overly optimistic reading of the faintly creepy tone of the narrator's invitations to trust him, to accept his blandishments and reassurances; it also ignores the fact that the oscillation between sincerity and manipulation in these closing lines emerges from an ambiguous source. As David Hering notes, though it is tempting to read this culminating monologue as emerging from a single narrator, or even from the voice of David ("Dave") Wallace speaking directly to the reader, "it would be more accurate to say that it is delivered in the first person by a narrator of uncertain diegetic status, an unidentified composite voice engendered by the preceding 'Armageddon-explosion' of metafictional narrators and authors."[19] As a result, the potential sincerity of the novella's conclusion—the sincerity of the novella itself—is shown to have a deeply uncertain relationship to the intentions of its author. Like his avatar Mark Nechtr, David Wallace doesn't know the ending of his own story; like Nechtr's tale, *Westward* remains "unfinished and basically unfinishable" (370).

It is a central claim of the present chapter (and of this book more generally) that the uncertainty captured in the form and content of *Westward*'s ending is a defining feature of what I am calling literary New Sincerity. The formal problem of "unfinishedness" so evident throughout Wallace's career as a writer—from the deliberately incomplete final sentence of *The Broom of the System* to the tragically incomplete manuscript of *The Pale King*—is likewise a structuring feature, albeit in varying ways, in the work of virtually every writer examined in subsequent chapters of this book. As *Westward* suggests, and as Wallace's 1990s fiction will reinforce, this formal incompletion constitutes an invitation to the reader to offer an aesthetic and ethical judgment that the text and its author cannot provide. In the Hegelian terms that emerge in *Westward*—and which, as we shall see, also frame *Infinite Jest*—the intentions of the artist can be judged only on the basis of the art itself, and only then by the beholder of the art rather than by its producer. But even this distinction is broken down in literary New Sincerity, which ultimately wants to invite the reader/beholder to become a kind of co-producer in the aesthetic process. If solipsism (which Wallace often claimed was his greatest fear) has morphed, under neoliberalism, into inescapable and all-consuming self-interest, then the only way to break down such self-interest is to break down the self and let the other in, as the narrative voice of *Westward* does at its conclusion. But this means that sincerity, if it is to characterize the aesthetic work, must derive as much from the outside as from the inside. Intention is realized in recognition; sincerity is achieved only in the other's response. In the love song of the New Sincerity, "I love you" becomes radically dependent on your acknowledgment that "you are loved."

Cycles of Freedom and Fascism

Infinite Jest, written across the early 1990s and published in 1996, returns with vigor to the End of History thesis, literalizing Hegel's and Fukuyama's metaphor in more than one way. The USA of the novel, now the leading partner in the Organization of North American Nations (O.N.A.N.), has exhausted the traditional Gregorian calendar, which had tracked the progress of history through year dates given as increasing ordinal numbers. The last year B.S., or

"Before Subsidization," appears to equate to 2001 in the old calendar. This has been followed by nine successive years named for corporate sponsors, beginning with the Year of the Whopper and ending with the Year of Glad, which an endnote tells us is "the very last year of O.N.A.N.ite Subsidized Time."[20] What follows this year is not made clear: it might be a return to linear, ordinal history, or it might be something closer to an apocalypse, an end to the end of history along the lines imagined by J. D. Steelritter in *Westward*. This apocalypse, if it does occur in the world of *Infinite Jest*, will likely be the result of widespread dissemination by Quebecois terrorists of "Infinite Jest"—known colloquially as "The Entertainment"—a film cartridge so absorbing it paralyzes viewers into doing nothing other than watching it on an endless loop. Such a looping apocalypse would indeed be an apt one: as an actual end to history, it would simply offer a logical extension of the post-historical world depicted in *Infinite Jest*, a world in which linear development has been supplanted by a series of seemingly unbreakable cycles.

Some of these cycles relate to the intersection of technology and commerce. In a consumer environment already gone far beyond Fukuyama's "easy access to VCRs and stereos," Wallace outlines in comically excruciating detail the rise and fall of millennial US network television and advertising (410–418), and the cycle in demand for videophones (144–151). Elsewhere, there are cycles associated with place, such as the "seven moons orbiting a dead planet" (193) that constitute the visual landscape of the hospital complex containing Ennet House, the drug and alcohol recovery house that is one of the novel's main settings. There are also the cycles that characterize the films of James O. Incandenza, patriarch of the Incandenza family and founder of Enfield Tennis Academy, the other primary setting in the novel. Incandenza's culminating work, the aforementioned "Infinite Jest," is revealed late in the novel to be made up of at least two looping scenes: in the first scene two characters cycle through revolving doors "for several whirls"; in the second a veiled woman stares into a camera bolted to a baby's bassinet, repeatedly apologizing with "at least twenty minutes of permutations of 'I'm sorry'" (939). On the thematic level, *Infinite Jest* frequently depicts endless cycles of drug and alcohol addiction, while on the formal level, even the novel's very structure can be understood as built on "cycles within cycles within cycles," as Katherine Hayles pointed out in one of the earliest scholarly analyses.[21]

The word Wallace employs most often to name these processes of recursive cycling and looping is "annulation," and perhaps the most intriguing of the cycles depicted in *Infinite Jest* is the process of waste production and recycling referred to as "annular fusion." This process is described by the mathematical savant Michael Pemulis as an emblem of stability and efficiency, "a type of fusion that can produce waste that's fuel for a process whose waste is fuel for the fusion" (572). But this seemingly hermetic cycle turns out to have damaging side effects. In the Great Concavity, the region north of Boston where annular fusion takes place, plant and animal growth have spiraled out of control, necessitating the constant catapulting of toxins into the area to counteract the growth. The stability of the initial cycle therefore turns out to contain an internal contradiction, and that stability can only be preserved through negation (annulation) of that contradiction. What fails to happen, however, is the overcoming of this self-contradiction at a higher level, the process named by Hegel as *Aufhebung*, or sublation. In Hegel's philosophy, sublation—the dialectical overcoming of logical or practical self-contradiction through the simultaneous negation and preservation of the contradiction at a higher level as part of a new determination—is the method through which history and thought move in the direction of the progressive realization of truth and freedom. In the cycle of annular fusion, the dialectical process has become stalled at one of its poles, annulation, resulting in a failure to overcome the contradiction and a doomed pattern of recursive repetition. This annular pattern— the tendency to self-cancel rather than self-overcome—can be observed in a range of other contexts in *Infinite Jest*.[22] The End of History depicted in the novel is thus stuck in a cycle, constituting the dark inverse of Hegel's vision of freedom as the ability (inseparable from communal acknowledgment) to recognize oneself in one's own deeds.

The detrimental political implications of this situation are brought out most clearly through *Infinite Jest*'s explicit discussion of freedom. This discussion takes place between two otherwise minor characters, the American federal agent Hugh Steeply and Rémy Marathe, a member of the Quebecois terrorist group Les Assassins des Fauteuils Roulents (A.F.R.). Their dialogue, excerpted in stages throughout the novel, occurs over a single night and early morning atop a mountain in Arizona, and centers around an opposition made famous by Isaiah Berlin in his 1958 lecture "Two Concepts of Liberty":

negative freedom (or negative liberty) versus positive freedom.[23] Negative freedom refers to the absence of external constraints on the individual agent, and Berlin associates it with classic liberal thinkers including Locke and Mill in England and Constant and de Tocqueville in France. These are thinkers for whom freedom from interference is valuable as an end in itself, and who argue that the state should permit the individual to pursue their own ends as long as these do not impinge upon the freedoms of others. In *Infinite Jest*, Hugh Steeply defends this conception of freedom as paradigmatically American: "'The United States: a community of sacred individuals which reveres the sacredness of the individual choice. The individual's right to pursue his own vision of the best ratio of pleasure to pain: utterly sacrosanct. Defended with teeth and bared claws all through our history'" (424). Rémy Marathe, for his part, agrees with Steeply that such a defense of negative freedom defines the American mindset, but counters with an argument for positive freedom, a tradition associated by Berlin with philosophers such as Rousseau, Hegel, and Marx. From this standpoint, the individual's goals of self-actualization and self-determination are assumed to require support from their connection to larger communal goals, goals that Marathe thinks have been lost in the American context. To make this point to Steeply, Marathe reiterates Berlin's distinction between "freedom from" (or negative freedom) and "freedom to" (or positive freedom):

> "Your freedom is the freedom-*from*: no one tells your precious individual U.S.A. selves what they must do. It is the meaning only, this freedom from constraint and forced duress. . . . But what of the freedom-*to*? Not just free-*from*. Not all compulsion comes from without. You pretend you do not see this. What of freedom-*to*. How for the person to freely choose? How to choose any but a child's greedy choices if there is no loving-filled father to guide, inform, teach the person how to choose? How is there freedom to choose if one does not learn how to choose?" (320)

The Quebecois spy's sentiments here and throughout the dialogue chime with certain views Wallace expressed in his nonfiction. In particular, Marathe's language of temples and worshipping—"'All other of our you say *free* choices follow from this: what is our temple?'" (107)—clearly resonates with positions the author would set out in his 2005 Kenyon Commencement Address: "There is no such thing as not worshipping. Everybody worships. The only choice we get is *what* to worship."[24] However, while Wallace might seem to support the spirit of Marathe's views, the methods employed by the A.F.R.—which involve killing motorists with mirrors and kidnapping innocent bystanders for lethal experiments involving "The Entertainment"—should give the reader pause. In showing such seemingly noble ends supported by such obviously nefarious means, Wallace is allowing us to glimpse, in fact, how easily the rhetoric of positive freedom can slide into the practices of fanaticism and even of fascism. This association is made more concretely through the account offered in *Infinite Jest* of the tennis philosophy of Enfield Academy's director, Gerhardt Schtitt. Introduced as a wearer of "high and shiny black boots" (79) and possessor of "skin so clean-sheet white it almost glows" (80), Schtitt has been, "like most Europeans of his generation, anchored from infancy to certain permanent values which—yes, OK granted—may, admittedly, have a whiff of proto-fascist potential about them, but which do, nevertheless (the values), anchor nicely the soul and course of a life—Old World patriarchal stuff like honor and discipline and fidelity to some larger unit" (82). Here the "honor" that served as the potential anchoring point of value in Mark's story about Dave in *Westward* becomes even more clearly situated in a neo-feudal context, as that neo-feudalism was made manifest in the twentieth-century politics of German fascism. Educated in "the rather Kanto-Hegelian idea that jr. athletics was basically just training for citizenship," Schtitt has been brought up to believe that the junior athlete must "sacrifice the hot narrow imperatives of the Self . . . to the larger imperatives of a team (OK, the State) and a set of delimiting rules (OK, the Law)" (82–83).[25]

Yet despite the association made here between the characters of Schtitt and Marathe and the historical specter of fascism—at one point in their dialogue, Steeply even accuses Marathe of seeking to establish "The National Socialist Neofascist State of Separate Québec" (320)—it would be a mistake to see *Infinite Jest* as outright condemning these figures. Rather, Wallace is depicting the traditional choice between negative freedom and positive freedom as having deteriorated in the world of the novel—a near-future version of the American present—into a choice between two forms of nihilism: the empty and isolating consumerism of neoliberal economy and the falsely authenticating reversion to a fascist state. Even calling this a choice is not accurate, moreover. What *Infinite Jest* really presents is a threatened historical continuum: unless neoliberalism is challenged, fascism will result.[26]

In a radio interview given soon after the novel's publication, Wallace offered the following assessment of Gerhardt Schtitt's role:

> The guy who essentially runs the academy now is a fascist, and, whether it comes out or not, he's really the only one there who to me is saying anything that's even remotely non-horrifying. Except it is horrifying because he's a fascist. And part of the stuff that was rattling around in my head when I was doing this is that it seems to me that one of the scary things about the nihilism of contemporary culture is that we're really setting ourselves up for fascism. Because as we empty more and more values, motivating principles, spiritual principles, almost, out of the culture, we're creating a hunger that eventually is going to drive us to the sort of state where we may accept fascism just because—you know, the nice thing about fascists is they'll tell you what to think, they'll tell you what to do, they'll tell you what's important.[27]

Given this bleak assessment of contemporary American culture, it makes sense that in the most celebrated strand of *Infinite Jest*, which deals with the recovery of addicts through the methods of Alcoholics Anonymous, Wallace's narrator describes "Boston AA's real root axiom," its core message, as "almost classically authoritarian, maybe even proto-Fascist" (374). Proto-Fascist authoritarianism here begins to look like—and will in fact become for characters such as the novel's hero Don Gately—the only means to address the desperate isolations and addictions that neoliberal hegemony has caused. Technological advances have played a significant role in creating the conditions for this isolation and addiction: Wallace's early version of the internet, InterLace, streams addictive content in a manner that leads to the endless lonely watching of TV. But Wallace evidently believed that technology was not the foremost determinant; its growing influence was rather the byproduct of an underpinning utilitarian ethos in American culture. As Marathe remarks of the apotheosis of technological development in the novel, the film "Infinite Jest": "'This is a U.S.A. production, this Entertainment cartridge. Made by an American man in the U.S.A. The appetite for the appeal of it: this also is U.S.A. The U.S.A. drive for spectation, which your culture teaches'" (318).[28]

Wallace's point is that "The Entertainment" has not arrived as a shocking event from outside the course of American historical development; rather, it has emerged immanently from within that development.[29] The nineteenth-century conditions that saw the formulation of Steeply's traditional argument for negative freedom—an argument that was affirmed by mid-twentieth-century liberals like Berlin—have now given way to the nihilism of the neoliberal "free market"; thus a form of positive freedom, Wallace implies, must emerge to counter this nihilism. The "good" Hegelian version of this freedom would be one that sees subjects become rationally self-legislating, collectively giving themselves the law and seeing their norms and principles embodied and reflected in the rationally constructed polity in which they live. In such a condition of freedom, what we "worship," in Wallace's terms, would be reason itself, identical with the collective good. The "bad" Hegelian vision of positive freedom offered by Marathe, by contrast, cannot provide an acceptable alternative to Steeply's model, given how closely it hews to fascism in its unquestioned acceptance of the dictates of the "Higher Power" of the state.[30] Yet within the world depicted in *Infinite Jest*, the contradiction between these two harmful models of freedom cannot be sublated to produce a new determination. Instead, in the annular cycles that reappear everywhere in the novel, the experiences of its characters approximate the effects produced by "The Entertainment," as described by Steeply: "'Stuck. Fixed. Held. Trapped. As in trapped in some sort of middle. Between two things. Pulled apart in different directions'" (647). Against the ethical impasse represented by its content (which recalls the aesthetic impasse of *Westward*'s ending), it will be left to the form of *Infinite Jest*—in conjunction, importantly, with the novel's reader—to create the conditions necessary for the nihilism of the End of History to be overcome. Over the remainder of this chapter, I argue that the crucial formal principle through which the novel aims to achieve this overcoming is the principle of absorption.

Absorbing Hal's Sincerity Crisis

"I am seated in an office, surrounded by heads and bodies" (3).[31] Thus begins *Infinite Jest* in the perspective of Hal Incandenza, an eighteen-year-old being interviewed for admission to the University of Arizona on a tennis scholarship. That we first find our protagonist amid "heads and bodies" rather than among "people" is an immediate signal that something is wrong. Some vital connection between the outer appearance of others and the intimation of their inner human lives has become opaque to Hal. Moreover, it seems that Hal's inner life may be equally opaque to others: "I am in here," runs the famous assertion, rather odd and desperate, that constitutes the whole of the novel's second paragraph. As the interview unfolds, we witness Hal endeavoring to "appear neutral," not attempting "what would feel to me like a pleasant expression or smile," leaving the talking to those present to support him (3). Hal's tennis prowess is undoubted, and his academic track record has been "off the charts," but following recent "subnormal" test scores, the admissions panel wants, understandably, to hear an explanation from the boy they are planning to admit (6). And so, as his silence becomes ever more excruciating and with his supporters banished from the room, Hal is left with little option but to speak. Among the first things he tells the panel is the following:

> "I am not just a boy who plays tennis. I have an intricate history. Experiences and feelings. I'm complex. I *read*. . . . I'm not a machine. I feel and believe. I have opinions. Some of them are interesting. I could, if you'd let me, talk and talk. Let's talk about anything. I believe the influence of Kierkegaard on Camus is underestimated. I believe Dennis Gabor may very well have been the Antichrist. I believe Hobbes is just Rousseau in a dark mirror. I believe, with Hegel, that transcendence is absorption." (11–12)

Attempting to convince his interviewers that he has an intricate and complex inner life, Hal states his opinions on some of the most celebrated figures in the history of philosophy. While Dennis Gabor, the inventor of the hologram, might not be a household name, the same cannot be said for Søren Kierkegaard and Albert Camus, two major existentialist philosophers, nor for Thomas Hobbes and Jean-Jacques Rousseau, two renowned political philosophers. And then there is G. W. F. Hegel, whom we have already encountered as a key framing presence in Wallace's conception of ethical action and aesthetic creation over the early part of his career.[32]

"I believe, with Hegel, that transcendence is absorption," Hal says aloud. Or does he? At this point *Infinite Jest*'s opening scene suddenly pivots, as it is revealed that the words we are reading in Hal's voice are not what his interviewers hear. "*Sub*animalistic noises and sounds" are what they afterwards profess to have heard instead (14), while what they see is something horrifying: "I look out. Directed my way is horror. I rise from the chair. I see jowls sagging, eyebrows high on trembling foreheads, cheeks bright-white" (12). We now understand that the first-person monologue we have been reading as Hal's speech to the panel bears no relation to the "vision of hell" these men claim to behold (14). Like his forebear Prince Hamlet, Hal Incandenza evidently has that within which passeth show, but Hamlet's worries about the deceptions of speech have been scaled up in this opening scene of *Infinite Jest* to a full-blown crisis in sincere communication—in the congruence between feeling and avowal—a crisis summarized by Hal's repeated remark, "I cannot make myself understood" (10).

Critics have offered various explanations for Hal's crisis at the beginning of *Infinite Jest*, the scene that in fact occurs chronologically latest in the novel. Hal's inability to make himself understood might be due to his withdrawal from marijuana, or his escalating depression, or his possible ingestion of "the incredibly potent DMZ," a drug with effects that are described as "almost ontological" (170). The crisis might even stem from Hal's exposure to "The Entertainment" at the hands of the Quebecois terrorists who are on the verge of capturing him at the end of the novel.[33] "Infinite Jest," as we have already heard, is a film so absorbing that no one who watches it can turn it off or turn away. And this description highlights the connection among all these plot possibilities: their shared reliance on the trope of absorption. Marijuana and DMZ are substances absorbed by the subject, with the consequence that the subject loses touch with the objective world. Clinical depression, as represented not only in Hal but even more powerfully in the minor character Kate Gompert, is similarly characterized by acute absorption in the self rather than the world. Conversely, exposure to "Infinite Jest" leads not to self-absorption but to absorption wholly in the object, to the radical extent of complete self-forgetting: watchers of the film urinate themselves and do not respond to painful stimuli. Absorption in all these forms heralds a crisis in the relationship of subject to object: at one extreme, complete absorption in the subject; at the other, complete absorption in the object, with no mediation between the two. Subsequent appearances of the word "absorption" in the novel seem only to underscore its association with damagingly polarized states of being.[34] Against this background, to "believe, with Hegel, that transcendence is absorption" looks like a serious error on Hal's part—absorption appears to equate not to transcendence of this opening scene's polarities but rather to their deepening. Yet as we shall see, Wallace's novel will in fact be driven by the project of reclaiming absorption—in a form I will term *refractive absorption*—as a redemptive and potentially transformative force.[35]

This project stems directly from Hal's broken state at the beginning of the novel. For it is already clear, I hope, that to explain Hal's sincerity crisis solely with regard to the contingencies of plot would be to miss the dialectical point. If the principal concern of Hegel's dialectic can be summarized, in Fredric Jameson's words, as "the adequation of subject and object, . . . the possibility of reconciliation of I and Not-I, of spirit and matter, or self and world," then *Infinite Jest* opens not with any such reconciliation but with a profound rending apart of subject and object, I and Not-I, spirit and matter, self and world.[36] A comparison might be made with Greek tragedy, the historical emergence of which was the sign, for Hegel, "that a great crisis in the basic institutions of that society had arisen and could not be resolved."[37] The communicative breakdown in *Infinite Jest*'s opening scene signals something similarly amiss in Hal's society. Yet it is to go too far to claim, as Allard den Dulk does, that there is in fact no longer anything amiss in Hal himself and that it is simply his "ironic community" of interviewers who cannot recognize his newfound "attitude of sincerity."[38] Since, as I argue throughout this book, sincerity must be understood as a social rather than individual achievement, it is not possible to be sincere without some communal recognition of that sincerity. The opening scene of *Infinite Jest* makes clear that Hal's capacity for sincerity depends not only upon an intentional alignment between inner feeling and outer avowal (as Lionel Trilling describes sincerity), but also on what Pippin calls "the conditions of social subjectivity necessary for mutual intelligibility."[39] Hal's repeated phrase, "I cannot make myself understood," rendered initially in first-person narration and then unsuccessfully spoken aloud, suggests the failure of this social subjectivity and mutual intelligibility in his historical moment.

The historical moment is crucial: Wallace viewed the isolation experienced by Hal as symptomatic, as he told an interviewer, of "what it's like to live in America around the millennium."[40] Neoliberal US society manifests subjectively in *Infinite Jest* as a kind of heightened loneliness and depressive solipsism, most extreme in the case of Hal but evident in a great many of the other competitors, educators, artists, and addicts that populate the novel's pages. As one critic has noted, Hal's story constitutes a failed Bildungsroman, which "suggests that the hyper-individualized and consumption-oriented worldview of neoliberalism fails to provide the possibility of fulfilling human development because it does not provide a framework for meaning and value beyond the individual."[41] Hal in fact displays many highly developed individual traits: as well as being "'a balletic athlete'" on the tennis court, his headmaster opines that "'he's fine when he's by himself.... Hal here is provably competent. Credentials out the bazoo, Bill. The boy reads like a vacuum. *Digests* things'" (15). But while Hal's human capital may be sky high, the "supportive situation" (15) that would allow his social individuality (rather than atomized individualism) to flourish has fallen away amid a cult of specialization and a Weberian disenchantment of the world.

In his classic *Theory of the Novel*, Georg Lukács argues that the novel emerged to articulate and address a fragmented modern condition in which there is a "rift between 'inside' and 'outside,'" an "essential difference between the self and the world, an incongruence between soul and deed."[42] *Infinite Jest*, a novel deliberately built from fragments and fractals, thus begins with Hal's sincerity crisis so that Wallace can spend the following thousand pages mediating the crisis, re-enchanting the world, and restarting the stalled historical dialectic—if not for Hal, then at least for the novel's reader. Underpinning this aesthetic attempt at mediation, enchantment, and dialectical revitalization is the central Hegelian insight that, as Pippin puts it, "there is a deep connection between understanding meaningful conduct, actions, and expressions of persons and understanding expressive meaning in artworks."[43] The symbolic breakdown in understanding between Hal and his interlocutors is therefore something that *Infinite Jest*, as a modern novel and modern artwork, must both represent and attempt to bridge.

It is in this context that we can return to Hal's (attempted) statement: "I believe, with Hegel, that transcendence is absorption." How might we interpret this claim in a more positive light? One possibility emerges from the knowledge that Hegel's signature term *Aufhebung*, usually rendered in English as "sublation," has alternatively been translated as both "transcendence" and "absorption" and contains both of those elements as "moments" within it. Thus the phrase "transcendence is absorption" could gesture to Hegel's dialectic of unfolding freedom, which in Wallace's *Westward* was heralded by "the revealed transformation of a present" that never came to pass in the story.[44] *Infinite Jest* builds on this gesture by portraying the dialectic as frozen at one of its poles: annulation. How, then, might it be made to start moving again—how might self-canceling transform into self-overcoming and eventually mutual self-realization? And what role might art play in this process?

Here it is important to note that alongside *Aufhebung*, Hegel employed other variations on the word "absorption"—most notably *Vertiefung* (deepening) and *Versenkung* (immersion)—with regularity in his compendious *Lectures on Fine Art*.[45] Dubbed "the father of art history" by the twentieth century's leading art historian, Hegel's story of the development of art emphasizes how it contributes to the coming to self-consciousness of *Geist*, or spirit.[46] "Things in nature are only immediate and single," he writes, "while man as *Geist* duplicates himself, in that (i) he is as things in nature are, but (ii) he is just as much for himself; he sees himself, represents himself to himself, thinks, and only on the strength of this active placing himself before himself is he *Geist*."[47] Hegel's treatment of absorption's thematic and instrumental role in this story of man "represent[ing] himself to himself" in art emphasizes two dimensions of absorption: its expression in the content of the artwork and in the relationship of the artist to the work.[48]

Infinite Jest, by contrast, is most interested in the theme of absorption with respect to the reader of literature or beholder of art. It is through its treatment of absorption in this sense that the novel attempts to address Hal's symptomatic crisis and to set out its own aesthetic and ethical project. In later sections we will see the notion of aesthetic absorption critically framed through the films of James Incandenza, as well as examining the absorptive aesthetics of *Infinite Jest*'s own narrative voice, language, and point of view in its presentation of Alcoholics Anonymous and the character arc of Don Gately. But first we must ask some basic questions that bear upon the relation between artistic practice and readerly absorption. What does it mean to create an absorbing work of art? What might be the risks and opportunities in doing so? What aesthetic techniques serve the ends of absorption? And how might the absorptive aesthetics of a novel like *Infinite Jest* relate to its project to heal the division at the end of history between subject and object, spirit and matter, self and world?

Absorbing Art

In approaching questions like these, I have found it useful to turn away from the traditions of literary criticism—in which readerly absorption has generally been considered only through its interruption, for instance in the alienation devices of Brechtian theater or postmodernist metafiction—and toward scholarship on the visual arts. In a series of studies beginning with his now-classic 1980 book *Absorption and Theatricality: Painting and Beholder in the Age of Diderot*, the art critic and historian Michael Fried uses the term "absorption" to describe an ideal and historically dynamic relation between artwork and beholder. Fried's initial thesis, briefly summarized, is that in French painting of the 1750s and 1760s there emerged, simultaneously and in combination, a *practical* concern with the representation of states of absorption and a *theoretical* concern with the status of the beholder. Fried reads a wide array of paintings through comments made upon them by critics at the time, and shows that painters like Chardin and Greuze, along with critics like Diderot, promoted an "anti-theatrical" aesthetics that "treated the beholder as if he were not there."[49] In Diderot's criticism, any implicit acknowledgment of the beholder represented a theatrical appeal for their attention, which had the converse effect of weakening the painting's hold on the beholder and therefore its aesthetic self-sufficiency as a painting. The goal of anti-theatricality was initially served by Chardin and Greuze depicting figures fully absorbed in their daily lives and seemingly unaware of the beholder standing before the painting. As French painting developed over the following century, major artists including David, Géricault, Courbet, and Manet, all of them forced to confront "the primordial convention that paintings are made to be beheld," could continue to defeat theatricality only by turning to ever more elaborate and complex techniques.[50] Fried's subsequent books then trace "the dialectical vicissitudes and modifications of the Diderotian paradigm up through its abandonment or rather its radical reconfiguration in the art of Manet and his generation" in the 1860s, at which historical point we have reached the dawn of modernist art.[51]

Although not always explicitly framed this way by Fried, his story about eighteenth- and nineteenth-century French painting intersects significantly with two contemporaneous strands in European thought and culture: the growing worries in Romantic circles concerning the (in)sincerity and (in)authenticity of life in modern societies; and the development of aesthetic theory in the German Idealism of Kant, Schelling, and Hegel. In the early Romantic tradition, represented by figures including Diderot and Rousseau, the notion of absorption was understood normatively, as an authentic identification with one's social role or activity, whereas theatricality "would be to act without such identification, to perform an activity controlled and directed by an anticipation of what others expect to occur."[52] Meanwhile, the normative underpinnings of German aesthetic theory—its concern with the truth or falsity of artworks as models for social being—are brought out by statements such as the following from Hegel's *Aesthetics*, which, while it doesn't employ the word "absorption" with respect to the relationship between artwork and beholder, is nonetheless concerned to outline in proto-Friedian terms what that relationship should ideally look like:

> Producing effects is in general the dominating tendency of turning to the public, so that the work of art no longer displays itself as peaceful, satisfied in itself, and serene; on the contrary, it turns inside out and as it were makes an appeal to the spectator that tries to put itself into relation with him by means of the mode of portrayal. Both, peace in itself and turning to the onlooker, must indeed be present in the work of art, but the two sides must be in the purest equilibrium. If the work of art in the severe style is entirely shut in upon itself without wishing to speak to a spectator, it leaves us cold; but if it goes too far out of itself to him, it pleases but is without solidity or at least does not please (as it should) by solidity of content and the simple treatment and presentation of that content.[53]

As we saw in relation to *Westward*, the reader's experience is importantly privileged in Wallace's fiction, and in a manner that would seem at first glance to go against Hegel's proscriptions against "appeal[ing] to the spectator." Yet, reverting to Fried's language, this apparent theatricality (in the sense of appealing directly to the reader) is in fact undertaken to the end of defeating theatricality (in the sense of artistic inauthenticity). Wallace's aesthetic approach thus gives him an equivalent position in the development of American fiction to the one held by Edouard Manet in Fried's narrative of French painting. For Fried, the century-long anti-theatrical battle to sustain "the supreme fiction of the beholder's nonexistence" came to necessitate in Manet a completely new approach, which involved painting figures looking out of the painting towards the beholder, yet without making a wholly intelligible appeal to the beholder.[54] Fried calls this Manet's "facingness" technique, and it saw him "systematically avoid or subvert absorptive or potentially absorptive motifs" in the service of interrogating (rather than appealing to) the beholder.[55]

Wallace's relationship to postmodernist art nevertheless differs in important ways from Manet's relationship to the realist painting that preceded him. Here we should note that, like Wallace, Fried emerged to public consciousness with an eye-catching critique of postmodernism, albeit one articulated at the dawn of postmodernism's reign rather than (as in Wallace's case) at its moment of eclipse. Fried's 1967 article "Art and Objecthood" defended the American modernist color field painting of Morris Louis, Kenneth Noland, Jules Olitski, and Frank Stella against the new minimalist (Fried calls it "literalist") sculpture by figures like Tony Smith, Robert Morris, Carl Andre, and Donald Judd. These sculptors saw painting "as an art on the verge of exhaustion," and in their own practice placed a new emphasis on "presence," "experience," "situation," and "objecthood," repositioning the ontological basis of the artwork in the beholder's experience rather than in the artist's manipulation of their medium.[56] This literalist espousal of objecthood, and concomitant privileging of the beholder, "amounts to nothing other than a plea for a new genre of theater," Fried writes, "and theater is now the negation of art."[57] American modernist painting had continued Manet's tradition of interrogating the beholder, Fried thought, whereas in minimalist sculpture the mode of interrogation had been replaced by the mode of appeal. Which is to say that Fried saw postmodernism, as it would come to be called, as a historical error—a sacrifice of the principles of aesthetic conviction and autonomy to the ends of flattering the views and sensibility of the beholder.

Wallace, by contrast, saw postmodernism as a historical necessity, a salutary engagement with its time, and therefore a paradigm that needed to be overcome rather than ignored or reversed. If postmodernism had become "theatrical," it had not started out that way but rather had failed to develop sufficiently in response to subsequent developments, primarily the incorporation of ironic modes of communication into television and advertising alongside the increasing commercialization of everyday life. This argument, incipient in *Westward*, is made explicitly, as we saw in my Introduction, in "E Unibus Pluram," an essay that culminates by calling for a "weird bunch of *anti-rebels*" who would ameliorate the situation by risking the appearance of outdatedness in their writing: "Dead on the page. Too sincere. Clearly repressed. Backward, quaint, naïve, anachronistic."[58] Wallace's paradoxical claim is that a technically up-to-date fiction is now required to serve a traditional moral outlook, one that has been lost in modern art's very emphasis on being technically up-to-date.

Critics have come up with various ways to explain this contrast between medium and message in Wallace, from the claim that his writing "turns irony back on itself"[59] to the view that his fiction's technical sophistication is necessary to gain the attention of a "self-consciously intellectual readership"[60] or "cultured postmodern reader"[61] who would balk at a more basically rendered self-help message. But these explanations all depend upon the idea that sincerity—in life and in art—is an attitude that one can simply will oneself to adopt.[62] My argument, by contrast, is that the achievement of sincerity in contemporary art has to elicit the response of the reader in order to attain the recognition it requires to be itself. In a fragmented world in which "the conditions of social subjectivity necessary for mutual intelligibility" are uncertainly available, sincerity cannot know itself without such recognition, and the artist must therefore address their audience as a partner in the search for certainty and meaning. This turns out to require a rethinking and reworking not only of theatricality but of absorption too, something we see most clearly in *Infinite Jest*'s presentation of other artworks, principally the films of Hal's father, Professor James O. Incandenza, Jr.

The Medium Is (Not Entirely) the Message

Judged according to the qualities Wallace regularly called for in contemporary art—passion, communication, intimacy, sincerity—James Incandenza's film career would seem to constitute a rather spectacular failure, and critics have uniformly regarded it as such.[63] In keeping with his initial description as "tall, ungainly, socially challenged and hard-drinking" (64), Incandenza—whose suicide precedes the main action of *Infinite Jest* by approximately five years—is depicted as silent and withdrawn during his few appearances in flashback scenes from the narrative present. Marshall Boswell describes him as "a cold, closed figure with serious paternal resentment, a man who has been trained to hide his emotions behind cold logic and surface objectivity," and suggests that "his films seamlessly reflect these psychological defenses."[64] Based on "JAMES O. INCANDENZA: A FILMOGRAPHY" (985n24), the eight-and-a-half-page endnote that reads like "an extended parody of the postmodern canon," it would be difficult to argue with this assessment of the films and the filmmaker.[65] Yet it is also true, as Mary Shapiro has observed, that the progression of the filmography "tells the only story that serves to illuminate the circumstances directly leading to Incandenza's suicide," with the films moving from "serious attempts to understand the world, particularly through experiments in optics," to "increasingly autobiographical attempts to understand only his own life."[66] And it is likewise true, as David Hering notes, that the descriptions in the filmography—often collated from dubious sources and harboring critical intent—do not always match up with the way the films are described ekphrastically in the main text of the novel.[67]

Taking both the filmography and ekphrastic textual descriptions into account, Incandenza's output can be said to oscillate among a number of modes, ranging from relatively realist early-career documentaries to work (such as the *Found Drama* series) that appears to be, in Hegel's phrase cited earlier, "entirely shut in upon itself without wishing to speak to a spectator."[68] More common in Incandenza's *oeuvre* are films that address the viewer in a heavily theatrical manner, refusing the Hegelian ideal of art as, in Pippin's summation, "a subject-subject relation, not some sort of subject-object relation."[69] The achievement of a sincere "subject-subject relation" in art is always under threat: "if 'theatricalized,'" Pippin adds, "that social relation is presented either in terms of submission to a collective subjectivity (in effect a self-objectification or an internalization of what 'they' want) or as an attempt by the artist to dominate or overwhelm and so objectify the artwork's audience."[70] Thus, in genre works by Incandenza such as *Very Low Impact* and *Blood Sister: One Tough Nun*, we get submission to the norms of entertainment and the desires of the audience, "an internalization of what 'they' want." And in films like *The Joke*, *The Medusa vs. the Odalisque*, and *Cage III—Free Show*, we see an aggressive attempt to dominate, overwhelm, and objectify the audience (often by depicting them *within* the film).[71]

Incandenza's life and film career end with his sixth and final attempt to make "Infinite Jest," the cartridge that will surface as the lethal "Entertainment." As Lee Konstantinou has observed, this film is not only (as its nickname suggests) "the ultimate expression of the recursive logic of U.S. consumer culture"; it is also an uber-experimental work that accomplishes the historical avant-garde's mission "to end art as an institution and to break down the barriers . . . that prevent art from changing consciousness."[72] In Fried's terms, "Infinite Jest" is both intensely theatrical and intensely absorptive. On the one hand, it is difficult to imagine a work more clearly designed to appeal to the subjectivity of its beholder, given that it has originally been created for a single beholder, Incandenza's son Hal, as "a magically entertaining toy to dangle at the infant son still somewhere alive in the boy, to make its eyes light and toothless mouth open unconsciously, to laugh" (839). On the other hand, "Infinite Jest" is wholly absorptive: indeed, its capacity to absorb is so extreme that no one who sees it can ever become unabsorbed again. Such lethal absorption was far from Incandenza's aim in making the film, which was—he professes late in the novel in his posthumous incarnation as the wraith—"to contrive a medium via which he and the muted son could simply *converse*" (838). While Wallace, in keeping with his vision of art as communication, italicizes the final word of this line, "*converse*," I want to suggest that it is equally crucial that Incandenza envisages this act of conversation as requiring a new "medium." If a new medium proves necessary for "Infinite Jest" the film/postfilm, then it raises a larger question for *Infinite Jest* the novel/post-novel: might it be that for an artwork to heal the nihilistic neoliberal division between subject and object, spirit and matter, self and world, a new medium will have to be contrived to achieve that purpose?

Here Wallace's critique of the avant-garde is indeed of equal importance to his more widely noted critique of the entertainment industry. Yet while Konstantinou reads "The Entertainment" in relation to the aims of the historical (i.e., early) avant-garde, I would argue that of even more relevance for Wallace is what avant-garde art became after it had been widely acknowledged institutionally as the leading edge of artistic practice. In the most canonical accounts of the avant-garde, beginning with Clement Greenberg's 1939 essay "Avant-Garde and Kitsch," the movement is described as emerging in nineteenth-century Europe in response to the decay of bourgeois society and "the first bold development of scientific revolutionary thought" (i.e., Marxism).[73] It then turned away, in the twentieth century, from "subject-matter or common experience" towards "pure" preoccupation with the medium of each particular art form.[74] In Greenberg's view, this development was justified by the fact that, in a society still capitalist rather than socialist, "by no other means is it possible today to create art and literature of a high order."[75] In Greenberg's later writing, the focus on capitalism dropped away, and heightened attention to the medium became understood as the only means of sincere art-making. With Romanticism, artistic sincerity had been envisaged as direct communication of sentiment, so that "the medium was a regrettable if necessary physical obstacle between the artist and the audience, which in some ideal state would disappear entirely to leave the experience of the spectator or reader identical with that of the artist."[76] By contrast—and in line with Hegel's counter-Romantic emphasis on mediation—modernist sincerity came to mean formalism: in an age when "the conditions of social subjectivity necessary for mutual intelligibility" were breaking down, the medium turned out to be the one thing an artist could successfully *mean*. In his *Aesthetics*, Hegel writes that "the work of art stands in the middle between immediate sensuousness and ideal thought. It is not yet pure thought, but, despite its sensuousness, it is no longer a purely material existent either."[77] For modernist critics like Greenberg and Fried, it is precisely from this "medium" position between ideality and materiality that avant-garde art can carry out its absorptive work. The downside, as thinkers such as Pierre Bourdieu and Stanley Cavell have acknowledged in different ways, is that avant-garde art becomes "a field of restricted production" in which "artist and audience are out of touch," with fewer and fewer potential beholders knowing enough about these mediums to be absorbed in modern art.[78]

James Incandenza is described in *Infinite Jest* as an "après-garde" artist. Beyond the evident humor of this phrase, it throws an interesting light on his attempts to "contrive a medium," since it suggests that neither the modernist project of medium-specific absorption nor the postmodernist embrace of intermedial theatricality will be sufficient to achieve his communicative goals, including the attempt to reach his son Hal.[79] And it is important, I would argue, to take those goals seriously: rather than interpret Incandenza's output as simply indexing his biographical weaknesses and failures, we should see the filmmaker as facing a parallel conundrum to Wallace—the question of how to communicate sincerely in an increasingly complex world and at a highly fraught aesthetic conjuncture. To pursue the implications of this parallel between the two artists, the next section shines light on a single film from the Incandenza *oeuvre*, one whose effects are likely to come as close as possible to those of "The Entertainment" (the content and form of which cannot be analyzed in detail, because it cannot be viewed without an experience of absorption that destroys the possibility of critical detachment). This comparison seems appropriate because the film in question—Incandenza's midcareer *Pre-Nuptial Agreement of Heaven and Hell*—features at its heart a work of sculpture at which, according to the historian Simon Schama, "we stare and stare . . . as we stare at no other sculpture ever made."[80]

The Ecstasy of Refractive Absorption

The sculpture in question is *The Ecstasy of St. Teresa*, completed in 1652 by the Italian artist Gianlorenzo Bernini. Held in the Cornaro Chapel, Santa Maria della Vittoria, Rome, the Baroque altarpiece depicts the moment when God penetrated Teresa of Ávila through the intercession of an angel with a golden spear. In her diary, the nun recalled the moment in vivid terms: "The sweetness of this intense pain is so extreme that there is no wanting it to end."[81] Expressing this intensity in sculptural form, *The Ecstasy of St. Teresa* has gone on to become one of the most celebrated works in the history of art. Yet its inescapable power has not protected Bernini from the criticism of later artists and critics. As Schama recounts of the altarpiece: "It's magic. And that was precisely why, after his death, Bernini would be attacked by artists such as Sir Joshua Reynolds for being a cheap sorcerer, a specialist in theatrical trickery, who—for the sake of wowing the worshipper—had, unlike Michelangelo, debased the purity of his chosen material."[82] In emphasizing the beholder's experience over the purity of its subject matter and medium, *The Ecstasy of St. Teresa* constitutes, in Michael Fried's terms, an eminently theatrical artwork.[83] And not only in Fried's terms: in her book *Bernini: Art as Theatre*, Genevieve Warwick shows how Bernini's engagements with the Roman theater—including writing and acting in plays—shaped his now more celebrated work in sculpture.[84] Schama comments on this theatricality in its connection with the beholder's experience of Bernini's earlier *David*:

> There's never a time when Bernini isn't conscious of the spectator, who becomes not just a silent starer, but an actively engaged participant, moving around the piece and seeing it work in different ways from different perspectives.... Centuries on, this understanding of sculpture as presenting not one but multiple images to us, each in a state of mutating motion as we move about it, might seem a truism; but in the 1620s it broke all previous conventions. Bernini had discovered a way to make marble movies.[85]

This invocation of the "marble movie" is pertinent to *Infinite Jest*. *The Ecstasy of St. Teresa* appears in Wallace's novel at four points, three of which have to do with the sculpture's role in Incandenza's *Pre-Nuptial Agreement of Heaven and Hell*. In the filmography endnote, the plot of *Pre-Nuptial Agreement* is described as follows: "God and Satan play poker with Tarot cards for the soul of an alcoholic sandwich-bag salesman obsessed with Bernini's 'The Ecstasy of St. Teresa'" (988n24). In the main text of the novel, the sculpture is discussed twice from the point of view of Joelle van Dyne. The first time, Joelle is freebasing cocaine, and her experience is narrated thus:

> The 'base frees and condenses, compresses the whole experience to the implosion of one terrible shattering spike in the graph, an afflated orgasm of the heart that makes her feel, truly, attractive, sheltered by limits, deveiled and loved, observed and alone and sufficient and female, full, as if watched for an instant by God. She always sees, after inhaling, right at the apex, at the graph's spike's tip, Bernini's "Ecstasy of St. Teresa," behind glass, at the Vittoria, for some reason, the saint recumbent, half-supine, her flowing stone robe lifted by the angel in whose other hand a bare arrow is raised for that best descent, the saint's legs frozen in opening, the angel's expression not charity but the perfect vice of barb-headed love. (235)

Joelle, the university girlfriend of Incandenza's son Orin and nicknamed the P.G.O.A.T. ("Prettiest Girl of All Time") by his peers, wears a veil in the novel, her face having reportedly been disfigured by acid thrown in rage at her father by her mother. Joelle's cocaine high in this scene restores her beauty not as the isolating factor it had formerly been (we later learn that her "almost grotesquely lovely" quality left her "almost universally shunned" [290]) but as a source of fullness, of Godlike attention and love. The feeling is paradoxical—she feels simultaneously "observed and alone"—and so intensely sweet and painful that it suggests comparison with St. Teresa's ecstatic encounter. That encounter is rendered at the culmination of the passage through a dense and provocative ekphrastic description that emphasizes a phallic quality in the "bare" and "barb-headed" arrow brandished by the angel, a heavily eroticized Cupid figure.

At this point in the novel, the reader might not connect Joelle's drug-fueled vision of Bernini's sculpture with its role in Incandenza's filmmaking—after all, the two references have appeared in unrelated scenes many pages apart. Much later, however, we discover that Joelle's knowledge of *The Ecstasy of St. Teresa* has developed (and may even have begun) through her viewing of *Pre-Nuptial Agreement of Heaven and Hell*. This information arrives in a passage when Joelle is thinking through Incandenza's films, and how she saw in their surface coldness "flashes of something. Very hidden and quick. Almost furtive" (741). These "flashes" are then made specific in a lengthy passage that describes Joelle's viewing of *Pre-Nuptial Agreement*, and particularly the "240-second motionless low-angle shot of Gianlorenzo Bernini's 'Ecstasy of St. Teresa'" that Joelle initially sees as "an annoying halt" in the film, but later, "on the fifth or sixth reviewing," comes to understand differently:

> The statue, the sensuous presence of the thing, let the alcoholic sandwich-bag salesman escape himself, his tiresome ubiquitous involuted head, she saw, was the thing. The four-minute still shot maybe wasn't just a heavy-art gesture or audience-hostile herring. Freedom from one's own head, one's inescapable P.O.V.—Joelle started to see here, oblique to the point of being hidden, an emotional thrust, since the mediated transcendence of self was just what the apparently decadent statue of the orgasmic nun claimed for itself as subject. Here, then, after studious (and admittedly kind of boring) review, was an un-ironic, almost *moral* thesis to the campy abstract mordant cartridge: the film's climactic statue's stasis presented the theoretical subject as the emotional effect—self-forgetting as the Grail—and—in a covert gesture almost moralistic . . . —presented the self-forgetting of alcohol as inferior to that of religion/art. (742)

This challenging passage brings together many of the themes I've been discussing in this chapter: art, absorption, mediation, self-forgetting, self-transcendence. "I believe, with Hegel, that transcendence is absorption," Hal tells us in the novel's opening scene, and here, 730 pages later, we have *Infinite Jest*'s most explicit discussion of the relationship between absorption and transcendence with regard to an artwork. Bernini's sculpture, an eminently theatrical work, is here viewed not from several perspectives, as in Schama's description of its intended effect, but from a single perspective, in stasis. Bernini may have made a "marble movie," but here that movie is reduced to one, static, four-minute shot. Note that this shot functions like a photograph, achieving what Fried calls "a certain essentially photographic distance from the film experience, a distance by virtue of which the automaticity of the avoidance of theatricality . . . is forestalled or undone."[86] While the theatrical effect of Bernini's statue might thereby seem to be accentuated, the multimedial element of this extended moment offers a complicating factor. Indeed, the moment involves the interaction among a whole range of traditionally separate arts: sculpture (Bernini's altarpiece), photography (the four-minute still shot), cinema (Incandenza's film), television (Joelle views the film on a small screen at home, rather than in the cinema space that is the traditional site of film theory), poetry (the reference to Blake's *The Marriage of Heaven and Hell* in the film's title), and prose fiction (Wallace's *Infinite Jest*).

While Wallace necessarily falls short of "contriv[ing] a medium" for the representation of this moment, therefore, he goes almost as far as one could imagine in refracting it through a series of mediums that modernist criticism in the Greenberg–Fried mode has typically construed as in competition with one another. It is this multiply mediated quality that reveals the oblique "emotional thrust" of the moment to Joelle, even if she does not exactly experience that thrust herself. But perhaps the "thrust" (the echo of the angel's arrow surely not coincidental) should not in fact be experienced by the beholder, since this would risk reducing the moment to the norms of melodrama, perhaps the most theatrical of genres in its overt intent to stir audience emotions.[87] Indeed, rather than accentuating the theatricality of Bernini's statue, Incandenza's technique would appear intended precisely to defeat that theatricality by inducing absorption—if not emotion—in the viewer in the same way that it induces absorption in the alcoholic sandwich-bag salesman, whose point of view we inhabit (and simultaneously escape) for the duration of the shot.

But here Joelle's description of the conditions under which she views Incandenza's films becomes important. Of the "flashes of something," the narrator remarks:

> She noticed them only when alone, watching, without Orin and his rheostat's dimmer, the living room's lights up high like she liked them, liked to see herself and everything else in the room with the viewer—Orin liked to sit in the dark and enter what he watched, his jaw slackening, a child raised on multichannel cable TV. (741)

Here we have two models of watching. One of them, Orin's, seems the height of absorption; the other, Joelle's, is very different. Even though she is watching the alcoholic sandwich-bag salesman undergo a kind of absorptive self-forgetting in front of Bernini's statue, Joelle herself is *not* engaged in absorptive self-forgetting in front of Incandenza's film. The medium is of particular importance here, since by watching alone on a small screen Joelle has the option of turning up the lights and refusing the invisibility of herself and everything else in the room.[88] Rather than wholly enter the film, she can retain perceptual awareness of herself and her surroundings as she watches the statue on the screen. This could indeed be described as an experience of "mediated transcendence of self" rather than an experience of fully absorptive self-forgetting.

Marking the difference between these two experiences constitutes, I would argue, a vital engagement by Wallace with the notion of *self-consciousness*, an abiding concern he shared with Hegel. To the Romantic sensibility, self-consciousness can only be understood as self-alienation, with the threat of inauthenticity and theatricality provoked by any awareness of others as desiring beings whose thoughts and actions impact upon the self. We can see this sensibility at work in famous statements such as the following by Rousseau: "The Savage lives within himself; sociable man, always outside himself, is capable of living only in the opinion of others and, so to speak, derives the sentiment of his own existence solely from their judgment"; and likewise in Diderot's claim that his art criticism was informed by the distinction between "a man presenting himself in company and a man acting from motivation, between a man who's alone and a man being observed."[89] Here it is again significant that Joelle, in the cocaine passage, describes feeling simultaneously "observed *and* alone," as if this Romantic picture of self-consciousness as self-alienation could be dialectically overcome by another view. This other view—the view Wallace could be said to be working towards in his representation of Joelle's viewing experience—resembles what Robert Pippin calls *reflective absorption*, which he explains as follows:

> A reflective embodiment is not one that in some way *thematizes* one's role and thereby distances oneself from it, but reflection is meant in the original Kantian sense of apperception, as *adverbial*. An apperceptive awareness of a room is not a direct awareness of a room *and* a second-order self-consciousness *of* one's perceptual state as a new, dual object. (This misunderstanding is the source of the unavoidable self-alienation worries). Rather one perceives the room *self-consciously*, aware in perceiving the room that one is in a perceptual state (not an imagined or remembered state) as one perceives but not aware of two intentional or separate objects. The idea would be to understand reflective absorption as *an intensification of such absorption*, not a thematizing and ultimately theatricalizing distance.... That sort of theatricalizing might be said to occur only when something like the normative structure of such mindedness begins to break down, fails to sustain allegiance, becomes a *reflected object of inquiry*, not a *mode of life*.[90]

Pippin is commenting here on Fried's reading of the nineteenth-century German painter Adolph Menzel, whose realism aimed to cure Romantic self-alienation by inducing reflective absorption. As David Hering has persuasively argued, however, "reflection" is a vexed term in Wallace's aesthetics, connoting mirror tropes that lead not to apperceptive awareness but to inescapably recursive loops back to the character, the author, and the surface of the text (the recursive quality of annular fusion is exemplary here). In Hering's four-stage model of Wallace's engagement with motifs of reflection, Orin Incandenza's mode of watching films would offer a good example of the third stage, narcissism: "the absorption of the character in the text within the reflective image, be it a mirror or screen."[91] The breakthrough fourth stage, "refraction," transforms watching into "a specifically communicative gesture between character and character, text and reader or authorial presence and reader."[92] Hering summarizes the contrast between reflection and refraction as one between "'looking at' (as one does to a mirror) and 'looking into' (as one does to another's eyes)."[93] While it never leaves reflection wholly behind, refraction directs the intentionality of the gaze toward self and other simultaneously.

Bringing Hering together with Hegel and Fried, I would argue that Joelle's mode of watching *Pre-Nuptial Agreement* is best described as *refractive absorption*. The multimedial quality of the film's presentation, combined with Joelle's account of how she chooses to watch it, dialectically transfigures both the theatricality of Bernini's sculpture and the absorptive self-forgetting of the film's protagonist, precisely via the beholder's "mediated transcendence of self." In contrast to Hal's failed reading of other texts and other minds throughout the novel—in the opening scene he "look[s] out" rather than looking into, and "*Digests* things" rather than responding to communicative acts (15)—we can see Joelle as a model for the ideal reader of *Infinite Jest*. Her mode of viewing/reading—a mediated immersion that does not equate to total self-forgetting—promises to recognize and thus realize the potentially sincere communication in James Incandenza's filmmaking, healing the division between subject and object otherwise as evident in that filmmaking as it is in his son Hal's breakdown.[94]

While Incandenza's aim to converse with Hal by contriving the medium of "Infinite Jest" thus ends in failure, Wallace's hope was that the medium of *Infinite Jest* would provide that healing experience of refractive absorption for the novel's reader. But attempting to induce such a state in the reader—to make them feel simultaneously "observed and alone"—was a delicate task, one that for Wallace was perennially threatened by a writer's temptation to anticipate and manipulate the reader's response, and to look for overly theatrical or overly absorptive effects on that basis. The connections with Wallace's later fiction are suggestive here: it would not be a stretch to say that the questions of how and to what extent the perceptions of others should be consciously taken into account—both in social action and aesthetic creation—serve as the driving concern of key stories such as "Octet" and "Good Old Neon." In *Infinite Jest*, these questions emerge in earnest for the first time, and they do so in escalated form, as nothing less than a matter of life and death. In Fried's work, the threat that theatricality posed was to the continued possibility of genuine art. For Pippin, channeling Hegel, the threat was to the possibility of authentic historical subjectivity. But Wallace further radicalized this originally aesthetic problem by building his novel around the great social discovery of his years since *Westward*. That discovery was the Alcoholics Anonymous twelve-step program, and it stands at the very heart of the life-and-death sincerity struggle in *Infinite Jest*.

Life, Death, and Sincerity

The Alcoholics Anonymous "commitments" depicted throughout *Infinite Jest* feature speakers telling the story of their personal journey, from initial drug use to addiction to total despair ("bottoming out") to finding AA and onto recovery and a tentatively rehabilitated life. The speaker's audience consists of fellow addicts, who range from skeptical new arrivals in recovery to older men and women whom the narrator refers to as Crocodiles, and of whom we are told: "Sincerity with an ulterior motive is something these tough ravaged people know and fear" (369). When they encounter this brand of "sly disingenuous manipulative pseudo-sincerity" in a speaker, these experienced listeners shift uncomfortably in their seats as they recognize the kind of theatrical performance that undermines the therapeutic prospects of both speaker and listener. "The thing is that it has to be the truth to really go over, here," we learn of the AA meetings. "It can't be a calculated crowd-pleaser, and it has to be the truth unslanted, unfortified. And maximally unironic" (369). These insights, and the stories that prompt them, are mostly focalized through the consciousness of Don Gately, resident staffer at Ennet House Drug and Alcohol Recovery House and the nearest thing that *Infinite Jest* has to a hero. Through flashbacks we see that Gately's struggle with drugs has indeed been a life-and-death matter, and he has found a path to sobriety by keeping things as simple and sincere as he can: "he tries to be just about as verbally honest as possible at almost all times, now, without too much calculation about how the listener's going to feel about what he says. This is harder than it sounds" (370).

Gately's reflections on the stories told at AA commitments, and on his own experiences with narcotics, stress the importance of anti-theatrical truth-telling, of a sincerity that does not pander or manipulate, that resists "figuring out what an audience wants to hear and then supplying it" (367). What is striking about the many transcriptions of these recovery stories in *Infinite Jest*, nevertheless, is their very similarity in structure and content, the way they must closely follow a narrative pattern and linguistic template laid down by AA. If an addict is to prove, to themselves and their audience, that they acknowledge their addiction and are genuinely committed to recovering, they must repeat clichéd mantras—"'Easy Does It!' and 'Turn it Over!' and 'One Day at a Time!'" (369)—and tell the same generic story about their journey that everyone else also tells. "All the speakers' stories of decline and fall and surrender," we are told, "are basically alike, and like your own" (345). Following this pattern leads to certain paradoxes, as Gately recognizes when he notes that a commitment to truth "doesn't mean you can't pay empty or hypocritical lip-service, however. Paradoxically enough" (369). With AA we thus find that we are no longer in a Wordsworthian realm of sincerity as spontaneous effusion, nor in a Byronic realm that treats sincerity as a social convention. Instead, we are somewhere in between: AA prioritizes a set of communally recognized generic forms and linguistic motifs, which retroactively frame the experience of the individual addict and create a familiar story with which everyone listening can identify (AA's motto in the novel is "Don't Compare, Identify").

From the outset of scholarship on *Infinite Jest*, the way readers should assess the role played by Alcoholics Anonymous has been a subject of dispute and a certain unease. While early critics saw AA as "possibly rescuing"[95] and a "tentative antidote,"[96] and many have continued to see its presentation by Wallace as "ambivalent,"[97] the first full-throated critique of the model was offered by Mary Holland. She saw the AA sections as an example of the novel's narcissism theme writ large, with each addict asked "blindly to submit his or her will to the universal experience of the program, . . . requiring them to empathize with this standard story that each member tells, with their own story, with themselves."[98] Conversely, the most thoroughgoing affirmation of AA's role has been presented by Jon Baskin, who claims that the tenets of the program replace a theoretical mode of reason with one that emphasizes "interpersonal contact, intellectual discipline, and a respect for clear and distinct boundaries, sometimes referred to as conventions."[99] Baskin adds that "language is conceived, in Wallace's AA, as a conduit for intention," and he contrasts this view of language with the one promoted by poststructuralist theory, where the "intentional fallacy" and the "death of the author" are shibboleths, and authorial intention is eclipsed by emphasis on the ambiguities of the text.[100]

As we saw in the Introduction to this book, Wallace's stated position with respect to poststructuralist ideas varied across his early essays. And while *Infinite Jest* is certainly critical of the consequences of a full embrace of "Theory," as Baskin rightly observes, the novel also retains some distance from the model that Theory challenged, the humanist conception of the self that—as we also saw in the Introduction—was closely associated by mid-twentieth-century American liberals with the value of sincerity. As defined by Trilling via Polonius's speech in *Hamlet*, sincerity named a congruence between avowal and feeling whose ethical basis required being true to oneself as a means of avoiding falsity to others. When authenticity came to challenge sincerity across the nineteenth and twentieth centuries, it was on the premise that truth to the self should be its own end, rather than serving as means to an end. With modernism, Trilling's "public end in view" came to be understood, in Friedian terms, as a gateway to theatricality. Nevertheless, in the case of neither sincerity nor authenticity was the possibility or value of self-knowledge placed in doubt. This is where *Infinite Jest* demurs: while defending the self against its poststructuralist and postmodernist eclipse, the novel remains skeptical about self-knowledge, at least when approached by means of self-reflection in the tradition of philosophy since Descartes. The novel can here be said to reverse the causal relationship between sincerity and the other set out in Polonius's formulation. With Wallace's AA, avoiding falsity to others now becomes not the end but the *means* of discovering the truth about oneself. Or, to put it in a way pertinent to this chapter's argument: in literary New Sincerity, the other becomes the *medium* for approaching the sincerity of the self.

As Gately says, "This is harder than it sounds" (370). If sincerity does not simply flow outwards from the self, then telling the self's truth to the other requires leaning on generic and linguistic conventions that risk falsifying—or at least evading the singularity of—the experiences of the self. Nonetheless, those very conventions, recognized and validated by a community of fellow addicts, constitute the only means one has for achieving sincerity. More than that, those conventions and that community become the support necessary to stay alive, since the self cannot rely on its own resources to do so. The tenets and prescriptions of AA are thus placed beyond question or assessment from a first-person point of view. This is captured most memorably in the recommendation that addicts get down on their knees every morning and night to pray to their chosen "Higher Power." Rather than placing us in the territory of *The Varieties of Religious Experience*, wherein sincerity would be viewed as the expression of personal belief, *Infinite Jest* stresses the formalism of this gesture: how belief in the divine recipient of the prayer is very much secondary to the process of undertaking the ritual. This is precisely Gately's experience, because "when he tries to understand something to really sincerely pray to," all he feels is "Nothingness" (444). But Gately is advised to continue to carry out the ritual even though he cannot rationally connect it to the progression of his sobriety. The director of his recovery house puts this in its bluntest terms:

> Pat had said it didn't matter at this point what he thought or believed or even said. All that mattered was what he *did*. If he did the right things, and kept doing them for long enough, what Gately thought and believed would magically change. (466)

In *Infinite Jest*, all the characters are addicts of a kind—whether to alcohol, drugs, sex, consumerism, television, or even the murdering of cats—and addiction is connected to a weakness of the will that cannot be overcome by the will itself. The only way through this paradox is to follow the advice and believe in the magic.

This resistance of AA's tenets to first-person challenge remains unacceptable to certain characters in the novel, as when an academic in recovery named Geoffrey Day, responding to the same paradoxes of truth and hypocrisy in the Program that Gately has acknowledged, asks the latter, "'Am I out of line in seeing something totalitarian about it? Something dare I say un-American?'" (1003). "Day's right about how it seems," Gately thinks to himself in response. "Yes, and if Geoffrey Day keeps on steering by the way things seem to him then he's a dead man for sure" (273). The deliberate echoes between Day's picture of AA and the fascist themes in *Infinite Jest* demonstrate that Wallace is making a broader point here than about how best to overcome addiction to drugs, or even—as Baskin would have it—addiction to damagingly theoretical forms of thinking. In placing neoliberalism and fascism on a continuum with one another, Wallace is identifying the origins of damaging thought patterns in contemporary forms of individualism that privilege the first-person point of view at the expense of a more dialogical and social perspective. Neoliberalism, with its signature making over of the capital-labor relation into an issue of human capital, thereby shifting the costs of social reproduction from the state to the competitive individual and their family circumstances, creates the conditions for poverty and despair. The antidotes offered by consumer society, the technocapitalist world of hyper-entertainment presented in *Infinite Jest*, are not antidotes at all, but accelerate the morphing of classic liberal freedom—the kind defended by Hugh Steeply—into a libertarianism that leaves individuals isolated but increasingly without sovereignty over themselves.

Infinite Jest turns for answers to this dilemma not to the educated young men of Enfield Tennis Academy, but to a set of characters defined by their dearth of human capital and their consequent lack of investment in the system they are trying to escape. For these characters, who circulate in and around Ennet House, AA provides the social support that neoliberal society has denied them. With no pretensions to believe they can think their way through their problems, these characters see no great reason to be worried about the dark side of the AA model. Responding to the question of what makes the AA program different from brainwashing, Don Gately thinks to himself that "the Program might be more like deprogramming than actual washing, considering the psychic job the Disease's Spider has done on all of them" (369). A minor character, Bruce Green, agrees: "if Boston AA is a cult that like brainwashes you, he guesses he'd got himself to the point where his brain needed a good brisk washing" (562).

Through its treatment of AA and recovery, then, *Infinite Jest* betrays skepticism concerning the reliability of the first-person point of view, highlighting the way in which one's own true intentions can remain a source of opacity and self-deception. But if it is not possible to be sure when one is being sincere, this does not mean that sincere acts do not take place in the world of Wallace's novel. As Severs points out, "people do it, people give, and one path to being sincere and generous for Wallace seems to lie in remaining absorbed in work and not recognizing a need to avow an intention at all."[101] But where a character—and here Severs is thinking of Gately cleaning feces from the walls of a homeless shelter—might remain fully absorbed in work, I have argued in this chapter that the aesthetic logic of *Infinite Jest* challenges this prescription. That logic suggests instead that its reader should be *refractively* absorbed in their reading, on the model of Joelle's viewing of Incandenza's films. Such a refracted reading experience is encouraged by the fragmented structure of

Infinite Jest itself, where readerly absorption is disrupted by basic confusions about the meaning of the action and the progress of the plot. But refractive absorption is also encouraged on the level of style, and it is with a close consideration of Wallace's prose that this chapter will conclude.

Achieving the Art

Most noteworthy among *Infinite Jest*'s many stylistic innovations is its characteristic brand of free indirect discourse. Wallace's use of the technique differs from canonical examples in the literary tradition, ranging from the novels of Jane Austen, where free indirect discourse is arguably invented, to the famous "Uncle Charles Principle" in James Joyce, where it is perfected.[102] These earlier examples are characterized by the seamless melding of narrator and character's points of view and linguistic registers ("the narrative point of view unobtrusively fluctuates," as Hugh Kenner puts it), meaning that the reader's attention is rarely drawn away from the imagined world to raise questions about the origins of the voice and language.[103] In *Infinite Jest*, the seams are more regularly exposed by collisions between the narrator's and character's views and registers, highlighting the impossibility of conclusively establishing the source of the words on the page. It is not only when reading closely, moreover, that it becomes unclear whether a character or narrator is having certain thoughts transcribed in the text's language; this lack of certainty is often made inescapable in the reading process.

These collisions in free indirect discourse culminate near the end of the novel when Gately, lying prone in a hospital bed and fighting off searing pain while refusing potentially addictive medication, is visited by the wraith of James Incandenza. A conversation between the two takes place via Gately's "brain-voice," where words in capital letters become part of Gately's conscious thoughts even though he has never heard or seen those words before. We understand that the words must be coming from Incandenza's wraith even though they also seem to Gately to be the product of his own thoughts, as in the following passage:

> [The wraith] holds one knee to its sunken chest and starts doing what Gately would know were pirouettes if he'd ever once been exposed to ballet, pirouetting faster and faster and then so fast the wraith's nothing but a long stalk of

sweatshirt-and-Coke-can-colored light that seems to extrude from the ceiling; and then, in a moment that rivals the Coke-can moment for unpleasantness, into Gately's personal mind, in Gately's own brain-voice but with roaring and unwilled force, comes the term PIROUETTE, in caps, which term Gately knows for a fact he doesn't have any idea what it means and no reason to be thinking it with roaring force, so the sensation is not only creepy but somehow violating, a sort of lexical rape. (832)

Andrew Warren has dubbed this stylistic innovation "free indirect wraith" and has offered a series of convincing close readings of the style's ambiguities, how it is rarely clear where the wraith's interventions end and Gately's own thoughts begin (from which consciousness, for instance, does the lowercase "lexical rape" derive?).[104] As a literal example of *ghostwriting*, this scene connects with a motif explored throughout *New Sincerity*, through which an author writing in the age of normative neoliberalism expresses their anxiety about acting as a medium for larger corporate entities. When twinned with this late scene involving Gately, Hal's "I am in here" in *Infinite Jest*'s opening scene might then be read as a plea from the author to recognize his agency in a neoliberal landscape, with the singular style throughout the novel offering the necessary evidence that Wallace is indeed "in here."

Moving from a key idea in this book back to a key idea in this chapter, we might also observe that it is this scene with Gately—rather than the film "Infinite Jest"—that marks the real culmination of Incandenza's attempt to "contrive a medium" to converse with his son. As Warren points out, this phrase need not be understood only as signaling a new artistic form of communication, but equally as "finding or waking or disturbing or stirring up (Latin, *turbare*) someone who could communicate for you (as in the occult sense of *medium*)."[105] Gately becomes Incandenza's medium in this latter sense, the means by which the father will attempt for one final time—now posthumously—to communicate with his son Hal.[106] And as many critics have noted, this scene between Gately and the wraith also serves as an allegory for Wallace's relationship to his reader, whereby the author's message can only be conveyed through the medium of its recipient. The fact that this process is described as "lexical rape" chimes with the uncomfortable ending of *Westward*, with the sincerity of the author's relation to the reader complicated by the ghostly origins and intentions of the words on the page.

That ending is likewise recalled by the most sustained passage of second-person address in *Infinite Jest*, which—as so often in New Sincerity fiction—heralds a significant textual moment. In this case the grammatical shift in address is used to introduce Ennet House and AA for the first time, through a five-page passage that begins: "If, by the virtue of charity or the circumstances of desperation, you ever chance to spend a little time around a Substance-recovery halfway facility like Enfield MA's state-funded Ennet House, you will acquire many exotic new facts" (200). Among these facts are the following:

> That having sex with someone you do not care for feels lonelier than not having sex in the first place, afterward.
> That it is permissible to *want*.
> That everybody is identical in their secret unspoken belief that way deep down they are different to everyone else. That this isn't necessarily perverse.
> That there might not be angels, but there are people who might as well be angels.
> That God—unless you're Charlton Heston, or unhinged, or both—speaks and acts entirely through the vehicle of human beings, if there is a God.
> That God might regard the issue of whether you believe there's a God or not as fairly low on his/her/its list of things s/he/it's interested in re you. (205)

This prose addressed to "you," the implied reader, draws attention to itself as alternatively spoken, for instance in the jocular reference to Charlton Heston, and written, as in the pedantic faux precision of "his/her/its list of things s/he/it's interested in re you," which is impossible to say out loud as printed on the page. This undecidable oscillation between speech and writing is one indication that the sincerity of the tone here—like the tone at the finale of *Westward*—is anything but simple; another indication is the liturgical quality of the passage, which is close to the familiar genres of mantra, litany, or catechism. The passage's stand-alone maxims, each granted its own single-sentence paragraph, deal with matters of profundity: the emotional repercussions of sex, the expression or repression of desire, the belief in individual uniqueness, the human relationship to God. And yet sincerity is inseparable here from its instantiation in a socially established genre: not only the genre of the liturgy, but the genre of the modern novel itself, which unlike religious verse understands itself to be irreducibly fictional.

This fictionality, emphasized by the novel's structure and style, is enacted through the secular medium of the reader. And the reader, like Gately and Joelle, must be active in the process, must become refractively absorbed. How better to described Gately's orientation in the scene with the ghost? Like Gately refusing the pleasure of drugs, the reader must resist being fully absorbed in entertainment, which for Wallace soothed the audience to sleep rather than keeping them awake and aware. Hence Wallace's refusal of the so-called plain style, which for him was marked by similar narcotic qualities. "He looked at the plain style," notes John Jeremiah Sullivan,

> and saw that the impetus of it, in the end, is to sell the reader something. Not in a crass sense, but in a rhetorical sense. The well-tempered magazine feature, for all its pleasures, is a kind of fascist wedge that seeks to make you forget its problems, half-truths, and arbitrary decisions, and swallow its nonexistent imprimatur. Wallace could never exempt himself or his reporting from the range of things that would be subject to scrutiny.[107]

Laying bare the techniques of his fiction through a singular use of free indirect discourse (and occasionally second-person address) was one way Wallace saw to resist the fascist impulses that stalk American culture throughout *Infinite Jest*. So too, as we saw in the debate between Marathe and Steeply, must the utilitarian impulses underpinning neoliberalism be resisted. As William Paulson wrote in a study that appeared just as Wallace was beginning his career, at the dawn of the age of normative neoliberalism: "If literature is to deviate from the utilitarian task of communication, it must be an imperfect process of communication, an act of communication in which what is received is not exactly what was sent. Rather than attempting to reduce noise to a minimum, literary communication *assumes* its noise as a constitutive factor of itself."[108]

Paulson's claim suggests why literature, above all other media, proved the most appropriate vehicle for New Sincerity aesthetics in millennial-era art. Literary writing was not faced with the choice that other modernist arts confronted in the twentieth century, where "noise" had to be reduced in favor of "pure" exploitation of the medium, but at the expense of audience understanding and engagement. Literature, enacted through a shared language, need not (and perhaps could not) aim to reduce noise in this way.[109] "Writers do not share the severe burden of modernism which serious musicians and painters and sculptors have recognized for generations," Wallace's teacher Stanley Cavell observed in a famous essay. "A writer can still work with the words we all share, more or less, and have to share; he still, therefore, has an audience with the chance of responding to the way *he* can share the words more than more or less."[110] Despite the complexity of his dialectical engagement with modernist and postmodernist art across a variety of media, this sharing of words was something Wallace testified to again and again when talking about his work. "The old tricks have been exploded, and I think the language needs to find new ways to pull in the reader," he told an interviewer during his *Infinite Jest* tour. "And my personal belief is a lot of it has to do with voice, and a feeling of intimacy between the writer and the reader. That sorta, given the atomization and loneliness of contemporary life—that's our opening, and that's our gift."[111] Whether voice or text, oral or written, in the end we might say that the medium for Wallace is not really "Infinite Jest" or even *Infinite Jest*. It is not the words he writes or speaks but the reader who reads or listens. The reader is, finally, the medium for a co-authored message, the intervening consciousness through which the art of sincerity can be recognized, enacted, and achieved.

New Economy, New Sincerity

Believing in the New Economy

In the sixth chapter of *A Heartbreaking Work of Staggering Genius* (2000), Dave Eggers recounts the story of the early months of *Might*, a magazine he founded and edited with two college friends in the mid-1990s. The "filthy corner of a shaky warehouse" in San Francisco's South Park that served as the publication's headquarters had previously been inhabited by *Wired* magazine, whose early success allowed it to move to a new (and presumably less filthy) space two floors higher in the same building.[1] A magazine that only a couple of years into its existence had already established itself as "the monthly bible of the 'virtual class,'" *Wired* is an object of simultaneous envy and scorn for Dave.[2] "There is no prestige like the prestige of working for *Wired*" (171), he acknowledges, while also claiming that one of the key missions of *Might* would be "ridiculing other magazines, especially *Wired* upstairs" (172). This posture of ridicule, which took the form of ironic parodies of *Wired* staples such as the What's Hot/What's Not list, underpinned the *Might* editors' strategy of denying that "we're part of this scene, or any scene." The point was not to negate the value of surrounding cultural trends but to affirm *Might*'s own distinctiveness as, in Dave's comically grandiose words, "the very first meaningful magazine in the history of civilization" (172).

When Eggers added an appendix, "Mistakes We Knew We Were Making," to the 2001 Vintage paperback edition of his best-selling memoir, he identified the *Might* chapter as the only place where irony could be found in a book that otherwise features "almost no irony, whatsoever, within its covers."[3] Yet rather than flat-out ironic, the tone of these pages in the memoir is deceptively layered. The narrator of *A Heartbreaking Work* is evidently poking fun at both the *Might* editors' youthful and irreverent attitude at the time, and the equally irreverent but more self-serious outlook of a magazine like *Wired*. But the retrospective ironizing is also laced with respect and even pride: the San Francisco Bay Area in the mid-1990s really *was* an exhilarating place to be, "not just a place where people are working but a place where people are creating and working to change the *very way we live*" (170). The emphasis Eggers puts on this latter phrase communicates a number of things simultaneously: the mid-1990s Dave Eggers's excitement at participating in this nascent but influential subculture; how that excitement is expressed through Dave's parroting of the hyperbole that characterizes the subculture; and the way in which, looking back a few years later, the Eggers of the memoir wants to express both his earlier excitement and the ironizing of that excitement—or, we might say, his sincerity and the ironizing of that sincerity—all at the same time. A significant element of that earlier sincerity, moreover, is expressed through economic disavowal. While work with *Might* magazine was not well remunerated, this fact only supported a philosophy, shared broadly among the South Park community, in which "money is suspect, the making of money and caring about money . . . is archaic, is high school, is completely beside the point" (171). By refusing to value their labor in conventional economic terms, the workers of South Park display a simultaneous nonchalance and exuberance that puts them at odds with the grim and grasping capitalism they find sadly characteristic of wider American culture.

The layers of the *Might* chapter only multiply when we read it from a perspective more than two decades after Eggers published *A Heartbreaking Work*. For the idea that this Bay Area subculture would change "the *very way we live*" turned out to be not at all an exaggeration. The technology that was created in and around San Francisco, and—perhaps just as importantly—the way that technology was imagined, narrated, marketed, and sold to the public of the United States and the globe, has had widespread and permanent effects. Moreover, the working model that Eggers describes—where work is about creating rather than earning, where the old industrial-era opposition between labor and leisure is imagined irrelevant—has become, if far from ubiquitous in fact, then at least widely held up as the ideal vision of what twenty-first-century work should be.[4] While this model of work emerged from the technology sector, Eggers's passing reference to *Might* magazine as a "start-up" shows how quickly this tech lingo migrated to other fields (169). Embedded in the idea of the start-up, too, is a particular orientation toward capital: while "money is suspect" as a moral value in the subculture Eggers is describing, in practice it remains a necessity. The funding model is one in which those with ideas pitch to those with money—the "angel investors" or "venture capitalists"—in order to build and sustain a business. Indeed, it was a lack of venture capital that eventually brought the curtain down on *Might* magazine. Three-and-a-half years on from its first issue, the publication folded following failed talks with a range of investors, among them—as Eggers relates at the end of his memoir (415–416)—none other than *Wired* itself.

This whole milieu—the work, the way of talking about the work, the non-capitalist (even anti-capitalist) ethos expressing itself through the capitalist start-up, the sense that value could be created by creativity itself—was emblematic of the so-called New Economy of the 1990s. An outgrowth of the "End of History" vision of liberal capitalist triumph set forth in the 1989 essay by Fukuyama that framed my opening chapter, the New Economy referred to specific developments in the technology sector as well as the wider implications of those developments for the notion of a post-industrial economic order. While the phrase itself dates back to a 1988 speech by Ronald Reagan in which the US president intoned, "In the new economy, human invention increasingly makes physical resources obsolete," it was over the second half of the 1990s that the idea gained serious prominence.[5] Chief among its champions was *Wired*'s founding editor Kevin Kelly, whose *New Rules for the New Economy* (1998) described the New Economy as "a tectonic upheaval in our commonwealth," a dispensation that was global, networked, and drew value from "intangible things—ideas, information, and relationships."[6] "Communication *is* the economy," Kelly went so far as to proclaim.[7] Together with his observations that the pension funds of ordinary citizens were now the biggest players on capital markets, and that "increasing amounts of wealth are now held in equity, and not in debt," Kelly's stress on the new centrality of communication even led him to summon the spirit of Karl Marx in an incongruous setting: "The workers of America really do collectively own the means of production."[8]

To critics of New Economy thinking, such utopian pronouncements did not square well with reality. Despite much-trumpeted rises in productivity, "for the majority of American workers, wages through the nineties either fell or barely kept pace with inflation."[9] Nevertheless, many economists at the time either ignored this reality or treated it as a positive sign, since "rising wages were by definition a form of inflation" and "inflation was declared the mortal enemy of national economic policy."[10] Some even became convinced that it was possible for the New Economy boom to be sustained over the long term. "The U.S. economy likely will not see a recession for years to come," wrote Rudi Dornbusch, a leading macroeconomist, in 1998. "This expansion will run forever."[11] Summarizing the fervor of the moment, Joseph Stiglitz later remarked that the New Economy "promised the end of the business cycle, the ups and downs of the economy that had, until now, always been part of capitalism."[12]

Even for those who sung loudest in praise of its coming, however, the New Economy was not all good news. Echoing Fukuyama on the End of History, Kelly concluded his paean to the New Economy with a surprising turn toward ambivalence, even resignation. While mostly sanguine and even celebratory of what he called "a widespread reliance on economic values as the basis for making decisions in all walks of life," Kelly nevertheless diagnosed the consequences of this new cultural worship of economics and technology in more mixed terms.[13] "Because the nature of the network economy seeds disequilibrium, fragmentation, uncertainty, churn, and relativism, the anchors of meaning and value are in short supply," he wrote. "In the great vacuum of meaning, in the silence of unspoken values, in the vacancy of something large to stand for, something bigger than oneself, technology—for better or worse—will shape our society."[14]

It was against this background of excitement and anxiety about the promise of the New Economy that *A Heartbreaking Work of Staggering Genius* was lived, conceived, and written. That what later became known as the "dot-com bubble" would burst with the crash in value of the NASDAQ index in April 2000—two months after the publication of his memoir—adds another layer of irony to Eggers's picture of mid-1990s San Francisco as a place and time working to change "the *very way we live*." The book's rhetorical register—its distinctive mix of ironic cynicism and exuberant affirmation, of sincere pathos and angry self-laceration—can come in retrospect to seem in keeping with the bubble of the times, doing precious little to deflate it. Many critics have read Eggers's early writing as a symptomatic artifact of this kind, complicit with the neoliberal outlook that underpinned the rhetoric of the End of History and the New Economy.[15] What I want to argue, by contrast, is that while *A Heartbreaking Work* and Eggers's first novel *You Shall Know Our Velocity* (2002) are indeed artifacts of their time, they contain important critical and dialectical resources for reading the consciousness of that time, for diagnosing key features of neoliberal economy and culture, and for recognizing the changing meanings of complicity and sincerity within that setting. While the seeds of New Sincerity were sown by David Foster Wallace's fiction and essays of the early to mid-1990s, this literary and cultural formation only came to fruition in the later part of the decade, alongside, and in dialogue with, the rhetoric of the New Economy. Dave Eggers—a literary entrepreneur as well as an experimental author—is an unavoidably central figure in this cultural ripening.[16]

Indeed, *A Heartbreaking Work of Staggering Genius* has long been recognized as "an Urtext for new sincerity."[17] Caroline Hamilton reads the memoir as exploring "the possibility that celebrity and sincerity need not be perceived as mutually exclusive," while Lee Konstantinou sees Eggers as asking readers "to believe in *him*, in the truthfulness of his memoir, the sincerity of his various enterprises."[18] Other critics have zeroed in on the literary techniques Eggers uses to convey the sincerity effects of his narrative, with the most extended analyses offered by European critics schooled in narratological traditions. These scholars have highlighted the "metareferential elements"[19] of Eggers's memoir as contributing to its "meta-honesty,"[20] all in the service of playing on "contemporary culture's contradictory injunctions: *Thou shall exhibit and share with us thy most private inner self*, while *Thou shall mistrust any exhibition of sentiment*."[21] In this collective critical reading, *A Heartbreaking Work* is often made a transitional text, with its sincere ironies "paving the way for more full-fledged sentiment" both in Eggers's own later writing and in post–9/11 American culture.[22]

The link between the early Eggers and a historically situated New Sincerity aesthetics—sometimes understood under related names—is thus well established in critical accounts. But an implicit assumption that all these accounts share, an assumption I want to challenge in this chapter, is that the sincerity effects of *A Heartbreaking Work* (and of *You Shall Know Our Velocity*, where critics discuss it) aim to solicit and inculcate readerly belief as an unequivocal good in itself. That is, although Eggers may be ironic or even cynical about the *possibility* of belief in our time, the overriding moral *goal* of his work is the successful reconstitution of belief among readers. As the critic for whom the category of belief is most central, Konstantinou makes this argument most explicitly. "Eggers means to make his readers into believers," he contends, noting that "what is paradoxical about this project is the *emptiness* of the proposed postironic belief. Postironists do not advocate a stance of belief toward any particular aspect of the world, but rather promote a general ethos of belief."[23] This promotion of belief is achieved by turning metafiction—a literary strategy traditionally associated with skepticism and the attack on naïve metaphysical and aesthetic beliefs—to new ethical ends. The literary result, which Konstantinou dubs "a kind of (nonprofit) retail avant-gardism," contains elements both conservative and radical, making its peace with the market while often involving "the elision of 'truth' and 'untruth' in pursuit of creating belief and reenchantment."[24]

Konstantinou's reconstruction of Eggers's aesthetic project is supported by many elements of Eggers's entrepreneurial and philanthropic work in the literary field, not least the naming of one his magazines *The Believer*. Yet if Eggers calls on readers to become believers, then this call to credence should, I argue, be understood against a specific historical-material background. In *The Market Logics of Contemporary Fiction*, Paul Crosthwaite argues that the rapid and widespread financialization of the US and world economy over the neoliberal period has served to position belief at the very center of contemporary economic life. While the use of money in modern society has always relied on "fiduciary exchangeability"—the faith among users that money will hold stable value in marketplace transactions—rarely, according to Crosthwaite, "has trust been installed so centrally . . . than in the fiat money regime that assumed *de facto* command of the international monetary system in the early 1970s," following the collapse of the postwar regime of fixed exchange rates.[25] Under this new regime, which for the first time divorced money entirely from the gold reserves that had traditionally been understood (however dubiously) to underpin its value, the requirement of belief was raised, as it were, to the second power, since "fiat money (in the form of cash deposited in bank accounts) is imagined as 'backing' some still less tangible form of value, despite lacking 'real' value itself."[26] This less tangible form of value is located in the new credit "instruments"—including securities, collateralized debt obligations, futures contracts, and other derivatives—that accompanied the expansion of finance over the neoliberal decades.

Writers of fiction have been directly impacted by this economic shift, not only because of the "fiduciary logic—a logic of trust or tacit belief—that marketable fictional texts and credit instruments have long shared," but also because of concomitant and far-reaching changes in the publishing industry.[27] The contemporary genre of writing that has emerged in response to these changes Crosthwaite dubs "market metafiction," and his overview of its various stages includes five pages covering the "trust, realism, sincerity" paradigm that is central to my own work in this book. Crosthwaite takes *A Heartbreaking Work of Staggering Genius* as his exemplary text for this paradigm, focusing on how the notorious preface of Eggers's memoir analogizes its reader to an investor open to persuasion by the financial capital that others—including a prestigious publisher—have already put into the book, and therefore liable to be swept along by the confidence of the author's product pitch. Accepting the image of Eggers as a proponent and avatar of belief, Crosthwaite argues that his metafictional memoir allows us to see "how the appeal to belief that is a hallmark of the wider 'postirony' or 'New Sincerity' generation partakes of . . . a dominant contemporary market logic of 'fiduciary exchangeability'—of faith, trust, and credit as the conditions of circulation in literary and financial markets alike."[28]

While the thrust of Crosthwaite's addendum to Konstantinou's argument is therefore to show that exposing his economic entanglements supports Eggers's aim to "make readers into believers," I offer an alternative reading of the author's New Sincerity. I want to suggest that alongside a market logic of fiduciary exchangeability, there is a counterlogic at work in Eggers's writing, one that indicates a less complicit, more dialectically responsive relation to the neoliberal economy and the demand for faith, trust, and credit that underpins it. The fact that Eggers may not be fully aware of this counterlogic does not derail my argument—this despite the authorial claim, made *ex post facto* about *A Heartbreaking Work*, that "SELF-AWARENESS *is* sincerity."[29] I want to show, in fact, that it is precisely the claim to full and present self-awareness that acts as both an animating force and a limiting ethical-aesthetic principle in the work of New Sincerity authors such as Eggers. *A Heartbreaking Work* and *You Shall Know Our Velocity* consistently thematize and interrogate this controlling self-awareness through their temporal and spatial features, producing a counterlogic to the call for belief. And this counterlogic has, I will argue, its own material relation to the economy of Eggers's time. In short, if Konstantinou, Crosthwaite, and others are describing in Eggers what we might call the sincerity of credit, then the counterlogic I am identifying could be dubbed the sincerity of debt.

Here it is useful to turn briefly to Annie McClanahan's *Dead Pledges: Debt, Crisis, and Twenty-First-Century Culture*, which argues that the rise to visibility of the neoliberal debt economy after 2008 has seen the appearance of a range of literary and aesthetic works that engage with the realities of debt and indebtedness. For McClanahan, the global financial crisis of that year brutally exposed the widespread myth—which we have seen Reagan endorse in his paean to human invention making physical resources obsolete—that the financialized credit economy could create value independently of material inputs, and that "some magical shared 'belief' either caused or could prevent the collapse, as if the economy were in the last instance . . . fully imaginary."[30] The neoliberal economy had in fact been operating "as if mere suspension of narrative disbelief could protect us against falling home prices or rising unemployment," but the financial crisis brought the falsity of this premise home.[31] Artists and writers responded by creating works that register the realities of debt in formal terms, including works that challenge realist conceptions of character, conceptions that have traditionally depended upon an understanding of the economy as functioning on credit.

In this chapter, I want to show that this registering of debt and challenge to literary credit in fact emerged earlier, not from a position outside the New Economy but from its very heart, in the early writing of Dave Eggers. In what follows, I will argue that exploring the neoliberal culture of indebtedness via *A Heartbreaking Work* and *You Shall Know Our Velocity* allows us to understand Eggers's New Sincerity aesthetics from a perspective that is not liberal or categorical, but dialectical. Building on the Hegelian conception of the dialectic that underpinned my examination of Wallace's writing in Chapter One, this chapter will add perspectives from thinkers influenced by Hegel's greatest student, Karl Marx. My primary emphasis will be on understanding credit and debt as means of managing time and space, so that the distinctive temporal and spatial dimensions of Eggers's writing can emerge through a reading of his work. But before we turn to this reading, we need a picture of how the neoliberal debt economy can be understood to challenge the primacy of belief in the economy of credit. Only then can we see how literary New Sincerity articulates a shift from the sincerity of credit to the sincerity of debt.

Crediting Debt

The status of indebtedness as the underpinning economic reality of the period since the 1970s has indeed become widely recognized only since the global financial crisis of 2008. In the decade and a half since the economic crash, a series of significant studies of debt have appeared across a range of disciplinary contexts.[32] Though not all of these texts—some primarily anthropological, some sociological, some political—take the neoliberal period as their main focus, those that do collectively narrate an economic history roughly along the following lines. The three decades after World War II—the so-called Golden Age or *Trente Glorieuses* of capitalism—had witnessed strong growth, rising wages, and high profitability throughout what we now call the Global North. Underpinning the stability of these years was the Bretton Woods Accord of 1944, partly designed by the economist who would go on to lend his name to many retrospective characterizations of the period, John Maynard Keynes. Replacing the gold standard whose collapse had contributed to the dire economic conditions that led to the war, Bretton Woods mandated that international currencies would operate on a system of fixed exchange rates. The US dollar, convertible into gold at thirty-five dollars an ounce, acted as the reserve currency.

Following a quarter century of success, this system was coming under increasing pressure by the late 1960s. Persistent full employment led to higher wages led to lower profits led to higher consumer prices led to claims for still higher wages: spiraling inflationary pressures were the result. Moreover, high deficit spending by the US government to support the Vietnam War abroad and Great Society reforms at home decreased confidence in the sustainability of the dollar's linkage to gold. By the turn of the 1970s, foreign governments were exchanging their dollars for gold at unprecedented rates, resulting in a substantial outflow of gold from the US Treasury's reserves. In 1971, President

Richard Nixon unilaterally suspended Bretton Woods by unpegging the dollar from gold. The "Nixon shock," which introduced a system of floating currency exchange rates that became permanent two years later, led to a depreciation of the dollar and steeply rising inflation. Then in 1973, the OPEC oil embargo—a direct response to the dollar's diminishing value and the resultant loss of income for oil-producing countries—heralded an economic crisis and the beginning of what Robert Brenner has called "the long downturn," a still-continuing period of decline in capitalist profitability.[33] With profits now increasingly difficult to realize in industry and manufacturing, capital shifted to grasp the new speculative opportunities available in finance under the regime of floating currencies. The resulting "financialization" of the US and global economy led to the creation of new speculative instruments that positioned value to be realized in the future as the basis for present wealth. These instruments impelled, and relied upon, the creation and spread of credit and debt.

For the Marxist geographer David Harvey, the extended crisis of the 1970s offers an exemplary case study in the problem of overaccumulation. Frequent occurrences in a system built upon the extraction of "ever-increasing quantities of surplus value" from living labor, crises of overaccumulation feature an excess of available labor (i.e., unemployment) alongside a surplus of capital (in the form of commodities, money, stocks, productive capacity, etc.), without any apparent means to bring them profitably together.[34] If the accumulated surplus capital is unable to realize its expected rate of profit, then it must be devalued or destroyed, an outcome that can only be avoided (in the short term) by constructing temporal and spatial arrangements that allow for that surplus capital to be profitably absorbed. What Harvey calls a "temporal fix" is accomplished through the credit system, involving "the creation of what Marx calls 'fictitious capital'—money that is thrown into circulation without any material basis in commodities or productive activity" (95). A "spatial fix," meanwhile, is achieved through locating new markets, including "the geographical expansion of capitalism through colonial and imperialist policies" (93).

The avoidance of crisis for one form of capital at one moment will lead to crisis for another form at another time and place. According to Harvey's updated 2006 preface to *The Limits to Capital*, this has been the key story of the neoliberal period: "Contemporary finance capital, with the aid of information technology, has radically reconfigured spatio-temporality over the last forty years in ways that have disrupted other forms of capital circulation as well as daily life" (xxi). Harvey acknowledges neoliberal capitalism's "astonishing record" in breaking down obstacles to accumulation by disciplining the global working class, reducing barriers to free trade, and inventing credit instruments to absorb capital through new forms of speculation in asset values. Surveying fiscal and debt crises in Mexico, Indonesia, Russia, South Korea, and Argentina over recent decades, alongside the fact that "the US is running a debt-economy on a scale never before envisaged in human history," he remarks ruefully on neoliberalism's capacity "to organize and orchestrate gigantic devaluations of capital worldwide without, up until now, crashing the whole system" (xxvi–xxvii).

"But all is not well with this system," Harvey's 2006 preface warns. "Capitalism increasingly lives on faith alone" (xxv–xxvi). The temporal fix of financialization means nothing more than a delayed reckoning, since "there is no substitute for the actual transformation of nature through the concrete production of use values" (285). The contradictions of capitalism can thus be resolved by the credit system "only at the price of internalizing those contradictions within itself," leading to concentrations of financial power that "can as easily de-stabilize as stabilize capitalism" (xxxii). This dialectical destabilization is the inevitable (albeit delayed) consequence of a temporal fix, since the credit system can only absorb overaccumulated commodity capital by producing an overaccumulation of fictitious capital, promising more production than will occur in the future and issuing more debt than can be repaid. The eventual result is a crisis of confidence in fictitious capital, with no more credit being issued and creditors calling in the debts they are owed. Less than two years after Harvey issued his warning, a credit crisis of precisely this kind occurred throughout the global financial system. The period of neoliberal expansion shuddered abruptly to a halt, and an age of austerity began across the heavily indebted societies of the Global North.

In the next two sections of this chapter, we will see how Harvey's temporal and spatial fix theses can underpin new readings of Eggers's first two books. But in the present section, the specificity of debt and indebtedness for neoliberal society bears further elaboration. In *Buying Time*, Wolfgang Streeck also invokes Marxist crisis theory (this time of the Frankfurt School variety) to argue that neoliberal financialization constituted a "delayed crisis of democratic capitalism" in the Global North, with the delay purchased at the cost of inflation in the 1970s, public debt in the 1980s, and private consumer debt from the 1990s on.[35] These debts finally fell due in 2008, but even following the crash this trend has continued: a recent account records that the world's total sovereign debt, which at the beginning of the 1980s hovered around $3 trillion, had by 2018 "skyrocketed to a record $60 trillion, or over 80 percent of global GDP."[36] The first debt crises of the neoliberal period stemmed in large measure from the "Volcker shock" of 1979–1982, when, in a bid to finally overcome the chronic inflation let loose by the Nixon shock of 1971, the newly appointed chair of the US Federal Reserve, Paul Volcker, engineered a steep rise in interest rates from 4 percent to over 20 percent.[37] This left many developing countries, which had absorbed the surplus capital of the Global North through low-interest loans from Wall Street banks through the 1970s—a classic spatio-temporal fix for capital—with unpayable debts denominated in US dollars. Facing bankruptcy, these countries were made to undertake IMF and World Bank structural adjustment programs shaped by "disciplinary neoliberalism," featuring demands for fiscal austerity, privatization of state assets, deregulation of the economy, and liberalization of trade.[38]

Yet despite the origins in American power of the disciplinary neoliberalism meted out to world's poorest economies—a policy regime that would later be dubbed the "Washington Consensus"—it was in the United States itself that the most pronounced shift to indebtedness occurred. In the 1970s, total US debt—owed by governments, corporations, and individuals—was approximately 125 percent of GDP. By the mid-1980s it had increased to 200 percent, and by 2005 was almost 350 percent, "not far from the $44 trillion GDP for the entire world."[39] Consumers bore the greatest burden: at the time of the 2008 crisis, US consumer debt had reached $13 trillion, more than thirty times the figure in the mid-1970s, leading one theorist to dub this development "Privatised Keynesianism."[40] In the face of prolonged stagnation in real wages, writes McClanahan, "US consumers have been using credit to pay not only for housing and automobiles but also, and historically unprecedentedly, for education, health care, groceries, clothes, and all manner of other daily necessities."[41] As we have seen, however, this underpinning reality of mass indebtedness was all but occluded by the New Economy rhetoric of the 1990s. Recall that for Kevin

Kelly, one of its foremost champions, much of the impetus of the New Economy rested on the idea that "increasing amounts of wealth are now held in equity, and not in debt."[42] This equity lay primarily in housing, and during this period "an impossibly huge home mortgage was not, consumers were told, a debt—it was 'an investment in the future.'"[43] And yet, when the financial storm hit the US and global economy in 2008, credit and debt were revealed to be two sides of the same coin. As Mauricio Lazzarato noted soon after the crash, "The 'new economy,' the information and knowledge societies, have all been absorbed by the debt economy."[44]

For Lazzarato, the key impact of the neoliberal culture of mass indebtedness has been on the nature and experience of time. Where Harvey and Streeck foreground how the economic and political systems "buy time" through issuing debt, Lazzarato concentrates on the subjective dimension, exploring the standpoint of both the creditor and the debtor. Acknowledging that "the neoliberal economy is a subjective economy" (37), he counsels that Foucault's entrepreneurial self must now give way in our imaginary to the indebted self: "The subjective achievements neoliberalism had promised ('everyone a shareholder, everyone an owner, everyone an entrepreneur') have plunged us into the existential condition of the indebted man, at once responsible and guilty for his particular fate" (8–9). This is not a sequential historical process—from entrepreneurship to debt—because mass indebtedness was always the underpinning condition of neoliberal entrepreneurialism, even if it was only the financial crisis that exposed this truth for all to see.

Addressing the fate of the indebted man, Lazzarato proceeds via Marx's and Nietzsche's interlinking of debt and ethical life. Marx offers a critique of the credit relation as a heightened form of subjective alienation, but it is Nietzsche's *On the Genealogy of Morality* that provides the beginnings of an analysis of indebted temporality. Pointing out that the German word for guilt, *Schuld*, is derived from the word for debts, *Schulden*, Nietzsche argues that "it is within the domain of debt obligations that memory, subjectivity, and conscience begin to be produced" (40). These human characteristics are defined by an orientation not toward the past but toward the future: "For Nietzsche, making a memory for man means being able 'to have . . . control over the future,' 'to view the future as the present and anticipate it,' so that he is answerable to his own future" (45). This anticipatory logic mirrors subjectively the credit relation in a money economy, as described by Jean-Joseph Goux: "A society dominated by banking activity, and therefore by credit, *uses* time and expectation, uses the future, as if all these activities were overwhelmingly calculated in advance, ahead of society itself, through anticipation and deduction."[45] On the systemic level, anticipation, deduction, and prediction become the key activities, reproducing the power structures of the present through temporal projection. "What matters is finance's goal of reducing what will be to what is," Lazzarato concludes, "that is, reducing the future and its possibilities to current power relations. From this perspective, all financial innovations have but one sole purpose: possessing the future in advance by objectivizing it" (46).

If temporal anticipation becomes the key systemic activity under neoliberalism, this is true on the subjective level for the creditor, who sets the terms of the debt relation. But for the debtor, Lazzarato contends (here contra Nietzsche) that the sense of time is neutralized. Describing a state of temporal suspension reminiscent of Fredric Jameson's evocation of postmodernism's eternal present, Lazzarato diagnoses that "the principal explanation for the strange sensation of living in a society without time, without possibility, without foreseeable rupture, is debt" (47). This is because the operations of debt rest on a promise to pay at a future moment that has not yet arrived, but that serves to discipline present conduct: "The system of debt must therefore neutralize time, that is, the risk inherent to it. It must anticipate and ward off every potential 'deviation' in the behavior of the debtor the future might hold" (45). Lisa Adkins describes this as "a contracted out future ... a future which is known before it has arrived."[46] "Debt, or the promise to pay," she adds, "therefore operates via a double move in regard to time: it defers the present but does so by counting on (and counting) the future."[47] Yet Adkins is critical of Lazzarato's conclusions, arguing that "what debt is and how it operates has shifted in the context of finance-led accumulation and especially in the context of the securitization of debt."[48] For her, rather than canceling time, "debt must be understood as productive of time."[49]

What this complex debate about time and indebtedness demonstrates is that while it is one thing to narrate the history of the neoliberal debt economy and point to some of the eye-popping numbers it has produced, it is another thing to fully decide the meaning and implications of this development. In

Debt: The First 5,000 Years, David Graeber highlights this interpretive difficulty, noting that "once the global system of credit money was entirely unpegged from gold, the world entered a new phase of financial history—one that nobody completely understands."[50] In McClanahan's view, any attempt to gain understanding of the "ubiquitous yet elusive social form" of debt should involve close examination of recent cultural production.[51] She has American culture particularly in mind, on the basis that it is "in the United States where we can most clearly see both the effects and the aesthetics, both the material signs and the ideological signals, of the global crisis that came to the surface in 2008."[52] Her book, nevertheless, tracks the implications and appearance of this crisis only in works published since 2008, whereas I will argue that the intersection of the New Economy and the debt economy is anticipated (this being the keyword) in the early work of Dave Eggers, published at the apparent high point of the neoliberal boom. *A Heartbreaking Work* and *You Shall Know Our Velocity*, on my reading, are books about the multiple origins and consequences of debt and indebtedness. They are the New Sincerity texts that best articulate a shift from the sincerity of credit to the sincerity of debt.

The Temporal Fix: Heartbreaking Futures

Early in the lengthy "Acknowledgments" section of Eggers's preface to his memoir, we encounter the following passage:

> Yes, it caught your eye. First you took it at face value, and picked it up immediately. "This is just the sort of book for which I have been looking!" Many of you, particularly those among you who seek out the maudlin and melodramatic, were struck by the "Heartbreaking" part. Others thought the "Staggering Genius" element seemed like a pretty good recommendation. But then you thought, Hey, can those two elements work together? Or might they be like peanut butter and chocolate, plaid and paisley—never to peacefully coexist? Like, if this book is, indeed, heartbreaking, then why spoil the mood with all the puffery? Or, if the title is some elaborate joke, then why make an attempt at sentiment? Which is to say nothing of the faux (real? No you beg, please no) boastfulness of the whole title put together. (xxvi)

Dave Eggers, the author-narrator of *A Heartbreaking Work of Staggering Genius*, cannot even get beyond his work's title without attempting to anticipate and preempt the reader's response to it. Using the second-person singular, the narrator here puts himself directly in the place of the reader, narrating that reader's reaction as if it were a past event, a stream of consciousness from the moment of first encounter with the book—"This is just the sort of book for which I have been looking!"—through the step-by-step process of decoding the intentions behind the title, culminating in the mock horror of "No you beg, please no." The tone is coy, playful, and humorous, and the littering of Eggers's memoir with similar gestures has led critics to focus on the interplay of irony and sincerity in the narrating voice of *A Heartbreaking Work*.

But it is the *temporality* at play in this quoted passage—the relationship staged between past, present, and future—that interests me here. We commonly think of the future as something other than the present: it is a time open to anticipation and hope, certainly, but its promise and its risk are not reducible to present information. The characteristic gesture of *A Heartbreaking Work*, however, is to narrate the future as if it were *already* present or even past. And this future is preeminently, as in this particular passage, the future moment of *reading*, an activity that is conventionally understood to come after, and depend upon, the necessarily earlier moment of *writing*. Eggers eliminates the gap between these two moments, inscribing the moment of reading into the moment of writing.[53] This we see both in the long quotation above, and more concisely in a line a few pages later, when the narrator claims that "he too is well aware of all of the book's flaws and shortcomings, whatever you consider them to be, and he tips his hat to you for noticing them" (xliii). This gesture might initially seem to be a humble one, allowing for the possibility of authorial error and readerly correction. When we look again, however, we can see that the effect is actually to *a priori* foreclose the reader discovering a flaw or shortcoming that has not *already* been identified and preempted by the author-narrator. "Mistakes We Knew We Were Making," the title of the appendix later added by Eggers, achieves the same effect: no future lies beyond what has been absorbed into the awareness and intentions of the original author, an author who claims to be "self-conscious about being self-referential, [and] also knowing about that self-conscious self-referentiality" (xxx). Eggers's preface thus instantiates what I call a pure economy of self-consciousness, an economy in which time appears to be neutralized or canceled as all future possibilities are absorbed into present awareness and authorial intent.

Yet perhaps time is not so much canceled here as speeded up to a dizzying extent, with experience preceding writing preceding reading at intervals so infinitesimal that they simply cannot be observed. This description seems better to capture the headlong quality of Eggers's prose, which is less static and all-knowing than restless and ever moving. Following the agonizing slow burn of the memoir's first chapter, where the deaths of his two parents leave Dave and his sister Beth to care for their younger brother Toph, the opening of chapter two offers a typical example of such accelerating prose:

> Please look. Can you see us? Can you see us, in our little red car? Picture us from above, as if you were flying above us, in, say, a helicopter, or on the back of a bird, as our car hurtles, low to the ground, straining on the slow upward trajectory but still at sixty, sixty-five, around the relentless, sometimes ridiculous bends of Highway 1. Look at us, goddammit, the two of us slingshotted from the back side of the moon, greedily cartwheeling toward everything we are owed. Every day we are collecting on what's coming to us, each day we're being paid back for what is owed, what we deserve, with interest, with some extra motherfucking consideration—we are *owed*, goddammit—and so we are expecting everything, everything. (47)

This paragraph of appeal/instruction to the reader is peppered with images of speed. Dave and Toph drive a "hurtling" car as if "slingshotted" from the moon, while the reader is asked to picture themselves on a helicopter or a bird, flying to maintain pace with the rapidly "cartwheeling" protagonists. The sentences themselves move at rapid pace, via urgent question marks and punctuating commas that extend those sentences beyond the completion of a single thought into a giddy accumulation of thoughts, recalling nothing so much as the Beat generation prose of *On the Road*.[54] But the classic American rhythms here combine a language of speed with an impatient rhetoric of entitlement, glimpsed in the repetition of "goddammit" and the insistent declaration that "we are owed." This entitlement is, moreover, figured in explicitly financial terms, with Dave and Toph "collecting on what's coming to us," "being paid back for what is owed . . . with interest," and "expecting everything, everything." Having suffered the trauma of their parents' loss, the children are imagined as creditors, collecting on the debts owed to them. But who or what will pay those debts?

One answer: US institutions of education. Dave reports that Toph will soon enter a Californian private school on a full scholarship, even though the money the children received from their father's life insurance policy and the sale of the parental home could easily have paid for his tuition. "But because we are owed," Dave affirms, "we take the free ride," adding that his sister Beth will also return to law school with her tuition waived: "Beth being as much or more owed than Toph and I, and she being gloriously adept at wringing money from our situation" (53–54).

Another answer: the natural world. The Eggers children's journey west from Illinois to California following the death of their parents is presented, as so often in American literature, as a rebirth and fulfillment of exceptionalist myths:

> Only here [in California] are you almost sure that you are careening on top of a big shiny globe, blurrily spinning—you are never aware of these things in Chicago, it being so flat, so straight—and and and we have been *chosen*, you see, chosen, and have been given this, it being owed to us, earned by us, all of this—the sky is blue for us, the sun makes passing cars twinkle like toys for us, the ocean undulates and churns for us, murmurs and coos to us. We are owed, see, this is ours, see. (50–51)

Here the rhetoric of speed migrates from the "careening" protagonists to the "blurrily spinning" planet itself, which is imagined as providing the sky, sun, and ocean as things "given," "owed" and "earned" by the Eggers children. The conflation of these transactional categories complicates the status of the debt—after all, a gift is not usually something "earned" or something one is "owed"—at the same time as the narrator's sense of entitlement is scaled up to ownership of nature itself.

A third answer: the real world—or, *The Real World*. This is the "seminal" MTV program for which Eggers auditions in the same central chapter of the memoir that details his years with *Might* magazine (167). His audition interview begins in a standard manner—"'Where did you grow up?' she asks"—before almost immediately undergoing "a format change . . . one where quotation marks fall away and a simple interview turns into something else, something *entirely so much more*" (184). While initially this interview continues to seem "real," in that we might be reading a transcript of questions that Dave was asked and answered, the realism eventually breaks down as the interview becomes an avowedly metafictional "device," drawing attention to its own "manufactured and fake" quality as "a catchall for a bunch of anecdotes that would be too awkward to force together otherwise" (197). The device likewise becomes a way for Dave to relay what he sees as the core messages of his memoir in the most direct manner possible, highlighting tropes of generational solipsism, the intersection of tragedy and fame, and the connective "lattice" that he imagines drawing together everyone he knows.[55] And the device is also a means for the impatient and demanding rhetoric of credit and entitlement to return at the conclusion of the interview. "Reward me," Dave tells the interviewer. "Put me on television. Let me share this with millions. I will do it slowly, subtly, tastefully. Everyone must know. I deserve this. I have this coming. . . . I know how this works. I give you these things, and you give me a platform. So give me a platform. I am owed" (235).

Yet while institutions, nature, and the "real world" of media culture are all conceived at different times in *A Heartbreaking Work* as the debtors that must pay Dave what he is owed, it is the real people he writes about, whose stories he appropriates as part of his own, who serve as the book's most identifiable debtors. First and foremost in this category are Eggers's parents, whose untimely deaths are converted—via the writing and publishing of *A Heartbreaking Work of Staggering Genius*—into a timely source of income and fame. Then there is a figure like Shalini, a friend in Dave's circle who suffers her own trauma when she falls off a balcony and receives a brain injury. In the memoir's preface, we learn that "this edition reflects the omission of a number of sentences, paragraph, and passages," only for those passages to be reproduced in the pages immediately following (xi). Among them is one in which the narrator visits Shalini: "p. 427: She was living in a sort of perpetual present. Always she had to be told of her context, what brought her here, the origins and parameters of her current situation" (xvii). The language used here recalls Jameson's description of a traumatized postmodern temporality (or Lazzarato's description of a temporality of indebtedness), where both history and futurity have been forestalled. Turning Shalini into a metaphor in this manner could be considered in bad taste, which could in turn suggest why the passage has been omitted from the memoir. But, of course, it has not been omitted, and in fact has arguably had more attention drawn to it by its placement in the preface, before we have even encountered Shalini in the text proper. In the closing pages of *A Heartbreaking Work*, another of Eggers's friends, John, indicts the author for exploiting "'the people whose tragedies you felt fit into the overall message'":

> "All to help make some point. I mean, isn't it odd that someone like Shalini, for example, who really wasn't one of your closest friends, is suddenly this major presence? And why? Because your other friends had the misfortune not to be misfortunate. The only people who get speaking parts are those whose lives are grabbed by chaos—" (423–424)

Dave responds to this criticism with his now familiar mantra—"'I am allowed. . . . I am owed'"—only for John to dispute this claim. "'You're not. See—You're just not. You're like . . . a cannibal or something'" (424).

John has good reason to make this complaint, since he is the friend whose own trauma—constituted by bouts of suicidal depression for which he frequently requires hospitalization—is cannibalized most heavily in *A Heartbreaking Work*; it seems that simply to know Dave is to "owe" him. But in fact John's complaint is an imagined one, since his scenes are among those in which what initially appear to be verbatim recordings of conversations with other people are revealed—through a repeated breaking of the fourth wall—as internal dialogues that Dave Eggers is staging with himself. In these scenes the voice of the other, rather than sustaining its otherness, is instead preempted and absorbed into the narrator's consciousness. The *Real World* interview is a prime example of this metafictional technique in action, thus making it the perfect scene to "complete the transition from the book's first half, which is slightly less self-conscious, to the second half, which is increasingly self-devouring" (200). In that first half, the technique appears most memorably in a conversation between Dave and his brother Toph, where the latter comically breaks with his initially realist presentation to draw attention to the impatient condensation of Dave's narration, "'as if a number of days had been spliced together to quickly paint a picture of an entire period of time, to create a whole-seeming idea of how we are living, without having to stoop (or rise) to actually pacing the story out'" (114). When Dave justifies his approach—since "'to adequately relate even five minutes of internal thought-making would take forever'"—Toph responds that what he observes is "less a problem with form, all that garbage, and more a problem of conscience. You're completely paralyzed with guilt about relating all this in the first place, especially the stuff earlier on. You feel somehow obligated to do it, but you also know that Mom and Dad would *hate* it, would crucify you—" (115).

Expanding on the religious dimension of his crucifixion image, Toph (or Dave as Toph) concludes that "'your guilt, and their disapproval, is a very middle-brow, middle-class, midwestern sort of disapproval. . . . You struggle with a guilt both Catholic and unique to the home in which you were raised'" (115).

This (self-)accusation of a guilty conscience tied to a religious upbringing recalls the Nietzschean account of the origins of debt. While for Nietzsche the relationship between creditor and debtor is "the oldest and most primitive personal relationship of all," in which "for the first time person confronted person . . . first *measured himself* against another person," this relationship is not initially to be understood in moral terms.[56] Moralization occurs only when categories of personal duty and guilt are introduced through a religious reinterpretation of the creditor-debtor relation, "the conflation of *bad conscience* with the concept of God."[57] On Lazzarato's Nietzsche-influenced account, the transition from the "finite debt" of primitive societies (where debts could be paid and canceled, with no moral hang-ups or hangovers) to the "infinite debt" of modern capitalist societies (where to be born is already to inherit debt) was made via the advent of monotheistic religions that turned indebtedness to God as creator into an underpinning fact of human existence. "Christianity, by introducing the infinite," Lazzarato writes, "completely reinvented the system of debt which capitalism would inherit."[58] While in the premodern imperial societies that succeeded primitive ones, debt was already infinite but still exterior to individual consciences, "the particularity of Christianity lies in the fact that it places us not only within a system of debt, but also within a system of 'interiorized debt.'"[59] Worldly indebtedness to other persons or institutions morphs into a feeling of guilt about one's indebtedness to God, a feeling that can never be fully relieved since it is perpetual and lifelong.

The Christian iconography of *A Heartbreaking Work*, glimpsed in Dave's self-haranguing through the voice of Toph, is prevalent and inescapable throughout the book. While this iconography is predominately Catholic—"a repurposing of Catholic practices, images, and dogma," as Benjamin Widiss puts it, "to a set of ends ranging from the manifestly secular to a twilight zone of uncertain belief"—the form of the memoir itself recalls the Protestant genre of spiritual autobiography.[60] In keeping with the key role played by that genre in the emerging "spirit of capitalism" of the early modern period, Eggers's spiritual autobiography tracks the further transition identified by Lazzarato, from Christian guilt to the capitalist relation.[61] It is the scenes with John that make this transition most explicit. In the longest scene, after Dave offers a detailed description of his friend tied to a hospital bed and medicated, the prostrate John suddenly breaks with the realist frame and stands up, exclaiming, "'Screw it, I'm not going to be a fucking anecdote in your stupid book'" (272). On the surface level, in line with Toph's earlier analysis, we are being given a window here onto Eggers's guilt—apparently religious in origin—at exploiting his friend's suffering for the purposes of dramatic storytelling. Yet on another level, following the temporal logic I identified in the book's preface, this guilt is being carefully stage-managed in order to anticipate and preempt a readerly hermeneutics of suspicion that would condemn Dave for such exploitation. The moment of reading is again being inscribed into the moment of writing, as a means to allay any future risk to the pure economy of the narrator's self-consciousness.

The link between this pure economy of self-consciousness and the financial economy is directly suggested by Dave's reaction to John's imagined protest:

"This is mine. You've given it to me. We're trading. I gave you the attention you wanted, I bail you out . . . now I get this, this is mine also, and you, because you've done it yourself, made yourself the thespian, you have to fulfill that contract, play the dates, go on the road. Now you're the metaphor." (274)

As part of the trade here, the present value of Dave's experience with John is understood to derive from the anticipated payoff from its future incorporation into his memoir. In other words, the contract the narrator imagines signing with John functions like a futures contract, a type of financial derivative. Derivatives are priced with reference not to the present but to the anticipated future, and their rapid proliferation in the financialized economy is an aspect of what one critic calls "the messianic turn in twentieth-century economics, where more and more intellectual energy is spent on theorizing the future, until the present comes to look insignificant except as its prefiguration."[62] This is exactly what happens in the economy of *A Heartbreaking Work*: the story of John becomes the capital "owed" to Dave, and his investment in his suicidal friend in the present—spending time at his hospital bed—is really just a prefiguration of his investment in the future moment of writing-selling-consuming-reading, when all the financial returns will be to himself. Dave has become an exemplary "entrepreneur of the self," with all external relations with others understood as transactions that return in profit to that self. In the temporal economy of Eggers's memoir, the possibility of a future *beyond* what can be anticipated by the writer-self has become structurally (and financially) unimaginable.

This is the temporal fix conceived by the entrepreneurial author of *A Heartbreaking Work of Staggering Genius*, the ingenious repackaging of a tragic past and chaotic present as an investment in a successful future. This temporal fix mirrors the neoliberal financialization of the economy, whereby a present crisis of devaluation is avoided through the issuing of fictitious capital as credit, treating the anticipated realization of value as if it has already happened. When John objects that his personal experience is being cannibalized and devalued, Dave responds that the fictionalizing of that experience is a means of ensuring its future (and therefore present) value, even if it is he rather than John who will recoup that value at the point of sale. In extending credit in this way, Dave becomes a kind of proxy God, the ultimate and all-knowing creditor; this parallel with Christianity as itself a kind of temporal fix accords, moreover, with a tradition of biblical scholarship that "reads the Eucharist as functioning proleptically, somewhere between promising and ensuring the Second Coming."[63] Yet this temporal fix—simultaneously financial and religious—is not the smooth solution that it promises to be. "The observation that financialization not only forestall[s], but also *foretells*, a structural crisis is critically urgent," McClanahan reminds us, and this structural crisis—marked by the return of material constraints to haunt the ideality of anticipated futures—rears its head at a number of moments in *A Heartbreaking Work*, not least in the book's startling conclusion, addressed in this chapter's final section.[64] But before reaching this point of (over)accumulated crisis, we must attend to the other way Eggers's writing registers and proposes to resolve the problem of indebtedness. This means supplementing the temporal fix of his memoir with the spatial dimensions addressed in his second book and first novel.

The Spatial Fix: Imperial Velocity

You Shall Know Our Velocity announces its central concern with speed in its very title. At the head of the odd-numbered pages of the book, that title is itself shortened to Y.S.K.O.V., almost as if these five words simply take too long to say or read in anything other than abbreviated form. This mark of impatience—the restless sense that nothing can wait and everything must be done right away—is further accentuated by the whole of the novel's opening paragraph appearing on the original hardback's front cover, as though the impulse to begin telling the story cannot be delayed long enough for the niceties of opening the book and turning the title pages to be observed. And that opening paragraph rushes us immediately from the beginning of the story right to its end, condensing the time of the narrative into a brief passage between two moments:

> Everything within takes place after Jack died and before my mom and I drowned in a burning ferry in the cool tannin-tinted Guaviare River, in east-central Colombia, with forty-two locals we hadn't yet met. It was a clear and eyeblue day, that day, as was the first day of this story, a few years ago in January, on Chicago's north side in the opulent shadow of Wrigley and with the wind coming low and searching off the jagged half-frozen lake. I was inside, very warm, walking from door to door.[65]

The conflicting temporalities of this passage are initially rather headspinning. We have the compression of the whole book—"Everything within"—between two traumatic events: "after Jack died and before my mom and I drowned." The second of these two events introduces another temporal frame, the afterlife, because these words render impossible our most conventional assumption when encountering first-person narration, that the words we are reading, even when they are in the past tense, express the present living consciousness of a narrator. To complicate the effect, this narrating consciousness is otherwise evoked in a strikingly sensual language: the alliterative rhythm of "cool tannin-tinted Guaviare River"; the doubly visual metaphor of "clear and eyeblue day"; the personification of "the wind coming low and searching";

the tactile adjectives of "jagged half-frozen lake." Equally particularizing are the spatial references—the river where the story ends is in "east-central Colombia," while the story begins in the shadow of Chicago's renowned baseball stadium, Wrigley Field. With the finale in Latin America connected back to the starting point in a major US city, this is a first hint that *Velocity* will be concerned with global circuits of power. The narrator, whose own sensual presence is registered in the description "I was inside, very warm," paces back and forth between doors, oscillating between the times and places of the story's beginning and ending, just as the passage does.

The "I" here, *Velocity*'s narrator, is a young Polish American man named Will Chmielewski. We first encounter him attempting to talk his friend Hand into a trip around the world, with the aim of giving away a significant amount of money. Hand agrees, and he and Will spend the novel flying to countries throughout Africa and eastern Europe, delivering US dollars in person to poor people. These dollars have been "earned" by Will through his silhouette appearing on the packaging of a lightbulb ("So I'd been given $80,000 to screw in a lightbulb. There is no way to dress it up; that's what it was" [41]). Spurred by an impulse to justice, the friends hope that by undertaking acts of direct generosity, they can circumvent the abstract economic structures that generate global poverty and inequality. Yet Eggers's two protagonists are forcefully confronted throughout the novel with the twinned legacies of financialization and US imperialism, and they are constantly brought up against the limits of their actions, in ways both functional and affective. Meanwhile, in its prose style, rhetoric, narration, and structure, *You Shall Know Our Velocity* provides a window onto the traumatic quality of contemporary capitalism, the speed at which it moves and the way its temporality outstrips human cognition and linguistic stability. By taking on themes—speed, time, and language—that so fascinated modernist writers, Eggers's novel sketches some useful contrasts between the artistic situation of the early twentieth and early twenty-first centuries. This only heightens the impression of difficulty attached to sincere living and writing in neoliberal times.

If Will's relationship to narrative time is complicated, even impossible, his relationship to speed can be characterized as two-sided. On the one hand, speed offers the narrator a way to escape from the traumatic daydreams that haunt his consciousness, which stem mostly from the death of his childhood friend Jack: "—The only times they are not with me are those times when speed overwhelms, when the action of moments supersedes and crowds out" (146). What he describes as the "overall idea" of his trip with Hand, "that of unmitigated movement, of serving any or maybe every impulse" (8–9), is therefore Will's attempt to lose the burden of traumatic consciousness through pure action, to ground his being in the body rather than the mind. Yet on the other hand, speed is the cause of his trauma in the first place, as we see when Will recalls reading the newspaper report on Jack's death: "From the local paper, a picture of the car, crushed, under the headline: YOUNG MAN DIES WHEN SEMI SPEEDS OVER CAR" (32). In his memories, Will recalls Jack as a young man who did not himself understand the need for speed, who puzzled at his friends' insistence that they should stay out late even when it means being tired all the next day, and who questioned why Will and Hand would want to jump from a garage roof like stuntmen:

> But [Jack] didn't see the point. Why not wait till we're older, when we'll get trained by actual *certified stuntmen*? What? we asked. He thought he was making sense but we were stunned. Certified? Stuntmen? We argued him into submission. (227)

Jack, then, wants to go slower, displaying what is usually called maturity; he assumes that he and his friends have all the time in the world and that tomorrow will always come. Jack, we might say, has sacrificed the present to the future, and yet he is cruelly cut down before that future arrives. Will, by contrast, instinctively sacrifices the future to the present, most explicitly by giving away the money that might have ensured his security over the long term. This is an impulse he laments toward the novel's end: "We should have saved the money, most of it, invested it, so there would always be more. I could have done this every year if I had planned it better. I planned nothing well" (334).

We can already see how the concerns with speed, guilt, futurity, and finance that characterized *A Heartbreaking Work* re-emerge in *Velocity*. Another technique that migrates from the memoir to the novel is that conversations held between Will and other characters are frequently revealed to be internal dialogues he is holding with himself. A telling example comes when, during a telephone call he makes home while in Senegal, his mother describes his charitable actions and impulses as condescending. Will responds with (imagined) fury:

> —What are you saying? That we're not allowed to see their faces? You're saying that. You're the type who won't give to a street person; you'll think you're doing them harm. But who's condescending then? You withhold and you run counter to your instincts. There is disparity and our instinct is to create parity, immediately. Our instinct is to split our bank account with the person who has nothing. But you're talking behind several layers of denial and justification. If it feels good it *is* good, and today, at the ocean, we met a man living in a half-finished hut, and he was tall and had a radio and we gave him about $700 and it was good. It can't be taken from us, and you cannot soil it with words like *condescending* and *subjective*, fey and privileged words, and you cannot pretend that you know a better way. You try it! You do it! We gave and received love! How can you deprive us of that? (123–124)

Will's trip has been premised on the idea that by cutting the distance between giver and receiver, by establishing proximity, the abstractions and moral uncertainties that plague the unequal interaction of subjects under global capitalism can be overcome in favor of a common human love. By rejecting, through an appeal to feeling, any theoretical or moral critique of his actions, Will offers an ethical justification—"our instinct is to create parity, immediately"—for his earlier embrace of "unmitigated movement" as a way of dealing with his own traumatic consciousness. Will's appeal to instinct and to feeling—"if it feels good, it *is* good"—is intended to short-circuit any such critique, with the parataxis of the passage—"and he was tall and had a radio and we gave him about $700 and it was good"—suggesting a natural link between action, feeling, and outcome. The culminating equivalence made between giving money and giving (and receiving) love is presented as equally natural, with any objection to that equivalence condemned as "fey and privileged."

Yet despite his protestations here, Will repeatedly finds to his dismay that the abstractions of capital are not overcome by proximity and direct action; indeed, the opposite is all too often the case. During his journey we see Will constantly disorientated and his mood made volatile by his discovery that the appearance of money turns any interaction into a transaction, sullying the positive feelings associated with what had seemed to be pure human contact. When he and Hand play basketball against a group of Senegalese children, Will considers whether to give them money at the end of the game:

> I still had some American hundreds in my shoes, but would that spoil everything? Would it pollute something pure—a simple game between travelers and hosts—by afterward throwing money at them? But maybe they did expect money; otherwise, why would they all gather by the car after the game? Maybe this was a common occurrence: Americans pull up, grab the ball, show them what's what, drop cash on them and head back to the Saly hotels—(115).

Here, in an activity Will had assumed was spontaneous and pure, he recognizes the possibility of ritual, and the taint of motives other than sincere fellow feeling. And even on those occasions when his reaction is less analytical, when what is at stake is simply the affective feelings involved in giving money away, these feelings prove anxiety-inducing and difficult to process. We see this when Will passes a woman begging on the street in Morocco and runs back to give her money. When he returns to Hand, he is distressed and exclaims: "'Why the *fuck* is that so weird? Why is it so hard?'" The incident seems too complex to parse: "We had no idea" is Will's concluding comment (173).

Because these moments of intellectual reflection prove traumatic for Will, his need for speed increases as the novel progresses—he wants to move faster than he can think. This in turn leads to frequent frustration with the technologies of travel that he and Hand are forced to employ on their trip, which leave too much time for reflection and not enough for action. Once the friends have established that they only have one week to undertake their trip—since this is the maximum leave Hand can obtain from his job as security supervisor in a casino—they assume that they will be able to get all the way around the world in the time allotted, traveling west. Will declares his motto: "We would oppose the turning of the planet and refuse the setting of the sun" (5). When they begin to examine the details, however, they discover the impossibility of this task: not only will they lose a day over the international dateline but, as an amused travel agent informs them, they will have to spend over 80 percent of their total time in planes. "'These planes are too fucking slow,'" Hand complains. "'When did planes get so slow?'" (7). Will's annoyance, as the organizer and ringleader of the trip, is even greater. Later, while stranded at a hotel waiting for a rental car to arrive, he thinks to himself:

> This, this unmitigated slowness of moving from place to place—I had no tools to address it, no words to express the anger it forged inside me. Yes I appreciated cars and planes, and their time-squanching capabilities, but then once in them, aboard them, time slowed again, time slowed doubly, given the context. Where was teleporting, for fuck's sake? Should we not have teleporting by now? (54)

The automobile and the airplane, the two great transport technologies of the twentieth century and the fetishized objects of Futurist modernism, are here relegated from the cutting edge of modernity to what Will dismisses as the "goddamned medieval" (55). But Hand's question ("When did planes get so slow?") is also one that the novel is trying to answer as it gets to grips with the structuring temporalities of contemporary experience.

We come closer to grasping these temporalities as Will expands on his exasperation over the impossibility of teleporting:

> Why were we spending billions on unmanned missions to Mars when we could be betting the cash on teleporting, the one advancement that would finally break us all free of our slow movement from here to there, would zip our big fat slow fleshy bodies around as fast as our minds could will them—which was as fast as they should be going: the speed of thought. (55)

Even space travel, the great utopian project of the American midcentury, pales here in comparison to the speed of thought, as Will imagines it. But in proposing the speed of thought as his ideal of global circulation, Will's imaginary here resembles nothing so much as that of capital itself, as described by Marx in notebook VI of his *Grundrisse*:

> Circulation time only expresses the velocity of circulation; the velocity of circulation only the barrier to circulation. *Circulation without circulation time*—i.e. the transition of capital from one phase to the next at the speed of thought—would be the maximum, i.e. the identity of the renewal of the production process with its termination.[66]

In the previous notebook, Marx's analysis makes clear that in order to avoid crisis, capital needs to circulate as quickly as possible or else "time passes it by unseized."⁶⁷ In notebook VI he clarifies that the ideal is "circulation without circulation time," a form of instantaneity that recalls neoliberal-era fetishizing of the "frictionless" movement of capital. The frictionless instantaneity of teleporting is what Will desires for his own circulation round the world, a temporal fix that would produce time but take no time at all.

But while both Will and Marx imagine that the maximum velocity of circulation is "the speed of thought," in the twenty-first century this is in fact no longer the case. As we can glimpse in the above passage's reference to "betting the cash," it is rather financial markets that provide today's model for maximum velocity circulation. And in the age of high-frequency trading, financial markets move multiple times faster than the speed of thought.⁶⁸ Yet financial markets—in their creation of fictitious capital that leaves behind the flesh-and-blood realities of human life—also lie at the core of the capitalist abstraction that haunts Will, and that he wants to reject. The temporal fix he imagines would thus leave him more deeply ensnared in the very system he is trying to escape.

Furthermore, teleporting and contemporary finance capital share a political context, something Will and Hand discover when they meet Raymond, an investment banker, while in Senegal. Hand and Raymond hit it off owing to their common background in finance; before his current job in casino security, Hand explains that he worked in "weather futures": "'. . . industries affected by the weather, like energy, insurance, agriculture . . . could hedge their risk . . . one industry wants rain, the other doesn't, they share the risk . . .'" (54). But Raymond eventually cuts through these familiar abstractions to provide some historical context. Originally from Chile, not coincidentally the site of the first American experiment in neoliberal economic policy abroad, he uses the example of *Star Trek* to inform the protagonists that "'teleporting was based on a Cold War mentality. This was the American foreign policy model then. This was based on the American strength, the American ability to move and change the worlds they touched into'" (67). The connections underpinning Will's imaginary—teleporting, velocity, financial circulation—are thus shown to have their basis in postwar American imperialism, a reality that becomes increasingly evident as their journey progresses. Before their meeting with Raymond has even ended, Hand has encountered some French sailors who, when told of his nationality, exclaim "'America! . . .

you pay for the world!'" (71). As their trip draws to a conclusion, Will has the insight that "every country now seemed to offer a little of every other country, and every given landscape, I finally realized, existed somewhere in the U.S." (253). "When I heard the word Portugal," he observes at another point, "I thought of Madagascar, scrubby, dry, poor, the trees crowded with lemurs" (74). Many empires, from the Holy Roman Empire onward, have been described as "the empire on which the sun never sets"; with this in mind, Will's imperialist imaginary can even be read back into his earliest motto for the trip: "We would oppose the turning of the planet and refuse the setting of the sun" (5).

What Harvey calls capital's "spatial fix" depends on this imperialist dynamic: the only way for a temporal fix to succeed in preventing devaluation over the long term is for new markets to be opened up that are capable of absorbing overaccumulated capital in the present and future. The global turn from productive investment to finance from the 1970s onwards—including the Nixon and Volcker shocks themselves—can be understood not only as a temporal but as a spatial fix of this kind, an extended American imperialist power play. McClanahan makes this link, observing that "since 1973 capital investment has entirely shifted from the kinds of direct investment that drove European imperial finance in previous eras into a purely speculative form of investment that gambles on and encourages volatility."[69] So too does Graeber, who argues that under the new regime when credit money is no longer underpinned by gold, it is only US military power that ensures that money is treated by people as if it possesses value; as he memorably puts it, "There's a reason why the wizard has such a strange capacity to create money out of nothing. Behind him, there's a man with a gun."[70] The United States is thus simultaneously the world's largest debtor state and the imperialist creditor that underpins the entire monetary system. Against this background, it becomes possible to see an analogy between Will's actions—flooding the developing societies he visits with unexpected injections of capital—and the transitions to free market capitalism that were instituted by American policy through the Washington Consensus, beginning in Chile in the 1970s, expanding to Latin America more generally in the 1980s, to the Soviet Union in the early 1990s, and to Iraq and Afghanistan in the 2000s.[71]

Caught in the claws of this analogy, Will comes to realize that his plan to give away dollars to deserving recipients is not the grand equalizing gesture he had envisioned. At one point, he imagines a conversation with a man whose rudeness has discouraged Will to give him money:

> —You do more harm than good by choosing recipients this way. It cannot be fair.
> —How ever is it fair?
> —You want the control money provides.
> —We want the opposite. We are giving up our control.
> —While giving it up you are exercising power. The money is not yours.
> —I know this.
> —You want its power. However exercised, you want its power. (117–118)

Even as he tries desperately to avoid conscious analysis of this kind, Will's political unconscious has been structured by the spatio-temporal fix of neoliberal capital and its source in imperialist power and control. His need for velocity, instantaneity, and circulation, conceived as an escape from personal trauma and financial inequality, thus winds up embedding him all the more deeply in the economic and political systems he is attempting to disavow. As it increasingly dawns on Will that "money is really the only tangible communication device we have" (187), he starts to intuit its vexing and paradoxical power, described forcefully by Marx in the 1844 manuscripts: "If *money* is the bond binding me to *human* life, binding society to me, connecting me with nature and man, is money not the bond of all bonds? Can it not dissolve and bind all ties? Is it not, therefore, also the universal *agent of separation*?"[72] Finding himself separated from others even while in closest bodily proximity to them, Will laments this shared condition: "—We've chosen money as our language, and I don't know if it was the right one" (301).[73]

Eggers's first novel can be read, then, as a metafictional reflection on the contemporary American novelist's own political unconscious, on the difficulties a complicit writer faces in writing with full sincerity about his own ethical stance toward the global economic system that supports his work. This metafictional element was highlighted and heightened when *You Shall*

Know Our Velocity was republished in 2003 as *Sacrament*, including a new section written in Hand's voice that questioned Will's original telling. According to Hand, not only did Will fabricate much of the content of the story—including the death of Jack and the phone calls to his mother, who had passed away eight years earlier—but his narrative emphasis on chaotic and instantaneous decision making leaves out an important dimension of their trip, its status as "Performance Literature": "what we had planned was a book conceived, then acted out, then transcribed, then ostensibly made into art. Thus, our actions in Africa and onward were predetermined to be transferred to the page, and we were therefore actors performing in a book not yet written."[74] This complicating of the protagonists' intentions by the premeditated quality of their actions might seem to lend itself to charges of inauthenticity and insincerity. In Hand's view, however, such details are made irrelevant by the overriding political message of their journey. Will's book turned out to be, he claims,

> a rather neat and tidy allegory for any sort of intervention, whether by governments or neighbors—but mostly the idea of humanitarian aid, on whatever scale, micro or macro—from NGOs to panhandlers and passersby. The story, when we lived it, was about economics, and about desperation, and about inequity brought to levels that are untenable.[75]

On Hand's account, the scriptedness of his and Will's interactions with poor people should ultimately be understood in religious terms, as a kind of sacramental ritual: "the exchange of the money was much, if I may be so bold, like the exchange of the Holy Eucharist, in that in each case it is preceded by a brief and seldom-changing dialogue."[76] Through this kind of sacramental transformation—"an outward symbolic act of an inward grace"—Eggers's work would seem to be aiming to elevate its own sincerity to a higher level.[77] Writing similarly of *A Heartbreaking Work*, Widiss argues that the tensions of Eggers's memoir are overcome through "a renovated sense of sacramental logic," even "a new Eucharistic calculus."[78] These religious (self-)readings of Eggers's early writing aim to resolve the contradictions of the text by appeal to a final transcendence in credit. In the final section of this chapter, I will counter the religious reading with a conception of Eggers's writing as instantiating a sincerity of debt.

The Sincerity Fix: Disowning (and Acknowledging) Debt

Following the example of Hand's allegorical interpretation of Will's narrative, the general critical consensus is that Eggers's first two books should be read jointly as an allegory of the author's relation to the literary world. From the earliest reviews, the plot of *Velocity* was interpreted as "a sendup of Eggers's embarrassment at the money he made from his memoir," while critics have connected specific elements of the novel to the reception of *A Heartbreaking Work* and Eggers's subsequent fame.[79] For many of these critics, the ultimate project of Eggers's early writing is the construction of an aesthetic gift economy—supported by a range of real-world literary and charitable institutions—that readers can believe in and invest in. They offer diverging takes on this aesthetic economy: while Brouillette accuses Eggers of economic disavowal, and Konstantinou criticizes the author's otherwise "laudable" institutional projects as "incapable of overcoming the depredations of the End of History," James Clements offers a more positive assessment.[80] Inspired by the model of Kurt Vonnegut, Eggers writes from the position that "the primary encounter facilitated by any work of art is not reader/text or reader/character, but reader/author."[81] If that encounter is to succeed in building community, then "it must be grounded in the reader's acceptance of authorial sincerity" (122). While fiction does not normally elicit judgment on the author's sincerity in this way, the metafictional and paratextual dimensions of *Velocity* encourage readers to approach the book "as Eggers's utterance rather than a mimetic illusion" (130), "not as a thing but as an *act*" (132). This act can, as Hand suggested, be understood as a sacramental gift, and "the value of each 'act' is dependent on the faith it engenders between giver and receiver" (133). Clements calls this "a Ricoeurian hermeneutics of faith, rather than suspicion" (133), and for him it offers a way to defeat the undecidability that otherwise underpins any gift. In dialogue with my work on New Sincerity, he argues that reading Eggers as sincere "may be delusional, but it is also an essentially moral choice, a decision to see good intentions rather than hold them up to suspicion" (134).

Eggers scholars, even those suspicious of his project, are therefore unanimous in reading that project as staging a kind of sincerity fix, through which crisis can be resolved or at least deferred by encouraging readers to "believe in the goodness and sincerity not only of Eggers as an individual but also of the various enterprises that he has helped construct."[82] Building on my explication of Eggers's early texts through the framework of the neoliberal economy, I now want to demonstrate how those texts in fact answer to an alternative logic, a sincerity of debt to counter the sincerity (fix) of credit. In her essay on Eggers's circulation of revised editions of his first two books—the "Mistakes" version of *A Heartbreaking Work* and the *Sacrament* version of *Velocity*—Jacqueline O'Dell moves us part of the way toward this reading. Rather than assume, as Clements does, that the sincere intentions of the author must underpin the status of the artwork as gift, O'Dell claims that intentions, affects, and gifts, "rather than being identifiable in and of themselves, register as surplus effects of circulation" in an economic network.[83] Instead of clarifying the intentional essence of the first editions they supersede, "Eggers's second editions construe original intentions as moving targets beyond definitive representation," thereby "ruptur[ing] the temporal movement towards closure."[84] Clements's claim that the undecidability of the gift can be overcome through a reader's faith in the sincerity fix is therefore misguided. "Clements looks to the individual reader to receive *Velocity* or *Sacrament* as sincere gifts," O'Dell writes, "when Eggers's thematic and material engagement with literary circulation suggests instead that the gift is an effect of coterminous financial and affective networks, not individual choices. *Sacrament* ultimately shows that the gift trades in riskier, non-transactional, forms of collective mystification."[85]

Despite the valuable insights offered here by O'Dell, the "forms of collective mystification" she identifies remain mystified in her account. What is missing from her analysis is the importance to Eggers's aesthetics of the neoliberal economy, precisely as that economy has historically functioned to mystify debt as credit. When collective belief props up a system that can only delay crisis through the temporal fix of credit and the spatial fix of imperialist finance, then that belief cannot be unequivocally celebrated. Despite their avowed re-enchantment of belief, Eggers's texts ultimately undermine the sincerity fix they propose, thus acknowledging (even in spite of themselves) that "in the twenty-first century, credit and debt are no longer two reversible perspectives on the same circular exchange (money passing from lender to borrower and back again); rather, they represent two fundamentally antagonistic subject and class positions."[86] We have seen in *Velocity* how Will, like the United States for which he comes to function as a synecdoche, simultaneously acts as creditor and debtor. When he tries to give a gift, he in fact chooses the terms and retains an element of control, just as a creditor does; meanwhile, his endless search for speed and movement do not allay his nagging sense of indebtedness as both a human and an American. Will's own breaking apart—culminating in his early death—thus allegorizes the impossibility of inhabiting both positions successfully, as well as the futility of imagining that offering credit can erase debt.[87]

It is in *A Heartbreaking Work*, however, that we witness the full psychological and material implications of simultaneously inhabiting the position of creditor and debtor, while also imagining that credit marks the erasure, rather than the creation, of debt. On the one hand, as we have seen, Eggers's memoir shows the frictionless futurism of neoliberal credit in operation through its recurrent structures of preemption and anticipation, most explicitly in the scenes with John. On the other hand, however, *A Heartbreaking Work* exposes the dark underside of this ideology, the troublesome material substrate of the debt economy that haunts the temporary fix of credit. We see this double movement in the way Dave exhibits wild mood swings, oscillating between emotional boom and bust. The instability reaches its apex in the book's final lines, when the narrator confronts his implied readers with equal parts anger and desperation:

> Don't you know that I am connected to you? Don't you know that I'm trying to pump blood to you, that this is for you, that I hate you people, so many of you motherfuckers—. . . oh when you're all sleeping so many sleeping I am somewhere on this stupid rickety scaffolding and I'm trying to get your stupid fucking attention I've been trying to show you this, just been trying to show you this—What the fuck does it take to show you motherfuckers, what does it fucking take what do you want how much do you want because I am willing and I'll stand before you and I'll raise my arms and give you my chest and throat and wait, and I've been so old for so long, for you, for you, I want it fast and right through me—Oh do it, do it, you motherfuckers, do it do it you fuckers finally, finally, finally. (436–437)

If we glance back to the long quotation from the preface to *A Heartbreaking Work* with which I began the temporal fix section of this chapter, we can see that there the "you" was merely a placeholder for the "I" who could presume to speak in place of the other ("Yes, it caught your eye"). In the book's concluding passage, by contrast, the "you" has become separated from the "I," with the link between the two having to be insisted on rather than assumed ("Don't you know that I am connected to you?"). Picking up on the crucifixion imagery in the passage, Widiss reads the ending in religious terms, observing that "the reader is cast not only as the agent of Eggers's demise, but also as that of his resurrection."[88] But while this reading suggests circularity and closure—what we might even call a "religious fix"—the sense of the writer's vexed indebtedness to the reader conveyed in the passage is better understood in the economic terms I have foregrounded throughout this chapter. In asking to have his body and consciousness penetrated by "you motherfuckers," the "I" in these lines—Dave Eggers—is appealing for the pure economy of self-consciousness that has dominated his text to be *finally* broken through. A future reader who is *truly* other to the writer, who can discover flaws in his text that the writer has *not* anticipated or preempted—mistakes he didn't know he was making—is both what is hated and feared by the writer (as a risk to the spatio-temporal fix that ensures his future gains), but also the only thing that can offer him relief from the burden of a hyper-aware preemptive consciousness. This consciousness is haunted by the creeping sense that the entrepreneur of the self is living (literally) on borrowed time, simultaneously inhabiting the role of creditor and debtor, endlessly pumping blood (credit) through the system while depending on future readers to be transfused by it in his place (debt).

From this complex structure of indebtedness to the reader—both needing and fearing the reader's judgment—emerges the fraught psychodynamics of the writer-reader relationship staged in New Sincerity fiction. These psychodynamics—the avowed coexistence of hatred and love—can be described in terms of an ambivalence that, as Freud famously argued, does not diminish but intensifies the libidinal relation to an object. Writing of the contemporary novelist's ambivalent relation to "market logics," Crosthwaite argues that "what arises from this position of ambivalence is not simply a trade off between critical insight, on the one hand, and unthinking affective attachment, on the other, but rather forms of insight that are only possible precisely at this vexed juncture of disavowal and attraction."[89] I would contend that the true object of Eggers's ambivalence is not the market but the reader, precisely to the extent that the reader represents something other than the market, something that cannot be preempted or anticipated in the way the market must be, since—in the ideology of neoliberalism—the market it is the ultimate and implacable source of truth.[90]

It is from just such a vexed juncture of disavowal and attraction toward the reader that Eggers's explosive prose registers the truth underpinning the financialized economy of credit. This truth, laid bare in Marxist crisis theory, is that the ideology of frictionless transition and messianic futurism that characterizes the neoliberal era masks accelerating instability and frenzied cycles of boom and bust. "The post-1973 era is defined not by smooth transitions," writes McClanahan, "but rather by the manic turbulence that characterizes all hegemonies in their autumnal period."[91] This insight, which draws on the analysis of *longue durée* cycles of imperialist accumulation in Giovanni Arrighi's *The Long Twentieth Century*, casts a new light on the very American qualities of Eggers's prose: its Beat Generation urgency; its aggressive parody of Whitmanesque pastoral reveries ("oh when you're all sleeping so many sleeping I am somewhere on this stupid rickety scaffolding"); its participation in an American tradition of confessional writing. This confessional tradition goes back to the poets of the postwar period, two of whom—Anne Sexton and Robert Lowell—Eggers quotes in his preface.[92] If the "American Century" began in that postwar moment, then perhaps Eggers's work of the early 2000s indexes the end of this century in more ways than one.[93] While its huge debt economy still places the United States unavoidably at the center of global power structures, that indebtedness—much of it inhering in a large trade deficit with China—also points to underlying weaknesses in its economic future. While the spatio-temporal fix of the US-sponsored neoliberal decades may not quite have ended in 2008, the global crisis of that year surely pointed to more of the same to come. "From time to time the conflict of antagonistic agencies finds vent in crises," Marx writes in volume 3 of *Capital*. "The crises are always but momentary and forcible solutions of the existing contradictions. They are violent eruptions which for a time restore the disturbed equilibrium."[94] But only for a time.

Neoliberalism is thus complicit in the onset of its own crisis. The temporal fix at its heart—the reduction of the future to the present—results in a short-termism that, as Bernard Stiegler notes, "has given rise to a *systemic stupidity* that *structurally prevents the reconstitution of a long-term horizon*."[95]

This is what New Sincerity texts like Eggers's ultimately have to teach us: that while contemporary capitalism has its winners and losers, the stupidity of the system makes us all losers in the long run. Yet the task of getting outside our complicity with the system—the task of acting sincerely without that sincerity being contaminated by anticipatory self-interest—remains far from an easy one. We can see this in my final quotation, which comes once again from the "Real World" interview at the center of *A Heartbreaking Work*:

> My heart is pure.
> I know what you're thinking.
> I know what I mean. (208)

These three sentences encapsulate the problem of personal sincerity staged by Eggers's early work more broadly. Having a pure heart and knowing what one means to say: these are core elements of the traditional understanding of sincerity. But the middle sentence of the three contaminates the other two with uncertainty. If I know what you're thinking, then how can my heart be pure of that knowledge? And how can what I mean and intend remain autonomous from my knowledge of your thoughts and my foreknowledge of your reactions?

My heart cannot be pure and my intentions cannot be autonomous. But this is not something to lament. The task set by *A Heartbreaking Work* is precisely to break our purity of heart. And why might we want this? Because it is precisely purity and autonomy that neoliberal ideology privileges: the purity of entrepreneurial self-relation; the autonomy of the market from production; the autonomy of the frictionless extending of financial credit; the purity of a future that is entirely a product of the present. Indeed, we might go so far as to call neoliberalism the last great utopian ideology of the twentieth century, following on from earlier and even more destructive utopian projects. New Sincerity writers like Eggers do not oppose these utopias with a pure sincerity: instead, the generation of American writers from which Eggers comes is firmly post-utopian, emphasizing contamination, impurity, contingency, the recognition of complicity. And emphasizing reading, because there is nothing, in the end, more temporally contaminated, more impure, than the process of reading, which must escape the pure logic of preemption, however much that preemption strives to outdo it.

For these reasons, I have argued that reading Eggers's early writing as a dialectical engagement with the underpinning realities of the neoliberal debt economy is the best way to historicize and evaluate his New Sincerity aesthetics. Understanding how and why issues of irony and sincerity arise in New Sincerity texts like Eggers's, and how and why they are (partially but never wholly) resolved within those texts, should lead us beyond a conception of New Sincerity as simply the expression of the artist's intention to communicate in an unironic manner. On my reading, literary New Sincerity is better understood as expressing an historical impasse, as bringing to light the erasures necessary to "fix" the contradictions of a neoliberal world. The disavowal of the neoliberal subject's true state of indebtedness is only one of the disavowals that New Sincerity writing trains its focus upon. In the following chapters, we will see how a range of New Sincerity writers examine neoliberal erasures of other kinds—erasures of gender, race, class, and politics.

3. Gendered Histories and Novel Genres

Late to the Party

The closing chapter of Jennifer Egan's debut novel *The Invisible Circus* (1994) sees its eighteen-year-old protagonist Phoebe O'Connor touching down in San Francisco following a summer spent in Europe. The year is 1978, and Phoebe has returned home with new knowledge concerning the death of her beloved older sister Faith, whose body had been found on the rocks below an Italian seaside village eight years earlier. Faith's full and tragic immersion in the tail end of the 1960s has always lent her brief existence a flavor of reality that Phoebe feels is absent from her own; "her present life," she reflects wistfully, "was nothing but the aftermath of something vanished."[1] *The Invisible Circus* opens with Phoebe arriving too late to a party marking the ten-year anniversary of the 1968 Festival of Moons in a San Francisco field—"She'd missed it, Phoebe knew by the silence" (3)— and as the novel draws toward its final pages, this sense of lateness to the scene of real life has not abated. As she walks the streets of her hometown reflecting on her time away, a "numbing depression" settles over Phoebe, the previous weeks coming to seem in retrospect no more than "a brief, hallucinatory flash" (327, 328). She feels more removed than ever from contact with reality, a reality she was able to experience only by tracing Faith's footsteps across Europe and reliving her sister's life, right down to a sexual relationship with the same man. In San Francisco Phoebe goes back to trying on Faith's clothes and visiting her sister's old haunts in the Haight. "She felt like the ghost of her former ghostly self," Egan writes, "flickering outside even the narrow, shadowy realm where she'd once been at home" (331).

What eventually lifts this pall over Phoebe is a visit to the offices of her older brother Barry's technology company in Silicon Valley. At twenty-three her brother is already a millionaire, and his company's workplace—"sprawling and flat, full of glass and light and dozens of the sleek, unapproachable computers"—is the "diametric opposite" of their late father's functional IBM office, with many exotic items including "a grand piano, plus two massive refrigerators stocked with exotic juices" (332). In the midst of this stylish contemporary space, "Barry's authority seemed effortless. After all, she reasoned later, the company was his own, all the people there his employees" (332–333). This entrepreneurial example inspires Phoebe, and she begins to spend more time in Silicon Valley, even learning to drive at the wheel of her brother's Porsche. She moves to a new apartment with her mother, and as she prepares to begin college at Berkeley in January 1979, a new hope finally emerges:

> Something was gone. But something was also beginning. Phoebe felt this more than understood it—a jittery pulse that seemed to flutter beneath the city. A new decade was upon them. In Barry's office the mood of manic anticipation infected Phoebe at times with a wild certainty that the world was in the grip of transformation. Everyone seemed to feel it—the clean, inarguable power of machines, the promise of extraordinary wealth. It filled them with hope. Phoebe was amazed that the world could ever feel this way again, much less so soon. Yet she felt it herself. (337)

Arriving on the penultimate page of this post-boomer Bildungsroman (Phoebe O'Connor was born in 1960, the similarly Irish-sounding Jennifer Egan in 1962), the question raised for the reader by this giddy passage is whether the conflation it offers between two moments of historical "transformation"—the equality and liberation movements of the 1960s, and the neoliberal embrace of technology and concentrated wealth beginning in the late 1970s—is solely Phoebe's conflation or whether the novel endorses it. Taken in isolation and at face value, it is tempting to read the passage as a heady expression of the "Californian Ideology" that—as my previous chapter outlined—would go on to underpin the 1990s culture of *Wired* and the New Economy, a culture crystallizing concurrently with the writing of *The Invisible Circus*. In a much later reflection on her yearlong relationship with Steve Jobs, which concluded when she declined his marriage proposal in the mid-1980s, Jennifer Egan remarked of the Apple boss's innovations, "Whether in the end he did us harm or good is an open question, from my point of view."[2] This kind of ambivalence is more difficult to detect in the culminating passage of Phoebe's story. Egan's close third-person realist presentation of her protagonist's youthful ingenuousness contains none of the multilayered ironic self-consciousness found in Dave Eggers's depiction of Silicon Valley culture in *A Heartbreaking Work of Staggering Genius*. In place of an authorial New Sincerity, what we appear to have at the finale of *The Invisible Circus* is a protagonist's sincere embrace of the new, without the self-reflexiveness that the former phrase should by now signal.

Phoebe's lack of ironic awareness has, nonetheless, been a theme of the novel to this point. During her European trip, her German boyfriend Wolf describes Phoebe as "so completely without irony—it's like discovering one of those tribes untouched by civilization" (184). This puzzles Phoebe—"She thought of irony as a purely literary concept, and an elusive one at that"—which leads Wolf to clarify: "I think irony might be one of those things you either can't see at all or can't see anything but" (184). But if it seems here that irony is to be understood as an innate facet of character (you either have it or you don't), Wolf goes on to link it to historical experience, specifically the experience of the 1960s and its aftermath. "When I think of that time," he tells Phoebe, "what I remember most was feeling like nothing could ever go wrong for me." "So how does irony fit in with that?" she asks, to which he replies, "Blows it to pieces" (185). In a treatment with strong elective affinities to David Foster Wallace's New Sincerity manifesto "E Unibus Pluram," irony is here depicted as a generational response to the disappointment of political hopes at the end of the 1960s. For Wolf as for Wallace, this kind of irony soon hardens into a disabling cynicism, a diagnosis that makes Phoebe's unironic, innocent, and ingenuous sensibility initially appear as an attractive alternative.

While the sexist character of this diagnosis is here implied (not least by Wolf's name), the message is complicated by Phoebe's lack of responsiveness to broader cultural ironies. The discussion with Wolf takes place while the lovers are visiting a Bavarian castle "whose dimensions were eerily familiar to Phoebe, like a vision from one of her dreams" (186). This familiarity becomes more explicable when Wolf informs her that "Disney used it as Sleeping Beauty's castle. In the movie" (186). Moreover, Phoebe's "dream" is a further step removed from authentic reality because the castle, while it recalls the days of King Arthur, is in fact an Industrial Revolution-era construction by King Ludwig II. Phoebe's dream is thus a media-derived image of a place that is already a copy with no original outside of myth. Notwithstanding this revelation, she announces that the artificial beauty of Ludwig's castle was worth its exorbitant price, which bankrupted the surrounding community. Phoebe's dearth of irony is consistently linked in this way to her willful preference for image and illusion over material realities. Her teenage identification with Patty Hearst, to cite another instance, is not diminished by later disclosures about the truth of the heiress's initially romanticized capture by the Symbionese Liberation Army: "Patty's later account of rape and torture and brainwashing had done little to alter Phoebe's vision of her: a dull, privileged girl drawn irresistibly toward an invisible border, then crossing it into a dark, transcendent world" (82). Phoebe's predilection for fictions over realities is not presented as singular or unusual, moreover. The novel's epigraph, from Ludwig Feuerbach, suggests her representativeness:

> ... for the present age, which prefers the picture to the thing pictured, the copy to the original, imagination to reality, or the appearance to the essence ... *illusion* alone is sacred to this age, but *truth profane* ... so that the *highest degree of illusion* is to it the highest degree of sacredness.

A central question raised by the novel is whether this preference for illusion over truth distinguishes Phoebe and her post-boomer generation from their predecessors in the 1960s, or whether this preference was shared by the older generation. The ambiguity here is most evident in the diverging significations of the novel's title. While for Phoebe "the invisible circus" evokes personal feelings of childhood nostalgia through its link to a special evening she spent with Faith, Wolf explains that the term originates with a Digger event in San Francisco that "was all about watching ourselves happen":

> The idea was for everyone to live out their craziest fantasies at once. Meanwhile these "reporters" were taking notes on everything that happened, then Richard Brautigan—no joke, Brautigan himself—would type up the notes into "news bulletins" and mimeograph hundreds of copies that got passed around instantly, so not only were people doing all this crazy shit, but a lot of times they were reading about themselves doing it before they'd even finished. (183)

Here the interpenetration of media and reality embraced by Phoebe is explicitly connected to the legacy of 1960s counterculture. In making this link, Egan follows a book whose influence she has acknowledged in interview, Todd Gitlin's 1980 treatise on the New Left and the mass media, *The Whole World Is Watching*.[3] Gitlin, a leading figure in the mid-1960s Students for a Democratic Society, summarizes his book's thesis about the period thus: "Journalism—especially television, with all its vividness—was not merely 'holding a mirror up to reality,' to use journalism's own favorite metaphor. It was at least in part *composing* reality, and the composition was entering into our own deliberations—and more, our understandings of who we were and what we were about."[4] "By the second half of the decade," he adds, "activists, counter-activists, and politicians of varying stripes seemed to have grown aware that events were in a sense doubled, cursed, or enchanted by auras of media representation."[5] This sense of doubling, cursing, and enchantment is deep in the literary DNA of *The Invisible Circus*, which draws frequently on gothic and (mediated) fairytale tropes to represent Phoebe's experiences in America and Europe in the summer of 1978. It seems that for both Phoebe and her generational predecessors, fictions enchant while enchantment delivers—paradoxically—the flavor of the real.

Gitlin's narrative of the penetration of 1960s counterculture by media representation offers an origin story for what we now call postmodernism. A signal feature of the postmodern condition, diagnosed most influentially by Fredric Jameson, is the waning of historical consciousness in the face of media proliferation.[6] Phoebe exemplifies this feature when she attempts to investigate the period that had absorbed and destroyed Faith:

> The sixties had been named and written about. In the public library Phoebe spent hours poring over old *Oracles*, leafing through scholarly and journalistic accounts of the "Love Generation." But she read with a restless, uneasy suspicion that these analyses were leading her further from the mystery's core, not toward it. Often she found herself drifting instead to the fashion magazines, leafing through *Vogue* and *Harper's Bazaar* where models lazed in their inadvertent beauty, Lisa Taylor and Patti Hansen, Janice Dickinson.... Yes! Phoebe would think, her breath quickening as she flipped the pages. Yes. Another world gleamed through these images. Phoebe searched the pages half expecting to find a picture of Faith. (29)

As the various passages above suggest, though not a formally postmodern novel, *The Invisible Circus* is concerned with typically postmodern themes: the penetration of reality by fiction, illusion, and mediation; the waning of historical consciousness; the intensification of consumer society and the cult of the image. The emphasis on image culture underpins the specifically gendered way Egan presents these themes. The magazines with celebrity models that so dazzle Phoebe and derail her historical investigations re-emerge in another form at the novel's conclusion, immediately following the earlier quoted passage about "the clean, inarguable power of machines, the promise of extraordinary wealth." "Women were cutting their hair," we learn. "Not the soft, blow-dried Dorothy Hamill cuts of a few years before, but sparser, tighter ones, emphasizing the angles and power of the head. In front of the mirror Phoebe would gather her own reams of hair and hold them behind her, away from her face. The idea of cutting it off appealed to her, the lightness of it, like stepping out from behind a pair of heavy drapes" (337).

The definitive end of the 1960s hangover and the coming age of technological entrepreneurship and "extraordinary wealth" are thus heralded by a shift in the female image. No longer defined by belatedness vis-à-vis their storied boomer sisters—with the famous Dorothy Hamill "wedge" lodged in that mid-1970s transitional space between past and future—Phoebe and her generation of women end *The Invisible Circus* at the anticipatory edge of the coming era, ready to embrace the new hairstyles alongside the new values of the late-century United States. Concluding with this seemingly unironized presentation of an unironic Phoebe, *The Invisible Circus*'s realist methods finally absorb its postmodernist themes, meaning that it cannot be considered a full-fledged example of literary New Sincerity. Questioning but still placing its ultimate emphasis on its protagonist's sincere ingenuousness about the future, the text does not work through an ironic dialectic. While Phoebe's lack of historical consciousness sees her embracing neoliberal technoculture as a reprise of political liberation—as well as finding in female image culture "another world" to replace "faith" in an earlier one—the Bildungsroman form offers no clear alternative to Phoebe's traditional re-absorption into the social order.

In Egan's second novel *Look at Me* (2001), the interweaving concerns of *The Invisible Circus*—fictionality, femininity, mediation, consumerism, realism, gothic, history, irony—will be recapitulated, with the theme of sincerity front and center once again. But this later exploration of sincerity is framed in a far more self-reflexive and metafictional formal structure, albeit one that retains strong ties to the classic realist novel. This hybrid approach to sincerity as a problem for the novel form leads me to describe *Look at Me* as perhaps *the* exemplary New Sincerity novel *qua* novel.[7] Egan's second novel is, moreover, a text that offers a distinctively feminist revision of the aesthetic innovations familiar to us from the work of Wallace and Eggers. The remainder of this chapter will therefore obey the titular plea/demand of *Look at Me* to examine it closely. But before doing so, we need to investigate the underpinning issue of how sincerity arises as a particular question for the novel as a form, from its historical origins to its gendered dynamics to its particular entanglement with fictionality.

Novel Sincerity

In an interview following the publication of her third novel *The Keep* (2006), Egan was asked about the ambiguous conclusion of that novel's plot, in which the reality of various characters' fates is not finally resolved. She replied to the question as follows:

> I wanted to be faithful to the gothic genre, but I also wanted to raise the issue in our modern world of telecommunications. I wanted to explore the question of how reality as a concept might have changed—or needs to change—in light of all the new states of being and new experiences that communications technology has created. My goal was not so much to decisively answer the question of what is real and what isn't, but to make the question no longer matter. In other words, I wanted to create a world that was simultaneously real and not real. I've been asked, sometimes angrily, "Well, was it real or not?" and a part of me wants to respond, "We're talking about a novel: of course it's not real."[8]

The interviewer's immediate reaction to Egan's claim was to question her sincerity in making it: "Oh, come on. You are a very good writer, and your readers become deeply involved with what started out as 'your' but what become 'our' characters. To us, they're real."[9] "Exactly," replied Egan, before going on to outline her fascination with the way fictional characters can be made real by the reader's imagination, and with how literature retains that capacity even in the changed reality of the digital telecommunications age. By making this imaginative process her theme, as she does explicitly in *The Keep* and implicitly in all her work, Egan is acknowledging a significant aspect of writing fiction in an age of media saturation: that such fiction shares properties of artifice with the contemporary world it takes as its subject. The brand of unreality that characterizes a literary text cannot be absolutely distinguished from the mediated reality of the world in which that text is written and read. One way to approach this situation is to privilege questions not about what is real but about what is valuable, in a range of senses of that word.

I want to suggest that the shift we witness in this interview excerpt—where a question about reality gets reframed as a question about sincerity—can stand as an apt synecdoche for the way Egan's fiction asks to be read more generally. Her novels begin from the viewpoint, delivered to us by the postmodernists, that reality is unstable, that we live in an age of artifice and rapid technological change, that things can seem (and be) both real and unreal at the same time. The critic Brian McHale defines postmodernist fiction as dominated by ontological concerns; Egan's fiction accepts as its premise a world where the category of reality no longer holds out the promise of orientating the self and moves to consider the ethical implications, asking how sincerity can continue to operate between people in such a world.[10] This is of necessity a question with formal implications as well as thematic ones. Within the broader scope of New Sincerity fiction, therefore, one specific concern that *Look at Me* brings to the table relates to the status of fiction itself as a means for addressing questions of sincerity. And this concern takes us right back to the early days of the novel.

For the modern novel begins with what, at first blush, appears to be a blatant act of insincerity. In his 1719 preface to the first edition of *Robinson Crusoe*, Daniel Defoe calls himself not the work's author, but its editor, and the first English novel is described in its own pages as "a just History of Fact; neither is there any appearance of Fiction in it."[11] Leading authorities on the origins of the novel highlight the crucial quality of this statement for understanding early eighteenth-century conceptions of truth, fiction, realism, and sincerity. Rather than deem Defoe insincere, Michael McKeon poses his sincerity as a question: "How can an author sincerely believe that he is telling the truth if he knows that he has invented the story to whose historicity he earnestly attests?"[12] According to Maximillian Novak, such a question can only be answered by taking into account the "sincerity crisis" of 1715–1724, which emerged in response to controversial comments made by Benjamin Hoadly, Bishop of Bangor, concerning the privilege of conscience over religious authority. Defoe had made an earlier contribution to this debate with his 1703 pamphlet *The Sincerity of the Dissenters Vindicated*, and he continued to write on the controversy alongside working on his major novels, all of which were published during this period of "sincerity crisis." Novak claims that Defoe's concern with sincerity impelled his literary realism, because "the discovery of a 'new' notion of sincerity [privileging personal conscience] tended to undercut stereotyped characterization in favour of a realistic assessment of personality"; thus, "it was the Bangorian Controversy and the debate over sincerity that turned Defoe toward a type of fiction that fused a vivid presentation of a real world of things, people, and events with a focus on the inner life."[13] Novak's emphasis on sincerity supplements the classic account of Defoe's realism offered by Ian Watt, who highlights the shaping cultural effects on the early novel of capitalism, Protestantism, philosophical empiricism, and, above all, individualism.[14]

In his influential study *Factual Fictions*, Lennard J. Davis concentrates less on Defoe's innovations in the sphere of realism than in the realm of fictionality. He points out that the author's denial of *Robinson Crusoe*'s fictionality was no more than a conventional gesture of the time, found in many works of a similar kind. What distinguished it from earlier instances was the unexpected response it received, when Charles Gildon, in *An Epistle to Daniel Defoe*, attacked the work as no more than a "fable."[15] The argument continued through Defoe's prefaces to subsequent Crusoe novels (often written in the voice of Crusoe himself) and their responses by Gildon, so that "for the first time the whole issue of a discourse based on fact or fiction as a discriminant is brought up front" (157).

Davis contends that the reason this happened in Defoe's case and not before is that the category of fiction in its modern sense—a story not factual but plausibly so—only emerged at this time. Earlier romances and candidates for the category of the novel from other cultures—notably Cervantes's *Don Quixote* (1615)—could never have been mistaken for anything other than made-up tales or fables, which leads Davis to deny the usual importance granted to these precursors in critical genealogies of the novel. Instead, he argues that the rise of news reportage in the seventeenth century led to a new pressure to distinguish genres of printed text by degrees of factuality and fictionality; it was only with the emergence of a legal category of truth as correspondence to real-world events that it became incumbent on authors to clarify the degree of veracity in their work. It was out of this "news/novels discourse" (51) that the novel—"an ambiguous form, a factual fiction that denied its fictionality" (36)—was born. "When *Robinson Crusoe* was written in 1719," Davis remarks, "there was no clear distinction between news and fiction, and Defoe's work rests uneasily in that world of a discourse which is more and more inclining to separate into two subdiscourses but which still has not broken apart" (155). Calling into question Defoe's sincerity, as Gildon did, therefore invoked not only the "sincerity crisis" of the time but also the emerging importance of a distinction between fact and fiction. Viewed theoretically, the emergence of this distinction between fact and fiction can be understood to render the question of Defoe's sincerity as much one of textual effect as of psychological cause.

In her essay "The Rise of Fictionality," Catherine Gallagher extends Davis's argument in claiming that "the novel is not just one kind of fictional narrative among others; it is the kind in which and through which fictionality became manifest, explicit, widely understood, and accepted."[16] Through the seventeenth and early eighteenth centuries, credible prose narratives could not be fictions, but "were meant to be read either as factual accounts or as 'allegorical' reflections on contemporary people and events" (339). Defoe's responses to Gildon's attacks marked the first step in the emergence of the concept of fiction, which only became necessary, according to Gallagher, when narratives began to seem plausible without referring to identifiable real-world referents. Fiction then began to assert itself as something different to a lie, and it did so by producing itself as a discursive mode whose reference was to "nobody in particular" (341). In *Joseph Andrews* (1742), for instance, Henry Fielding was able to describe his novel as being about "not men, but manners; not an individual, but a species" (quoted on 341). Thus a new mode of truth developed in the mid-eighteenth-century novel, based on a "nonreferentiality that could be seen as a greater referentiality" (343). And by the end of the century, "disclaimers like Fielding's were no longer necessary, for the public had been trained to read novels as stories about thoroughly imagined (if representative) people, names without singular, specific referents in the world" (344). Noting the centrality of realism or verisimilitude to this development,

Gallagher concludes that "the widespread acceptance of verisimilitude as a form of truth, rather than a form of lying, founded the novel as a genre. It also created the category of fiction" (341).

By the middle of the nineteenth century, this new category of fiction was no longer problematic but "became the norm," Gallagher writes, "throughout Europe and America" (336). And realism was now very much the dominant trend, gaining such prominence and popularity that the realist novel came to embody, in Pam Morris's phrase, "the code of sincerity in the public sphere."[17] Dickens, Eliot, and the Brontës in England; Stendhal, Balzac, and Flaubert in France; Turgenev, Dostoevsky, and Tolstoy in Russia—in each of these major writers a new code of sincerity replaces an older and more formally embedded code of civility. This shift provides a kind of interpersonal and ethical glue for rapidly industrializing societies, "a public interpellative code based upon an assumption of common human interiority."[18] The public quality of this sincerity (also emphasized, as we have seen, in Lionel Trilling's classic account) becomes prominent in a way less applicable to the early modern concern with individual religious conscience; as Morris notes: "The novels I discuss are more thematically concerned with sincerity as a public mode of discourse than as a personal attribute of interiority. In addition, by means of narrative voice they contribute to the elaboration and popularization of a code of sincerity within the public sphere."[19] The narrative voice of which Morris writes—the so-called omniscient narrator—is the key to this convergence of sincerity, fictionality, and realism in the mid-nineteenth-century novel. The editors of the volume *Romanticism, Sincerity and Authenticity* relate these categories as follows: "Through verisimilitude the realist novel attempts to resolve questions about the sincerity of characters and the earnestness of the form itself."[20] On this reading, the persistent quest for sincerity in content leads fiction to embrace realism in form. It leads the novelist towards what George Eliot famously defined as "the humble and faithful study of nature," placed in the service of uncovering "a definite, substantial reality."[21]

As part of their elaboration of a public code of sincerity, nineteenth-century novelists frequently had recourse to what Garrett Stewart refers to as the "dear reader" trope. Drawing on a tradition of direct address in Western literature that extends back to Dante's *Divine Comedy*, these novelists updated this tradition for a cultural context in which the reader, the emerging self of bourgeois liberal capitalist society, related to literary narrative "not only as mass product but as supposedly private pleasure."[22] *Jane Eyre*'s "Reader, I married him," discussed in my Introduction to this book, is the "master sentence" of the genre, "minimal but in its own way exhaustive" of the possibilities of direct address as the founding of an aesthetic of novelistic sincerity in liberal society.[23] And yet by the end of the century, this trope of direct address had fallen out of favor. With the coming of modernism, the address to the reader, a move that had been "faintly anachronistic even in its earliest appearances and self-consciously dated in its later uses," now virtually disappeared from consciously cutting-edge fiction, "wiped clean," as Stewart puts it, "from the burnished surface of a modernist text that stresses inscape over outreach, as well as from a vision of community too besieged for the gesture of familiarity and affiliation sketched by address."[24]

This privileging of the interior individual over the exterior community is in line with Trilling's claim that authenticity replaced sincerity as the defining ethos of modernism. And when direct address returned in postmodernist fiction, it was in parodic and often transgressive form. Rather than a writer speaking to a reader or a narrator addressing a narratee, postmodernist fiction habitually features contraventions of the normal planes of fictional communication, such as when a narrator addresses one of their characters, or a narrating character directly addresses the reader. "The reader! You dogged, uninsultable, printoriented bastard, it's you I'm addressing," writes John Barth in *Lost in the Funhouse* (1969), while in Pynchon's *Gravity's Rainbow* (1973) the regular uses of second person "hover ambiguously among several alternative communicative situations, or switch disconcertingly from one to the other."[25] *You*, that "most reliable sign of narratorial 'voice,'" is employed in these postmodernist texts in the service not of sincerity but of "ontological scandal."[26] Fictionality is transgressed; realism is revoked; sincerity and authenticity are subordinated to parabasis, or irony.

Generic Realism

Look at Me, a novel that—as we will see in the next section—fashions a gothic relationship to its postmodernist predecessors, will serve to exemplify the New Sincerity legacy of the nineteenth-century novel's braiding of realism, fictionality, and sincerity, after and in response to the unbraidings of modernism and postmodernism.[27] The fact that Jennifer Egan seems at once to be operating in the mode of traditional realism—with rounded characters, a vividly drawn social web, satisfying narrative arcs, and predominately transparent language—and at the same time to be writing a kind of speculative fiction, in which technological change fundamentally alters how language signifies and identity is shaped, means that her work offers a telling example of this kind. The best place to begin is a scene midway through *Look at Me*, in which the main narrator and protagonist, a thirty-five-year-old fashion model named Charlotte Swenson, is discussing the creation of a "PersonalSpace™" web page—a blogged account of her life—with two colleagues, the would-be internet entrepreneur Thomas Keene and the journalist-cum-cultural-studies-academic Irene Maitlock. The proposal under review is that Charlotte's blog entries for Thomas's "Ordinary People" platform be ghostwritten by Irene, and the purpose of the meeting is to find a way to tell, in the most eye-catching manner possible, the story of Charlotte's rise and fall (before the novel opens, she has gone from successful New York fashion model to suffering a horrific car accident followed by extensive reconstructive surgery to repair the shattered bones in her face).[28]

While Charlotte mostly remains mute and on the sidelines of the weblog debate, Thomas and Irene find common ground in their shared knowledge of the literary canon. In musing upon the correct representation of Charlotte's "tragedy," they name and briefly discuss a range of novelists and their work. The following is a representative excerpt:

> "Tragedy, okay. Yes," he said. "But not Greek. Too cold. Has to be something warmer."
> "Nineteenth century."
> "Bingo. Hardy. The Brontës. Tolstoy. Sad things happen but they happen for a reason."
> "Zola."
> "Exactly. Stendhal. Or Dickens, for God's sake."
> "George Eliot," Irene said. "*Adam Bede*."
> "That's the one where he—"
> "Gets her pregnant," she said. "And then tries to find him after his regiment moves to Scotland."

"Oh, my God, where she's hitching rides on carts and sleeping in the fields? That was the saddest book . . . ," Thomas said, his whole face opening at the memory. "But only the second half. The first half was kind of—"

"That's amazing!" Irene said, and she did look amazed. "I thought exactly the same thing."

"—schmaltzy."

I listened, my frustration at finding myself ignorant of these books offset by my wonder at the abrupt change in Irene; she was smiling, cheeks flushed. Books, I thought; she loved books. It made perfect sense.

"Edith Wharton," she said.

"Yes! Wharton is perfect. *Age of Innocence. House of Mirth.* Or Flaubert," he added, but then changed his mind. "Nah, *Madam B.*'s too dark, too modern."

"Too ironic," Irene said.

"Exactly, exactly. See, irony we don't want—there's too much of it out there! We just want the story without the built-in commentary."[29]

The final line brings out the metafictional irony of this scene, which offers as much "built-in commentary" as it does story. Yet amid the evident comedy there is also a serious point being made: what we are witnessing in this passage is the great tradition of the nineteenth-century novel, from Stendhal to Edith Wharton, signifying directly for these two avid readers as a kind of shorthand, a set of soothing generic narrative arcs. The realist novel—a form that began its existence, on Watt's canonical account, with the task "to convey the impression of fidelity to human experience" so that "attending to any pre-established formal conventions can only endanger [its] success"—has morphed for Thomas and Irene precisely into such a set of preestablished conventions ("sad things happen but they happen for a reason").[30] These conventions can now be exploited to map an emotional trajectory for the website's reader and to manipulate the way a story is pitched and sold: in other words, literature has become a branch of advertising. We might recall here the cynical J. D. Steelritter's words in Wallace's *Westward the Course of Empire Takes Its Way*: "'Stories are basically like ad campaigns, no?'"[31] And yet neither of the two discussants in this passage is represented as cynical, or obviously insincere, in the way they approach this issue, as indicated by the descriptions of Thomas's open face and Irene's flushed cheeks. Indeed, Thomas's earnest cyber-utopianism is evident in many other passages of the novel; as Charlotte notes, Thomas "truly believed he was making the world a better place. And maybe he was," she adds. "What did I know?" (206).

The pace of technological change, and its intersection with market values, has evidently outstripped Charlotte's sense of right and wrong, altering human relationships in ways that challenge ethical norms. For Thomas and Irene, however, the question of right and wrong is simply a matter of generic fit; and in the preordained "realist" formula, it turns out that the conventions of fiction must sometimes overrule the contingencies of fact. Hence Charlotte finds her homeless black friend Pluto written out of her online narrative, when Irene and Thomas agree that such a relationship, despite its empirical existence, "may be kind of a stretch" in narrative form (262). And they are not exactly wrong: the norms of nineteenth-century realism would indeed militate against the occurrence of a genuine friendship between a poor character and a rich one, not to mention two characters from different racial backgrounds. In fact, submission to narrative convention helps to eliminate knotty problems of social justice altogether, even when Pluto himself later becomes the subject of a PersonalSpace page. The relevant conversation between Thomas and Irene is reported by Charlotte as follows:

> "I have three words for you on Pluto," Thomas told her during one of our many recent visits to his office. "Dickens. Dickens. Dickens."
> "You mean . . . victim of circumstance," Irene said.
> "Exactly."
> "Living below his—"
> "You got it."
> "So his fortunes will improve. They have to."
> "Bingo," Thomas said. (318)

In these central scenes in *Look at Me*, literary realism has morphed into precisely the object that its original pioneers set out to defeat: a form of narrative representation that ignores contemporary realities in favor of preordained generic norms, a set of conventions that can be exploited for instrumental ends rather than placed in the service of truth. The realist novel has been reduced not only to the status of advertising, in other words, but also to the character of the classically inspired romance that predated it historically, a form the purpose of which had been to "depict the world not as it is (or was) but as it should have been."[32] This replacement of realism by romance in *Look at Me* offers an early and prescient glimpse of the perfected image of "real" life that would go on to characterize the *gestalt* of what we now call social media.

Yet at least the conventions of classic realism, even when instrumentalized in this way, do promise some larger and potentially cathartic payoff for a contemporary audience. But fiction in *Look at Me* does not simply mean Hardy and the Brontës; it also refers, more regularly and more banally, to the conventions of the best-selling genre thriller in its familiar, twentieth-century forms. Irene Maitlock's online narrative of Charlotte's life may aim for a tragic arc, but the ghostwriting itself more often resembles the standard prose of sensationalist pulp. And one of the conceits of Charlotte's first-person narration is that this pulp version begins to preempt and infect her own sensibility, so that events in her life get turned into dramatic material and submitted to narrative conventions even as she is processing her own thoughts:

> I tried to consider the question. How did it *feel*? But almost immediately, the breathless narrator who had taken up a pampered existence in one lobe of my brain . . . began piping in her own treacly reply: It had been nearly a year since the devastating event, and oh, the pain Charlotte felt on returning to the scene, the anguish of seeing those same fields scarred by terrible memories . . . (315)

The shift in typeface signals the dividing consciousness that increasingly marks Charlotte's narration as the novel progresses. Her awareness of past and future transcription distances her from intuitive feeling, and generic conventions begin to substitute for spontaneous experience, so that feeling gets immediately instrumentalized rather than felt. *Look at Me* shows us a world in which the female self becomes gradually suffocated by the discursive forms and norms of popular culture. With her inner life evacuated of organic feeling, all that remains are standard stories, familiar images.

This standardization seems to move us far from the philosophical realism defined by Watt, which "begins from the position that truth can be discovered by the individual through his senses," and from a consequent literary realism which hails individual experience as "always unique and therefore new."[33] And yet the metafictional conceit is actually functioning here in the service of an updated brand of realism, in which Charlotte's experience still conforms to Watt's definition of "particular individuals having particular experiences at particular times and at particular places."[34] It is just that Charlotte's experience of her own particularity has combined in a new way with the novelistic representation of "nobody in particular."[35] As the publicist Victoria Knight puts it when encouraging Charlotte to see her life in terms of a formulaic narrative of punishment and redemption, "'Right now, as far as the world is concerned, you're a tabula rasa. You don't exist'" (196).

One of the casualties of *Look at Me*'s updated brand of generic realism is therefore a traditional understanding of sincerity. Trilling's ideal of "a congruence between avowal and actual feeling" appears to lose purchase in an age when the "actual feeling" of the subject has always already been infiltrated by the conventions of prior and future "avowals." Despite, or perhaps because of this waning of its very possibility, *Look at Me* is a novel obsessed by sincerity. "The truth. I wanted to see it," Charlotte admits early on.

> Everyone was a liar, blah-blahing their way through life, pretending to be good and constant, to have and to hold and all that. Everyone was a politician, wearing a pious face until the last possible moment when the press unearthed a taste for child amputees and a beheaded mistress chained to a radiator. (41)

As we shall see later, the gothic excess here is not coincidental, and it is not only the reader to whom our narrator discloses such darkly cynical assessments. In Charlotte's first meeting with Irene, she informs the journalist: "'everyone is a liar. Including me. . . . You're selling me a line of bullshit and you want me to sell you a line of bullshit back so you can write a major line of bullshit and be paid for it'" (76). Later, she admits to the detective Anthony Halliday that one of the things she likes about New York nightclubs is that "'nobody pretends to tell the truth, they just go ahead and lie. It's a relief'" (154). But the relief for Charlotte is not in the evasion of truth, rather in the lack of pretense that it will be revealed through the sincere use of language, either her own or that of others. "If I cared about someone, I did my best to mean what I said when I said it," she acknowledges elsewhere. "But I'd given up on the whole truth, much less my ability to tell it" (84).

If for Charlotte something like "the whole truth" remains accessible, it is through the visual rather than linguistic realm. "'I watch everyone,'" she tells Halliday. "'It's how I learn'" (160). Significant moments of connection in the novel often happen through sight, as for instance when Charlotte and a silent North Korean model share their reactions to painful exploitation at the hands of the photographer Spiro: "I felt the engagement of her sight physically, as if she'd grabbed me. While the shutter clicked, we stared at each other, our gazes interlocked, and something passed between us, a wordless acknowledgement of the depravity that surrounded us" (146–147). Often these moments of connection are sought out by Charlotte through the novel's titular refrain, "look at me." "'Can you look at me and swear that everything you've said is absolutely true, that none of it is bullshit?'" she petitions Irene (77), while elsewhere she asks a man leaving her apartment to "'look at me . . . . If you were going to describe me, what would you say?'" (42). His answer is verbal—"'You look tired,' he said"—but its sincerity is revealed through the visual realm, as "the two halves of him fused in a moment of humanity" (42).

Yet the ambiguities of this moment—what is Charlotte really *seeing* when she claims to see two halves of a person fusing?—lie at the heart of Egan's New Sincerity aesthetics. We have seen how this aesthetics revises the traditional conjoining of realism, fictionality, and sincerity in the nineteenth-century novel. To further analyze and historicize Egan's literary New Sincerity, the next sections explore the intersections in *Look at Me* among the postmodern, the gothic, female experience, and the visual realm.

Uncanny Postmodernism

Although Jennifer Egan's early novels—those published before her breakout hit *A Visit from the Goon Squad* (2010)—have been relatively overlooked by critics to date, few American writers around the turn of the millennium more directly addressed the task of responding to postmodernism and postmodernity. In one of the earliest substantial considerations of her work, Pankaj Mishra identified Egan as one of the "oddly few successors" of Thomas Pynchon and Don DeLillo, the two American novelists who had most ably chronicled "the strange new mutations in individual and social life caused by the reorganisation of work, consumption and war."[36] Mishra praised Egan's fiction, and *Look at Me* in particular, "for still being able to register incredulity at the weirdness of this process."[37] Given this directness of engagement with recognizably postmodern themes and forms in her early writing, Egan's neglect by critics might seem surprising. And yet, ironically, it may be the very directness of her engagement that has contributed to the overlooking of her work: at first glance, it can be difficult to identify what exactly Egan's early fiction brings to the postmodern table that we haven't seen before, how she builds upon and departs from the tradition of Pynchon and DeLillo, as well as other authors regularly included in the postmodern fold such as Paul Auster, J. G. Ballard, John Barth, Jorge Luis Borges, William Burroughs, Italo Calvino, Angela Carter, Umberto Eco, Bret Easton Ellis, Vladimir Nabokov, Ishmael Reed, and Jeannette Winterson. Of course (as this list of names unavoidably suggests), another and perhaps more obvious explanation for Egan's relative critical neglect is her gender, with the canon of postmodernist fiction still often appearing to be, even in many revisionist accounts, predominately a (white) male preserve.[38]

What I want to suggest is that surface similarities between Egan's novels and key texts in the postmodern tradition owe much to the relation her fiction maintains to that tradition as a whole, a relation that can best be characterized as gothic. While *The Keep* makes the gothic underpinnings of Egan's fiction explicit, it is *Look at Me* that provides the more significant case study in postmodern inheritance. This is because *Look at Me*, late as it is to the postmodern party, plays a similar role for mid- to late-twentieth-century postmodernism that an earlier novel to which it alludes, Edith Somerville and Martin Ross's *The Real Charlotte* (1894), played for nineteenth-century realism. Both novels, characterized by smooth surfaces concealing darker processes of decay, repeat the most identifiable tropes of the immediately preceding literary tradition, but do so in a manner that produces a sense of the uncanny.[39] In the case of *Look at Me*, the effect of this uncanniness is to reintroduce resonances and specters of history into the novel's form (alongside, as we shall see later, its content), allowing its contemporary prose to be haunted by texts and techniques from the postmodernist canon. And one reason why this effect can be powerful is because the most influential accounts of postmodernism and its exemplary texts have consistently stressed the prominence of space over time—the contemporary loss of history and emergence of an endless present—in the totally administered and technophilic postmodern society.[40]

Look at Me's postmodern specters emerge as early as its second paragraph, wherein Charlotte recounts the car accident in which almost every bone in her face was broken. "In my memory," she tells us,

> the accident has acquired a harsh, dazzling beauty: white sunlight, a slow loop through space like being on the Tilt-A-Whirl (always a favorite of mine), feeling my body move faster than, and counter to, the vehicle containing it. Then a bright, splintering crack as I burst through the windshield into the open air, bloody and frightened and uncomprehending. (3)

This aestheticized description of a physically brutal event recalls the openings of J. G. Ballard's twin car crash novels *Crash* (1973) and *Concrete Island* (1974). In particular, the notably filmic representation of Charlotte's memory as a series of clashing images—"dazzling beauty," "white sunlight," "splintering crack," "bloody and frightened"—answers to the mix of horror and beauty, fear and desire, which typifies Ballard's work and is encoded more generally in what one critic has termed the "adrenaline aesthetic" of modern cultural engagements with the automobile.[41] Moreover, the crash that opens *Look at Me* will later be reconstructed within the novel precisely as a film, the making of which is recounted in the penultimate chapter, with the story of the film shoot simultaneously transcribed at the scene by Irene Maitlock.[42] In that same chapter the buildup to the crash will also be recounted for the reader in a separate thriller-like narration in a "first-person" account set in different type and produced by Irene as Charlotte's ghostwriter. While any sexual element to the crash, or any relation to the feeling of driving at speed, are played down by Charlotte's opening narration of the accident, Irene's ghostwritten account will certainly suggest the combination of adrenaline, sexuality, and deadened affect associated with Ballard's postmodern *oeuvre*. The allusion to Ballard is sharpened by Irene's surname, Maitlock, recalling the protagonist of *Concrete Island*, Robert Maitland.

Yet the suggestion that there might be something fictional about all these retrospective renderings of memory is highlighted by Charlotte as early as the paragraph that follows the quotation above:

> The truth is that I don't remember anything. The accident happened at night during an August downpour on a deserted stretch of highway through corn and soybean fields, a few miles outside Rockford, Illinois, my hometown. I hit the brakes and my face collided with the windshield, knocking me out instantly.... The shatterproof windshield did indeed hold fast upon its impact with my head, so although I broke virtually every bone in my face, I have almost no visible scars. (3)

It now appears that the "memory" related by Charlotte in the first quotation has a different status from that recounted in the second. The latter account, which contradicts the first in language that is less dreamlike and more denotative, is associated with "the truth," and the truth is that there exists for Charlotte no memory of the event, if memory is to be associated with the recall of experience rather than its (re)creation from generic models. But can memory and experience function in this traditionally sincere manner, through the outward avowal of inner feeling?

Not, it seems, in the postmodern moment, as Irene will later imply at the point when she reveals to Charlotte her "true" identity, as a cultural studies professor rather than the *New York Post* journalist she had initially posed as:

> "I'm an academic," she went on, "a professor of comparative literature.... My area is cultural studies. Specifically, the way literary and cinematic genres affect certain kinds of experience." I sensed her straining to put this in language I would understand. "For example, the Mafia. How do cultural notions of the so-called wiseguy affect the way people like John Gotti dress and move and speak? How does that extra layer of self-consciousness impact experience? The same for cops; they watch cop shows, too. And how does their experience of those shows affect their experience as cops?"
>
> "Detectives," I said, addressing the cigarette in my hand.
>
> "Exactly. Detective stories. The genre is almost as old as the profession, the two have been intertwined practically from the beginning."
>
> "Detectives write books," I said ruefully.
>
> "That's right," she said. "A surprising number try to write detective novels, as if writing books were a corollary of the experience of being a detective." (279)

As with the allusions to Ballard, there is little pretense to literary innovation in these gestures by Egan, rather the opposite. Perhaps the most obvious precursor to Irene Maitlock in her role as cultural studies academic is Murray J. Siskind in Don DeLillo's *White Noise* (1985), who theorizes about Elvis, car crashes, and, in his most Baudrillardian moment, "The Most Photographed Barn in America."[43] Similarly, the insights that Irene and Charlotte share about detectives, the idea that "writing books [is] a corollary of the experience of being a detective," could come straight from many a Paul Auster novel, for instance *City of Glass* (1985). Irene's ghostwritten accounts of Charlotte Swenson's life are "fed by the cheap detective novels she still gulped down when she had time" (244), and the other allusion in her surname is to the popular TV detective Matlock. From the outset, then, Egan's approach to representing the world her characters inhabit acknowledges prior fictional treatments of similar themes and worlds, and she deliberately builds upon those treatments.

Nonetheless, these lightly metafictional allusions to postmodernist texts by Auster, Ballard, and DeLillo—as well as to others by Barth, Burroughs, Ellis, and Pynchon, to which I will come—always remain relatively implicit throughout *Look at Me*, unlike the novel's explicit naming of realist authors and texts. This sense of quietly resuscitating postmodern tropes, in a novel that more overtly invokes the conventions of classical realism, helps to account for *Look at Me*'s uncanny quality. In a story concerned with how the fictional layering of the protagonist's world renders her identity ethereal and uncertain, those qualities of fictionality and ethereality are heightened for the reader by the sense that Charlotte's otherwise realistically presented surroundings may exist only as a patchwork of postmodern genres, genres that are themselves *already* characterized by qualities of parody, intertextuality, and what Jameson identified as "pastiche," an aesthetic that offers surfaces with no referential depth.[44] This underlying web of allusions to postmodern literary texts creates the effect of a "double life" and "mirrored room" (the titles of Parts One and Two of *Look at Me*), providing an additional layer of mediation beyond the levels associated with those technologies of representation—television, film, writing—that were a critical focus of postmodernist fiction in the first place.

As we have seen, a key technique Egan uses to signal the preempting of Charlotte's narrative by popular and literary tropes and conventions is to enact in the novel's typeface the division of consciousness increasingly experienced by its protagonist. A postmodern precursor for this technique can be found in the text that also inspired Wallace's *Westward*, John Barth's coming-of-age story "Lost in the Funhouse" (1968). There is a notable difference, however, in Egan's use of this conceit. When the typeface alters in Barth's story, the agency seems to emanate from Ambrose as writer: "*Italics mine.*"[45] Ambrose can thus negotiate the "*place of fear and confusion*" that is the funhouse of consciousness at the story's opening by claiming ownership of the act of creation by its end: "he will construct funhouses for others and be their secret operator."[46] For Charlotte, by contrast, the funhouse—of writing, of consciousness, of image culture as represented by the mirrored room—can only be more passively endured, with little opportunity for agency. "I was peeling apart in layers," Charlotte tells us at one heightened moment:

> I was breaking into bits. She was coming apart at the seams . . . my head buzzing with a confusion of junk noise, white noise, space junk, a junkyard of noisy thought that made me long instead for a lovely, petaled silence. (329)

Here the protagonist's "peeling apart" is reinforced not only by the specter of gendered cliché ("coming apart at the seams") but also by the "junk" of Burroughs, the "white noise" of DeLillo, and the "space junk" of science fiction. The effect is accentuated by the pronominal shift: the split between "I" and "she" enacts in the material type the sense of splitting and doubling that haunts Charlotte's sense of self throughout the novel. For Charlotte, the playful, comic spirit that animated the "literature of exhaustion" practiced by Barth gives way to a more oppressive sense of enclosure.[47] Even the "lovely, petaled silence" for which Charlotte yearns offers an image that seems derived from earlier literature, calling to mind the Romantic poets, the early Pound or e e cummings, or moments of lyrical texture in the later Beckett.

This lack of an outside to fictionality and transcription suggests the scriptedness of Charlotte's life, the haunting of her sincere self-relation by texts prior and to come. This emphasis on the material word, the elusive manuscript, is a classic trope of the gothic tradition, as is the foreclosure of escape from the institution, the claustrophobia that results from the lack of an outside.[48] As *Look at Me* demonstrates, postmodernist fiction and commercial culture can combine to constitute a mirrored room that encloses the subject, helping to induce the passivity suggested by the novel's title. We can deepen and complicate our reading of the gendered dimensions of this passivity by considering further the theme of visibility in the context of Charlotte's experience of the novel's gothic-inflected world.

Gothic (Post-)Feminism

Emerging in the late eighteenth century—the historical midpoint between the initial rise of the realist novel and its dominance by the middle of the nineteenth century—the "modern romance" (as the first gothic novelist Horace Walpole dubbed the genre in 1765) saw the re-embrace of non-realistic elements of romance writing that had predated the advent of realism.[49] While the "big five" male authors of the eighteenth century—Defoe, Richardson, Fielding, Smollett, and Sterne—were already canonical by the time gothic fiction arrived on the literary scene, the latter genre was developed particularly successfully by women writers, notable among them Clara Reeve, Ann Radcliffe, and Mary Shelley. Moreover, from Ellen Moers's 1976 coinage of "Female Gothic" onward, critics have observed in gothic writing a powerful vehicle for representing the historical experience of women in patriarchal societies, as well as for querying (and queering) gender distinctions and how they are instituted.[50] Summarizing the development of the field of gothic literary studies in the 1990s and 2000s, one critic notes "the transformation of the gender debate from the biologically driven term 'Female Gothic' to the more culturally driven agenda of 'Feminine Gothic.'"[51] This turn to more cultural conceptions of gender included a consideration of the intersections between gothic narrative and so-called postfeminism, a developing discourse around the turn of the millennium.[52] This is the complex cultural field into which *Look at Me* arrived: concerned with female experience in the overlapping eras of postmodern image culture, postfeminism, incipient social media, and neoliberal capitalist exploitation at home and abroad, Egan's second novel develops the gothic impulses of her first as part of a continued thematic concern with personal sincerity and a more articulated formal concern with writing "sincere" fiction after postmodernism.[53]

The gothic atmosphere of *Look at Me* does not stem only (or even primarily) from the allusions to literary texts that help to build the novel's artifice-embroidered world. In a more palpable sense, gothic and uncanny imagery is everywhere in the novel. In the opening chapter, images of death and disease are recurrent: Charlotte's father's lungs are "slowly dissolving from emphysema" (5); the house where she is recovering "smelled of dust and dead flowers" (6); the trees outside are "slowly expiring from Dutch elm disease" (7); Charlotte sits on a gravestone "among legions of dead Swedes" (11); she remembers the mother of her childhood best friend, Ellen Metcalf, as "a quasi-invalid, cloistered in a darkened master bedroom, consumed by some malady whose exact nature no one seemed sure of" (12). Later in the chapter Charlotte recalls her teenage sexual tryst with Ellen as a doppelganger experience: "She felt both familiar and strange—someone else, but like me. . . she was less a separate person than a variant of myself—that together, we made one thing" (20). The chapter concludes with the present-day Charlotte sneaking uninvited into Ellen's home and encountering her daughter, "a sadly average-looking girl" also called Charlotte (25). As she hurries away from the house, the extremity of the protagonist's emotional response is typical of the gothic mode:

> I was gripped by jealousy so sharp and unexpected that it felt like sickness. I wanted that girl. She was mine, she should have been mine; even her name was mine. I wanted that house, that life; the kid with cancer—I wanted it. I wanted children, people around me. I wanted to send a young Charlotte into the world to live a different life from mine. (27)

"Double Life," the title of the novel's first part, evidently refers to the uncanny feeling the narrator's encounter with this other Charlotte imbues in her. But "double life" also refers to the lives of Charlotte Swenson before and after her car accident. In keeping with the gothic preference for ambiguous realities, the opening sentences of *Look at Me* highlight the indeterminacy of Charlotte's visual status following the crash:

> After the accident, I became less visible. I don't mean in the obvious sense that I went to fewer parties and retreated from general view. Or not just that. I mean that after the accident, I became more difficult to see. (3)

The exact relationship between Charlotte's pre-crash and post-crash facial features is never fully clarified. Her initial reconstructive surgery at the hands of the splendidly named Dr. Hans Fabermann—surely a nod to Victor Frankenstein, the gothic *homo faber* whose attempt to control destiny through technology unleashes dark forces—is described in gruesomely precise detail:

"I'd been sliced from ear to ear over the crown of my head so Dr. Fabermann could peel down the skin from my forehead and reattach my cheekbones to my upper skull" (4). On her return from Rockford to New York, Charlotte is operated on again, this time by a surgeon defined less by Promethean skill than by class allegiance: "Dr. Miller, who was married to a model, normally devoted his reconstructive powers to making wealthy, attractive people look even more attractive—not scrapping with the 'gross disfiguration' that follows cataclysmic trauma to the face" (29). Charlotte has given Dr. Miller a set of old photographs to help him recreate her image, yet the results of the surgery are inconclusive, or at least they become increasingly so as the novel muddies the subjective and objective realms:

> I'd spent as long as an hour staring through the ring of chalky light around my bathroom mirror; I'd held up old pictures of myself beside my reflection and tried to compare them. But my sole discovery was that in addition to not knowing what I looked like now, I had never known. The old pictures were no help; like all good pictures, they hid the truth. (32)[54]

At least since *Frankenstein* (1818), gothic fiction has registered a haunted anxiety at the effect of technological developments on human relations. Following the invention of the camera, observes one critic, "the emergence of telegraphy, radio, television and computers each in turn produced fantasies of spectral presence and an otherworldly space."[55] Moreover, gothic responses to these technologies have typically centered on women, who "frequently provide a hinge between the embodied human subject and a pure realm of disembodiment."[56] While rehearsing the traditional gothic engagement with the gendered impact of new technologies, *Look at Me*'s intersecting themes of visibility, medical intervention, and wealth also speak directly to the novel's 1990s writing and setting. In their introduction to *The Visible Woman* (1998), the editors note that the 1990s witnessed a widespread embrace by the medical profession of new imaging technologies—MRI, computerized tomography, DNA sampling, video endoscopy—which promoted "women's health" to the center of "research agendas, academic curricula, and policy mandates."[57] Setting out their feminist response to these developments, the editors argue that "visibility is itself a claim that must be carefully examined: in acknowledging what is seen, and newly seen, we need to be equally vigilant about what is not seen, or no longer seen."[58] Among the things no longer seen are "existing networks of power, cultural values, institutional practices, and economic priorities," which shape the representation and treatment of the "visible woman."[59]

In highlighting these networks, values, practices, and priorities—which by the 1990s were broadly neoliberal in their rationale and orientation—*The Visible Woman* updates a longer feminist tradition in the study of cultures of visuality and visibility, a tradition for which "'Woman' is, in semiotic terms, a signifier of 'to-be-looked-at-ness.'"[60] In light of this tradition, much of *Look at Me* reads like a literal rendering of classic tropes of female subjectivity and objectivity derived from visual culture. In *Ways of Seeing* (1972), an originating text in this lineage, John Berger writes of "a woman's self being split in two": "A woman must continually watch herself. She is almost continually accompanied by her own image of herself. . . . From earliest childhood she has been taught and persuaded to survey herself continually."[61] For Berger, the classic male/female binary—"*men act* and *women appear*"—has been shaped by the tradition of European painting, albeit he also acknowledges that "today the attitudes and values which informed that tradition are expressed through other more widely diffused media—advertising, journalism, television."[62] To this list, *Look at Me* adds the technologies of internet and social media, which update but do not alter the classic gender binary. For women, this socially produced division in the self destabilizes the integrity assumed by the traditional notion of sincerity, in which a coherent inner feeling is avowed to the outside world.

Shadows and Signs

Charlotte finds an alternative route to sincerity, as I noted above, through the visual realm, and particularly through what she calls "the shadow self," a gothic-inspired trope that connects the protagonist's ambiguous visibility to an equally ambiguous capacity to see. Charlotte claims to be able to see shadow selves "by looking at people when they thought they couldn't be seen—when they hadn't arranged themselves for anyone" (42). Yet it is never clear whether the reader should take this claim literally or metaphorically. On the one hand, the shadow self seems to be objectively visible as "that caricature that clings to each of us, revealing itself in odd moments when we laugh or fall still, staring brazenly from certain photographs" (34).

On the other, seeing shadow selves requires a subjective power apparently available to Charlotte alone: "After the accident, I had lost the power to see people's shadow selves, but as my vision improved, and as the fog burned off whichever cerebral lobe I required for this visual archeology, the shadows had slowly been returning" (34). Intriguingly, this power—so often used by Charlotte to assess the sincerity of men—arises initially from her own act of insincerity, after she cheats on her beloved boyfriend Hansen while on a modeling trip to Paris. "He would lie in bed watching me for whole minutes," she reflects on her final days with Hansen, when her infidelity still remained secret. "I would look back into his eyes and wonder, What does he see? How can he not see the truth? Where is it hidden? It made me ask, when I looked at other people, what possible selves they were hiding behind the strange rubber masks of their faces" (83).

To truly see, in *Look at Me*, means to see shadows, the realities obscured by surface images such as those in the glossy fashion magazines that so beguiled Phoebe in *The Invisible Circus*. Indeed, shadow selves are particularly prevalent in the fashion world through which Charlotte moves, "where beauty, the best disguise of all, was so commonplace" (34). But this ability to see shadows also connects to the wider gothic project of Egan's novel, its attempt to gain access to a history that has been repressed by the gleaming surfaces of postmodern society. Early in the novel, Charlotte and her fashion agent Oscar walk out onto the New York streets after meeting for the first time since Charlotte's surgery. In response to a wry joke by Oscar, Charlotte recalls that she

> laughed, my head back, so that suddenly I was looking above the buildings, up at the winter sky. And then I saw the sign. It snagged my gaze and held it, an old advertisement painted on the side of a brick building. Griffin's Shears, it read. The paint was faded but still legible, a faint chalky blue, and beside the words I made out the silhouette of a pair of scissors. . . .
> Oscar looked up and down, then swiveled his head. "What?"
> "That old ad! Griffin's Shears."
> Oscar looked at me.
> "It's like a ghost," I said.
> We stood there, looking at the ad. I felt moved by it in some way I couldn't explain. It reminded me of Rockford, of its factories and smokestacks and industry. A glimpse of New York's shadow face. (38)

The visual advertisement is the postmodern symbol *par excellence*, usually connoting, for Jameson, Baudrillard, and others, a free-floating, intensifying, seductive quality. Such a sign can sometimes take on a religious or pseudo-religious aura—as for example does the billboard at the finale of DeLillo's *Underworld* (1997)—but although it might (falsely) promise transcendence, what the sign is usually taken to deny is any kind of coherent historicizing impulse. Egan is obviously engaging with these postmodern ideas and discourses, but with a subtle difference. Here the sign suggests to Charlotte not a depthless simulacrum but the ghost of an identifiable history, specifically the faded industrialism of her hometown of Rockford, which we are told elsewhere remains known for the production of manufacturing tools, "for dull, invisible things that no one in the world would ever know or care about" (10). The material reality of these tools, represented in the old sign with uncommon directness by the ghostly image of the shears, is here glimpsed by Charlotte as the "shadow face" of postmodern New York, a reality metonymically connoted by the image rather than simply replaced by it in a process of metaphorical transfer. In a world obsessed with image over reality, and with lying over truth, these "shadow selves," whether at the level of the person, the sign, or the city, offer Charlotte the comfort of accessing something authentic, a sincere reality that is not being simulated.

And yet, just as the shadow selves of others are identified solely through Charlotte's potentially unreliable first-person narration, it remains unclear in the quoted passage whether Charlotte really is seeing the image of Griffin's Shears on a New York wall, or, more accurately, whether the image really exists to be seen. It is notably uncertain, for instance, whether Oscar also sees the sign—he looks up and down, and then at Charlotte, but his silence does not confirm whether or not he shares her vision. This uncertainty also marks a similar passage from a little later, when Charlotte, now on her own, sees another of these signs, this time for Hollander Ladies Underwear:

> It's a sign, I thought, the wind gulping my laughter. A sign in the form of a sign.
> At the corner of Sixth Avenue and Twenty-eighth Street I stopped and turned slowly around. They were everywhere—signs and the possibility of signs, many faded to translucence, as if I'd gained some new power that allowed me, finally, to see them. "Harris Suspenders Garters Belts." "Maid-Rite

Dress Co."; mementos of the gritty industrialism I'd come to New York to escape. But today the signs looked honest, legible in a way that the negligéed models I'd seen this morning in *Vogue*, prone in a parking lot surrounded by broken glass, would never be. (71)

On this occasion the change is more firmly located not in the object of Charlotte's gaze—the built environment of New York—but in Charlotte's own subjectivity: "as if I'd gained some new power that allowed me, finally, to see them." Charlotte feels empowered by interpreting her vision as "a sign in the form of a sign," thereby turning that vision into something other than a postmodern in-joke. The suggestion in Egan's passage is that seeing "signs and the possibility of signs," and connecting them to historical referents, to the depth they might connote, involves an ability to see the world as characterized less by the loss of history than by its suppression, its retreat to the status of a haunting that can return. Yet the ambiguous existence of these images means that it remains significantly uncertain whether reality in these scenes exists primarily on the side of the subject or on the side of the object, the historical mark on the wall.[63]

This is where the titular appeal/demand of the novel, "look at me," shades into its other key refrain, "we are what we see." This latter phrase is associated with a character who appears predominantly in the third-person strand of *Look at Me*, the academic historian Moose Metcalf. Moose's award-winning PhD dissertation at Yale was entitled *Bathe the World in Light: How the Dissemination of Clear Glass Altered Human Perception*, and his interest in the topic is explained as follows:

> It transfixed Moose to imagine those early years of quickening sight made possible by the proliferation of clear glass (perfected in Murano, circa 1300)—mirrors, spectacles, windows—light everywhere so suddenly, showing up the dirt and dust and crud that had gone unremarked for centuries. But surely the most shocking revelation had been people's own physicality, their outward selves blinking strangely back at them from mirrors—*this is what I look like; this is what other people see when they look at me*—Lacan's mirror phase wrought large upon whole villages, whole cultures! And yet, as was the case with nearly every phenomenon Moose observed (his own life foremost), a second transformation followed the first and reversed nearly all

> of its gains, for now the world's blindness exceeded that of medieval times before clear glass, except that the present blindness came from *too much sight*, appearances disjoined from anything real, afloat upon nothing, in the service of nothing, cut off from every source of blood and life. (109)

We travel, in this Foucauldian reading of history, from the medieval to the postmodern, from visual ignorance to the birth of modern self-consciousness to its overbearing quality in the present day. Even Lacan's mirror stage—posited by psychoanalysis as a universal experience in infancy—is historicized, presented as originating in historical advances in the technology of looking. And here again, as in the passages involving Charlotte, a paradoxical blindness has resulted from the suppression of shadows brought about by the dream of visual perfection in the contemporary age. The dishonesty Charlotte sees in the negligéed *Vogue* models—the way their metaphoric relation to beauty replaces the more grounded metonymy of the ugly sign—is repeated here in Moose's denunciation of the postmodern image disjoined from its referent and its history, "cut off from every source of blood and life."

As with the ambiguities surrounding Charlotte's first-person testimony, however, the parenthetical reference in this passage to Moose's view of his own life hints at doubts about the objective reliability of his account. Early in *Look at Me* we learn that in his twenties Moose had an epiphanic vision that he believes revealed the objective truth of the present age to him, derailing in the process his promising academic career. The content of this vision is withheld from the reader until a moment late in the novel when Moose returns to the vision's original site, a hill overlooking a motorway interchange:

> The answer lay in the vision itself: a different man than Moose was the one who thrived in this new world, a sociopath who made himself anew each afternoon, for whom lying was merely persuasion. More and more they ruled the world, these quicksilver creatures, minotaurs who weren't the products of birth or history, nature or nurture, but assembled for the eye from prototypes; who bore the same relationship to human beings as machine-made clothing did to something hand-stitched. A world remade by circuitry was a world without history or context or meaning, and because we are what we see, *we are what we see*, such a world was certainly heading toward death. (390)

Moose's account of the insincere man of the postmodern era, the "sociopath who made himself anew each afternoon," recalls no literary figure so much as Patrick Bateman, the protagonist of *American Psycho*. Bret Easton Ellis's novel, published in 1991, is one of the latest American novels that could be considered classically postmodern, reminiscent of the fiction of the early postmodernist John Hawkes in the blankness of its parody, the lack of ethical distance that it offers to its reader. Moose, by contrast with Bateman, is a character whose self-conscious doubt encourages empathy in the reader, a character who engages with his own postmodernity and strains to find a sincere way beyond its limits.[64]

As with Charlotte, however, this effort to see sincerely is haunted by the threat to metonymy by metaphor:

> What proof did Moose have that his vision was not, itself, just a metaphor? His mind wheezed like a bellows as he attempted to grasp the implications of this query: that the revelation he'd devoted his life to understanding might not exist in itself, might be a metaphor for something within Moose—a mistake, a mutation, a disorder of the brain. (395)

The inability to know the objective truth of one's vision and express it sincerely is connected here to the prevalence of metaphor, that defining element of literary language and literary fiction. And with fiction re-introduced into our discussion, it is with an eye to resolving its connection to femininity and sincerity that I turn in my final section to the conclusion of Charlotte's story, which is also the conclusion of Egan's novel.

Afterlives of Sincerity

Part Three of *Look at Me*, which takes up less than five pages of a novel of more than four hundred, is titled "Afterlife." It opens with a sentence that foregrounds lifestyle, branding, mediation, and audience, as well as their disavowal: "That woman entertaining guests on her East River balcony in early summer, mixing rum drinks in such a way that the Bacardi and Coca-Cola labels blink at the viewer haphazardly in the dusty golden light—she isn't me" (411). At the foot of the page, following an exhausting (though probably not exhaustive) list of sixty-two sponsors of Charlotte Swenson, most of them well-known consumer brands including Doritos, Calvin Klein, Kodak, and K-Y Jelly, the disavowal is repeated:

> That woman whose veins and stomach and intestines have opened their slippery corridors to small exploratory cameras; whose heart, with its yawning, shaggy caverns, is more recognizable to a majority of Americans (according to one recent study) than their spouses' hands; the first woman in history to both conceive and deliver a child on-line, before an international audience more than double the size of those assembled for the finales of *Cheers* and *Seinfeld* combined—she isn't me.
>
> I swear. (411)

What the reader soon comes to understand is that the colonization of the private Charlotte Swenson by the public persona, a colonization first threatened by the packaging of Charlotte's "real" experience for online consumption (and symbolized by the encroachment of third-person typeface into her narration), is now a completed fact. Nevertheless, in these closing pages of *Look at Me*, when the public Charlotte has become the protagonist of webcams, TV series, movies, chat shows, video games, books, photo shoots, and even an academic symposium—"The Semiotics of Physiognomy in Post-Deconstructive Visual Discourse" (412)—Egan holds out the possibility of a residual form of sincerity that resists the mediated world of public consumption, albeit a sincerity rather fragilely and dubiously figured in the isolated performative, "I swear."

These final pages of *Look at Me* depict a neoliberal dystopia, a near-future world in which the subject as human capital is entirely on display and on sale. It is also a highly gendered vision, in which Charlotte's on-screen conception and birthing of a child are only the most extreme manifestations of an overwhelming media focus on her face, body, relationships, and consumption patterns. "Could it be that neoliberalism is always already gendered, and that women are constructed as its ideal subjects?" asks Rosalind Gill in an influential article on postfeminist media culture.[65] Reading neoliberal capitalism through a Foucauldian lens, as characterized by self-surveillance and self-branding in a culture where everything can and will be commodified, Gill notes a high level of convergence "between the autonomous postfeminist subject and the psychological subject demanded by neoliberalism."[66] The public Charlotte is a paradigm of this postfeminist subject, combining in one person the various elements—"lifecaster," "voyeurtainment" entrepreneur, social media celebrity—that Sarah Banet-Weiser has anatomized in the branded postfeminist self.[67] Indeed, Charlotte Swenson has become such a perfect synecdoche for neoliberal culture and postfeminism that her agent Oscar's gothic-inflected words from early in the novel ring newly accurate by its end: "It's truly uncanny; if you didn't exist they would have to invent you" (72).[68]

In *Desire and Domestic Fiction*, her classic text of literary feminism, Nancy Armstrong revises Watt's "rise of the novel" thesis (as well as Davis's revisionist argument about the novel's emergence from a "news/novels discourse") by highlighting the importance of marriage manuals to early novelists in England, most of whom were not men but women. This analysis leads Armstrong to the provocative and much-cited claim that "the modern individual was first and foremost a woman."[69] The "Afterlife" section of *Look at Me* makes an implicit claim along similar lines, that the subject of literary New Sincerity is first and foremost a woman.[70] Confronting her protagonist with the full glare of media objectification and capitalist commodification, Egan constitutes the New Sincerity subject by interrogating and rejecting the move by which, in Gill's words, "the female body in postfeminist media culture is constructed as a window to the individual's interior life."[71] The narrator of "Afterlife" refuses to connect the media visibility of Charlotte Swenson with the narrator's own interior life, and indeed has attempted to keep that interiority private, "hoarding my occasional dreams and what few memories she hadn't already plundered, camouflaging my hopes and future aspirations in a palette of utter blandness lest they be caught in the restless beam of her overhead camera and broadcast to the world" (413). "She isn't me" and "I swear," phrases that disavow public image and affirm private integrity, seem to indicate the residual existence of an authentic and sincere self, a "real Charlotte" under all the media layers.

Yet there is a final twist: the terms of her contract with the "Ordinary People" website—excerpted at length on the penultimate page of the novel, in a final burst of alternative typeface—allow the narrator to complete a "Transfer of Identity" for a negotiated price: "I sold Charlotte Swenson for a sum that will keep myself and two or three others comfortable for the rest of our lives, although not (I'm told) for nearly what she was worth" (414). Even in refusing to privately affirm her public image and postfeminist brand, Charlotte benefits financially from the terms of the contract, while—not insignificantly—her reaffirmation of a residual sincerity morphs into its own kind of literary brand, one in which the novel's reader can invest. Egan's protagonist might well be attempting to challenge what Brooke Erin Duffy and Emily Hund have called "the post-feminist ideal of individual success obtained through inner self-discovery," but her author nevertheless allows Charlotte to have her sincerity and eat it too, eschewing any conclusive rejection of the cultural ideal that "making money could be just a bonus added to one's natural expression of self."[72]

As Michael Szalay has pointed out, this culminating gesture in *Look at Me* can be read allegorically in relation to Egan's own position in a contemporary literary marketplace transformed by the rise of huge transnational and transmedia conglomerates. Riffing on Walter Benjamin's "The Author as Producer," Szalay claims that for Egan and her generation, "the media corporation oversees 'a mighty recasting of literary forms' that collapses 'the distinction between author and reader' to reflect what these writers take to be a more general collapse between consumers and producers."[73] The leveling of the author-reader relationship that we have seen modeled in the literary New Sincerity of Wallace and Eggers—where neoliberal self-interest is deliberately unsettled by opening the text to the judgment of the reader as other—is here reframed by Szalay as a self-serving response to the shifting industrial relationship between producers and consumers. On this reading, moreover, the particular aesthetic model to which these authors look for inspiration in responding to this shift is the contemporary genre of "quality television," wherein the "author as executive producer" can function as both a key brand and a kind of middle manager in the production process, with all the contradictions this entails: "[the author] provides the template that coordinates otherwise far-flung media. Real agency and control nevertheless elude her. With her managerial responsibilities comes the corresponding sense that she is a conduit or channel, her body a vessel rather than a point of origin" (257).

With Charlotte Swenson's body acting as a conduit for media and commercial forces beyond her control, it is certainly possible to see her fate in the light of Szalay's analysis, and to see the implications for her author too. It then becomes possible to read a kind of authorial self-affirmation into the conclusion of *Look at Me*, as Szalay does when he notes of the multiple versions and sources for Charlotte's story: "What might otherwise seem a broadly postmodernist multiplication of authors takes on a more industrially pointed cast: Charlotte can sell her life Identity Rights, finally, because her branded persona no longer needs her attached to it" (268). With television and branding providing the new paradigms for literary production, Egan's representation of real divisions in Charlotte that are obscured by the singularity of the Charlotte Swenson brand becomes, for Szalay, less a lament by the author about the divisions in her own literary voice than an embrace of those divisions as a selling point of her own brand: "the 'death of the author' is less a theoretical fact than an industrially propitious one" (272).

The question framed by this critical reading is what it means to write from within these new material conditions of production. Does a novelist's apparent complicity with the neoliberal media ecology that publishes and promotes her work constitute a mode of selling out or a form of immanent critique? Here it is relevant to note Szalay's tendency to read backward from the importance of "quality television" for Egan's breakthrough novel *A Visit from the Goon Squad*—which the author has expressly acknowledged was inspired by HBO's *The Sopranos* (1999–2007)—to make similar claims about the earlier *Look at Me*. This despite the fact that all references to TV in Egan's second novel—from the explicit mentions of *Unsolved Mysteries* and *The Making of the Making of*, to the more buried allusions to *Matlock* and various other popular detective shows—make very little claim for the quality of such television or its potential as a model for literary quality. Television seems in the earlier novel less an inspiration than a threat, aligned with the pulpy ghostwriting by Irene that imperils Charlotte's ability to process her own experience in anything other than generic terms.

This sense of genre as threat can help us to add precision to the historical trajectory of literary aesthetics traced across *New Sincerity*. As I have argued in the present chapter, *The Invisible Circus* should be read as a realist Bildungsroman with postmodern inflections and *Look at Me* as an archetypal New Sincerity novel published at the high point of that paradigm's literary significance. Egan's later fiction, however, marks a shift away from the unstable balances that characterize New Sincerity—between originality and genericity, between sincerity and performance, between experimentation and communication, between aesthetics and commerce—toward a series of proceeding literary developments. *The Keep* participates prominently in what has been called the "genre turn" in contemporary American fiction, a development from the mid-2000s onward that sees literary authors turn to popular genre forms to articulate contemporary concerns and open up new markets.[74] *A Visit from the Goon Squad* then marks a turn to Szalay's "author as executive producer" model, with quality television now providing a powerful new aesthetic (and financial) inspiration for novelists.[75] Egan's fifth novel, *Manhattan Beach* (2017), seems to bring things full circle, re-embracing the literary realism that characterized *The Invisible Circus* but that *Look at Me* had suggested was outmoded and open to commercial manipulation. A historical Bildungsroman set in the Brooklyn Navy Yard during World War II, featuring another Irish-sounding authorial surrogate named Anna Kerrigan, *Manhattan Beach* offers the pleasures of realism alongside the unmarked deployment of genre tropes, such as the sentimental depiction of Anna's disabled sister in the early parts of the novel and the seafaring adventures of her father in the later parts.

Look at Me belongs to an earlier cultural moment than these novels, a moment when the full literary embrace of genre forms and televisual models was not yet a done deal. While the concern with sincerity does persist in the later works, the problems that sincerity presents to literary form are no longer so central. If in *Goon Squad*, as Szalay suggests, "Egan struggles to resolve contradictions inherent in the opportunities now afforded novelists by the rise of a newly prestigious and ostensibly literary television format" (258), I would argue that the contradictions in *Look at Me* have less to do with television in particular and more to do with a broader neoliberal culture comprised of material and ideological components that bear upon the status and possibility of sincerity. Among these components is postfeminist media culture—for which, as Gill notes, "irony has become a way of 'having it both ways,' of expressing sexist, homophobic or otherwise unpalatable sentiments in an ironized form, while claiming this was not actually 'meant.'"[76] The critique of irony underpinning literary New Sincerity thus centrally contributes to the feminist critique that Egan pursues in *Look at Me*. As we have seen, this feminist critique is also a critique of the politics of visibility in a culture where reality and fiction have become visually indistinguishable.[77] In such a culture, where the uses of fiction are tied in with contemporary political economy and specifically with platform capitalism, visibility becomes both increasingly important and increasingly problematic. "In a media context," Banet-Weiser observes, "in which most circuits of visibility are driven by profit, competition and consumers, simply *becoming* visible does not guarantee that identity categories will somehow be transformed, or will deeply challenge hegemonic power relations."[78]

So it is that visibility is finally rejected in *Look at Me* in favor of language, embodied experience, and the voice, all reclaimed in its conclusion as potential markers of sincerity. Despite Charlotte and Moose's earlier critiques of metaphor, on the novel's final page we are presented with an elaborate metaphorical language that denigrates the visual realm as claustrophobic and constricting. "As for myself, I'd rather not say very much," the narrator tells us:

> When I breathe, the air feels good in my chest. And when I think of the mirrored room, as of course I still do, I understand now that it's empty, filled with chimeras like Charlotte Swenson—the hard, beautiful seashells left behind long after the living creatures within have struggled free and swum away. Or died. Life can't be sustained under the pressure of so many eyes. Even as we try to reveal the mystery of ourselves, to catch it unawares, expose its pulse and flinch and peristalsis, the truth has slipped away, burrowed further inside a dark, coiled privacy that replenishes itself like blood. It cannot be seen, much as one might wish to show it. It dies the instant it is touched by light. (415)

The metaphors here connect the organic body—the chest, the pulse, the blood—with the world of liquid nature: seashells, air, swimming, peristalsis. Physical, bodily, natural processes are emphasized; the previous privilege afforded to sight—with cameras even within Charlotte's own body—is negated. The tone is poetic and unironic: it aims for beauty alongside the "congruence between avowal and actual feeling" that marks sincerity in its traditional sense.

When the final lines of the novel move to reclaim the voice, however, a nagging division remains:

> Once or twice a year I still call my old voice mail, just to see if the outgoing message is the one I recorded myself. My hand shakes as I dial the phone, and I wonder who will answer.
>
> "Hi, it's me," comes her childish, cigarette voice from the digital void. "Leave a message, but keep it short."
>
> "Hello," I say. "It's me." (415)

The brevity and directness of these closing words stand in contrast to almost everything that preceded them. We have moved in *Look at Me* through layers of irony and commerce and image—even through different printed fonts—only to arrive at a moment of apparently simple dialogue. Of course, as was the case with the closing passage of Wallace's inaugurating New Sincerity novella, *Westward*, the underpinning complexities have not in fact diminished: this is a fictional narrator, whose divisions have been exposed throughout the novel, speaking through "the digital void" to the recording of her own voice, attached to an identity she has sold and now disowns. Moreover, this is a female narrator, faced with an entire cultural history that has denied sincerity to the female subject and the woman's voice and has enforced division in that subjectivity and voice, in a manner that goes far beyond their male counterparts. The difference between the claustrophobic quietness of Charlotte's ending and the explosive aggression of Dave's monologue at the finale of *A Heartbreaking Work* is telling in this regard: the archetypal male confidence that allows Dave to demand (however tongue in cheek) to be seen as the genius of his book's title has its counterpart in the title of *Look at Me*, with its demand that Charlotte should be looked at, but now *how* she should be seen.

Nevertheless, as we saw not only with Eggers's Dave but also with *Infinite Jest*'s alcoholics before him, the key gesture of literary New Sincerity is to turn the apparent weakness of self-division into an opening to the other. In the ending of *Look at Me*, therefore, self-division is reframed as the intimacy of self-dialogue, performed through a second-person address that invokes intimacy between the two Charlottes and simultaneously between the novel's author and its reader. This is the central and repeated gesture of literary New Sincerity, the culminating moment when the world drops away, and the intimacy of the transcribed voice speaking to the reader is all that remains. Whether this gesture marks a successful immanent critique of neoliberalism's implications for women, or even a successful resolution of the contradictions of fictionality, femininity, and sincerity in *Look at Me*: these are questions left to answer for the reader, the ultimate receptacle of the novel's afterlife.

4 Freedom Struggle, Class Struggle, Sincerity Struggle

Professional-Managerial Consciousness

Early in Colson Whitehead's fourth novel *Sag Harbor* (2009), the narrator Benji Cooper, a privileged black teenager in the mid-1980s, tells the story of how W. E. B. Du Bois entered his life. Rather than encounter the eminent African American sociologist through his writing, perhaps in a classroom or on the bookshelves of a friend or relation, Benji repeatedly hears the man's name on his mother's lips. With evident pride she recounts the rumor that, sometime in the 1950s, Du Bois visited Sag Harbor to eat dinner near the house where Benji's family now spend their summers. Sensing that his mother is referring to a person "who had struggled and suffered for every last comfort I enjoyed," Benji is too embarrassed to admit that he doesn't know who the man is.[1] "What I did know about DuBois," he tells us, "is that he fell into the category of Famous Black People":

> The respectful way my mother pronounced *DuBois* told me that the man had uplifted the race. Years later in college I'd read his most famous essay and be blown away. And I quote: "It is a peculiar sensation, this double consciousness, this sense of always looking at one's self through the eyes of others, of measuring one's soul by the tape of a world that looks on in amused contempt and pity. One ever feels his two-ness,—an American, a Negro; two souls, two thoughts, two unreconciled strivings; two warring ideals in one dark body, whose dogged strength alone keeps it from being torn asunder. The history of the American Negro is the history of this strife,—this longing to attain self-conscious manhood, to merge this double self into a better and truer self." I thought to myself: The guy who wrote that was chowing fried fish behind my house! (18)

The embedded lines from "Of Our Spiritual Strivings," the opening chapter of *The Souls of Black Folk* (1903), are indeed among the most famous ever written by a Famous Black Person. They have been interpreted and reinterpreted again and again by readers, artists, critics, and intellectuals, producing a "respectful" scholarly tradition that has connected Du Bois to figures like Hegel, Emerson, and William James, as well as to prior and later black American and diasporic thinkers. Needless to say, the satirical grace notes that begin and end the passage are Whitehead's own: in Du Bois commentary, phrases like "blown away" are almost as rare as references to the consumption of fried fish in a resort town in the Hamptons.

Having discovered double consciousness, Benji runs with the notion, applying it to the experience of listening to the car radio while his father drives. "It was potholes of double consciousness the whole way," he recalls. "There were only two things he would listen to on the radio: Easy Listening and Afrocentric Talk Radio" (18). Here Du Bois's tragic account of black "twoness"—"an American, a Negro; two souls, two thoughts, two unreconciled strivings"—mutates bathetically into the father's oscillation between radio channels. "Every time Karen Carpenter moved her mouth," Benji remembers of the typical song on the Easy Listening station, "it was like the lid of a sugar bowl tinkling open and closed to expose deep dunes of whiteness. Then the next song would send my father's fingers to the preset stations and we were knee-deep into police brutality, the crummy schools, the mechanistic cruelty of city hall" (19). Through this "pothole of double consciousness" the reader not only gains insight into Benji's father's sensibility, divided between white ease and black oppression; we also catch a glimpse into the growing polarization in African American life during the 1980s, when an upwardly mobile post–Civil Rights middle class—those like Benji's family who could afford a summer home in Sag Harbor—found their social contrast in the so-called underclass, the creation and target of Reagan-era welfare cuts, the War on Drugs, and mass incarceration.

Yet this glimpse of class disparity in *Sag Harbor* remains just that—a glimpse. Though the novel will demonstrate some interest in the attractions and repulsions of "deep dunes of whiteness," and more substantially in the complex negotiations of "real" blackness, we will hear little further about police abuse, educational inequality, or political corruption. Instead, in a series of lightly meandering and loosely connected vignettes set during the summer of 1985—a summer in which the major event seems to be the invention of a new brand of waffle cone—*Sag Harbor* depicts the significant personal freedoms experienced by fifteen-year-old Benji. Describing himself and his friends as "the definition of a paradox: black boys with beach houses" (71), we follow Benji as he manages successfully, in Du Bois's terms, "to be both a Negro and an American, without being cursed and spit upon by his fellows, without having the doors of Opportunity closed roughly in his face."[2]

Fifteen is likewise the age that Colson Whitehead would have been that same summer. Considering that the author has described *Sag Harbor*—currently the only one of his nine novels narrated in the first person—as "autobiographical," it's not hard to imagine Whitehead, the son of entrepreneur parents who owned an executive recruitment firm and a summer house in Sag Harbor, encountering Du Bois's passage during his years at Harvard College in the late 1980s and connecting that reading experience to his own teenage summers.[3] Significantly, the late 1980s was also the time when "Of Our Spiritual Strivings" became canonized as Du Bois's "most famous essay," a stature it had not always held. When Du Bois's early work was initially revived during the 1960s against the background of the Civil Rights and Black Power movements, the third chapter of *The Souls of Black Folk*, which stages a political critique of Booker T. Washington's post-Reconstruction program of "adjustment and submission," was understood to be the center of the book.[4] As Adolph Reed, Jr., points out, no reference to the double-consciousness passage appears in introductions to editions of *Souls* produced in 1961, 1965, and 1968, an absence in keeping with the evidence that "Du Bois dropped the double-consciousness idea early in his career."[5] Across four editions of the book published in 1989 and 1990, by contrast, the passage about double consciousness is treated as central. This newly fashionable quality of the idea underpins a contemporary political and cultural project, Reed argues, to unearth and delineate a tradition of African American thought in which "differentiation, tension, and conflict among black Americans recedes into a dim background."[6] He attributes the prominence of this project to two factors: the self-justificatory aims of the "post-segregation-era black petit bourgeoisie" and the centrality of literary studies to African Americanist scholarship in the period.[7] The first of these developments is attacked by Reed for its "fundamentally conservative and depoliticizing effects on black American intellectual life"; the second for its privileging of "text-based notions of tradition, or canons," which tend to be "idealist and ahistorical."[8]

The implication of Reed's analysis is that any attempt to define and describe a transhistorical tradition of American literary blackness must be inimical to analyses of African American life that pay close attention to class antagonism and inequality. In his much-debated 2011 polemic *What Was African American Literature?*, Kenneth Warren provides further support for this view. Like all modern literatures, Warren argues, African American literature was from its inception "the product of an elite for whom the connection with a broader public was less than given"; the identity of this literature was thus sustained only by the assumption that "the welfare of the race as a whole depends on the success of black writers and those who are depicted in their texts."[9] But while the belief that all black Americans shared a "linked fate" might have held a certain validity during the Jim Crow era—a time when "the black literary voice could count for so much because, in political terms, the voice of black people generally counted for so little"—the idea's survival into the post-segregation period constitutes an ideological mystification of present-day realities.[10] Warren here shares with Reed—along with other scholars including Walter Benn Michaels, Cedric G. Johnson, and the novelist Charles Johnson—a conviction that the ongoing emphasis in African American studies on issues of racial identity, "black exceptionalism," and "the black American narrative" has only served to draw attention away from the signal impact of neoliberal hegemony: a rising wealth gap between rich and poor, both within and beyond racial groups.[11] In this context of widening inequality, continuing to harp on Du Bois's double-consciousness motif is taken by these scholars to speak of nothing more than "the neurasthenia of the black professional-managerial class," in Reed's acid phrase.[12]

Where does Colson Whitehead's fiction sit within this debate about the relative importance of race, class, and the black literary voice in contemporary African American life? In this chapter, I address Whitehead's early fiction—with its distinctive combinations of irony and sincerity, elite art and pop culture, individuality and collectivity, along with its acute analysis of racial capitalism—as a valuable example of how literary New Sincerity has addressed the intersecting subjects of race and class under neoliberal conditions. *Sag Harbor* was Whitehead's fourth novel, and its early scene of racial identification with a historical precursor—in this case Benji with Du Bois—provides a comic recapitulation of the plot of his three preceding novels. Each describes a modern-day African American protagonist discovering a racial forebear whose work bears upon his or her own life, albeit in ambivalent ways. In the case of Lila Mae Watson in *The Intuitionist* (1999), it is the realization that James Fulton, the founder of her sect of Intuitionist elevator inspectors, was a "colored" man passing for white. For J. Sutter, the journalist in *John Henry Days* (2001), it is the recognition that the industrial-era heroism of black folk figure John Henry shadows Sutter's irony-soaked existence in the information age. And for the unnamed "nomenclature consultant" in *Apex Hides the Hurt* (2006), it is the recovery of the views of Abraham Field, a freed slave whose pessimistic take on the human condition has been written out of triumphalist histories of American and African American progress. These novels turn on present-day acts of historical interpretation, in other words, and in each case the contemporary black protagonist is made to confront history in ways that lead to reflection on the relationship between their class position and their racial inheritance.

These scenes of interpretation are likewise scenes of reading, and as such they allegorize the reader's relationship to the novels in which they appear. Although the rapport Whitehead constructs with his reader does not immediately recall the psychologically freighted tug-of-war we have seen in Wallace, Eggers, and (to a lesser extent) Egan, the author nevertheless asks of readers a high degree of critical engagement.[13] In particular, Whitehead's political aesthetic works by "signifying"—to cite a critical term I'll return to—on prior texts and genre conventions, a method that in turn raises intricate questions about the contemporary African American author's relationship to the literary tradition and the literary marketplace. With these questions in mind, Whitehead's fiction has been read in generational terms as contributing to "post-soul," "post-black," and "postrace" aesthetics.[14] Critics have also connected Whitehead's work to Trey Ellis's 1989 manifesto, "The New Black Aesthetic," an essay that Reed and Warren have both heavily criticized.[15] In a more positive recent assessment of Ellis's text, Rolland Murray praises it as "one of the first coherent articulations of a historical transition from the autonomous arts organizations of Black Power nationalists to the corporate-based aesthetics of the 1980s."[16] Murray nevertheless acknowledges the manifesto's limitations, arguing that it "suggestively raises, yet cannot sufficiently address, the historical question of what happens to African American cultural expression once it is no longer an emergent subfield vying for legitimacy and becomes established at the center of the dominant culture."[17]

To the extent that Whitehead's fiction takes up this question of contemporary African American art's accession to mainstream success, we can understand it as displaying a revised form of double consciousness, one shaped not by rejection by the dominant culture but by that culture's recognition and even embrace. The conventional way to read the implications of this form of double consciousness is in terms of the problem of racial authenticity, of striving to embody "real" blackness rather than selling out to (white) commercial norms.[18] In preferring to read the revised double consciousness of Whitehead's writing in terms of literary New Sincerity—and thereby in conversation with the fiction of white generational contemporaries like Wallace, Eggers, and Egan—I do not aim to downplay the author's specific contribution to the traditions of African American writing. On the contrary, I want to draw on Whitehead's highly nuanced engagement with literary blackness to illuminate more sharply and from a different angle the claims about contemporary literature, neoliberalism, and sincerity made over my opening chapters. Specifically, I will explore how the movement of African American art from cultural marginality to commercial centrality over the neoliberal period—at the same time as class divisions within the black community were becoming more evident and intensely felt—raises new problems of complicity and sincerity for black writers, problems that threaten the kind of critical work that black art has traditionally been asked and understood to do.

Critical responses to *Sag Harbor* make these problems and tensions particularly clear. Read as a Bildungsroman, the novel can seem to be doing no more than replacing the famous question that opens *The Souls of Black Folk*—"How does it feel to be a problem?"—with a less obviously urgent contemporary version—"How does it feel to be bourgeois?" For some critics, such an emphasis on "racial individualism" is refreshing;[19] for others, it represents a lamentable capitulation to neoliberal ideals.[20] Read as a novel of manners, by contrast, *Sag Harbor* has seemed to still other critics to be indicting "the monstrous nature of class society and the logic of its reproduction."[21] How to decide among these readings? Whether one reads *Sag Harbor* as a celebration or critique of neoliberal norms and developments seems to come down, in these responses, to the question of how to interpret the novel's "sarcastic, clever voice"—in other words, how to read its irony.[22] Whether the irony is being affirmed as a feature of Benji's own consciousness, or that consciousness is itself being ironized for the particular values it unthinkingly affirms, becomes the test question. Given the first-person frame, however, this question remains difficult to answer when *Sag Harbor* is considered in isolation from Whitehead's other early fiction.

The remainder of this chapter therefore looks to this fiction, focusing in particular on Whitehead's first and third novels. In the next section I read *The Intuitionist* as an exploration of black complicity with, and resistance to, technological and capitalist modernity, and thereby as an allegory of the challenges posed by the African American writer's new mainstream positioning within the neoliberal culture industry. Lila Mae Watson is the first of the highly skilled black professionals that populate Whitehead's early fiction, and her individual success—along with that of her mixed-race mentor James Fulton—invokes debates around racial uplift that also underpin the novel's core metaphors of elevation, verticality, and freefall. The third section continues the focus on the significance of black individual success and its relationship to racial progress by turning to *Apex Hides the Hurt* and examining discourses of human capital in racial capitalism both in and out of that novel. In the fourth section I consider the role played by "freedom" across Whitehead's early fiction, and the ironic rather than sincere ways he tends to invoke the term. Addressing this ironic stance in the context of the importance of freedom as a signifier for black American struggle, particularly during the Civil Rights era, I ask why Whitehead might want to resist its lure. The final section returns to the theme of uplift, and the role of the black writer, in the context of growing African American political and economic power—black faces in high places—across the post–Civil Rights and neoliberal decades, culminating in the "postracial" presidency of Barack Obama.

Uplifting the Race

From the moment of its publication, *The Intuitionist*—a noir-inflected anti-detective story with a quixotic interest in philosophies of elevator inspection—was praised for its innovative combination of irony and sincerity. "Whitehead doesn't just travel back and forth between irony and sincerity, between the naturalistic novel of race and the imaginative novel of ideas," wrote one reviewer, "he simply occupies all territories at the same time."[23] "Poised between irony and sincerity," another critic remarked years later in an almost identical formulation, "the metaphor of vertical transport drives the narrative up and down between the narratival levels of the naturalistic protest novel of race and the metafictional postmodern imaginative novel of ideas."[24]

That critics have found the irony–sincerity dialectic in *The Intuitionist* worthy of repeated comment is notable. But it is also somewhat surprising, since African American literature would seem always to be "poised between irony and sincerity," given its defining propensity for what Henry Louis Gates, Jr., following Mikhail Bakhtin, has termed "double-voiced discourse." In black writing, on Gates's influential account, sincerity must always work its way through irony, just as for Bakhtin a speech act's "hidden polemic" at the level of the referent emerges through "parodic narration" at the level of the sign.[25] "Much of the Afro-American literary tradition," Gates explains, "can be read as successive attempts to create a new narrative space for representing the recurring referent of Afro-American literature, the so-called Black Experience."[26] This sincere attempt to update the narrative of "Black Experience" proceeds via ironic relation to older narratives. African American texts thus adopt a "signifying" relationship to precursor texts—both black and non-black—creating meaning via a process of revision.

The Intuitionist signifies on prior texts in a classically double-voiced manner. The novel begins with Lila Mae Watson inspecting an elevator at 125 Walker, an address that signifies on Alice Walker, author of *The Color Purple* (1982), and on Toni Morrison, whose *Beloved* (1987) opens in a "spiteful" house numbered 124.[27] Morrison's *The Bluest Eye* (1970) and *Jazz* (1992) provide further reference points for *The Intuitionist*'s representations of color and urban imagery, while allusions to Ralph Ellison's *Invisible Man* (1952) are laced throughout the novel, informing its critique of optical sight as "white people's reality" and "the business of Empiricism."[28] The tradition of "passing" novels—from James Weldon Johnson's *Autobiography of an Ex-Colored Man* (1912) and Nella Larsen's *Passing* (1929) forward—offers another important precursor genre, with Larsen's scenes of blacks in high buildings resonating particularly strongly with Whitehead's treatment of racial uplift in an urban cityscape that resembles midcentury New York.[29] An even earlier tradition invoked in *The Intuitionist* is the slave narrative. The "noble struggle" of Fanny Briggs, an enslaved person who taught herself to read, is fundamental to Lila Mae's self-understanding (12); meanwhile the slave narrative origins of what Gates calls "the trope of the Talking Book" inform Lila Mae's re-reading of James Fulton's work, as she learns to make "the white written text speak with a black voice."[30] Another important forerunner is once again Du Bois: the novel's repeated mantra, "*There is another world beyond this one*" (63, 134, 240), recalls Du Bois's famous image of the veil that separates the white and black worlds, while the notion of double consciousness underpins Lila Mae's application of the principles of what Stephen Soitos has termed "double-consciousness detection."[31] Alongside these black precursors, *The Intuitionist* also signifies on canonical texts by white American postmodernists including Thomas Pynchon, Robert Coover, Paul Auster, and Don DeLillo.[32] The urban setting and noir stylings of the novel, as well as its depiction of the taciturn Lila Mae Watson and her search for a McGuffin-style "black box," recall the earlier hardboiled detective fiction of Raymond Chandler and Dashiell Hammett.

Arguably the most important literary precursor for *The Intuitionist* is Ishmael Reed. In early interviews, Whitehead hails Reed as a key postmodern forebear, and his debut novel signifies continually on Reed's anti-detective fiction, *Mumbo Jumbo* (1972).[33] In the opening scene the white building superintendent of 125 Walker calls Lila Mae a "voodoo inspector" and "witch doctor" (7) when he observes the Intuitionist methodology through which she communes with the elevator in order to inhabit its perspective, aiming to "separate the elevator from elevatorness" (62). The Empiricist chair of the Elevator Inspectors Guild, Frank Chancre, likewise refers to Intuitionism as "heretical and downright voodoo," and we learn of "some nicknames Empiricists have for their renegade colleagues: swamis, voodoo men, juju heads, witchdoctors, Harry Houdinis. All terms belonging to the nomenclature of dark exotica, the sinister foreign" (26, 57–58). As well as associating Intuitionism with the racialized other, these epithets recall the "Neo-HooDoo" philosophy (which "believes that every man is an artist and every artist a priest") that underpins Reed's professed aesthetic.[34] "Jes Grew," the song-and-dance epidemic that moves through the United States in *Mumbo Jumbo* with the encouragement of its HooDoo-practicing protagonist PaPa LaBas, contains similar radical potential to the black box that Intuitionism founder James Fulton was apparently developing in order to bring about the "second elevation" of the modern city (61). Reed wanted this radical potential to be embodied in the aesthetic of *Mumbo Jumbo*, so that the novel provides, in the words of one admirer, "an ingenious dissertation on the nature of Afro-American art, a dissertation with a program for the revival of that art."[35]

Like the radical texts at their center that get divided into parts and dispersed through the mail, both *Mumbo Jumbo* and *The Intuitionist* move through a series of narrative fragments that ask readers gradually to piece together the two novels' respective worlds. Though marked by present-day racial and aesthetic concerns, those worlds exist in the past—in Reed, the Harlem of the 1920s; in Whitehead, "a vaguely post-Civil Rights era metropolis with distinctly pre-Civil Rights era racist sensibilities."[36] Noting the reference to skyscrapers in the final line of *Mumbo Jumbo*, one critic observes that "Whitehead literally picks up where Reed ends."[37] Whitehead's novel is, nevertheless, a critical revision of Reed's, rather than an unwavering tribute. This fact becomes particularly clear when one considers the character of Mr. Reed, a white spokesman and activist for Intuitionism who enters the novel when he appears at Lila Mae's apartment to rescue her from intruders. We later discover, however, that he has in fact staged the intrusion, and that although he represents Intuitionism, he is also acting on behalf of the Arbo elevator company, one of the two international corporations in pursuit of the blueprint for Fulton's black box.

Whitehead here signifies on Ishmael Reed as simultaneously an intuitive aesthetic visionary and a proponent of capitalist enterprise. The former view has been the one emphasized in Reed scholarship, most notably in Gates's account of *Mumbo Jumbo* as the postmodern apex of the signifying tradition in black writing.[38] The latter view has emerged more recently in a revisionist reading of Reed as a "proto-neoliberal."[39] Excavating the story of Reed's literary and cultural entrepreneurship in the 1970s, Nicholas Donofrio outlines the writer's support for "black capitalism," the popular philosophy of the time that Richard Nixon described as a bridge to "black pride, black jobs, black opportunity, and yes, black power."[40] In Reed's view, any answer to the question we saw framed by Trey Ellis's "New Black Aesthetic"—what happens to African American artistic expression when it moves from margin to mainstream?—was inseparable from the issue of black ownership of that artistic expression. But rather than lead Reed to a radical critique of the capitalist system that had denied ownership to blacks (and that indeed had permitted blacks to be owned as property), the author's "studies of voodoo and hoodoo" led him instead to reject "anti-business psychology" as "slave psychology" and to embrace "free enterprise's liberatory potential."[41] Interpreting Reed's early novels as aesthetic allegories of his various publishing ventures in the 1970s, Donofrio argues that the "commercial epiphanies" of Reed's Neo-HooDooism can make even the battle between good and evil in *Mumbo Jumbo* read like "an encounter between two competing businesses with widely divergent corporate cultures."[42] The historical irony is that under neoliberalism, which began its rise to hegemony in the same decade that saw the flowering of his aesthetic and entrepreneurial work, Reed's preferred notion of "free enterprise"—with its focus on independent production—would be transformed into the "free market," which emphasized consumption and sidelined the consideration of questions around ownership. "Reed's inveterate antiauthoritarianism, coupled with his cheerleading for businesses and cultural diversity," Donofrio concludes, "was largely compatible with the antistate, promarket neoliberal policies that would soon restructure the culture industries, along with many other areas of American life."[43]

Reed's support for "black capitalism" contrasts with Whitehead's focus on what has come to be termed "racial capitalism."[44] One site of difference is their respective attitudes toward technology: where Reed's multicultural capitalist vision displays "profound techno-utopian leanings," *The Intuitionist*—a novel whose science fictional bearing might initially seem to offer "a way of extending rather than recoiling from the project of urban modernity"—does much to question such utopianism.[45] For instance, in a scene Whitehead includes from the 1853 Exhibition of the Industry of All Nations, the vice president of the United States makes a speech proclaiming that the technology on display "cannot fail to soften, if not eradicate altogether, the prejudices and animosities which have so long retarded the happiness of nations" (80). This paean to "the realization of the unity of mankind" through "the stimulus of competition and capital" (80, 81) is offered, one critic points out, "three years after the reinstitution of the Fugitive Slave Law and four years before the US Supreme Court's decision in *Dred Scott v. Sanford*."[46] Such a juxtaposition not only emphasizes the lack of alignment between technological progress and social equality; it also alludes to the ways that capitalism can (at best) operate by ignoring racism and (at worst) mobilize it in the service of accumulation.

Through a series of revelations across its second half, *The Intuitionist* draws continual attention to the way capital accumulation pervades all the explanations—racism, philosophy, politics—that Lila Mae looks to as a solution to the novel's central conundrum: why the elevator in the Fanny Briggs Memorial Building fell. Lila Mae was the last person to inspect the elevator before the accident, and she initially suspects that she has been set up to take the blame as part of an electoral fight between Empiricists and Intuitionists for control of the Elevator Inspectors Guild. The racial (and gender) stereotypes associated with the opposition between Empiricism and Intuitionism mean that Lila Mae's status as the only black female elevator inspector in the city becomes a factor in the political battle, with Frank Chancre giving speeches full of conservative dog whistles following the Fanny Briggs accident and at the guild banquet later in the novel. When Lila Mae discovers that James Fulton, father of Intuitionism, passed as white, she has even more reason to believe that race will be the key to solving the mystery. But she is disabused of this belief by Raymond Coombs, a black operative for Arbo who had posed as a comrade (and potential love interest) for Lila Mae in an attempt to get hold of Fulton's blueprint for the black box. "'The rank and file in the industry won't believe [that Fulton was black],'" he tells her, "'and those who know care more about his last inventions. His color doesn't matter once it gets to that level. The level of commerce'" (250). The importance placed by Lila Mae on the opposition between Empiricism and Intuitionism is likewise challenged by the muckraking journalist Ben Urich. "'Did you think this was all about philosophy?'" Urich asks her.

> "Who's the better man—Intuitionism or Empiricism? No one really gives a crap about that. Arbo and United are the guys who make the things. That's what really matters. The whole world wants to get vertical, and they're the guys that get them there. If you pay the fare." (208)

In racial capitalism, black people may have built the elevators and even designed them, but they rarely get to ride them. Corporations, on the other hand, become "the guys" who earn the profit from taking those customers who can pay to a higher floor.

Whitehead's emphasis on the pervasive workings of racial capitalism underpins the novel's signifying on the notion of racial uplift. Emerging after the collapse of Reconstruction, racial uplift was the ideology through which, as Kevin Gaines writes, "elite blacks sought the cooperation of white political and business elites in the pursuit of race progress."[47] Where antebellum and early post-emancipation notions of uplift had signaled "collective social aspiration, advancement, and struggle," for the post-Reconstruction black elites, "uplift came to mean an emphasis on self-help, racial solidarity, temperance, thrift, chastity, social purity, patriarchal authority, and the accumulation of wealth."[48] This is where racial uplift ideology intersects with Du Bois's notion of double consciousness, with their "unconscious internalized racism" leading these black elites into "repressing anger toward whites" and thereby "leaving a psychic residue of self-doubt and shame."[49] Drawing attention to the "bitter contradiction" between uplift ideals and "the suffocating realities" of the period, Gaines dubs racial uplift ideology "a faulty construction."[50] In its central motif of an elevator in freefall, Whitehead's novel literalizes the faultiness of that construction.

As well as signifying on uplift through its central metaphors of verticality, elevation, and freefall, *The Intuitionist* also does so through its presentation of the bearing, beliefs, and actions of its central character. Lila Mae Watson is not the paradigmatic protagonist we have come to recognize from the literary New Sincerity of Wallace, Eggers, and Egan. Unlike the other-directed protagonists of those texts, anxiously responsive to the cultural norms surrounding them, Lila Mae appears more inner-directed. She takes her lead from the example of her parents (especially her father) while mostly ignoring the influence of her peers.[51] But while her outward bearing aligns her with the archetypal hardboiled detective, her gender means that Lila Mae's bearing also signifies differently, in line with what the historian Darlene Clark Hine has called "dissemblance," her name for "the behavior and attitudes of Black women that created the appearance of openness and disclosure but actually shielded the truth of their inner lives and selves from their oppressors."[52] From the opening scene onward, we see Lila Mae navigating white racism by relying on her inspector's uniform, using this badge of attainment to project an air of quiet confidence. But we also see her—in an unexpected congruence with Egan's fashion model Charlotte—treating her face as a kind of machine for "calibration" when dealing with the world, a "rigid concoction" that "accorded with her own definitions" (57): "Dressed, she's in front of the mirror. Armed. She puts her face on. In her case, not a matter of cosmetics, but will. How to make such a sad face hard? It took practice" (180).

Gaines describes dissemblance as a potential weapon, "the psychic armor enabling the survival of the powerless," but also notes that "this self-protective withholding of one's true feelings from more powerful others might also work too well, sundering African Americans from a history of group oppression and struggle."[53] Lila Mae's character has been interpreted in line with both sides of this dichotomy. Some critics see her individual strength and quiet intelligence as a model for black negotiation of "the machinery of white supremacy," and argue that she "functions as a representative figure, much as the authors of slave narratives typically speak for a collective set of interests."[54] Others see her commitment to completing the final text of her mentor Fulton (himself a figure who left behind familial, racial, and class affiliation in order to advance) as leaving her cut off from other African Americans and her working-class roots, "increasingly isolated from black community, progressively alienated from her own body, and ever more in thrall to the seductive attractions of uplift."[55] Faced with these opposing critical perspectives on Lila Mae, we are back with a version of the problem we encountered in *Sag Harbor*: how to interpret Whitehead's relation to his individual protagonist. But here there are two differences, interconnected but distinguishable: the narration of *The Intuitionist* is third person rather than first person; and Lila Mae's situation—working in isolation as she rewrites and revises past texts—more explicitly allegorizes her author's own.

The third-person narration matters because it inscribes an ironic distance between Lila Mae's self-perception and that of *The Intuitionist*'s narrator. The most dramatic example comes when Lila Mae discovers that Fulton had written the words "*Lila Mae Watson is the one*" in the margin of the notebook for his work-in-progress on the perfect elevator (253). Like the corporations chasing her, Lila Mae assumes that this phrase signals her special status as the inheritor of Fulton's mantel. In fact, as we learn in the novel's penultimate scene when the narrator enters Fulton's perspective for only the second time, the phrase signifies no more than that Lila Mae is the only other person awake when Fulton, working on his manuscript, looks out the window from the library at the Institute of Vertical Transport. This culminating example of narrative irony builds on the novel's more thoroughgoing tonal irony, with the narrative voice oscillating among a number of modes, including ambiguously situated free indirect discourse—"Now we're cooking" (10), "Keep cool, Lila Mae" (16); partially informed speculation—"She may be concerned at this point" (104); and a mode of omniscient insight—"She doesn't know yet" (9); "She tricks herself" (156)—that sometimes shades into outright correction of the protagonist's mistaken beliefs. Critics have grappled with how to describe this unusual narrative voice; in one of the more minimal classifications, Alison Russell calls the narrator "omniscient but reticent."[56] A more fitting phrase might be *flexible and intuitive*, and in this sense it is not a stretch to compare the narrator of *The Intuitionist* to the "neo-manager" in the neoliberal economy, a persona who, "like the artist," is "a creative figure, a person of intuition, invention, contacts, chance encounters, someone who is always on the move, passing from one project to the next, one world to another."[57] If, as Fulton's text tells us, "there is another world beyond this one," then the narrator's intuitive flexibility would seem to make them worthy of our trust as a guide to this other world, even if we are never quite certain where the narrator is speaking from and what their relation to this story really is.

This lack of readerly certainty is important, because by ending with Lila Mae's lonely revising of Fulton's text for the changed world she believes is coming—"She will make the necessary adjustments. It will come. She is never wrong. It's her intuition" (255)—Whitehead figures his own situation as a black writer in the era of neoliberalism. Although Gates doesn't acknowledge it, his theory of black literary signifying depends upon the marginality in American culture of the African American writer, and on their consequent ability to avoid abject complicity with the status quo by ironically subverting dominant linguistic and symbolic norms. But in the transition of black art from cultural margin to commercial center under neoliberalism's "new spirit of capitalism," the black writer's capacity to create new linguistic worlds can no longer be assumed to exist at an autonomous distance from the systems of signification and exchange through which those worlds are consumed. Nor can the writer's intimacy with ongoing collective struggles against racial capitalism be taken as read, given that they are writing from a vantage point underpinned by successful uplift.[58] The final scene of *The Intuitionist* emphasizes this distance between individual writer and collective struggle, as we are twice told that the room in which Lila Mae writes "looks out on a factory" (254, 255). The space most associated with socialist revolution, to be achieved collectively by the proletarian class, is thus contrasted with the technological revolution planned in secret by Lila Mae, who in this moment resembles no figure so much as a Silicon Valley entrepreneur, the heroic individual rewriting past code to shape the future.

Whitehead's ironic experimentation in his early fiction demonstrates his recognition of the challenges facing an African American writer who wants to avoid complicity with a system that uplifts the few—mostly, but not only, the white few—at the expense of the many. In this, at least, he is not alone. As one critic has observed,

> Whitehead joins a cohort of contemporary black writers whose texts also bespeak powerful affinities between the material forces of political economy that are now "making" race in the networked global market, and the textual and social materials they themselves deploy in their task to "make" racial identities within the space of literary culture.[59]

It is this contamination of the "textual and social materials" available to the black novelist by the "material forces of political economy" that raises the problem of authorial sincerity so acutely, given that these material forces are precisely what such a novelist would seek to challenge. In the next two sections I examine Whitehead's reckoning with this problem in more detail by addressing issues of work, education, and human capital in his fiction.

Specimens of Human Capital

Lila Mae's father Marvin Watson had wanted to be an elevator inspector. Taking his degree in engineering at "the colored college downstate," he aimed to move from his southern home to the North, "the big cities he knew were coming, the citadels pushed from the planet's guts like volcanoes and mountains to take the sky." Upon arriving at his interview for the role of inspector, however, he is promptly informed, "We don't accept colored gentlemen." Instead he takes a job in a hometown department store that "needed some colored boys" to operate its elevators, a role he inhabits for the next twenty years (160–161). As this dichotomy between "boys" and "gentlemen" suggests, there is a significant distinction in *The Intuitionist* between the role of elevator operator and elevator inspector. Operating an elevator requires skill and experience—as we see when Marvin tries to explain the technical idiosyncrasies of his elevator to a dismissive white inspector—but it is indisputably a working-class job, with presumably commensurate remuneration. Elevator inspection, on the other hand, is "a government job," and elevator inspectors are "civil-servant to the core," even if they are not so comfortably middle class as to turn their noses up at a $1.25 raise, since "anything that brings their salaries into closer proportion to their contributions to the American good are accepted cheerfully, election-year ploy or no" (13). Just as trying to identify the precise period setting of *The Intuitionist* is beside the point, neither is it important to identify exactly the class stratum into which the role of elevator inspector fits.[60] What is more significant is its public sector character. Lila Mae is an early pioneer in the black accession to government jobs, an area of the US economy in which African Americans would be strongly represented by the beginning of the 1970s.[61] Black Americans were therefore affected disproportionately by the public sector cuts of the 1970s and 1980s, one of many reasons—along with exposure to automation, deindustrialization, declining welfare, and scaled-up policing—why neoliberalism as a phase of capitalism has resulted in unequal racial outcomes among the US population.

If one could not obtain or retain a public sector job during the neoliberal period (and the jobs themselves became relatively worse paid than they had been at the height of the postwar boom), then middle-class status required success in the private sector. One route to such success—suggested by the examples of Ishmael Reed and Whitehead's own parents—was the embrace of entrepreneurship and black capitalism. Another route was to become a professional in one of the many private corporations that sprang up over the period, particularly in the service sector and most notably in the culture industries. The protagonists of Whitehead's second and third novels are professionals of this kind. J. Sutter in *John Henry Days* is a freelance journalist who writes mostly for magazines that resemble *The Village Voice*, where Whitehead was a

TV critic throughout the 1990s. The unnamed protagonist of *Apex Hides the Hurt* works for an advertising firm as a "nomenclature consultant," someone who comes up with names for new consumer products. Whereas in *The Intuitionist* Whitehead had deliberately written a female protagonist so as to avoid the "stock ironic black man character" he had developed in his earlier journalism, his subsequent novels center on exactly this kind of ironic male figure.[62] And as these novels—building on the narrative voice of *The Intuitionist*—make clear, ironic cool is inseparable from maleness and membership of the contemporary black bourgeoisie.

We can investigate the characteristics of this "stock ironic black man character" by looking closely at a passage from early in *Apex Hides the Hurt*. In the midst of undertaking the "one last job" that forms the present action of the novel—the task of renaming a Midwestern town—the nomenclature consultant reflects back on his early days working in advertising. This was the period when he began to discover that his aptitude for naming products could open unexpected doors:

> But the names. After two weeks of listening he was full of them. Every day the door cracked another half inch and he could see beyond the tiny rooms he had stumbled around in his whole life. He pictured it like this: The door opened up on a magnificent and secret landscape. His interior. He clambered over rocks and mountain ranges composed of odd and alien minerals, he stepped around strange flora, saplings that curtsied eccentrically, low shrubs that extended bizarre fronds. This unreckoned land of his possessed colors he had never seen before. Flowers burst petals in arrangements never considered by the natural world, summoned out of dirt like stained glass. These beautiful hidden things scrolled to the horizon and he walked among them. He could wander through them, stooping, collecting, acquainting himself with them until the day he died and he would never know them all. He had a territory within himself and he would bring back specimens to the old world. These most excellent dispatches. His names.[63]

This passage's concern with naming, interiority, and natural imagery all resonate with a key precursor text in the African American literary tradition—one likewise centered on the founding of a black town—Zora Neale Hurston's 1937 novel *Their Eyes Were Watching God*. Whitehead's protagonist's discovery of his innate facility with names recalls Hurston's heroine Janie Crawford's revelation that "she knew things that nobody had ever told her. For instance, the words of the trees and the wind."[64] The nomenclature consultant's finding a "territory within himself" parallels Janie's trajectory forward from the moment "her conscious life had commenced at Nanny's gate" (23) to her full inhabitation of subjecthood as the storyteller of Hurston's novel. Whitehead's imagery of nature—the "secret landscape" of "flora," "saplings," "shrubs," and "fronds"—likewise evokes Janie's celebrated scene of awakening to sexual self-consciousness: seeing "her life like a great tree in leaf" (20); lying under the "blossoming pear tree in the back yard" (23); watching bee and flower in a "love embrace" (24); imagining herself at sixteen as a pear tree kissed by such a bee: "Oh to be a pear tree—*any* tree in bloom! . . . She had glossy leaves and bursting buds and she wanted to struggle with life but it seemed to elude her" (25).

Precisely through these parallels between the two passages, however, important differences emerge. In *Their Eyes Were Watching God*, Janie is unambiguously close to nature, and nature is unambiguously natural.[65] In the passage from *Apex*, by contrast, minerals are "odd and alien," flora is "strange," saplings are "eccentric," fronds are "bizarre." Moreover, across two sentences at the center of Whitehead's passage, we move from "This unreckoned land of his possessed colors *he had never seen before*" to "Flowers burst in arrangements *never considered by the natural world*" (emphasis added). The shift here from subjective discovery of a new interior land to an objective statement about the natural world begins to foreground the colonialist undertones of the passage, which soon become overtones in the lines that follow. We learn of "beautiful hidden things" that the protagonist "collects," a "territory" from which he brings back "specimens" to "the old world." Through the connection to Hurston, these images of colonization and expropriation are implicitly linked to images of masculinity, with the "beautiful hidden things scrolled to the horizon" recalling the famous opening of *Their Eyes*:

> Ships at a distance have every man's wish on board. For some they come in with the tide. For others they sail forever on the horizon, never out of sight, never landing until the Watcher turns his eyes away in resignation, his dreams mocked to death by Time. That is the life of men. (9)

These impulses of masculine colonialism—figured in Hurston's distant ship and Whitehead's territory of "specimens"—extend not only to nature but to language itself, which in Whitehead's passage becomes subject to the will of the colonizer. Whereas in *Their Eyes* we witness "words walking without masters" (10), this paragraph in *Apex* moves from "The names" at the beginning to "His names" at the end. This recapitulates the move from discovery to ownership and emphasizes the Adamic origins of the myth of naming. The connection to Adam reminds us, too, that the story being told in this passage—of "most excellent dispatches" from the new world to the old—is originally a white story; indeed, with colonial slavery coming into view on the "horizon," it can even be called the originating story of whiteness.

Of course, analyzing the language and imagery of Whitehead's passage in this way does not tell us much about its mode of narration and the perspective and tone that characterize it. Here the comparison with Hurston offers further illumination, since *Their Eyes* is the subject of perhaps the most celebrated analysis of free indirect discourse in any African American novel, in a widely reprinted chapter of Gates's *The Signifying Monkey*. "It was Hurston who introduced free indirect discourse into Afro-American narration," Gates argues, and he gives three reasons for her innovation.[66] First, the developing narrative style of *Their Eyes*—where the omniscient third person (as in the novel's opening lines) gradually merges with the black vernacular speech that is initially found only in quoted dialogue—mirrors Janie's coming to self-consciousness through the alignment of her outer and inner lives. Gates here connects the divided origins of free indirect discourse—the way the language seems to emerge simultaneously and undecidably from both narrator and character—with Du Bois's notion of double consciousness, so that in Hurston's novel, free indirect discourse becomes "a dramatic way of expressing a divided self" (207). Second, Hurston employs free indirect discourse to bring together a high register of literary language with a black orality that has escaped literary representation up to that point, except in patronizing or parodic terms. This enables the novel to develop a "speakerly" quality that Gates sees as crucial to subsequent black literature: he notes that free indirect discourse represents "an utterance that no one could have spoken, yet which we recognize because of its characteristic 'speakerliness,' its paradoxically written manifestation of the aspiration to the oral" (208). Third, free indirect discourse allows Hurston to employ irony to indicate to her reader how they should feel about different characters. "When [free indirect discourse] is used in conjunction with Joe Starks," Gates writes of Janie's first husband, "irony obtains and distancing results; when it is used in conjunction with Janie, empathy obtains and illusory identification results, an identity we might call lyric fusion between the narrator and Janie" (209).

Whitehead's passage can be read as signifying on Hurston not only in its imagery and themes but also in its mobilization of free indirect discourse and irony. Rather than the revelation of a divided consciousness that will eventually be reconciled, Whitehead's free indirect discourse conveys the discovery of an interior that can be colonized and exploited. In neoliberal terms, this interior "land" or "territory" can be mined for human capital: the intense objectification of the self that underpins neoliberal theory is here given an exaggerated spin, with the colonization of the protagonist's "natural" talent explicitly foregrounded.[67] Furthermore, rather than the merging of a high literary register with an organic black vernacular, in this passage we have the combination of a subtly distorted rhetoric of nature with a comic language of mock-heroic archaism, most notable in the line, "These most excellent dispatches." This is a "speakerly" phrase—indeed, its air of quotation accentuates its orality. Its fragmentary quality, lacking a main verb, also marks the moment in the passage when the free indirect discourse cleaves closest to the character's point of view rather than the narrator's. This in turn makes the ironic consciousness of the line difficult not to attribute directly to the protagonist. But unlike in Gates's reading of Hurston, it is hard for Whitehead's reader to know how to feel about this irony. Does it produce distance or empathy? Perhaps, in fact, we are supposed to empathize with the distance, recognizing the protagonist's self-mocking irony as signaling not only (or even primarily) his racial consciousness, but also his membership of the professional-managerial class in a neoliberal corporation, and the kind of divided consciousness required in that context rather than in the racial one made famous by Du Bois.

The conclusion to this scene in *Apex* makes the comfortable alignment of this mock-heroic irony with a language of market utility abundantly clear:

> As one of the guys scrambled after the takeout menus so they could haggle over lunch options, he [the protagonist] slapped his hands on the table. Not

too loud, but enough to draw their attention. They assumed he was going to lobby for Thai. They looked at him and he said it: *Redempta*. It was the name. It stuck. They got paid. Not long after that he got his own office. He had to admit, it was pretty cool. (36)

Here the bathetic squabbling over takeout food gives way to an almost mystical tone of revelation—"They looked at him and he said it: *Redempta*. It was the name"—before the passage collapses again into the mundane quotidian, this time with the ring of capitalist triumph: "They got paid. Not long after that he got his own office." As in Ellis's "New Black Aesthetic," there is no class or racial anxiety involved here in the bridging of aesthetic intuition, individuality, and commodification: the ascent of a solitary black man within the domain of the neoliberal corporation is, simply, "pretty cool." In its use of a common vernacular phrase, this final flourish emphasizes the "speakerly" quality of the passage, its aspiration to the oral. But this orality is clearly not the previously unliterary territory of black idiom explored by Hurston; it is rather the ironic citation—from the perspective of a black member of the professional-managerial class—of the originally idiomatic but now abundantly commodified notion of "cool."[68]

The ultimate purpose of Whitehead's signifying on Hurston's novel in such an intricate and playful manner is to allude to a significant historical shift, and its meaning for African American literary expression. In the aesthetic universe of *Their Eyes Were Watching God*, the freedom of consciousness achieved and experienced by Janie implicitly stands in for the freedom of other black Americans—or at least other black women—through the literary conceit of "linked fate," just as in an earlier period Frederick Douglass's journey to freedom is understood to speak to the fate and hopes of all enslaved Americans. But the racial solidarity assumed by such examples is undermined by the individualism of the protagonist in *Apex Hides the Hurt*, whose personal freedoms—substantially underpinned by economic success—bear no necessary connection to the freedom of other black Americans at the same historical moment.[69]

We see this disconnection in the protagonist's relationship with the two black working-class characters in the novel: the barman and the cleaning lady at the hotel where he is staying as he makes his decision about the name of the town. The protagonist thinks of these people not as his racial brethren but as passengers on a ship he is naming. When the bartender, whom the protagonist has secretly named Muttonchops, tells him that "this is my home," the protagonist thinks:

> Already this job was different. Time was, you christened something, broke the bottle across the bow, and gave a little good-luck wave as it drifted away. You never saw the passengers. But there were always disgruntled passengers out there, like Muttonchops. It was simple mathematics. (23)

This abstraction of human life to "mathematics," a classic move in liberal governmentality and neoliberal thought, is both extended and undermined in the protagonist's relationship with his hotel cleaning lady. Although he never meets this woman face-to-face, she becomes a comically threatening specter outside his hotel door, a reminder of the mostly invisible working-class labor that enables the protagonist to live his comfortably bourgeois existence. All of this satirical material in the novel anticipates the central claim of Warren's *What Was African American Literature?*: that in the era of neoliberal hegemony, the success of what Du Bois called the "talented tenth," or what Warren calls the black elite, has "less and less to do with the type of social change that would make a profound difference in the fortunes of those at the bottom of our socio-economic order."[70] The protagonist's successes in *Apex Hides the Hurt* make no black life better except his own.

In foregrounding issues of class as well as race, Whitehead's novel alludes to the debates in African American intellectual culture that I sketched at the opening of this chapter and that first emerged in and around sociologist William Julius Wilson's *The Declining Significance of Race* (1978). Wilson's study was the first explicitly to make the claim that in the post-segregation era, the experience of well-educated members of the rising black middle class was diverging sharply from that of the unskilled black poor, whom Wilson referred to—in a term that would go on to become bleakly influential—as the "underclass."[71] Whitehead's allusion to Wilson may even be direct, since when pressed in an interview to offer a solution to the problems he was diagnosing, Wilson claimed that he could only "suggest programs such as full employment which provide the band-aids and don't really get at the basic fundamental cure."[72] Thus a band-aid that hides but does not heal the hurt becomes the central metaphor in Whitehead's novel. "Apex," the coinage that earns the nomenclature consultant fame in his field, is the name he gives to a "multicultural adhesive bandage" that is made to cover wounds on different shades of human flesh. The idea that the invention and commercial distribution of this bandage does not provide "the basic fundamental cure," as Wilson put it, but instead merely contributes to a superficial culture of identitarian individualism, is something the novel has persistent fun with. "The deep psychic wounds of history and the more recent gashes ripped by the present, all of these could be covered by this wonderful, unnamed multicultural adhesive bandage. It erased. Huzzah," reads one passage (90). "In the advertising," goes another,

> multicultural children skinned knees, revealing the blood beneath, the commonality of wound, they were all brothers now, and multicultural bandages were affixed to red boo-boos. United in polychromatic harmony, in injury, with our individual differences respected, eventually all healed beneath Apex. Apex Hides the Hurt. (109)

Neoliberal multiculturalism and racial uplift ideology are closely intertwined, and both place education at the center of their social vision.[73] The education that the protagonist of *Apex* has received has certainly uplifted him, albeit into a sphere otherwise dominated by white people. As critics have noted, he seems unperturbed by this fact.[74] It is telling that of all the people the nomenclature consultant meets in Winthrop, the one he instinctively feels himself most drawn toward is the white patriarch Albie Winthrop, scion of the family of barbed-wire magnates who incorporated the town in the nineteenth century. Albie shares with the protagonist an educational background at Quincy College, the "third oldest university in the country," whose graduates "formed the steel core of many a powerful elite, in politics, business, wherever there were dark back rooms" (69). "There was no secret handshake," we learn when the two characters first meet. "The two syllables sufficed. Quincy was a name that was a key, and it opened doors" (71).

This concluding phrase echoes the earlier passage I analyzed, in which doors open to lead beyond "tiny rooms" to "a magnificent and secret landscape" (34). That unusual metaphor for the protagonist's inner life is here connected to the more common metaphor of elite education opening doors to high-class people and positions, a "magnificent and secret landscape" of a more rarified kind. In the earlier passage, I noted the colonial imagery employed to convey the protagonist expropriating his "natural" talent as a source of human capital. Education is crucial to the enhancement of human capital, and here again Whitehead makes the link to a colonial past. Quincy is "structured on the classic British model," its graduates provided with metaphorical "royal titles" so that they become "prows to pulverize the swells of middle-class oceans" (69). The only subject the protagonist is described studying at Quincy is "Modern European History," while the sons of foreign presidents return home to spread the good news, "articulating American and Quincian directives in their native tongues" (69). The nomenclature consultant's acquisition of human capital in all its forms is thus shot through with imperial—and therefore implicitly racialized—imagery. It is thus worth closing the present section with a reflection on the racial heritage of the idea of human capital itself.

As noted in the Introduction to this book, the concept of human capital was developed by Chicago School economists in the early 1960s, and from the outset was elaborated "with special reference to education."[75] But when Theodore Schultz initially advocated for the term in his presidential address to the 1960 meeting of the American Economic Association, he acknowledged that it possessed certain associations that economists would do well to shake off. "Our values and beliefs inhibit us from looking upon human beings as capital goods, except in slavery, and this we abhor," Schultz claimed. "Hence, to treat human beings as wealth that can be augmented by investment runs counter to deeply held values. It seems to reduce man once again to a mere material component, to something akin to property."[76] The task begun by Schultz's lecture was thus to recuperate "human capital" from a context "haunted by the phrase's evocation of slavery" to one that would speak of neutrality and colorblindness.[77] This recuperative project was taken up with gusto by Gary Becker, and the extent of his success is indicated by the fact that, rather than evoking slavery, human capital analysis has become a primary tool used in the measurement of racial disparities in income and wealth, with public policies formulated on that basis.[78]

Despite the appearance of colorblind neutrality, however, "race is far from absent in Becker's formulas."[79] As one of the most significant "endowments" an individual possesses, but one that cannot be upgraded through education or training in the way of other endowments, race is not transcended but simply rendered invisible as a factor in Becker's theory of the labor market. Because he deemed racial discrimination "irrational" for corporations concerned with their bottom line—since it reduces the pool of potential employees—Becker's view was "that state programs aimed at redressing racialized economic inequality were less effective than a colorblind and competitive labor market."[80] But while the competitive labor market envisaged by Becker and his neoliberal colleagues has in many ways come to pass, rather than improve the outcomes for most black Americans— and here the protagonist of *Apex* is unrepresentative—this development has further exacerbated racial inequality through exacerbating class inequality (given that African Americans are disproportionately represented among the poor and working class). Moreover, the supposed neutrality of human capital theory has been used to argue that the lower classes—like all social groups—are simply getting what they deserve. Rather than a solution to racial disparities, human capital theory thus becomes a justification for them. This leads one critic to go so far as to suggest that "the theory of human capital might be understood as a global strategy for rationalizing American racism."[81]

For its adherents, the neoliberal project was a moral one rooted in a belief in individual freedom. Within this moral framework, the recuperation of "human capital" as a core idea could serve as a means of "righting the wrongs seeded by previous uses of humans as capital."[82] Now, investing in human capital would signal the righteousness of freedom rather than the evils of slavery. But who would do the investing? The employer? The state? "By investing in themselves," Schultz writes a few sentences after his mention of slavery, "people can enlarge the range of choice available to them. It is one way free men can enhance their welfare."[83] Over the course of a single paragraph, then, the first modern theorist of human capital has not only rebranded the phrase to signal freedom rather than slavery, but has used it to delimit the notion of freedom to a quality supposedly possessed by individuals as entrepreneurs of themselves, unencumbered by wider forms of collective constraint (or support). If we are to judge by the evidence of his third novel, Colson Whitehead has taken careful note of this highly influential sleight of hand.

Freedom to Struggle

Approximately a third of the way through *Apex Hides the Hurt*, Albie Winthrop tells the nomenclature consultant how the latter came to be hired to choose a name for the town. Despite its link to a successful industrial past, the continued value of the town's current name, "Winthrop," has been questioned by local tech entrepreneur Lucky Aberdeen, who believes it doesn't reflect the "new market realities, the changing face of the community" (74). Wanting to rename the town "New Prospera," Lucky brings his proposal to the three-person town council on which he sits, and they vote two-to-one in favor of change. But Regina Goode, the African American town mayor who voted with Lucky, now demurs on the new name. As Albie recounts to the protagonist: "'We sat there deadlocked. Every name—mine, Lucky's, Regina's—had one vote, and no one would budge'" (75). The result is that the protagonist is brought in to have the casting vote. Alongside Winthrop and New Prospera, the third name being touted is the original one given to the town by its first settlers, a group of formerly enslaved people. This name—Regina's choice—is revealed to the protagonist and the reader as Albie continues:

> "It was only a settlement really," Albie said, "where Regina's family decided to stop one day. There wasn't any thought to it. They just dropped their bags here."
> "But what was it called?"
> "Oh. They called it Freedom."
> Freedom, Freedom, Freedom. It made his brain hurt. Must have been a bitch to travel all that way only to realize that they forgot to pack the subtlety. (76)

"Freedom was so defiantly unimaginative as to approach a kind of moral weakness" (83), the protagonist reflects a few pages later. It could only be the work of "the laziest namers he'd ever come across" (95).

The protagonist's sarcastic dismissal of "Freedom" runs starkly counter to the word's centrality in postwar African American politics and culture. As Richard King has argued, "the search for freedom" was "the essence of the civil rights movement," and no word has come to be more identified with the movement's goals, attitudes, and legacy.[84] "Freedom" could offer a unifying banner because its significations and connotations crossed religious and secular boundaries. On the religious side, as conveyed most memorably in the rhetoric of Martin Luther King, Jr., "were two powerful and compelling stories of the move from slavery to freedom," the Old Testament journey of the children of Israel to the Promised Land and the New Testament story of Christ's spiritual deliverance of man from sin.[85] The more secular uses of "freedom" by Civil Rights activists and thinkers drew on a wide range of sources, from postwar liberal pluralism to radical Marxism to the thought of Hannah Arendt and Frantz Fanon. In both these senses, religious and secular, "Freedom Now" underpinned the possibility of collective action. The era saw the advent of freedom songs, freedom schools, freedom rides, and the freedom summer of 1964. Yet in the years following the major legal gains of the movement, and over subsequent decades, the mobilizing power of "freedom" for black activists and the broader Left notably declined. The term's originally inspiring mix of progressive teleology, open utopian possibility, and collectivist resonance began to wane in the face of economic retrenchment, capitalist realism, and a rising individualist ethos. In the preface to his book's second edition, King notes that in the wake of the conservative turn in American political life after 1968, any attempts to revive the rhetoric of Civil Rights—including the clarion call of "freedom"— had come to seem "counterproductive, mere exercises in nostalgia."[86]

While the ubiquity of freedom discourse in the United States hardly diminished over the post–Civil Rights decades, the neoconservative and neoliberal takeover of the term meant that by the time Whitehead began publishing in the late 1990s, it had become common for those interested in collective politics to be skeptical about the provenance and ideological uses of "freedom."[87] This was as much the case for African Americans as for other groups: describing "freedom" as "a word that has been steadily disappearing from the political language of blacks in the west," Paul Gilroy found himself asking "why it seems no longer appropriate or even plausible to speculate about the freedom of the subject of black politics in overdeveloped countries."[88]

In keeping with the rebranding of "freedom" by conservatives and its steady disappearance from progressive politics, the word barely features in Whitehead's first two novels. In *The Intuitionist*, "freedom" arises only once, and then not in the context of black struggle but of white captivity. When the journalist Ben Urich is abducted and tortured by thugs, we read that one of the men "loosens his grip on Ben's hand to remind his captive of freedom, the ease of mobility from which he has just been exiled" (74). This "ease of mobility"—historically felt far more by white than black Americans—does characterize the life of J. Sutter, the black protagonist of *John Henry Days*, but even in this novel about the legacies of Reconstruction, the word "freedom" is conspicuous by its relative absence. It appears four times in total, but only two of these relate to black freedom and only one reads non-ironically, when we learn of Paul Robeson that "his great-great-grandfather was born into slavery, purchased his freedom and became a baker."[89]

Apex Hides the Hurt, Whitehead's third novel, was his first written following the events of 9/11, and it is perhaps no surprise that it should convey a more actively jaundiced view of "freedom," the keyword of the US government's military response to the attacks.[90] While the nomenclature consultant's dismissive reaction to the name "Freedom" can certainly be viewed skeptically by the reader—given his status as a figure even more distant from a community of fellow black Americans than *The Intuitionist*'s Lila Mae Watson—the other names being touted for the town nevertheless suggest that the "freedom" brand itself is being satirized, rather than simply the protagonist's views on it. "Winthrop," the town's current name, points us to John Winthrop, a leading early Puritan settler in the New World and the first American theorist of freedom.[91] In an insightful discussion of the allusions to the Puritan context within *Apex*, Christopher Leise argues that from the Reagan presidency forward, any reference to Winthrop "has been programmed to trigger American ideals such as 'freedom' and the promise that wealth is the reward of hard work, while strategically suppressing the historical Winthrop's faith in the need for class hierarchies to promote a healthy body politic."[92] "New Prospera," meanwhile, has even more the ring of branding, echoing John F. Kennedy's "new frontier" rhetoric and repurposing it for a Reaganite idea of freedom as prosperity through (deserved) wealth. "New, new," the protagonist thinks to himself regarding the name, "new money, new media, new economy. New order. New Prospera. He reckoned it would look good on maps" (52). Much like "freedom," the "new" is evidently not what it used to be. Once the slogan of an oppositional modernism that aimed to "make it new," it has morphed into the watchword of a massively expanded culture industry that has subsumed modernist experimentation as simply one style among others. Less a challenge to capitalist hegemony, the new has become its very motor.[93]

None of these three names is finally the one chosen by the protagonist, however. While researching the town's history in its former public library, he uncovers the forgotten voice of one of its two original founders, whose preference for naming the town "Struggle" found little support among his fellows and was set aside in favor of "Freedom." The nomenclature consultant rebrands this history by choosing "Struggle" as the new name for the town. In doing so, he divides up a phrase—"freedom struggle"—that became prevalent with the Civil Rights movement and has recently regained prominence during the renewed protests of the Black Lives Matter era. *Apex* brings out the inherent tension between these two normally inseparable terms by making them the subject of a debate between the town's co-founders, Abraham Goode ("The Light") and William Field ("The Dark"). This debate is in turn mapped onto a distinction between "human nature" and "the human condition":

> Given the choice between Freedom, and [Field's] contribution, how could their flock not go with Goode's beautiful bauble? Field's area of expertise wasn't human nature, but the human condition. . . . Freedom was what they sought. Struggle was what they had lived through. (210)

Human nature is here associated with optimism—an optimism, the novel implies, that under neoliberal hegemony has become merely ideological, a "cruel optimism" that serves corporate and political interests rather than the interests of all.[94] The human condition, with its echoes of Hannah Arendt, seems by contrast to point to a role for struggle specifically in the realm of political action. Confronting this climactic decision in favor of "Struggle," it becomes tempting to read *Apex Hides the Hurt* as the story of the protagonist's developing racial consciousness, his journey from initially identifying with Goode and Field only as "a common business pair: a marketing, vision guy teamed up with a bottom-line, numbers guy" (143), to asking himself near the end of the narrative, "What did a slave know that we didn't? To give yourself a name is power. They will try to give you a name and tell you who you are and try to make you into something else, and that is slavery. And to say, I Am This—that was freedom" (206).

With an apparently new faith in the meaningfulness of language beyond its manipulative power to attain corporate ends, the protagonist finds himself imagining the effect his new name will have on the inhabitants of the town:

As he fell asleep, he heard the conversations they will have. Ones that will get to the heart of this mess. The sick swollen heart of the land. They will say: I was born in Struggle. I live in Struggle and come from Struggle. I work in Struggle. We crossed the border into Struggle. Before I came to Struggle. We found ourselves in Struggle. I will never leave Struggle. I will die in Struggle. (211)

This passage has an undeniably rousing quality, and it concludes the novel's penultimate scene. But in the short final scene, the reader is brought back to more material realities. First we witness the protagonist tipping "the white guy at the desk" while giving the finger to Muttonchops, the black bartender, as he leaves the town (211). Cross-class racial solidarity seems as far away as ever. Then we are reminded that the town library, where the protagonist made his momentous discovery, is to be replaced by an "OUTFIT OUTLET." The old library sign lies symbolically "cracked over shards of broken bookcases," while the gigantic new sign "possessed a certain majesty, and would be visible from even farther away," perhaps even "from space" (212). Finally, we learn that the act of renaming the town has not healed the protagonist's infected toe, which has been covered by an Apex bandage for much of the novel. "There was a moment a few hours ago, as he was lying in bed waiting for the morning to come, when he thought he might be cured," we read on the final page. "That if he did something, took action, the hex might come off. The badness come undone." But this has not happened, and in the novel's closing sentence, we are told that it will not happen: "As the weeks went on and he settled into his new life, he had to admit that actually, his foot hurt more than ever" (212).

Throughout *Apex*, the importance of finding the "true" name for things—rather than the "right" name, the one that sells—has been floated as a way to delve beneath the ironic surface and counteract the idea that success in life "came down to good marketing skills" (85). We are continually reminded, nevertheless, that even the notion of revealed truth cannot escape the ambit of marketing: of the original Band-Aid bandage, for instance, the protagonist observes that "the name was the thing itself, and that was Holy Grail territory" (87). The novel's final scene suggests that when the name is the only thing that is taken to matter, it becomes all too easy to overlook the underlying material realities of race, class, commodification, privatization, and even the body in pain—each of which is touched on in the scene. With this closing reminder of the stark limitations of symbolic action—the action of naming and renaming—in a world of racial disparity, class inequality, and corporate hegemony, the novel significantly places in ironic relief its own postmodern aesthetics, where action on language is conceived as the primary action a text can perform.

Indeed, by ending with the image of the consultant's injured foot, Whitehead may well be signifying on the very trope I have followed Henry Louis Gates in situating at the heart of African American writing—the trope of signifying itself. While Jesse Cohn has drawn attention to the Oedipal connotations of the protagonist's injury, observing that the name "Oedipus" can be taken to mean "swollen foot," the limping figure also has African origins.[95] As Gates notes, no less a figure than the Signifying Monkey—the trickster Esu-Elegbara in Yoruba mythology—"is said to limp as he walks, precisely because of his mediating function: his legs are of different lengths because he keeps one anchored in the realm of the gods while the other rests in this, our human world."[96] By giving his protagonist a pronounced limp, Whitehead aligns the nomenclature consultant—a kind of god in his own realm—with the trickster figure Esu. But he does so only to underline how the originally marginal and subversive practice of signifying has become central to the commercial and far from oppositional practice of advertising. In this racially inflected variation of the story told for his generation by Wallace in "E Unibus Pluram," irony—once the tool of subversion and liberation—has been captured by advertising and has become the guarantor of the status quo.

This claim leads us back once again to the author himself. The "stock ironic black man figure" developed in Whitehead's journalism and avoided in his first novel is placed center stage in his third, and it is hard not to feel the self-reflexivity of this gesture, especially when the nomenclature consultant finds himself unable to contradict his boss's claim that "you *are* the product" (146). "What happens to black identity when it is more mainstream than marginalized?" Stephanie Li asks in her chapter on *Apex Hides the Hurt*, and this question echoes the one we have seen framed by Rolland Murray regarding Trey Ellis's essay: "what happens to African American cultural expression once it is no longer an emergent subfield vying for legitimacy and becomes established at the center of the dominant culture?"[97]

The apparent answer to these questions offered by Whitehead's early fiction is that the freedom of the newly mainstream black writer is an ambivalent freedom, since the black artist's authentic expression of collective struggle—rather than their more mundane exemplification of professional-managerial consciousness—is no longer something that can be assumed. While Lila Mae Watson's name recalls Zora Neale Hurston's, the isolated and technologically driven rewriting that Lila Mae engages in at the close of *The Intuitionist* seems less to resemble than to contrast with Hurston's project, which involved transforming her personal experience and anthropological work in black communities into a lyrical literary voice. And while Colson Whitehead has inherited the mantle of the departed Toni Morrison as the most significant and celebrated black writer of his era, the early Whitehead doesn't much sound like Morrison, so confident from the outset that her rich metaphorical language could successfully and sincerely express not only the lives of her African American contemporaries but the tragic fates of their "sixty million and more" enslaved ancestors.[98] Like Hurston's colloquial soulfulness, Morrison's intimate sincerity could seem in its time a natural and organic literary expression of the consciousness of the black community. Whitehead's distancing irony, by contrast, continually calls attention to the unnatural, the inorganic, the insincere.[99] To understand more fully the structure of feeling that his writing expresses and engages, we need to return for a final time to consider the wider contradictions of African American life in the neoliberal age.

Black Faces in High Places

One prominent African American who does often sound like Toni Morrison is Barack Obama. In his 1995 memoir, *Dreams from My Father*, he describes his first attendance at Trinity United Church of Christ in a passage that recalls Morrison at her most lyrically and biblically rhapsodic (albeit with a didactic edge more reminiscent of Martin Luther King):

> People began to shout, to rise from their seats and clap and cry out, a forceful wind carrying the reverend's voice up into the rafters. As I watched and listened from my seat, I began to hear all the notes from the last three years swirl about me....
>
> And in that single note—hope!—I heard something else; at the foot of that cross, inside the thousands of churches across the city, I imagined the

stories of ordinary black people merging with the stories of David and Goliath, Moses and Pharaoh, the Christians in the lion's den, Ezekiel's field of dry bones. Those stories—of survival, and freedom, and hope—became our stories, my story; the blood that spilled was our blood, the tears our tears; until this black church, on this bright day, seemed once more a vessel carrying the story of a people into future generations and into a larger world.[100]

The speaker in this passage—who at the beginning remains seated and separate, watching and listening rather than clapping and crying out—becomes increasingly absorbed into the body of "ordinary black people" until, with the phrase "our stories, my story," the first-person singular is left behind. As is often the case in Morrison's writing, this process of absorption is conveyed through imagery drawn equally from nature—the forceful wind, the blood and tears, the bright day—and from biblical myth. The influence is doubtless direct: when awarding the Presidential Medal of Freedom to Morrison in 2012, Obama remarked that her 1977 novel *Song of Solomon* had helped him "to figure out how to write, but also how to be and how to think."[101] Though a generational contemporary of the writers featured in this book—born in 1961, he is a few years older than Whitehead and younger than Helen DeWitt and George Saunders, the subjects of my next chapter—Obama takes his stylistic lead from a writer born fully thirty years before.

One thing that nevertheless distinguishes Obama from figures like Morrison and King, according to Zadie Smith, is that this son of a white mother and black father is biracial, and is thus possessed of a distinctive brand of double consciousness, being "black and, at the same time, white."[102] Rather than trap him in a tragic bind, this double consciousness enables Obama to be "a genuinely many-voiced man," which in literary terms translates into "an enviable facility for dialogue" and in political terms into a capacity to speak the register of different audiences: "This new president doesn't just speak for his people. He can speak them" (136–137). Smith admits that Obama's brand of double-voiced discourse can suggest, in the context of politics rather than literature, "a sense of the double-dealer, of someone who tailors his speech to fit the audience, who is not of the people (because he is able to look at them objectively) but always above them" (140). She nonetheless dismisses accusations of insincerity and double-dealing as a "fear campaign" by the "single-voiced

Obamanation crowd" (140), while acknowledging that "a lot rests on how this president turns out—but that's a debate for the future" (147).

Writing from this future, at a less enchanted moment near the end of Obama's second term, Lee Konstantinou reads the president's many-voicedness as the key to his remarkable success as an electoral brand. Highlighting the Obama campaign's unprecedented use of "microtargeting" in order to appeal to different kinds of voters—which led to admiration and awards from marketing consultants up and down the land—Konstantinou transforms Smith's praise into a more cynical account of Obama's mastery of "the many different reified languages of the people—their identities anatomized in some vast Catalist databank of his soul."[103] Like the nomenclature consultant in *Apex*, Obama—the arch signifier—becomes the product to be sold, which has the political effect of "subordinating issues, interests, and policies to values, attitudes, and character."[104] Indeed, in a seemingly unintentional echoing of Whitehead's novel, Konstantinou even describes Obama as "something like the apex of branding theory."[105]

Konstantinou's demystifying account of Obama as brand dovetails with mounting critiques of the former president offered by figures on the African American Left. Adolph Reed was the first to skewer Obama from this standpoint, famously writing in a 1996 *Village Voice* article of "a smooth Harvard lawyer with impeccable do-good credentials and vacuous-to-repressive neoliberal politics."[106] More recently, Reed's son Touré Reed is one of a number of younger critics who have called attention to the failures of the Obama presidency. Arguing that Obama's "postracial" message made him palatable to white voters, Reed observes that the president's rhetoric regularly "shifted the blame for contemporary inequities away from both neoliberal economic policies and racism to the alleged cultural deficiencies of the black and brown poor."[107] At the same time, Obama kept black voters onside by speaking their language, "performing" authentic blackness as a way to avoid thorny questions that might highlight his class privilege and biracial background.[108] Reed's 2018 analysis offers something like the inverse of Smith's 2008 view. For Smith, Obama's multi-voicedness constituted a sustained performance that was nevertheless sincere, with the moral of *Dreams from My Father* being "that each man must be true to his selves, plural."[109] For Reed, Obama's multi-voiced quality instead signifies a performed blackness that is not only insincere but also paves the way for damagingly regressive policies, evidenced by the fact that "the percentage of African Americans living in poverty was actually higher when Obama left office than when he assumed it."[110]

For this younger generation of critics, the disappointments of the Obama presidency mark nothing less than the culminating failure of "black faces in high places" as a decades-long strategy for ameliorating the general condition of African Americans. "The most significant transformation in all of Black life over the last fifty years," writes Keeanga-Yamahtta Taylor, "has been the emergence of a Black elite, bolstered by the Black political class, that has been responsible for administering cuts and managing meager budgets on the backs of Black constituents."[111] The electoral turn in black politics at the conclusion of the Civil Rights era resulted in a significant transfer of legislative power to African Americans. Against the background of neoliberal restructuring, however, this did not lead to improved outcomes for most black Americans but simply widened class divisions among them. As a cover for this development, "personal stories of achievement and accomplishment began to replace the narrative of collective struggle" (82). So while Henry Louis Gates could call Obama's election "the symbolic culmination of the black freedom struggle, the grand achievement of a great collective dream,"[112] Taylor presents it as proof that the turn to the electoral and the personal was ultimately a failure, pointing to Obama as one of a number of "'new,' 'post-Black,' or 'third wave' Black elected officials who brandish their distance from the freedom struggle" (104). Explaining how the Black Lives Matter protest movement could emerge at the same time as an African American inhabited the White House, Taylor views this convergence as a sign that the post–Civil Rights period in black politics has come to a close:

> What seemed then like an alternative—greater Black inclusion within the political and economic establishment—has already come and failed. In this sense, the election of Obama completed that political project and has brought us back to this point. (218–219)

The grand gestures of Obama's writing and speechmaking, seen from this leftist standpoint, serve only to turn Morrisonian sincerity into a brand of political ideology. With this in mind, we can begin to understand more fully Colson Whitehead's reluctance to embrace words like "freedom" and "struggle" in his early fiction, as well as his reservations about assuming Morrison's legacy as the literary spokesperson for all African Americans. Writing in the glow of Obama's first term, it was possible for Stephanie Li to play down Whitehead's reluctance and reserve in order to rope together this prominent trio of black cultural figures. "Whitehead names the racial house Morrison envisions 'Struggle,'" she writes. "It is defined not by the apex of a racial utopia but by the hard work necessary to achieve it. Obama offered a similar vision of the United States in his most famous speech, 'A More Perfect Union' . . . . Our president seems to understand the necessity and beauty of living in Struggle."[113] As we have seen, this not only romanticizes Obama's mobilization of Morrisonian sincerity; it also misreads the invocation of "Struggle" in Whitehead's novel. Rather than embrace a symbolic politics of naming and branding, the ending of *Apex* emphasizes the distinct *absence* of a politics oriented toward actions and outcomes. By critically signifying on the trope of signifying, we might even say that Whitehead's early writing offers a skeptical rejoinder, *avant la lettre*, to precisely the figural and symbolic brand of politics that Obama would come to exemplify.[114]

In his essay on Obama, Konstantinou connects the president's potency as a brand and his skill as a brander to the form of his memoir, reading *Dreams from My Father* as a "postironic *Bildungsroman*." Stylistic differences aside, this generic designation brings Obama the writer and public figure into alignment with the literary generation of Whitehead, Wallace, Eggers, and Egan. The postironic Bildungsroman—"a post-Boomer commonplace"—sees its protagonist "grow beyond self-absorption, anger, and cynicism of youth toward sincerity, passionate involvement, and the philanthropic subordination of personality beneath larger, public concerns."[115] This is the journey taken by the protagonist of *Dreams from My Father*, who eventually becomes the writer capable of moving beyond tropes of difference, identity, and disillusionment in favor of embracing universal values, but without laying aside his innate multi-voicedness. "To move from corrosive irony toward a reconstituted sincerity," Konstantinou writes, "is not, for Obama, simply to return to one's former preironic innocence, but rather to harness one's many different voices in a new way, toward new personal and collective goals."[116] Like other postironic Bildungsromane—Konstantinou here names works by Dave Eggers, Jonathan Franzen, and Jeffrey Eugenides, and elsewhere adds novels by Jennifer Egan, Zadie Smith, and Jonathan Lethem—"*Dreams from My Father* likewise reflexively announces that it is the final product of a similar journey—from naïve sincerity (Barry) through bitter irony (Barack) to transcendent postirony (Obama)."[117]

At first blush, Whitehead's first four novels can read like postironic Bildungsromane in this vein. As I noted at the outset of this chapter, each novel tells the story of a racially ambivalent protagonist coming to a new understanding of African American history and its relationship to their own life. Each of these stories is narrated, however, from a marked critical distance. "My narrators generally have a certain kind of critical faculty," Whitehead has claimed in interview. "They're analyzing what the characters are doing in larger social structures."[118] I have demonstrated how this distance functions in *The Intuitionist* and *Apex Hides the Hurt*, neither of which presents their protagonist as unproblematically completing the journey from irony to sincerity exemplified by Obama's memoir. With this evidence in mind, even *Sag Harbor*—the most obvious candidate among Whitehead's early novels for the category of postironic Bildungsroman—should be read, I argue, precisely for its undercutting of the Bildungsroman and the vision of social totality that the genre proffers. Moreover, not only does Whitehead resist presenting his protagonists coming into alignment with a wider community, à la Obama, he also foregrounds the role of human capital in constituting these characters as subjects of neoliberalism. Whitehead therefore ensures a certain readerly *disinvestment* in character, precisely the opposite of the affect Obama's memoir aims to produce. While "Obama brings irony into the public sphere, when he does, in order to dissolve it," as Konstantinou correctly observes, Whitehead's fiction suggests that irony cannot be dissolved so fully and completely.[119] Nor should it be. Whereas Obama's nonfiction wants to move beyond irony so as to reconcile contradictions, Whitehead's early fiction works to express those contradictions as the inescapable condition of that fiction's own emergence.

Whitehead's novels of the first decade of the twenty-first century thus explore historically determined forms of double consciousness that take us beyond Du Bois's original framing, and thereby challenge Adolph Reed's dismissal of double consciousness as no more than bourgeois ideology. If Du Bois's famous passage is read as setting forth an eternal division in the souls of black folk, psychologically true regardless of historical circumstance, then it is not hard to share Reed's skepticism. In Whitehead's fiction, however, we see that the forms of double consciousness can alter over time and need not be based on notions of essential or transhistorical blackness. Where Du Bois was writing primarily about a post-Reconstruction African American (male) subject who was striving for uplift and thus felt torn between identities—"an American, a Negro . . . longing to attain self-conscious manhood, to merge this double self into a better and truer self"—Whitehead is writing about African American subjects in a neoliberal moment with its own very different racialized class structure. This is a moment where the cultural embrace of a certain class of black Americans—the professional-managerial class, notably including black artists—sits alongside the pathologization, incarceration, and state terrorization of a large and "disposable" black underclass.[120] The potential complicity of the African American artist in the perpetuation of this class situation is a notably different challenge to the one presented to artists throughout most of the twentieth century, where the pressing need was to provide a voice for a marginalized people understood to share a "linked fate."

The self-division that results from taking this challenge seriously is a source of the play of irony and sincerity that we find in Whitehead's fiction. Another source is the double-voiced quality of the African American literary tradition itself, now placed in the service of tackling a new aesthetic and political situation. Whitehead's distinctive mode of free indirect discourse in his early novels remains "a dramatic way to express a divided self," in Gates's phrase, but the causes of these divisions—or antinomies—have changed. Recognizing this change can allow us to acknowledge the importance of the critique of identarian thinking offered by Reed, Warren, Michaels, and others, while still highlighting that their position is characterized by its own nagging antinomies: between class and race, between structure and agency, between formalism and historicism, between aesthetics and politics. Whitehead's dialectically dynamic fiction aims to bring these antinomies to consciousness, allowing the African American literary tradition to renew itself for a new era. The forms of double consciousness expressed in this fiction still involve "looking at oneself through the eyes of others," as Du Bois puts it, but as I have been arguing throughout the present book, the self-division that results cannot (and should not) be resolved or eradicated by rejecting the other. While neoliberalism promotes an ideology of individual sovereignty, for Hegel every identity already has the structure of internal differentiation. The Hegelian vision of *Bildung* therefore involves a subject learning from experience that any projects of sovereignty or autarky must fail. This is, in sum, the lesson for the reader (rather than the protagonist) at the end of *The Intuitionist* and *Apex Hides the Hurt*.

In reading Whitehead's early aesthetics as expressing the growing contradictions of African American life over the neoliberal period, I therefore read his literary New Sincerity *against* what Konstantinou calls postirony. Oriented toward the resolution of self-division, postirony can function successfully as a brand, whereas literary New Sincerity (as we saw in Chapter Three) draws anxious attention to self-branding as a problem of complicity. In highlighting this complicity, writers like Wallace, Eggers, Egan, and Whitehead take seriously the ways in which the intentions and beliefs of an author intersect with material conditions and the affordances of literary form. Sincerity as "a congruence between avowal and actual feeling" comes into conflict with sincerity as an acknowledgment of the chasm between avowal and action, as well as with literary fiction as a realm of multiple and layered signification. In literary New Sincerity, the author's internal divisions emerge through style and are eventually displaced onto the relation between author and reader. But they are not, in the process, overcome: instead they offer a telling remainder that points to the fundamental bind of literature—its ambivalent relation to collectivity and emancipation—in the neoliberal age.

For Wallace, Eggers, and Egan, this bind is felt and expressed as a kind of urgent anxiety about purpose and self-serving performance. Whitehead's tone is both more sanguine and, arguably, more bleak: his early fiction prefers to dwell in ironic cynicism rather than attempt to move beyond it to the uplands of postironic sincerity gloriously achieved. Konstantinou's postirony, as an achieved state, is placid rather than anxious, reconciled rather than unstable. And, of course, the Bildungsroman is precisely the genre of reconciliation, the genre wherein the emerging contradictions of capital were first reconciled. This makes it, fundamentally, a bourgeois genre—perhaps *the* classic genre of the bourgeoisie.[121] And here Whitehead's early novels, despite their undercutting of Bildungsroman tropes and their articulation of the ideological problem of the exceptional individual existing apart from wider struggle, can only take us so far, since they still hold at their center a black middle class and professional-managerial consciousness. This consciousness is shadowed in Whitehead's fiction by a working-class alternative that, like the cleaning lady in *Apex*, never comes wholly into focus. In Chapter Five I turn to this alternative consciousness, examining how literary New Sincerity has addressed the human lives, and human capital, of the working class under neoliberalism.

Seeing Like a Neoliberal

Classing Shame

Early in Helen DeWitt's second novel *Lightning Rods* (2011), the salesman protagonist Joe parks his car by a beach and, looking out at birds flying over the sea, is struck by the question of shame: "He thought: an animal has no shame. It hunts what it eats and eats it. It shits when it needs to. . . . It doesn't understand the concept of bathroom. It just goes when it needs to."[1] When he immediately finds himself considering the contrary case of dogs and cats that look embarrassed while defecating and scrape dirt over their waste, he cuts the reflection short: "Instead of getting side-tracked the way he usually did he just thought: Screw that. In other words, when something was genuinely important he didn't get side-tracked" (23). The genuinely important element in this case, Joe decides, is that the shamelessness of animals contrasts with the bearing of people: "Humans do nothing without shame" (23). This leads him seamlessly to the question of sex, and its paradoxical relationship to selling: "Because you can sell people just about anything if you can convince them it will give them a better chance to get sex. You can sell people just about anything if you can convince them it's a *substitute* for sex. The only thing you can't sell is the thing itself. That is, obviously people sell it, but you can't sell it without shame" (23–24). Bothered by this frustrating inefficiency, Joe makes what we quickly learn will be his characteristic move. He starts to glimpse, in the inefficiency, a new opportunity:

> Well, just look at how much time people waste because they *can't* get [sex] without shame! Look at how much time people waste in conversations, asking people about their interests. Look at how much time people waste fantasizing.

And just look at the risks people take! Because he had read about a case where a man had harassed a woman by dropping M&M's in the pocket of her blouse and getting them out, and his firm had to pay her a million dollars. Or it might have been more.

Well, if people are willing to take those kinds of risks you *know* there's got to be money in it. (24)

The social and imaginative lives of individuals, from their interpersonal conversations to their intimate fantasies, are figured in Joe's thought process as no more than the waste product of their thwarted sex drives. This tragedy of sexual repression—which owes everything to "shame, false shame" (26)—is counted in time wasted, money wasted, and higher risk for corporations and their employees. But all of this is unnecessary, Joe will conclude. If allowed to flourish unchecked, the free market can cut through the problem of shame and give the people what they want. And if a genius happens to make a lot of money giving the people what they want? "Well, if an opening for a product has arisen, *entirely* thanks to you," he reflects late in the novel, "it's only fair that you should be the first to profit from it" (259).

Lightning Rods takes us from Joe's early epiphany about shame through the story of his rise from door-to-door salesman of encyclopedias and vacuum cleaners to owner and manager of the largest temping agency in the United States, the Lightning Rods corporation. In so doing, the novel tracks its protagonist's journey from one paradigm of neoliberal subjectivity to another—from a precariously employed and indebted service worker to a successful entrepreneur. While this journey involves a substantial improvement in Joe's material circumstances, to his mind the change is less material than ideological. The point is not that his fundamental situation has altered but that his perception of it has been transformed: following his epiphany, he comes to see service work and entrepreneurship not as hierarchical alternatives but as bound up with one another. In other words, Joe is learning to *see like a neoliberal*, ignoring structural constraints in favor of an outlook that embraces personal responsibility. When one sees like a neoliberal, the determining factors in any individual's life are not economic but psychological.[2] To rise through the social system, what needs to be overcome is not one's structural position in a class hierarchy; it is only the mental barrier of "shame, false shame."

Class and shame have, nevertheless, been closely connected by scholars. Summarizing the views of Helen Merrell Lynd, shame's original theorist in social psychology, Mark McGurl describes shame as "a fundamentally self-reflexive feeling, associated with negative feedback."[3] Unlike its close psychological counterpart, guilt—which involves internal self-reproach for an action undertaken with some element of choice—shame concerns a more inadvertent transgression of social codes and the consequent fear of exposure and potential humiliation. Deriving from an Old English word meaning "to cover up, to envelop," shame is "a simultaneously external and internal phenomenon, capable of being elicited by even the notion—the prospective imagination—of exposure to negative judgment."[4] One prominent example is the negative judgment that those of a lower social class anticipate being passed on them by those of a higher class: as another critic puts it, "those most likely to feel shame are those made to feel 'inappropriate' by dominant cultural norms."[5]

While shame is not absent from the work of the four writers considered to this point in *New Sincerity*, none of their main protagonists can be described as members of the traditional working class, the subject of much of the most prominent cultural scholarship on shame. Nor are they members of the lower middle class, the class McGurl positions as crucial to understanding the specific role played by shame in postwar American literary aesthetics. In *The Program Era*, McGurl records how the massive expansion of US higher education at midcentury served the needs of an economy requiring "a vast body of workers to fill jobs in the lower and middling orders of the corporate and public sector workforce, college graduates all."[6] These graduate workers—many of them the first from their family to attend university—are highly susceptible to feelings of shame and guilt. Aspiring to the culture and manners of upper-middle-class peers for whom "higher education is understood as a virtual birthright," they are vulnerable to exposure for not fitting in; striving to leave behind their roots in the "ethnic or post-ethnic traditional working class," they can always be made to feel guiltily inauthentic, that they have betrayed themselves and their community.[7] The difficulty and danger, for members of this class stratum, of practicing sincerity as the outward avowal of inner feeling is therefore manifest: they must constantly strive to hide their true selves. For McGurl, these constraints mean that the representative literary output of this class has been the minimalist short story. In the stories of an influential figure like Raymond Carver, minimalism serves to turn shame into aesthetic form, simultaneously hiding and exposing it, becoming a way "not of explaining, but of beautifying shame."[8]

This chapter examines two writers, Helen DeWitt and George Saunders, who develop these connections between class and shame for a neoliberal era in which the category of class has undergone an ideological transformation. Their work depicts fictional scenarios in which the deepening class inequalities of neoliberal economy are masked and justified by the prevailing narratives of neoliberal culture. While both are comic writers and satirists, they are not otherwise the most intuitive pairing: where DeWitt has built an underground reputation as a literary genius unfairly sidelined by the conservatism of the publishing industry, Saunders is a darling of the American literary establishment, with virtually every new story appearing in its house journal, *The New Yorker*. We will find, nevertheless, that in the connections they make among sincerity, shame, and the way in which working people have been taught to see like neoliberals, DeWitt and Saunders draw out and deepen aspects of the literary New Sincerity heretofore explored in this book.

The next two sections address Saunders's breakthrough second story collection, *Pastoralia* (2000), reading its opening and closing stories as meditations on the exploitation of sincerity and shame under neoliberalism, and as aesthetic responses to the dominance of Carverian minimalism in treating the subject of lower-class American life. The section that follows returns to DeWitt's *Lightning Rods* and considers in detail the figure of the sincere entrepreneur as paradigmatic for neoliberal ideology. Taking DeWitt's and Saunders's respective responses to the death of David Foster Wallace as a jumping off point, the final section addresses all three writers' ambivalent orientation toward capitalist society. The chapter thus concludes with a consideration of the extent to which literary New Sincerity can be said to resist or participate in the ideological project of seeing like a neoliberal.

Exploiting Sincerity

In George Saunders's "Pastoralia," the unnamed narrator holds down a job impersonating a Neanderthal caveman at a theme park. His co-worker cavewoman, Janet, consistently refuses to play by the rules of their bizarre employment—smoking cigarettes, doing crosswords, and speaking English to the narrator as well as to the vanishingly few customers who "poke in their heads."⁹ Every evening the narrator retires to his "Separate Area" to complete a "Daily Partner Performance Evaluation Form." Every evening he writes an inaccurate but positive account of his partner's performance, choosing to lie in order to cover for her errors of judgment. "Do I note any attitudinal difficulties? I do not. How do I rate my Partner overall? Very good. Are there any Situations that require Mediation? There are not. I fax it in" (4).

While the story's dark comedy lies in the absurdity of this employment situation, its drama revolves around whether and when the narrator will stop lying and covering for Janet. To encourage him on his way to making that fateful decision, his employers send an emissary from management. "'I want you to speak frankly,'" Greg Nordstrom tells him. "'Are there problems? Problems we can maybe help correct?'" (19). When the narrator denies having noticed any such problems, Nordstrom turns to biblical analogies, counseling his interlocutor to "'remember that part of the Bible where Christ or God says any group of two or more of us is a body.'" "'Our body,'" he continues, "'has a rotten toe by the name of Janet, who is turning black and stinking up the joint'" (21). If the narrator can just come clean it would allow the corporation to treat this toe with "'antiseptic'" or "'a nice sharp saw'" (22). The narrator continues to hold out, however, leading Nordstrom to conclude with an exasperated appeal to the truth: "'For us to know, what must you do? Tell the truth. Start generating frank and nonbiased assessments of this subpar colleague. That's it. That is all'" (22).

When, following a further forty pages of "unprofessional" behavior by Janet, the narrator finally does tell the truth in an evaluation form, his coworker is summarily dismissed. The corporation that runs the park then releases a memo to its employees, containing the following reflections:

> *Because what is truth? Truth is that thing which makes what we want to happen happen. Truth is that which, when told, makes those on our team look good, and inspires them to greater efforts, and causes people not on our team to see things our way and feel sort of jealous. Truth is that thing which empowers us to do even better than we are already doing, which by the way is fine, we are doing fine, truth is the wind in our sails that blows only for us. So when a rumor makes you doubt us, us up here, it is therefore not true, since we have already defined truth as that thing which helps us win.* (63)

The famous question put to Jesus Christ by Pontius Pilate—"What is truth?"—is here answered by the Pastoralia corporation in a comically, because blatantly, ideological manner. Given the severe power imbalance between "us up here" and the theme park employees down there, the latter have no way to respond to this might-makes-right philosophy other than to acquiesce. At the story's end—when Janet is replaced by a disturbingly professional young cavewoman whose competitive bearing looks set to make his working life ever more stressful—the unfortunate narrator will indeed discover that Christ's own renowned line about truth, "The truth will set you free," has become no more than a tragic joke at his expense.

"Pastoralia" thus depicts the exploitation of the narrator's sincerity in a context of threatening precarity and rank inequality. Sincerity is encouraged when it benefits his employer, when it can be mined for surplus value and can help to improve productivity by justifying "Staff Remixing" (16). But when it involves the narrator expressing his grievances, or even avowing his inner feelings to himself, such sincerity must be automatically and immediately (self-)corrected. "I have to admit I'm not feeling my best" is how the story opens, before the narrator remembers that he must admit no such thing and begins to backpedal:

> Not that I'm doing so bad. Not that I really have anything to complain about. Not that I would actually verbally complain if I did have something to complain about. No. Because I'm Thinking Positive/Saying Positive. (1)

The internalization of a thoroughgoing surveillance culture—"reminiscent," as one critic notes, "of Foucault's analysis of Bentham's Panopticon"—is here achieved via a parodically blunt self-help mantra, "Thinking Positive/Saying Positive."[10] The mantra will later reappear in the corporation's memo on truth (63), as if the reader needed reminding of where the encouragement to replace sincere self-reflection with blind positivity has come from. The narrator tries to channel this positivity when reflecting on a fax from the wife he never sees about their son's severe illness and the family's increasingly dire financial situation. "Dwelling on problems doesn't solve them," he thinks to himself as he lies alone in his Separate Area for the umpteenth night in a row. "Although on the other hand, thinking positively about problems also doesn't solve them. But at least then you feel positive, which is, or should be, you know, empowering. And power is good" (35).

In talking himself into feeling powerful without actually having power, the narrator might appear to be suffering from a classic case of false consciousness, failing to understand the real determinants of his situation and thus acting against his own enlightened self-interest and that of his class. By making the corporation's statements about its power so blatant and lacking in the kind of slick marketing polish we would expect, Saunders seems on the one hand to encourage such a reading. "*Feel no guilt*," Nordstrom writes to the narrator after he finally sends in the incriminating evaluation form. "*Are you Janet? Is Janet you? I think not. I think that you are you and she is she. You guys are not the same entity. You are distinct*" (59). Christ's metaphor of the group as body, like his invocation of truth as freedom, has here been given a distorting corporate twist, so that any notion of worker-to-worker solidarity is replaced by the individual worker's bodily identification with his employer. Such identification appears to be nothing but the misrecognition of class interests, the purest expression of ideology as "the imaginary relationship of individuals to their real conditions of existence."[11]

On the other hand, it is also here that the false consciousness reading—and its Althusserian revision—fall short in grappling fully with a neoliberal scenario in which the structural position of the worker has changed. When Nordstrom takes the narrator out to lunch to discuss the situation with Janet, the manager opens the conversation as follows:

> "You'll be getting your proxy forms in your Slot soon," he says, spreading out some bagels on a blanket. "Fill out the proxy as you see fit, everything's fine, just vote, do it boldly, exert your choice, it has to do with your stock option. Are you vested? Great to be vested. Just wait until you are. It really feels like a Benefit. You'll see why they call Benefits Benefits, when every month, ka-ching, that option money kicks up a notch. Man, we're lucky." (18–19)

Given what we go on to learn about the Pastoralia corporation, it is hardly surprising that we never see these forms arriving in the narrator's "Slot" during the story. Nevertheless, the subsequent discussion of truth-telling and corporate identification has been prefaced by Nordstrom's appeal to the narrator not as a wage worker but as an investor. It is not simply that the language of votes, choices, and options opens onto an insidious discourse of "responsibilization," the notion that the narrator is responsible for his own fate. It is that his financial interests have been brought into alignment with those of the corporation, so that when, in the memo on truth, the pronouns "we," "us," and "our" appear, they have a double reference, both to "us up here" (as opposed to "you down there") and to "us" the corporation, which includes the workers not only as wage laborers but as investors. "*If we make money, we can grow,*" reads another memo from management, "*and if we grow, we can expand, if we can expand, we can continue to employ you, but if we shrink, if we shrink or stay the same, woe to you, we would not be vital*" (47–48). The worker's income stream from employment and their benefits stream from investing in the company would both be negated by any blockage in the project of capital accumulation, so that any worker who threatens the success of the company also threatens their own vitality. Seeing like a neoliberal involves perceiving, and acquiescing to, this capitalist reality.

Saunders draws comic attention to the incongruity between this interpellation of the worker as investor and the worker's increasingly precarious status. The narrator of "Pastoralia"—a service sector laborer in the "experience economy"—is plausibly a member of what Guy Standing, among others, have dubbed "the precariat," a term that combines the notion of precariousness or precarity with the Marxist category of the proletariat, the original carriers of revolutionary promise against the bourgeoisie. Standing calls the precariat "the new dangerous class," positing that in the neoliberal era it has taken on this mantle from a working class pacified by its acceptance of postwar compromises with capital.[12] Other scholars have criticized the viability of this notion of the precariat as a coherent, never mind dangerous, class, questioning "whether precarity can serve as a new political identity or whether it reproduces social exclusions and upholds normative modes of life."[13] Lauren Berlant and Isabel Lorey, among others, have explored the various connotations of precarity—labor condition, class identity, ontological experience—and have highlighted the psychological and physiological effects of neoliberal governmentality on the precarious worker.[14] Saunders extends this critical work by highlighting how the experience of precarity intertwines with discourses of investment. He makes clear that while precarity is an objective condition with affective consequences, so too is the investor identity both objective and affective. The promises of that identity, moreover, even when unrealized, can be made to obscure the class consciousness that might otherwise emerge through the experience of precarity.

In a passage that chimes with the image of Janet as a rotten toe that the Pastoralia corporation must "lop off" in order to thrive (20), Wendy Brown describes a shift under neoliberal capitalism away from Adam Smith's "invisible hand" model—which assumed a liberal subject of interest and exchange—toward a newer brand of subjectivity:

> Rather than each individual pursuing his or her own interest and unwittingly generating collective benefit, today, it is the project of macroeconomic growth and credit enhancement to which neoliberal individuals are tethered and with which their existence as human capital must align if they are to thrive. When individuals, firms, or industries constitute a drag on this good, rather than a contribution to it, they may be legitimately cast off or reconfigured—through downsizing, furloughs, outsourcing, benefit cuts, mandatory job shares, or offshore production relocation.[15]

Brown's mention of "human capital" reminds us that the Pastoralia workers are expected to invest not only in the company but also in themselves. Whereas the liberal subject was understood to own his/her labor power—a relationship famously defined by C. B. Macpherson as "possessive individualism"—the relationship between the neoliberal subject and his/her human capital is, as Michel Feher argues, not possessive but "*speculative*, in every sense of the word."[16] Because "my human capital is me, as a set of skills and capabilities that is modified by all that affects me and all that I effect," I cannot exchange it for income or commodities, but must invest in it in a context of precarity and uncertainty, hoping to succeed as one of neoliberalism's winners rather than losers.[17] Faced with low wages and diminishing income from Social Security, those who lack hard assets in an asset economy "must try to turn their flexibility and availability into valuable assets."[18] On the one hand, this model is a rather ridiculous fit for the narrator of "Pastoralia," whose immediate need is not what Feher calls "self-appreciation" but rather income to pay his mounting debts, detailed in the faxes he receives from his wife. On the other hand, "flexibility and availability" are the most valuable "assets" the narrator shows himself to possess: as someone who never leaves his place of work, who proves willing to obey the most ludicrous and draconian mandates without protest, and who channels his sincerity solely in the interests of his employer, the narrator proves himself worthy of investment, of becoming a "vested" interest.

The liberal model of wage labor that might have spurred the narrator's class consciousness in the classic Marxian manner is shown to be further outdated in "Pastoralia" by the erosion of any clear separation between the sphere of production and the sphere of reproduction. The former is the realm of creation, circulation, and consumption of commodities; the latter realm "values selfless giving (whether in one's relation to God or to one's neighbor), exalts people's unconditional ties (with their family, with their nation, and with humanity), and justifies the social services required for the physical and psychological upkeep of individuals, to prepare them for their entry into the market."[19] As Foucault observed, even the early neoliberals associated with the Ordoliberalism project in postwar Germany considered a separate realm of reproduction necessary to ensure the healthy functioning of the productive sphere.[20] But Chicago School neoliberals wanted to extend market principles into the realm of reproduction too, so that the project of treating people as subjects of interest would be thoroughgoing in every aspect of life.

In "Pastoralia" we see an extreme consequence of this logic in the "Disposal Debits," or "Shit Fee," that the theme park workers must pay in order to dispense with their bodily waste. Whereas a liberal model would understand defecation to reside in the sphere of reproduction, necessary for (re)generating a working and consuming subject of interest and wage labor, the Pastoralia corporation treats bodily excretion as an unnecessary "business expense": *"Do you think your poop is a legitimate business expense? Does it provide benefit to us when you defecate? No, on the contrary, it would provide benefit if you didn't, because then you would be working more. Ha ha! That is a joke"* (47). The conception of defecation as a voluntary act not only redefines it as an expense, but also allows the introduction of market incentives to encourage the reduction of such waste, producing cost savings for both the worker and the company. "And by the way," the memo adds, *"we are going to be helping you in this, by henceforth sending less food. We're not joking, this is austerity. We think you will see a substantial savings in terms of your Disposal Debits, as you eat less and your Human Refuse bags get smaller and smaller"* (48).

As we can see, Saunders's dystopian theme park is a site of exploitation on multiple levels: from the worker's body to their mind to their speech to their remuneration. It is exploitation that conceals itself, nevertheless, not through propounding the classically liberal values of equality and exchange (which

Marx encouraged the working class to use in their favor) but through the neoliberal values of competition, growth, and human capital. The implications for class consciousness of this shift in the justification of exploitation are substantial; as Brown notes: "when everything is capital, labor disappears as a category, as does its collective form, class, taking with it the analytic basis for alienation, exploitation, and association among laborers. Dismantled at the same time is the very rationale for unions, consumer groups, and other forms of economic solidarity apart from cartels among capitals."[21]

Saunders makes blatant the fact that such "cartels among capitals" are simply another expression of class hierarchy: the "Disposal Debits" memo sees the managers, who do not have to pay the "Shit Fee," asking the workers: "*What would you have had us do? Negotiate inferior contracts? Act against our own healthy self-interest? Don't talk crazy*" (48). But the workers' identification with—and investment in—the company and its structures, in a context where their jobs and livelihoods are always on the line, ensures that these coercive elements do not lead to organized protest. Moreover, in having its workers sign up "freely" to the terms of their own subjugation, whether through investing in stock options or by carrying out seemingly mundane bureaucratic tasks such as filling out the "Daily Partner Performance Evaluation Form," the neoliberal corporation can reject the notion that any coercion is involved. The narrator of "Pastoralia" thus becomes what Jane Elliott calls a "suffering agent," the quintessential "loser" subject of neoliberal governmentality for whom "choice is experienced as a curse without simultaneously becoming a farce."[22] The narrator's options are never good ones, but he is continually put in the position of having to make a choice.

This emphasis on choice is why Nordstrom's counsel to the narrator to "*Feel no guilt*" for informing on Janet is darkly appropriate (59). Guilt, as I noted earlier, implies a willed moral transgression, and the condition of suffering agency creates in the narrator a sense of responsibility for the outcomes of his choices and actions, even as the reader can see that those choices and actions arise in a context of serious coercion and constraint. Shame, on the other hand, derives from class consciousness (or, more precisely, "class awareness") and is not an emotion we readily observe in the narrator of "Pastoralia."[23] This is not true of all the stories in *Pastoralia*; as David Rando has demonstrated, shame is a crucial emotion in "Sea Oak," and as we shall see in the next section, it will be important to the collection's closing story "The Falls" too. In his essay, perhaps the most influential consideration of Saunders's work to date, Rando considers "how shame might be emancipatory," how it might serve a demystifying role in drawing the subject's attention to their interpellation by the dominant ideology, and how that ideology might thus be challenged.[24] In this vein, Rando reads the narrator's key statement in "Sea Oak" about the return from the dead of his zombie Aunt Bernie—"I for sure don't plan on broadcasting this" (124)—as offering a performative contradiction, an expression that exposes shame to the reader even as it hides it from others in the narrator's world. The reader, then, becomes the vector of possible emancipation, even as the narrator seems to use his writing not in order to work to emancipate his class but to transcend it. As Rando puts it, "'Sea Oak' associates the act of writing with both social power and class betrayal."[25] The story's narrator, one might say, learns to exploit his own sincerity in the service of personal advancement.

If "Sea Oak" seems to bear out the core premise of Rando's essay—that "among other forms of marginalization, Saunders's subject is above all the American working class"—then that premise should be nuanced by our reading of "Pastoralia."[26] Rando's claim is correct only to the extent that we recognize that the status of the working class was transformed during the neoliberal period. This happened not only through increased racial and gender diversity (making it a "postmodern working class"), but also, as we have seen, in its structural and ideological relationship to capital, in terms of precarity, investment, and entrepreneurship. If this has an impact on the affective dimensions of class experience—because the suffering agency characteristic of neoliberal subjectivity blurs the boundary between guilt and shame—then it also impacts the aesthetic forms through which these structural, ideological, and affective changes are represented. This is where the writer's own labor becomes significant—particularly, in Saunders's case, the work of revision.

Revising Shame

A creative writing teacher at Syracuse University since 1996, Saunders has had plenty to say in print and in person about the writing process, above all about the importance of revising one's prose. "The best stories proceed from a mysterious truth-seeking impulse that narrative has when it is revised extensively," he opines in the title essay of his 2007 nonfiction collection *The Braindead Megaphone*.[27] Another essay in the book, "Thank You, Esther Forbes," pays tribute to its subject by using her novel *Johnny Tremain* as a case study in the power of revision. Forbes was the first writer to teach Saunders "that the sentence was where the battle was fought," a lesson he would learn again "in Hemingway, in Isaac Babel, Gertrude Stein, Henry Green" (61). These authors all wrote sentences "that had been the subject of so much concentration, they had become things in the world instead of attempts to catalog it," conveying to the reader that even a minimalist sentence "could have a thrilling quality of being over-full, saying more than its length should permit it to say" (61, 59). "Thank You, Esther Forbes" builds a veritable theology around such sentence writing. The essay is framed by Saunders's experience at Catholic school, where *Johnny Tremain* was first lent to him by Sister Lynette, a young nun whose attention he craved. Toward the essay's end, in a variation on "Godwin's Law"—where a hyperbolic comparison to the Nazis will eventually arise in any attempt to win an argument—Saunders contrasts Forbes's sentences with those of an SS officer whose passive constructions disclaimed his responsibility for the extermination of Jews, meaning "he accepted an inauthentic relation to his own prose, and thereby doomed himself to hell" (63). In contrast to this purveyor of malignant bureaucratese, "Forbes had fully invested herself in her sentences. She had made them her own, agreed to live or die by them, taken total responsibility for them. How had she done this? I didn't know. But I do now: she'd revised them" (62).

As we can see, Saunders's contentions about revision tend to escalate rapidly from the aesthetic to the moral and even theological realms. Revision not only makes a sentence more memorable, vivid, or interesting, it is the key to discovering subjective truth: "Working with language is a means by which we can identify the bullshit within ourselves (and others)" (63). One thing Saunders learned from Forbes was that "by honing the sentences you used to describe the world, you changed the inflection of your mind, which changed your perceptions" (62). Rather than *stemming* from a sincere attitude—knowing what one means to say and saying it—the process of revision therefore *produces* sincerity through a discovery process: "the process of improving our prose disciplines the mind, hones the logic, and, most important of all, tells us what we really think" (64). In this morally freighted realm, the work of revision is about the revelation, the exposure, of truth; more precisely, it is about overcoming those facets of one's own character that prevent revelation and militate against exposure.[28]

Saunders not only teaches at Syracuse but also studied there, taking his MFA under the tutelage of Tobias Wolff, himself a student of Raymond Carver. Saunders has inherited Carver's mantle as the most influential practitioner of the short story on the American literary scene, and has done so by writing about lower-class experience in a way that often echoes Carver.[29] Dubbing Saunders "one of the premier minimalist writers of the second generation," McGurl remarks that his stories "can be thought of as the crossing of Carver's lower-middle-class 'loser' aesthetic with some of the surreal craziness and violent public-sphericity . . . of Donald Barthelme."[30] Saunders has acknowledged the problem of overcoming Carver's influence, alongside that of Hemingway and other writers associated with minimalist writing.[31] He has also written a detailed appreciation of Barthelme's story "The School," in which he remarks that "writing short stories is very hard work."[32] As it was for Carver, "work"—along with "revision"—is a crucial term for Saunders.[33] This is something emphasized by the autobiography on his author's website, which unusually lists a series of jobs Saunders held before landing his post at Syracuse: an oil field geophysicist, a technical writer, "a doorman, a roofer, a convenience store clerk, and a slaughterhouse worker (a 'knuckle-puller,' to be exact)."[34] This extensive work experience "contributed," Saunders writes, "to my understanding of capitalism as a benign-looking thing that, as Terry Eagleton says, 'plunders the sensuality of the body.'"[35]

The reluctantly reflective and understated narrative voice of "Pastoralia" showcases Saunders's minimalist leanings, his Carverian belief that the body's sensuality—and the mind's energy—have been plundered before the story even begins. But the influence of Barthelme's antic postmodernism is equally evident in Saunders's willingness to display the continuing process of plunder in all its grotesque and maximalist detail. The combination of these opposed styles of writing has led McGurl to also describe Saunders's second-generation minimalist stories under the category of "miniaturism," which "might be described as maximalism in a minimalist package, or . . . as the becoming-maximal of Carverian minimalism."[36] Rather than minimalism's "resistance to the self-assertive blare of modern American gigantism," miniaturism indulges that blare, while at the same time refusing to gainsay the minimalist emphasis on revision and craft; indeed, "miniaturism could be said to intensify the commitment to craft that one finds in minimalism, or at least the commitment to *showing off* the intricate clockwork of its results."[37]

McGurl's categories are helpful here, but I want to supplement them with the findings of the previous section regarding the shifting character of the worker's status and subjectivity wrought through the category of human capital. Rather than see Saunders's revision of minimalism as simply the result of his stylistic influences—though it is of course partly that—I want to argue that the shift from describing lower-class working experience through Carverian minimalism to describing it through Saunders-esque miniaturism tracks a material transformation in that experience itself, its exposure not to the upward tide of the postwar boom that carried Carver to college but the downward pressure of neoliberal austerity that pushed Saunders near the breadline.

Here the story Saunders tells about the beginnings of his writing career is illuminating. In a 2013 preface written for a new edition of his first book, *CivilWarLand in Bad Decline* (1996), Saunders sets the composition of the stories in that collection in the context of his family and working life between 1989 and 1996. This was a period in which, as a father of two young girls, he worked for the Radian Corporation as a technical writer, having graduated from his Syracuse MFA without a clear literary identity or project. Saunders amusingly recalls writing Hemingway-inspired stories at Syracuse that "were stern and minimal and tragic and had nothing to do whatsoever with the life I was living or, for that matter, any life I had ever lived."[38] His initial attempts to depart from this approach culminated in a draft novel called "La Boda de Eduardo" ("Ed's Wedding"), the story of a wedding in Mexico where the people who attend "are described in Joycean/Lowryesque prose, which, in my hands, meant: as few verbs as possible, so as to ensure that nothing appeared to be happening, and if something inadvertently did happen, it didn't happen with any clarity." His wife's wounding response to this failed literary effort marked a turning point for Saunders, and the miniaturist stories of *CivilWarLand* were the eventual result.

Saunders presents this change not primarily as an aesthetic decision but as a truthful confrontation with the real conditions of his life. Throughout the preface, he combines comments on his literary development with observations on the economic challenges his family faced at the time, remarking "how close we were to the edge financially (we lived check to check, were running up huge credit card debt), feeling ourselves bringing up the back of the pack in terms of what kind of life we were making for our daughters relative to the lives of their peers." Worrying that "we'd missed the boat in terms of this thing called upward mobility," Saunders ponders how this state of affairs had come about:

> Don't get me wrong: it wasn't the Gulag. But I was puzzled by how difficult it was proving for me (a nice guy, an educated guy, a guy who loved his wife and kids) to put together a middle-class, or even lower-middle-class, livelihood for our family, and what it was costing me in terms of personal grace.

Although it doesn't comment directly on literary matters, this is perhaps the key passage in the preface. It suggests that if Carver's minimalism is the aesthetic of the American lower middle class circa 1970, at the tail end of the postwar economic surge that had seen that class uplifted from traditional working-class roots, then Saunders's miniaturism responds to altered historical conditions. It is the aesthetic of those striving, circa 1990, to *retain* lower-middle-class status, while constantly facing the threat of falling back into the precariat (or worse, the ranks of the unemployed) as they fight the tide of downward mobility that we now call neoliberalism.

"The Falls," the closing story in *Pastoralia* but the first from the collection to be published, can be read as a fictionalized reflection on this same formative period in Saunders's life.[39] The story appeared in *The New Yorker* in January 1996, only a few days after the publication of his debut collection, but it already signaled another turning point in the author's writing. All the stories in *CivilWarLand* had been first-person narratives, whereas "The Falls" is written in a free indirect style that switches between the focalized viewpoints of more than one character, a narrative mode the author would repeat many times thereafter. The story details an incident involving two characters inhabiting a small town somewhere in the American Midwest. The first of these is Morse, whom the story introduces in its opening lines as follows:

> Morse found it nerve-wracking to cross the St. Jude grounds just as school was being dismissed, because he felt that if he smiled at the uniformed Catholic

children they might think he was a wacko or pervert and if he didn't smile they might think he was an old grouch made bitter by the world, which surely, he felt, by certain yardsticks, he was. Sometimes he wasn't entirely sure that he wasn't even a wacko of sorts, although certainly he wasn't a pervert. Of that he was certain. Or relatively certain. Being overly certain, he was relatively sure, was what eventually made one a wacko. So humility was the thing, he thought, arranging his face into what he thought would pass for the expression of a man thinking fondly of his own youth, a face devoid of wackiness or perversion, humility was the thing. (175)

Though presented in an overtly comic register, Morse is only a heightened version of a character by now familiar to us from New Sincerity fiction: an anxious subject whose interiority is defined overwhelmingly through his internalization of the gaze of others. Morse's decision whether or not to smile at the Catholic children is denied any transparent relationship to interior feeling, with the staccato multi-clause conclusion to the opening sentence mimetically capturing his uncertainty as to what he feels and what he really is, independent of imposed social categories like "wacko" or "pervert." Indeed, variations on the word "certain" (and its close cognate, "sure") appear a comic eight times in this short paragraph, emphasizing through ironic repetition the insecurity of Morse's relationship to his social world.

In the works by Wallace, Eggers, Egan, and Whitehead that we have examined up to now, the pressures of society's gaze are felt mostly by middle-class characters. Morse's social insecurity, by contrast, is significantly linked to his precarious economic position. Living in a postindustrial town with "a nail salon in a restored gristmill and a café in a former coal tower," Morse works for a company called BlasCorp and "spends the best years of his life swearing at a photocopier," even as he wishes he could do something heroic like "discover a critical vaccine," "be a tortured prisoner of war," or "witness an actual miracle or save the president from an assassin or win the Lotto and give it all to charity" (180, 182). These pipe dreams contrast with Morse's actual circumstances: residing with his wife and two children in an "embarrassingly small rental house" to which he walks home from work "along the green river lined with expensive mansions whose owners he deeply resented" (176). As he walks on the day depicted in the story, he thinks of his son Robert's upcoming piano recital and recalls with pain that their family piano has been repossessed. Not only that, but his daughter Annie "had eaten the cardboard keyboard he'd made for Robert to practice on" (177), a detail that captures both the challenging economic situation of Morse's family and the unguarded quality of his thoughts.

Morse's straitened circumstances and limited self-awareness (exploited by Saunders for simultaneously comedic and discomforting effects) not only distinguish him from many middle-class subjects of literary New Sincerity, but also prevent him from confidently or unquestioningly inhabiting his own consciousness in the way the bourgeois subjects central to modernist free indirect discourse—Clarissa Dalloway, Isabel Archer, Leopold Bloom—were able to do. Whereas these characters certainly performed for the outside world— Mrs. Dalloway might "arrange her face" for a party, for instance—they did so confident of what the world required of them, intuiting the social forms that passed for good conduct.[40] Morse, as we learned in the story's first paragraph, can in contrast only perform "what he thought would pass for the expression of a man thinking fondly of his own youth," trying desperately to avoid the tag of "wacko" or "pervert." His social insecurity expresses itself not only in panicky thoughts but in agitated behavior, driven by the experience of shame:

> At work he was known to punctuate his conversations with brief wild laughs and gusts of inchoate enthusiasm and subsequent embarrassment, expressed by a sudden plunging of the hands into his pockets, after which he would yank his hands out of his pockets, too ashamed of his own shame to stand there merely grimacing for even an instant longer. (176)

The recursive and self-reflexive quality of shame is palpable in Morse's thoughts and actions, albeit his anxious thought patterns mark him out not as narcissistic and self-absorbed but as painfully earnest and sincere. Yet Morse's shame-filled brand of sincerity is not easily grounded in expressive subjectivity, in Trilling's "congruence between avowal and actual feeling." This is instead a sincerity that avows uncertainty as to "actual feeling," that betrays skepticism regarding the ontological priority of interior selfhood to the exterior gaze (to put it in a way that Morse himself never would). Confident expressions of interior feeling can only evade anxiously self-reflexive subjects like Morse, a character "ashamed of his own shame," worried about his own worry: "It worried him that Cummings might not like him, and it worried him that he was worried about whether a nut like Cummings liked him. Was he some kind of worrywart? It worried him" (177).

The Cummings whose possible dislike worries Morse is the other viewpoint character in the story. He is the parodic representative of another kind of modernist subject, the self-styled struggling artist—Stephen Dedalus, Tonio Kröger—and it is no coincidence that he is named after the American poet whose fragile word collages mark the lyrical edge of modernist experimentation. The free indirect style of Cummings's passages suitably break with grammatical correctness more than do those of Morse:

> To an interviewer in his head, Cummings said he felt the possible rain made the fine bright day even finer and brighter because of the possibility of its loss. The possibility of its ephemeral loss. The ephemeral loss of the day to the fleeting passages of time. Preening time. Preening nascent time, the blackguard. (179)

Taking up the archetypal modernist theme of time, Cummings's self-consciousness is linguistically oriented and poetically framed, and we see him carrying out the revisions in his head that Saunders encourages in his students. But here these revisions have the opposite effect to those counseled by his author, serving to amplify rather than evade cliché: "He thought with longing ardor of his blank yellow pad, he thought. He thought with longing ardor of his blank yellow pad, on which, this selfsame day, his fame would be wrought" (179). If Morse is the Saunders who struggled to support his wife and two children through deadening labor, then Cummings is the Saunders who wrote "La Boda de Eduardo." "In grad school I had grown suspicious of conventional literary beauty," the author writes in his *CivilWarLand* preface, but none of that suspicion is evident in Cummings, whose overblown aestheticism is heavily twinned with his narcissism, and whose comic delusions of grandeur are inseparable from his aesthetic outlook on the world.

Saunders spends the majority of the story setting up a contrast between these two characters before introducing the catalytic event toward the story's end. This is the moment when both characters see two young girls floating rapidly down the town's river in a disintegrating canoe toward the vertiginous falls of the story's title.[41] Saunders's use of free indirect style means that the characters' respective initial perceptions of this moment are registered in contrasting ways. When Morse hears the girls calling out to him with a cry for help, he initially assumes they must be yelling an insult. This leads him into another long interior monologue about the shameful woes of his life, before he eventually snaps out of it and is "stopped in his tracks, wondering what in the world two little girls were doing alone in a canoe speeding toward the Falls, apparently oarless" (183). Cummings, on the other hand, perceives the danger the girls are facing immediately, but he perceives that danger in a certain way, as follows:

> He rounded the last bend before the Falls, euphoric with his own possibilities, and saw a canoe the color of summer leaves ram the steep upstream wall of the Snag. The girls inside were thrown forward and shrieked with open mouths over frothing waves that would not let them be heard as the boat split open along some kind of seam and began taking on water in doomful fast quantities. (185)

The poet, "euphoric with his own possibilities," instinctively receives the girls' distress not as an occasion for action but as an occasion for literary impressionism. Cummings cannot help but take in the color of the canoe through its metaphoric resemblance to "summer leaves," cannot help but mentally append adjectives such as "frothing" and "doomful" that aestheticize the scene while drawing attention away from the urgency of action. This is a critique of art as spectatorship, of an implicit commitment to the priority of detached perception at the cost of real lives. As a result of this orientation, Cummings, despite his dawning awareness that he must do something, remains beautifully paralyzed: "Cummings stood stunned, his body electrified, hairs standing up on the back of his craning neck, thinking, I must do something, their faces are bloody, but what, such fast cold water, still I must do something, and he stumbled over the berm uncertainly, looking for help but finding only a farm field of tall dry corn" (185).

The contrast with Morse is drawn in the final section of the story, which begins not with thinking but with action: "Morse began to run" (185). Yet this active impulse does not keep Morse's self-consciousness in abeyance, as his thoughts move rapidly from the fate of the girls, to the hope that "several sweaty, decisive men were already on the scene," to the idea that his connection with such decisive men might cause his wife "to regard him in a more favorable sexual light," to berating himself for even entertaining such thoughts of sex:

> What kind of thing was that to be thinking at a time like this, with children's lives at stake? He was bad, that was for sure. There wasn't an earnest bone in his body. Other people were simpler and looked at the world with clearer eyes, but he was self-absorbed and insincere and mucked everything up. (186–87)

The reader knows by this point in the story, of course, that clarity of vision—the painterly precision of a Cummings—is not necessarily the key to sincerity, and that in fact Morse's suspicion of his own insincerity is the very thing that marks him out as sincere. But Saunders further complicates this reading in the story's closing lines, once again focalized through Morse:

> They were dead. They were frantic, calling out to him, but they were dead, as dead as the ancient dead, and he was alive, he was needed at home, it was a no-brainer, no one could possibly blame him for this one, and making a low sound of despair in his throat he kicked off his loafers and threw his long ugly body out across the water. (188)

In the sentence that ends the story and the *Pastoralia* collection, Saunders offers a stark division between thought and action. The first half of the sentence, ending with "no one could possibly blame him for this one," is a straightforward transcription of Morse's thoughts into third-person discourse, and its message to himself is to do nothing about the girls, to think of his own family and not risk himself for a lost cause. In the second half of the sentence, however, we move from Morse's thoughts to his actions, with the striking keyword being the conjunction "and." If the word here was "but," and the line therefore read, "but making a low sound of despair in his throat he kicked off his loafers and threw his long ugly body across the water," then Morse's consciousness could still be said to govern his action. That action would be taken despite his better judgment but would nonetheless still fall within his conscious intention. However, the "and," somewhat paradoxically, divorces thought from action, so that there is no way for Morse to narrate his actions to himself. His "long ugly body" acts for him, with the story thereby completing its dismantling of the traditional hierarchy of beauty and ugliness. Beauty has been corrupted as a virtue through Cummings's shameless glorying in freedom of consciousness and passive aestheticism. Through Morse's and the story's final thoughtless gesture, ugliness—and the shame it arouses—are redeemed.

Although it will be difficult to discover the truth of the following suggestion until Saunders donates his archive to an institution (and perhaps not even then, depending on the survival of his drafts), this replacement of "but" by "and" strikes me as the typical product of the work of revision, the process that according to Saunders "disciplines the mind, hones the logic and . . . tells us what we really think." Retaining "but" in the sentence would have meant that what Saunders "really thinks" is that shame can be consciously challenged by a subject, that the subject can take the steps suggested by Helen Merrell Lynd, using shame as a route to emancipation and the overcoming of (not simply escape from) class hierarchy.[42] By substituting "and," Saunders suggests that what he "really thinks" is the opposite: that the only way beyond shame is through the oblivion of consciousness in the pursuit of action. In this scenario, only the reader remains conscious at the end of the story, thus discovering themself to be the true subject of what, drawing on one of Saunders's own phrases, I will call his "shock methodology." The character and implications of this methodology will be taken up in the final section of this chapter; before then we must return to Saunders's partner in shock comedy, Helen DeWitt, and to the figure of the neoliberal entrepreneur.

Selling Shamelessness

The precariously employed service workers that populate George Saunders's stories represent one paradigm of the neoliberal subject, both empirically (there are increasingly many of them in neoliberalism's expanding "gig economy") and imaginatively (they are the newly "liberated" managers of their own human capital). Yet these subjects are merely the shadow images of the true neoliberal hero: the entrepreneur. While the Chicago School neoliberals wished to reconceive all adult humans as "entrepreneurs of themselves," in Foucault's famous phrase, the vision of the entrepreneur that inspired this idea did not originate with Gary Becker or Milton Friedman, nor even with Friedrich Hayek, but with an older Austrian economist: Joseph Schumpeter. Schumpeter saw the entrepreneur as the central protagonist in capitalism's historical rise, the individual genius without whom this modern mode of production would never have prospered. Unlike most of his peers and inheritors,

Schumpeter was willing to outline his argument in dialogue with the diagnosis of capitalism laid out by Karl Marx. Granting the correctness of Marx's insights about the "automatism of accumulation" and the extraction of surplus value that spurs capitalist production, Schumpeter rebuked what he saw as Marx's lack of attention to the way that surplus value gets reinvested into a successful business. "Manifestly, the captured surplus value *does not invest itself* but must be *invested*," he averred in a 1927 essay. "This means on the one hand that it must not be consumed by the capitalist, and on the other hand that the important point is *how* it is invested. Both factors lead away from the idea of objective automatism to the field of behavior and motive—in other words, from the *social* "force" to the *individual*—physical or family; from the *objective* to the *subjective*."[43]

The individual entrepreneur that Schumpeter works so hard to make space for in his theory of capitalism is, nevertheless, "one of the more enigmatic characters in modern social theory."[44] His features—and for Schumpeter the entrepreneur is always a he—include "hard-headedness, concentration on profit, authority, capacity for work, and inexorable self-discipline, especially in renouncing other aspects of life."[45] He is a person of "extraordinary physical and nervous energy," one whose most productive work often "falls into the evening and night hours, when few men manage to preserve their full force and originality."[46] His trademark is "departure from routine," and his most valuable skill is "critical receptivity to new facts."[47] The "critical" here is as important as the "receptivity," since the entrepreneur must know what to disregard as well as what to attend to, must be able "to evaluate forcefully the elements in a given situation that are relevant to the achievement of success, while ignoring all others."[48] This entrepreneur need not be a charismatic figure; as Schumpeter writes elsewhere, "A genius in the business office may be, and often is, utterly unable outside of it to say boo to a goose—both in the drawing room and on the platform."[49] The entrepreneur is rather a pragmatist, a man whose contribution "does not essentially consist in either inventing anything or otherwise creating the conditions which the enterprise exploits. It consists in getting things done."[50]

Joe in *Lightning Rods* is certainly a man who gets things done. He fits Schumpeter's description in most other ways too, displaying inexorable self-discipline, copious energy, laser-like focus on his goals, alertness to opportunities, and critical receptivity to new facts (alongside a willingness to disregard facts that don't suit him, and invent others that do). His path to success begins when, following his epiphany about "shame, false shame," he resolves to turn his recurrent sexual fantasy—which he masturbates to in a rented trailer when not out trying and failing to sell vacuum cleaners—into a product for the workplace. Joe's fantasy involves an image of the upper half of a woman's body visible above a wall or leaning out of a window, with her lower half invisible while she is secretly penetrated by a man from behind, or, in Joe's terms, is given "the old Atchison Topeka," "the full-service 24-hour Revco from the rear," "the old Triple Jeopardy," "the old Roto-Rooter."[51] As these phrases suggest, Joe thinks of this furtive sex act through folksy euphemisms, a mode of thought that extends to his view of the business world.

The product he comes up with based on his fantasy—the "lightning rod"—is a prime example. It names a woman employee of a firm who is "bi-functional," hired to carry out both a standard secretarial role in the office and to disappear every so often to the disabled bathroom, where her lower half is carried through the wall by a "transporter" so that one of her male colleagues can have sex with her from behind, with both parties remaining anonymous in the transaction. The ostensible purpose of this striking "departure from routine" is to reduce the level of sexual harassment at the firm, on the basis that "high-performance" male employees will not be distracted from their "results-orientated" work by sexual impulses (108), while female employees—whether "single-function" secretaries or lightning rods who "provide an outlet" (59, 25)—will no longer receive unwanted sexual advances from their male colleagues (and will thus no longer bring claims against their employer). Remarkably, Joe's innovation is a big success: the men who avail of the service find their focus and productivity increasing, while the female employees receive less harassment, and their absentee rates significantly diminish. As Sianne Ngai notes, Joe turns out to have come up with "the perfect idea for increasing the profits and protecting the assets of American corporations."[52]

On this basis, Ngai describes Joe as an embodiment of capital itself—specifically, "a white male heterosexual American personification of capital"—and reads *Lightning Rods* as an allegory of how capital relentlessly pursues economic incentives while also finding "ingenious way after way to capitalize on cultural and noneconomic factors, much of it based on civil rights legislation protecting the rights of women and minorities in the workplace."[53] While this reading makes evident sense of much of the novel's peculiar comedy and power, I want to challenge elements of it by pointing to those dimensions of *Lightning Rods* that relate to neoliberal capitalism in particular rather than capitalism in general. These dimensions include the novel's striking narrative voice, its historical setting, and its representation of class and entrepreneurship. My reading will also draw out the novel's ambivalence around the figure of the entrepreneur, an ambivalence underplayed in Ngai's analysis.

Joe's penchant for cliché and euphemism evidences the widespread dissemination, in the world of *Lightning Rods*, of neoliberal norms at the level of discourse, what Brown calls neoliberalism as "a normative order of reason."[54] Take for instance this early passage, which explains Joe's willingness to move across multiple states—from Eureka, Missouri, to Eureka, Florida—to take up his vacuum cleaner salesman job:

> It's important to give that new job 101%, 25 hours a day, 366 days a year. You simply can't afford to have any distractions. If the reason you gave up your old job was that it was not sufficiently remunerative to enable you to meet your commitments, you may well find yourself with some debts which it would be distracting to deal with at this time. It's absolutely vital to start the new job in an area where any difficulties you may have experienced in the past are unlikely to lead to unwelcome distractions. He needed to be based in a locality presenting no foreseeable distractions, and he selected the nearest Electrolux office which would enable him to meet that need, and he walked straight in. (6)

This paragraph captures in microcosm the distinctiveness of the novel's free indirect discourse. Joe's perspective is articulated through a blend of popular self-help rhetoric and corporate management dictums, a discourse that serves—through a seamless oscillation between second and third person, "you" and "he"—to constantly abstract from Joe's personal experience to the general principles he takes to underpin his action. The result is a simultaneously transparent and euphemistic discourse that seems to speak of things straightforwardly and directly even as it can distract the reader from noticing what is being revealed: in this case, that Joe is a man escaping from his debts, portrayed here as "unwelcome distractions." The comedy of the style derives from its combination of urgency—sentences begin "It's important,"

"You simply can't afford," "It's absolutely vital," "He needed to be based"—with overfamiliar positive-thinking cliché—"101%, 25 hours a day, 366 days a year," "meet your commitments," "meet that need." Much of this comedy is accumulative, not just at the level of style—the reader's delight at DeWitt's ability to sustain this combination of urgency and cliché without ever becoming boring—but also at the level of plot. Escalating through a series of logistical problems that Joe finds ingenious ways to solve, *Lightning Rods* proceeds from the protagonist's revelation about shame to become what David Flusfeder calls "a comedy of procedure," a study "of how goods and people are engineered into becoming parts of a functioning world."[55]

In this world virtually everyone thinks and speaks exactly like Joe, so that "the style and tone of narration stays remarkably consistent regardless of which particular character's subjectivity inflects it" and "all points of view seem to converge."[56] While one can read this convergence as an allegory of capital's rhetorical dominance, as Ngai does, it can also be read as a neoliberal revision of the entrepreneurial function identified by Schumpeter, a function whose erosion in midcentury monopoly capitalism led him to believe that capitalism itself was in inexorable decline and would not survive. Neoliberals beginning with Ludwig von Mises, on the other hand, increasingly "saw entrepreneurship as a general feature of human behavior due to the need to make choices under conditions of unavoidable uncertainty. For Mises, the entrepreneur was literally everyone."[57] Or, at least, the entrepreneur *could* be everyone: rather than fatalistically write off entrepreneurs as a dying breed, one could work to produce them, sometimes by combining individuals into functioning units. Herbert Giersch, president of the Mont Pelerin Society during the 1980s, speculated on the value of "forming teams": "there is no shortage of entrepreneurial talent, but institutional resistances and technical requirements may create so complicated situations that no single person, but only a combination of persons, can successfully perform the entrepreneurial role."[58]

One notable element of *Lightning Rods*, in this respect, is that despite his own ingenuity and critical receptivity, Joe does not solve all the problems he faces by himself. Indeed, he comes to rely particularly heavily on the interventions of Lucille, the "woman in a thousand" (145) who proceeds from a successful stint as a lightning rod to become Joe's personal assistant and who considers herself "about *thirty* times as good as the average PA, and ten times as good as the average senior PA" (93). A good example of his reliance on Lucille occurs when Joe invites her back to his penthouse apartment. The reader is led by the setup to expect a romantic liaison between the two, but instead we witness Lucille, in a virtuoso monologue, solving a problem that had been bugging Joe, which in turns leads Joe, in the final line of the scene, to "an incredibly brilliant idea" (253). The coming together of these characters turns out to be intellectual rather than physical: the point is that in a world where sex is no more than a commodity, the sexiest thing is a brilliant idea profitably shared.

Apart from profitable ideas, what Lucille shares most closely with Joe is the ability to transcend the problem of shame, something she does by psychologically bypassing narratives about class and gender exploitation. These narratives occasionally surface in the text—in the usual euphemistic vocabulary—only to be quickly swept away by the propulsive can-do attitude of the protagonists. We learn, for instance, that aside from Lucille, "the other early lightning rods found the practicalities of the job harder to adjust to. In later years, looking back on their experiences, a common theme was a feeling that they had been inadequately prepared [by Joe]" (95). This departure through prolepsis from the novel's chronological "comedy of procedure" is a regular occurrence, but usually, as Jasper Bernes observes, it is a technique used satirically, allowing successful characters like Joe and Lucille to retrospectively narrate their triumphs to an implicitly awestruck audience.[59] So it is that, in this case, we move quickly from these nameless other women to Lucille's perspective:

> Lucille by that stage had put it all behind her and was making a million a year as a litigation lawyer, but every once in a while she would pick up a paper and see a story about someone who hadn't been able to put it behind her. Someone who had spent an unpleasant three weeks back in 1999 and had never recovered from the shock. Well, just reading between the lines Lucille could tell that this was someone who should never have gone in for that kind of work in the first place. (95)

The question of exploitation is banished from such considerations. Freedom of contract places the onus on the female employee to prepare herself psychologically to act as a lightning rod and to deal with any trauma that results from the experience. To even have a psychological reaction, moreover, is to be responsible for misunderstanding the experience: "the whole point of lightning rods was that it was a purely physical transaction, with no *social* transaction of any kind" (244). By removing any element of the social, one also removes shame, a feeling that is "associated with involuntary subjection to social forces, and marks the inherent priority and superiority of those forces to any given individual."[60] In a neoliberal world where there is, notoriously, "no such thing as society," seeing like a neoliberal means acknowledging no such thing as shame.

The reference to 1999 in the quotation above suggests that DeWitt sets the main action of her story in a specific historical moment. Ngai seems to miss this in her claim that the novel's "historical indefiniteness" makes it less temporally situated and "more like a story of the 'perpetual present' [Moishe] Postone associates with the 'apparently eternal necessity' of the production of value."[61] The present of *Lightning Rods* is more accurately described, I would argue, as the present of capitalist realism, when "capitalism seamlessly occupies the horizon of the thinkable."[62] A useful way to locate the novel in its historical moment is to compare it to perhaps the canonical text in the tradition of American literature about salesmanship, Arthur Miller's *Death of a Salesman*, performed for the first time exactly half a century earlier in 1949. The play's protagonist Willy Loman is a victim of postwar capitalism's nascent cult of personality: misunderstanding its vectors of power, he converts his need to be "impressive, and well liked" into a source of weakness rather than strength.[63] "The only thing you got in this world is what you can sell," his friend and sponsor Charley tells him. "And the funny thing is that you're a salesman, and you don't know that."[64] The ostensible point of Miller's play is to allow his audience to see that "this world"—the capitalist world that brings shame to a man like Willy and provokes his tragic suicide—is fundamentally unjust and should give way to a socialist alternative.[65]

As with many an American text, however, the full force of this anticapitalist message is somewhat undercut at the play's conclusion, when Willy's life is romanticized in Charley's eulogy at his funeral:

> Nobody dast blame this man. You don't understand; Willy was a salesman. And for a salesman, there is no rock bottom to the life. He don't put a bolt to a nut, he don't tell you the law or give you medicine. He's a man way out there in

the blue, riding on a smile and a shoeshine. And when they start not smiling back—that's an earthquake. And then you get yourself a couple of spots on your hat, and you're finished. Nobody dast blame this man. A salesman is got to dream, boy. It comes with the territory.[66]

While Joe in *Lightning Rods* would likely admire the sentiment of Charley's words, his own way of putting things is substantially less poetic and more pragmatic. Ironically for a man whose success stems from commodifying his own fantasy, Joe sees the delusion of dreaming as the salesman's enemy. "Any salesman knows that you have to deal with people the way they are," he thinks to himself early on. "Not how you'd like them to be" (17). This realist perspective is underlined countless times by Joe, and applies to himself as much as to others: "If you're a salesman, you have to deal with yourself the way you are. Not how you'd like to be" (21). At the same time Joe has no problem transforming Willy's beliefs about being "impressive, and well liked" into successful self-commodification: "When you're in sales you've always got one thing to sell, and that's yourself" (6). The death of the salesman as deluded dreamer is transfigured in the birth of the salesman as capitalist realist.

This shift from dreaming to realism might seem to indicate that Willy Loman's sincerely deluded shame is rewritten in *Lightning Rods* as Joe's undeluded and shameless cynicism. But Joe is the opposite of a cynic: indeed, his sincerity is crucial to the novel's singular effects. As Bernes notes, in his requisition of disabled bathrooms for the use of lightning rods, Joe "displays a surprisingly sincere desire to meet the needs of disabled users of such bathrooms, and invents fully adjustable fixtures, including a variable height toilet that can be automatically stowed away under the floor."[67] It is important that Joe's imaginative sympathies extend only to men—his invention of the "Adjusta" toilet is inspired by his sympathy with the plight of a male dwarf he encounters on a bus—but it is likewise important that DeWitt presents this less as personal misogyny on the part of Joe than as the systematic way in which seeing like a neoliberal assumes a kind of male gaze. When women are willing to adopt that gaze in seeking their fortune as individuals, Joe has plenty of respect for them: "The more people sincerely want to do what's right, the more important it is to help them" (253).

Thus, and despite the dark consequences of Joe's innovations for the workplace and the role of women within it, Lee Konstantinou is surely right to observe that "the unexpected depth of Joe's pathos is the most powerful element of *Lightning Rods*, and makes the book far more than a toss-off, a virtuoso stand-up routine."[68] The key to evoking this pathos is to present Joe's shamelessness as sincere rather than cynical, and as linked to a vision of classlessness that has both neoliberal and more traditional American roots.[69] Rather than embrace Willy Loman's dream—what his son Happy calls "the only dream you can have—to come out number-one man"[70]—Joe rejects the selfish ethos of capitalism even as he embraces its classless can-do ethos. "I'll try to be more considerate in future," he thinks aloud to himself late in the novel. "I'll try to be a better person. I'll try to let my success be a force for good. After all, all any of us can ever do is try. All you can *ever* do is do the best you can" (269). The peculiar challenge of *Lightning Rods* is that it sells its reader the idea that neoliberalism can speak sincerely, and leaves us to locate the untruths underpinning this sincerely held worldview. For his own part, Joe does not think he is selling his audience anything. Indeed, he comes to feel that, like Schumpeter's entrepreneur, he lacks the personal charisma for such a task: "Basically, he wasn't a salesman. He was an ideas man. And those are two very different animals" (109).

This could easily be an admission on Helen DeWitt's own behalf. *Lightning Rods*, "the great office novel of the decade," was published in 2011, more than ten years after the author's critically and commercially successful debut *The Last Samurai* (2000).[71] Yet 1999 is not only the moment in which DeWitt's second novel is set, but also the moment, according to its author, when it was written. As DeWitt struggled to sell her first book to publishers, she wrote *Lightning Rods* in a hurry, in a way that "was originally supposed to pave the way for *The Seventh Samurai* (original title)" by being "completely UNLIKE *Samurai*."[72] Asked about the connection between these seemingly contrasting projects, DeWitt mused that *Lightning Rods* was

> probably some kind of subconscious reaction to the initial resistance [among prospective publishers] encountered by *Samurai*, all those people who insisted that readers didn't want all this extraneous material: so Joe is a guy who starts out selling Encyclopaedia Britannica, then moves to vacuum cleaners, and finally commodifies his sexual fantasies because there just weren't enough people buying the Encyclopaedia Britannica.[73]

That DeWitt reads her second novel as an allegory of the problem of selling her first will not surprise readers familiar with the stories of publishing travails that litter not only this and many other interviews, but also DeWitt's personal blog and the majority of the stories in her collection *Some Trick* (2018). Indeed, the allegory runs deeper still. The salesman who works on commission, as Willy Loman is shamefully forced to do at the end of his life, is the forerunner of the gig economy worker, the "entrepreneur" of his or her own human capital. And both these figures find their reflection in the late-twentieth-century novelist who lacks a supportive infrastructure, for instance a creative writing position that can pay the bills. As perhaps the contemporary writer who most clearly calls back to the autonomy and experimentation of earlier literary moments, DeWitt is certainly an ideas person: surely no American writing today has newer and better ideas. The problem under neoliberalism—and despite the official story it sells us—is that unless you can surround yourself with a team, you just can't make it on your own.

Commencing with Capitalism

When she learned of the death of David Foster Wallace in September 2008, DeWitt posted a tribute on her blog. "DFW lies in the arms of sleep's cousin," she began, going on to praise the author's "ravishingly lovely gift for voice," his willingness "to write texts that would challenge readers but be enjoyable enough to encourage them to take up the challenge," and his belief "that many people could be brought to surpass what they thought they could do, if someone was willing to take the trouble." "We were lucky to have had him," she signed off.[74] A few days later, following intermediate posts about the financial crisis exploding at the same time, she returned to the subject of Wallace, and specifically the commencement speech he gave at Kenyon College in 2005, a speech that appeared in many places in the period following his death (and was later repackaged as the short book *This Is Water*). The central premise of Wallace's speech is that the frustration we feel with other people as we experience a "consumer-hell-type situation," such as a lengthy traffic jam or crowded supermarket, is really a reflection of our "natural, hard-wired default setting, which is to be deeply and literally self-centered, and to see and interpret everything through this lens of self."[75] The thrust of his advice is that the way to escape this "default setting" is to choose to see the other people involved in these hellish scenarios less as sources of anger than as vessels for imaginative empathy: it then becomes possible to experience these situations "as not only meaningful but sacred, on fire with the same force that lit the stars—compassion, love, the sub-surface unity of all things." "Not that that mystical stuff's necessarily true," Wallace stressed. "The only thing that's capital-T True is that you get to decide how you're going to try to see it." Retaining your default setting might be comforting—and, in our system, even profitable—but it is really the road to spiritual ruin.

In her post, DeWitt criticizes Wallace's invitation to concentrate on our own psychological processes in response to the frustrations he outlines. "It's a bit demoralizing," she remarks, "that a speech cited for its inspirational qualities should be one that offers acquiescence as the first port of call (nothing to be done, might as well make the best of it)."[76] Instead of turning our attention inward, we should turn it outward to the problem at hand, and see how it might be solved for the good of the many:

> What if there is a solution, something that would make lines in stores move faster, reduce crowds? If there is a solution, a really good solution, surely it will be a successful meme—it will spread through overcrowded grocery stores across the city! the state! the country! the world!

DeWitt goes on to concoct a kind of madcap alternative commencement speech, one that imagines what would happen if everyone responded to their hatred of peak-time shopping and driving by choosing instead to buy food in bulk. This might lead, she considers, to the establishment of a bartering economy at the local level, where people would knock on each other's door when they needed to swap or borrow items of food. "Well, I'm just going around and around in my head," she writes at the conclusion of this lengthy thought experiment:

> But the point is, there are things I can do that will tell me more about the world than I already think I know. I can find something out by unilateral action; I can find out more by sharing ideas with my fellow man. And I can start with something that has an extremely high probability of being true: most people hate peak-time grocery shopping, most people hate traffic jams. To me that looks more attractive than making life bearable by inventing highly improbable backstories about the people I run up against in a crowd.

In the terms of this chapter, DeWitt is here accusing Wallace of seeing like a neoliberal. Combined with the thoroughgoing irony that characterizes *Lightning Rods*, her alternative commencement speech might thus seem to open onto a coherent anti-neoliberal politics. But things are not quite so straightforward. "DeWitt is the rare chronically impecunious writer who speaks in praise of bankers and Wall Street lawyers," we learn in a profile of the author. "She thinks the publishing industry would improve if it took lessons from Michael Lewis's *Moneyball* and imposed a system like sabermetrics on authors."[77] On her blog DeWitt has expressed admiration for Lewis's work, sharing her delight when, googling his name, she came across a piece of his that criticized the "extraordinary anticommercial attitudes" he found in 1980s Britain. "The genius of Lewis," DeWitt remarks,

> is to enable the reader to appreciate the ingenuity of persons capable of spotting a market inefficiency and exploiting it—Bill Walsh developing the passing game in football, Billy Beane using statistics to get the most out of the cashstrapped Oakland A's. And with this genius comes incredulous outrage: incredulity, outrage, at those who have institutionalized sheer lumpen stupidity.[78]

DeWitt here extols two kinds of genius: the savant who exploit market inefficiencies, and the writer who conveys the stories of those market savants. This recalls, of course, both *Lightning Rods* itself—a novel concerned with a person who exploits a "shameful" market inefficiency with spectacular results—and the genius of the writer who is able to bring us this story in an original way. But the praise of Lewis and his ingenious subjects also gives us another way to make sense of the tone of DeWitt's novel and the pathos it affords to Joe: there is, amid DeWitt's critique of capitalism's calumnies, a sneaking regard for the entrepreneurial genius who takes the risks necessary to master the system and make it work.[79]

This ambivalence about capitalism and risk—which I see less as particular to DeWitt and more as a symptom of the period in which she and her cohort are writing—can be explored more fully with respect to another book she praises in similar terms to Lewis's *Moneyball*. In an author's note appended to a story in *Some Trick*, DeWitt describes her text as an attempt to "show the way mathematicians think" and to "make non-intuitive ways of thinking about probability visible on the page."[80] Naming Peter Bernstein's 1996 book *Against the Gods: The Remarkable Story of Risk* as an "inspiration" for this attempt, she quotes a line from its opening page: "The revolutionary idea that defines the boundary between modern times and the past is the mastery of risk: the notion that the future is more than a whim of the gods and that men and women are not passive before nature."[81] As it happens, David Foster Wallace underlined precisely the same sentence in the copy of Bernstein's book held in his archive at the Harry Ransom Center. He also wrote "Moneyball" in the margin of a later page, indicating further overlap with DeWitt's chosen reading. Yet what is most interesting about *Against the Gods*, for our purposes, are passages that Wallace doesn't always underline and DeWitt doesn't quote, but that indicate the underpinning—and historically specific—assumptions of Bernstein's approach in writing his history of risk. "This book tells the story," we read on the opening page, "of a group of thinkers whose remarkable vision revealed how to put the future at the service of the present." These same thinkers "converted risk-taking into one of the prime catalysts that drives modern Western society." "Like Prometheus," they "converted the future from an enemy into an opportunity." We owe to their insights into risk nothing less than "economic growth, improved quality of life, and technological progress."[82]

Against the Gods is written, in other words, from a perspective that assumes that Western capitalism and its mode of risk-taking is the driver of all that is good in contemporary life. When Bernstein writes proudly of "our modern market economy that nations around the world are hastening to join," since "the free economy, with choice at its center, has brought humanity unparalleled access to the good things in life," he recalls Fukuyama at his most triumphalist.[83] "If we had no liquid capital markets that enable savers to diversify their risks," Bernstein claims in a passage starred by Wallace, "if investors were limited to owning just one stock (as they were in the early days of capitalism), the great innovative enterprises that define our age—companies like Microsoft, Merck, DuPont, Alcoa, Boeing, and McDonald's—might never have come into being."[84] Now, just because Wallace underlines and stars many of these passages does not mean he agrees with their sentiments. *Westward* is, after all, in large part a satire of McDonald's and the McDonaldization of culture that late capitalism portends. Nor does DeWitt's citing of *Against the Gods* as an inspiration serve to out her as any kind of dyed-in-the-wool neoliberal. But what I want to suggest is that any reflex assumption we might make that literary New Sincerity—whether in the work of Wallace, DeWitt, or any other writer featured in this book—can be straightforwardly distanced from the neoliberal values of its historical moment would be mistaken. In the age of capitalist realism, even work that challenges the boundaries of literary realism does not necessarily articulate (or even aim to articulate) an alternative to capitalism.

This is even clearer in the case of George Saunders. Like Wallace, Saunders has given a commencement speech that went viral and was later turned into a short book. Speaking to graduating students at Syracuse in 2013, and implicitly recalling Wallace's conception of the "default setting," Saunders identified "a series of built-in confusions that are probably somehow Darwinian," the first of which is that "we're central to the universe (that is, our personal story is the main and most interesting story, the *only* story, really)."[85] Saunders counseled his audience to resist such confusions, and to do so through practicing kindness: "It's a little facile, maybe, and certainly hard to implement, but I'd say, as a goal in life, you could do worse than: *Try to be kinder.*"[86] Commenting on this speech, Kasia Boddy observes that, for Saunders, "being kind is both a personal and political imperative."[87] As she also recognizes, however, there is no clear division between the personal and political in Saunders, something the author has acknowledged in an interview: "whatever political content my stories have comes out of the personal."[88] Saunders thinks of the object of his satire as "human tendency, rather than one particular political or cultural manifestation of that tendency"; what this means, in effect, is that "the enemy is us."[89] What Saunders calls "our public institutions—our companies and our government and our media" are merely reflections of our internal processes: "these institutions absolutely do not exist separately from ourselves, but exist within us, and the 'real' media/government/corporations are only manifestations of these internal ones."[90] This is, as Boddy notes, an uncomfortable position to adopt for a writer whose stories depict "hostile environments which oppress and exploit workers."[91] It can seem to make those workers responsible for their own oppression, diminishing class conflict in a way that dovetails with official neoliberal narratives.

Elsewhere, Saunders has been more explicit about his views on capitalism. "Now, profit is fine; economic viability is wonderful," he writes in "The

Braindead Megaphone." "But if these trump every other consideration, we will be rendered perma-children, having denied ourselves use of our highest faculties."[92] This suggests that Saunders objects primarily to the neoliberal form of capitalism rather than capitalism per se, an idea corroborated by interview comments in which he contrasts a present-day form of capitalism "that says 'if you've got it, you deserve it, no guilt, don't worry about it,'" with what he calls "the Emersonian, Whitmanesque form which says 'there's no point in any of this democracy and capitalism if we're not simply making more citizens, making better citizens, making the lives of the least among us better.'"[93] Saunders argues for the need to "rejigger" contemporary capitalism "to somehow at least think of" society's poorest members: "Otherwise there's going to be a revolution—or a suppressed revolution, which is even worse."[94] These sentiments return us to Saunders's views on kindness: kindness and empathy are the qualities we must cultivate in ourselves in order to avoid revolution (successful or suppressed). Literature offers a means to enhance those qualities because it "ennobles us."[95] Here it is telling, as Boddy astutely points out, that the line we earlier saw Saunders attribute in more than one place to Terry Eagleton—"capitalism plunders the sensuality of the body"—is in fact a quotation from the playwright Naomi Wallace, whereas Eagleton says something different: "The goal of Marxism is to restore to the body its plundered powers." "Eagleton is presenting Marx's *solution* to the problem of capitalism—communism," Boddy writes, whereas "Saunders is not a communist, but a self-described 'Eastern liberal,' and for him, the restoration of feeling, taste, smell, and touch is the work of literature."[96]

Of course, it has not been my practice in *New Sincerity* to privilege an author's statements about their beliefs and practices over the evidence of their work—quite the opposite.[97] As this chapter has shown, however, and as a small number of critics have acknowledged, the evidence of the work is mixed. Saunders's stated agenda of kindness and empathy places him firmly, Daniel Hartley observes, in the liberal humanist tradition. This is a tradition "which poses structural political and economic problems in individualist, ethical, and inter-personal terms, and which sees in literature and culture a repository of transhistorical moral values which are widely unavailable in the society at large."[98] Saunders's affinity for this tradition means that while his fiction shows acute attentiveness to "the social fabric of neoliberal America," his response to social problems "is individualization and moralization."[99] Yet Hartley stills sees something radical in the symbolic contradictions of Saunders's fiction: "whether intentional or not (and I imagine it is not), he has produced nothing so much as a *reductio ad absurdum* of the liberal-humanist position under neoliberalism."[100]

Hartley may well be right that the symbolic contradictions of Saunders's fiction are not intentional, but we should also recall that the complex relationship between authorial intention and aesthetic articulation has been central to the account of literary New Sincerity I have advanced throughout this book. Recognition of this complexity has underpinned my treatment of the new form of class-inflected double consciousness in Whitehead's early novels, and of the gender- and genre-derived divisions in the narrative voice of Egan's *Look at Me*. I have shown how the writer-reader relationship in Eggers's early work is imagined through a logic of credit and debt, whereby the writer simultaneously embraces and disavows a reader who can resist the intentional consciousness that would attempt to profit from the future by reducing it to the present. And I have explored how, for the Hegelian Wallace, the artwork embodies the expression of an authorial intention that can only be established retrospectively through an act of reader recognition. Whence the fraught dynamics of the writer-reader relationship—the oscillation between control and its relinquishment—addressed in psychological and libidinal terms at the finale of *Westward* and dramatized in the art of James Incandenza in *Infinite Jest*.

The instantiation and relinquishment of control is likewise central to Saunders's fiction, and is intertwined with his aesthetic investment in shock. In his own public remarks following Wallace's death, delivered not in a blog post but at an official memorial service, Saunders described the effect of reading for the first time Wallace's 1999 short story collection *Brief Interviews with Hideous Men*. "I found the book was doing weird things to my mind and body," he told the audience, "a kind of ritual stripping away of the habitual" that derived from Wallace's "shock methodology," the *"terrified-tenderness"* induced by his prose.[101] Despite Saunders's proclamations about kindness, his own fiction can be described in similar terms; as Jurrit Daalder observes, "Saunders can hardly write a single story without resorting to shock tactics."[102] Daalder contends that Saunders's adoption of such tactics carries more risk to readers than his "cruel-to-be-kind justifications" would suggest, with his belief that readerly shock will engender compassion "based on a false presumption that the artist does have the ability to anticipate these feelings and that the reading experience can, therefore, be micro-managed" (183). Moreover, Daalder traces the fault line in this aesthetic ideology to Saunders's praise of revision: "This work of revision, he believes, makes 'the narrative logic ironclad so that anything the reader objects to will have been taken into account in some way by me'" (184). Noting Saunders's own vacillation regarding this claim—"But 'that "reader,"' he quickly admits, 'is actually just me . . . trying to read/edit as if I have no existing knowledge of the story'"—Daalder nevertheless records many examples of Saunders's dismissal of the comments of actual readers. Such contradictions lead the critic to conclude that "Saunders's art of cruelty, with its attempts to anticipate and micro-manage the effects of its shock treatment, is far from emancipating" (184–185).

This claim leads me to a concluding set of questions. What would emancipation—whether achieved through kindness or cruelty—actually look like? What do we need to be emancipated *from*? And what are we being emancipated *to do*? For her part, DeWitt in *Lightning Rods* is honest enough not to attempt to offer any emancipation from the experience of seeing like a neoliberal. Having traced the growth to monopoly power of Joe's Lightning Rods corporation followed by its extraordinarily rapid integration with the security state and the operations of law and politics, her novel ends with the sentence, sublimely ironic in context, "In America anything is possible" (273). Saunders's regular paeans to American values suggest, meanwhile, that despite the darkness of his satire of the neoliberal present, he believes strongly and unironically in American possibility. Kindness is the route he recommends for achieving that possibility, but, as Boddy notes, this is a route most notable for its compensatory rather than emancipatory character: "If, or perhaps because, a different life is rarely possible, kind words are essential."[103]

Looking to Saunders's fiction, we certainly find little evidence that the possibility of a truly different, emancipated life can be *consciously* achieved. Indeed, the divorce from conscious intention that ends "The Falls," when Morse dives into the water despite what his mind is telling him to do, suggests that, in literary New Sincerity, it is not only class consciousness but consciousness *tout court* that has become questionable. "Consciousness is Nature's

Nightmare," writes Wallace near the conclusion of his last story collection, the ominously titled *Oblivion*.[104] When we also remember that in *Infinite Jest* addiction to drugs is figured as a spider in one's head that one feeds, then the implication of a later Saunders story, "Escape from Spiderhead," becomes clearer.

But this escape—like the escapes from consciousness that structure, in varying ways, the imaginaries of Eggers's *You Shall Know Our Velocity*, Egan's *Look at Me*, Whitehead's *Apex Hides the Hurt,* and Benjamin Kunkel's *Indecision*—should not be confused with emancipation. These escapist gestures must instead be read both critically—as informed by skepticism of earlier literary claims to the emancipation of individual consciousness—and dialectically, as an admission of present uncertainty about the "actual feeling" on which sincerity depends and the actual solutions on which politics is based. Highlighting but not necessarily overcoming the temptation to see like a neoliberal, New Sincerity writers frame the outlines of a political project, one not fully articulated but waiting to be taken up "*off* the page, *outside* words."[105] As we shall see in my final chapter, any route to emancipation must grapple with the imaginative limits imposed on political possibility by capitalist realism, so shamefully dominant in the moment these writers inhabit in their lives and in their work.

The Politics of Sincerity and the Sincerity of Politics

Neoliberalism in Common

In the Spring 2014 issue of *n+1* magazine, the law professor Jedediah Purdy published an autobiographical essay about his early career as a political writer. Dealing mostly with his first book, *For Common Things: Irony, Trust, and Commitment in America Today* (1999), Purdy's essay is notable for being glossed for readers in multiple ways. The issue's front cover trails the essay with the phrase "After the New Sincerity." The title on the table of contents is "The Accidental Neoliberal," with the phrase "Against the Old Sincerity" directly below (the same format is used for the online version of the essay). On the opening page of the essay itself, the words "Politics: Memorandum" appear in the top left-hand corner, with "The Accidental Neoliberal" directly below but no mention of sincerity—whether old, new, or otherwise.[1] These somewhat contradictory designations for the essay chime with the historical confusions being traced within it. Looking back at his 1990s self with the hindsight of a decade and a half, Purdy moves back and forth among a set of intertwining issues: his intentions in writing *For Common Things*; the choices he made in presenting his arguments; the character of the book's reception; how the era felt to live through at the time; and how all these things look in retrospect. At the essay's root is a diagnostic, historicizing impulse, very much in keeping with the aims of the present book: "I am trying to understand my writing as a symptom of the time, a way in to what it meant to write between 1989, when I was 14 and the Berlin Wall fell, and 2008, when the financial crisis brought capitalism into fresh question" (16).

From the point of view of an aspiring political writer and activist, this period—the era of normative neoliberalism, as I have been calling it—was a disillusioning time: "There were no movements then, and campus politics were tiny and self-involved" (15). Reacting against the prevailing mood of capitalist realism, *For Common Things* set out to offer a critique of the trends that Purdy saw poisoning the political climate, including "libertarian fantasies," "New Age notions," and, "above all, a debased form of irony that amounted to preemptive dismissal of public speech, institutions, and efforts as a mere game of thrones" (15). In the face of these trends, the politics that Purdy called for were classically of the Left:

> I defended the politics of structure, a politics about shaping the social world we all have to inhabit. That meant a politics in the tradition of democratic socialism, about the division of wealth between capital and labor, about workplace conditions and the balance of work and leisure; a politics in the voice of feminism, about who pays the cost of caregiving and how leave policies can break the grip of gender roles; an ecological politics that set limits on profit-making to preserve natural ecologies and inhabited landscapes. (15)

Purdy believed that, in a 1990s context, such a universalist politics could only gain a hearing if articulated from a particularist position. Hence he grounded *For Common Things* in his upbringing on a West Virginian farm, arguing that the realities he experienced in that setting led to the embrace of a collectivist democratic politics based around a natural world held in common. The earnest tone in which the book set out these personal details and political viewpoints was intended to underscore the seriousness of its message.

The problems began with the book's reception: financially speaking, a big success; intellectually speaking, a dispiriting failure. "*For Common Things* was reviewed in all the places," Purdy writes, "and there were long author profiles in the *Times* magazine, which called my project 'the new sincerity,' and the *Washington Post* style section, which pounced on the commodification of the new sincerity" (15–16). He notes the connections made between his book and a contemporaneous memoir that—as we saw in Chapter Two—addresses precisely this sincerity/commodification dynamic: "When *A Heartbreaking Work of Staggering Genius* appeared, NPR styled the sincere ironist Dave Eggers as 'the anti-Purdy'" (16). The comparison strikes Purdy as typical of how reviews ignored or downplayed the political claims of his book to focus instead on the tone of their presentation, "lean[ing] heavily on words like *earnest* and *serious*." This led different commentators to position Purdy alternatively and confusingly on the political Left, as a young conservative, and as aiming to go beyond left and right. "Aesthetics and sensibility had replaced substantive and structural politics," he muses. "That had been my complaint, and now I was an instance of it" (16). In welcoming him warmly into its most prestigious venues and channels of publication, the establishment had neutralized his critique of its prevailing ideology. "Saying structural politics was one thing; acting, another," Purdy reflects ruefully. "Action was what brought me back into the neoliberal end of history" (15).

Purdy's essay identifies an important feature of sincerity as an ethos, practice, and tone: that it has no necessary politics. Indeed, where sincerity is taken to be the end goal, rather than simply the means by which a goal is articulated or achieved, political considerations risk being underplayed or evacuated altogether. This is a risk run (or a deliberate decision made) in much art and culture that has been addressed under the moniker of New Sincerity: the films of Wes Anderson and Charlie Kaufman; TV shows including *The Office* and *Modern Family*; plays like *Tomorrow's Parties* and *The New Sincerity*; poetry by Dorothea Lasky and Tao Lin; indie music by Bright Eyes and The Pains of Being Pure at Heart.[2] These works are not devoid of politics, of course—no cultural artifact can be—but any conscious politics they express are implicit, inchoate, and often beside the point. The point is rather, as much commentary on these and similar works avers, to simultaneously invoke and defy the constraints of form, genre, modes of dissemination, and a jaded cultural environment in order to elicit moments of sincere affect against the odds. As one critic writes of the reality TV show *Nathan for You* as an example of the New Sincerity aesthetic, the show achieves an "expression of genuine humanity" that is "extraordinarily moving, and in ways that seem to go well beyond what we have come to take as the possibilities of the genre."[3]

The writers I have addressed throughout this book have often been approached in a similar spirit—this is particularly true of David Foster Wallace and Dave Eggers. Yet such an approach often comes at the expense, I have argued, of an appreciation of the full complexity of their literary art, its ambivalence regarding the value of sincerity, and the dialectical work such ambivalence undertakes in its historical moment. It would nevertheless be fair to say of these writers that the political sphere is not their primary topic or domain of interest. The present chapter thus constitutes a necessary final move in this book's argument by turning to a trio of novels by post-boomer writers that are explicitly *about* politics, and specifically the kind of left-wing political activism that Purdy was trying (and by his own admission failing) to revive in *For Common Things*.

These three novels from the mid-2000s—Susan Choi's *American Woman* (2003), Dana Spiotta's *Eat the Document* (2006), and Benjamin Kunkel's *Indecision* (2005)—address themselves to the intersections of sincerity, commodification, protest, and politics in the American past and present. Choi and Spiotta portray the early 1970s and the unraveling of leftist protest movements in spates of revolutionary violence, while Spiotta and Kunkel examine the legacies of this era for political activism in the millennial moment three decades later. All three authors thus participate in a generational project of reassessing the long 1960s. These years—of the New Left, Civil Rights, and counterculture—were marked by major tribulations and ruptures in the US public sphere, with previously marginalized voices entering mainstream consciousness through intersecting political movements including Black Power, second-wave feminism, Gay Liberation, the American Indian and Asian American movements, and the anti-imperialist Vietnam War protests. In literary terms, these years of protest have been extensively chronicled—both at the time and subsequently—in the fiction of the generation of American novelists born in the 1930s, including such luminaries as Robert Coover, Don DeLillo, Joan Didion, E. L. Doctorow, Ernest J. Gaines, Toni Morrison, Joyce Carol Oates, Marge Piercy, Thomas Pynchon, Ishmael Reed, and Philip Roth.[4]

Yet while this generation—the precursors to the boomers who would provide the core of the protest movements—had attained writerly consciousness by the time of the 1960s, the post-boomer writers at the heart of my book came to maturity in a later America, in an era when radical leftist politics and egalitarian social hope increasingly came to seem like relics from a distant past. As we saw in my Introduction, the locus of expression and sincerity in this post-1970s period shifted from the realm of political activism to the sphere of the market, which Friedrich Hayek and his fellow neoliberals depicted as a space that allowed "for the arrangement of our own life according to our own conscience," a sphere "in which alone moral sense grows and in which moral values are daily re-created in the free decision of the individual."[5] While all the writers explored in *New Sincerity* question this vision of the market in various ways, the novelists at the heart of this chapter counter it directly. They do so by revisiting and reconsidering the realm of political activism, particularly in the crucial historical window before neoliberalism became their generation's common inheritance.

Revisionist Histories

When post-boomer American novelists come to consider the long 1960s in their work, they do so partly as memoirists and partly as cultural historians. In this sense they inhabit a position akin to Phoebe O'Connor, the protagonist of Jennifer Egan's *The Invisible Circus* (1994), who in Chapter Three we saw researching the already historical 1960s as an eighteen-year-old in 1978. Egan's novel has been identified as the first entry in the wave of post-boomer historical fictions that address the radical years.[6] Its driving contrast between childhood enchantment and adult realities would go on to characterize many later examples of the genre, including Jeffrey Eugenides's *Middlesex* (2002), Jonathan Lethem's *The Fortress of Solitude* (2003), Spiotta's *Eat the Document*, and the Chris Fogle novella at the heart of Wallace's posthumous *The Pale King* (2011). In writing about the long 1960s, these novelists are simultaneously recreating the things of their youth and inquiring into the meaning of a history that is not quite theirs. Their fictions display a complicated nostalgia for an era when collective political agency still seemed possible, when individual acts—both good and ill—could make a difference in the public realm, and when notions of responsibility, while difficult and pressing, appeared comparatively well-defined. But those days—the days of Civil Rights, of people power, of radical protest but also radical violence—are gone, and what remains is political passivity and a shrinking of revolutionary consciousness that can look, from another perspective, like a growth in social harmony. The paperback cover blurb for *The Fortress of Solitude* neatly encapsulates this structure of feeling:

> This is the story of 1970s America, a time when the simplest decisions—what music you listened to, whether to speak to the kid in the seat next to you, whether to give up your lunch money—are laden with potential political,

social and racial disaster. This is also the story of 1990s America, when nobody cared anymore.[7]

Or as the 1990s teenager Jason marvels upon discovering his mother's secret radical past in *Eat the Document*: "What a world that must have been where ordinary people actually did things. Things that affected, however tangentially, history."[8] With their psyches soaked in this stark comparison between eras, post-boomer novelists address the long 1960s in American life with knowledge of the conservative retrenchment that followed and are concerned to understand the earlier period in the light of that retrenchment. The signs of the times are read, in other words, less in a mode of heady expectation than as part of a sober search for historical understanding. The crucial question that underpins this work is: how did we get from there to here?

In asking this question, these novelists also participate in a broader intellectual development that has become prominent over the last two decades and more. This is a revisionist project that critically reexamines the new social movements of the long 1960s with regard to their unheeded intersections with the neoliberalism to which they gave way. An early landmark in this scholarship, written before the term "neoliberalism" became current in contemporary study outside of the Latin American context, was Thomas Frank's *The Conquest of Cool*, which argued against the commonsense view that commercial enterprise had cynically co-opted the aims of the counterculture, in favor of a picture of 1960s business corporations as driven by countercultural sympathies *avant la lettre*.[9] Another mid-1990s publication already mentioned in this book, Richard Barbrook and Andy Cameron's essay "The Californian Ideology," examined the same nexus of forces from the other side, contending that many in the counterculture were effectively proto-neoliberals in their reflexive anti-statism and exaltation of individual freedom over collective class politics.[10]

This complicity between countercultural and neoliberal trends would go on to become a theme of several major works in the years that followed. Two publications in particular stand out for their influence on subsequent discussion. Luc Boltanski and Ève Chiapello's *The New Spirit of Capitalism*, which appeared in French in 1999 and in English translation in 2005, argued that the 1960s had seen the coalescing of two traditions in the critique of capitalism, which the authors dubbed the artistic critique and the social critique. The neoliberal transformation of capitalism had successfully internalized the artistic critique—which emphasizes "disenchantment and inauthenticity" and "shares its individualism with modernity"—while sidelining the social critique, with its focus on exploitation and inequality.[11] David Harvey's *A Brief History of Neoliberalism*, meanwhile, introduced its titular term to a broad audience via a similar criticism—albeit a sympathetic one—of the 1960s social movements for their failure to anticipate the neoliberal counterrevolution. "Any political movement that holds individual freedoms to be sacrosanct," he warned, "is vulnerable to incorporation into the neoliberal fold."[12]

In literary criticism, revisionist accounts of this kind began to emerge during the same period, notably in influential polemics such as Walter Benn Michaels's *The Shape of the Signifier* and Sean McCann and Michael Szalay's essay "Do You Believe in Magic? Literary Thinking After the New Left."[13] These critics attacked the literature and theory of the post-1960s period for emphasizing symbolic over structural politics, for promoting identity politics and multiculturalism over class politics and anti-capitalism, and for providing ineffective opposition to the steep rise in economic inequality over the neoliberal years. More recent studies have nuanced this view of post-1960s literature in various ways, but an earlier scholarly consensus about the leftist credentials of postmodern writing has by now been well and truly challenged.[14] In social and cultural scholarship more generally, high-profile interventions by figures including Michel Feher, Nancy Fraser, and Slavoj Žižek, alongside much fine-grained work on the intellectual history of neoliberalism, have thoroughly embedded the revisionist reading of the radical years.[15] As the recent appearance of titles like *The Countercultural Logic of Neoliberalism* and *Foucault and the End of the Revolution* make clear, the relationship between significant strains of the New Left and the neoliberal New Right now appears tighter than ever.[16]

Here it is useful to return to Purdy's account of the fate of *For Common Things*. His 2014 essay not only indicts the "accidental neoliberalism" of his ostensibly oppositional early writing, but also raises the question of what genuinely oppositional writing and action could look like in the period of normative neoliberalism. In trying to "say structural politics" in his debut work, Purdy was following the example of marginalized voices in the 1990s such as Adolph Reed (whose work I explored in Chapter Four), while anticipating the worries about individualism and identity politics articulated in the 2000s by Harvey, Michaels, Boltanski and Chiapello, McCann and Szalay, and many others. But the reception of *For Common Things* suggested either that such a message could not be heard by the US cultural mainstream or that it needed to be delivered in a different way. Purdy's essay oscillates between these two interpretations, alternately blaming his work's inability to meaningfully oppose neoliberalism on the character of the work itself and on the conditions of its publication and reception. On the one hand, he notes that his "signal failure in the book was refusing to decide between nostalgia and alienation," a failure that meant that his message about structural politics "fell nonetheless into the idiom of identity politics, a story about commitments that tied them essentially to origins," a story that "this world knows how to market" (18). On the other hand, he suggests that this was the inevitable fate not only of his book but of all public writing in the period. "The neoliberal public writer can't help being on the market, because the market is what any possible public has become," he opines, concluding on this basis that "critics of neoliberalism tend to confirm it even as they denounce it— making them more interesting and, in some ways, deeper supporters than the most shameless market-utopian hack" (17). Purdy here comes close to endorsing what Mitchum Huehls and Rachel Greenwald Smith term "ontological neoliberalism," whereby "neoliberalism becomes what we are," and critique can no longer be coherently articulated from an external position of non- or anti-neoliberal reason.[17] As Purdy himself puts it, "The naturalness of neoliberal premises comes in the way that, in a neoliberal world, to act is to accept them. I suppose I simply mean that I couldn't do anything but accept them myself" (17).

From the perspective of an Adolph Reed or a Walter Benn Michaels, such an argument would look like an act of bad faith, an assertion of insincere fatalism made to avoid the burden of ethical and political choice. But perhaps we can put Purdy's question about the possibility of oppositional writing and action in sharper and more productive terms by asking it as follows: *what does it mean to oppose sincerely a system from which one comparatively benefits?* Versions of this question—where the notion of opposition becomes inextricable from issues of complicity and relative privilege—we have seen posed again and again in the work of the writers this book has examined. We have seen the question articulated via the anxious intersection of art and commerce in Wallace's *Westward*. We have seen it in the way Purdy's media nemesis Dave Eggers connects ethical to economic debts in exploiting his own suffering to produce *A Heartbreaking Work*. We have seen it in Jennifer Egan's framing of the attempt to escape publicity as itself an act of publicity at the conclusion of *Look at Me*. We have seen it in Colson Whitehead's foregrounding of the African American writer's position as a member of the professional-managerial class as a complicating factor in any claims to racial solidarity. And we have seen George Saunders and Helen DeWitt pose the question seemingly inadvertently, by endorsing a form of capitalism in their nonfiction and interviews while seeming to critique it in their fiction.

In the case of all these writers, I have described their literary New Sincerity as an aesthetic means of attempting to address their complicity with normative neoliberalism and its reigning paradigm of human capital. Rather than foreground the ways their writing bypasses politics, I have highlighted their efforts to read the political unconscious of their own work. I have read the direct invocation of the figure of the reader in their fictions—the way in which free indirect discourse so often gives way at crucial moments to second-person address—as a means of signaling the foundational priority of the other's perspective, a way to reverse engineer Trilling's classic formulation of sincerity by aiming instead to be true to others as a means of discovering the truth about oneself. In analyzing the uncertainties that result from this aesthetical-ethical impulse toward sincerity, I have built on but also countered other critics in this area by arguing that something more than psychological ambivalence is at work, that in fact what literary New Sincerity most tellingly exposes is a structuring tension between the liberal emphasis on individual intention and conscience on the one hand, and the Marxist and Bourdieusian accounts of determining class interest on the other. It is when this tension is acknowledged that the question of sincerely opposing a system from which one benefits becomes a pressing one. And the realm in which this question becomes most pressing of all is the one that concerns Purdy: the realm of radical political activism. This realm is the primary concern of the New Sincerity novels addressed in this chapter.

Speaking Bodily

American Woman is Susan Choi's imagining of the "lost year" in the fugitive life of Patricia "Patty" Hearst, the Californian granddaughter of newspaper magnate William Randolph Hearst. Kidnapped by the Symbionese Liberation Army, a revolutionary left-wing organization, in February 1974, the nineteen-year-old Hearst notoriously converted to her captors' cause, renaming herself "Tania" and participating in an armed robbery before going on the run following the death of her comrades in a shoot-out with police. Having taken part in further criminal acts that resulted in the death of at least one citizen, Hearst was arrested in September 1975 and put on trial a few months later. She was found guilty but later had her sentence commuted by President Carter. The whole episode was a huge media event at the time and remains a subject of fascination for artists and historians of American culture. Core to this fascination is how the story centers on the question of Hearst's sincerity at two conflicting points in the saga. Was Hearst sincere when she claimed on tape to be joining the cause of the SLA and then took part in its violent activities? Was she sincere when she later claimed in court to have been coerced into joining the group through entrapment and rape? Or was she in fact sincere at both moments, with the contradiction mediated through the idea—new at the time—that she had been "brainwashed"?[18]

Choi's novel remains faithful to the outline of the Hearst saga while enfolding it into a broader story about underground revolutionary politics in the mid-1970s, a story with transnational as well as domestic dimensions. The novel's protagonist is not Hearst—called Pauline in the novel—but Jenny Shimada, based by Choi on the real-life comrade with whom Hearst was arrested, Wendy Yoshimura.[19] Before she meets Pauline and the other remaining SLA cadre members in a remote farmhouse in upstate New York, where she has agreed to help them hide out from the FBI, Jenny's role as a political radical primarily involved building and planting explosives. In protest against the war in Vietnam, she "had bombed several government targets, mostly draft offices, always deep in the night when no one would be killed."[20] Her small group of radical associates included her boyfriend William, whose arrest has left Jenny alone and on the run. By adopting Jenny's perspective on the events of the "lost year," the novel foregrounds the intersections of race, class, gender, and sexuality in the radical movements of the time, as well as highlighting the boomer generation's engagement with their parents' experiences of World War II, in Jenny's case her father's time in the Japanese internment camps in California. It is within these overlapping contexts that we see Jenny reflecting—mostly in free indirect discourse focalized through her point of view—on her own history and political choices. Choi presents her protagonist as someone sincerely concerned with understanding her personal motives and the motives of others, and with how those motives inform and relate to their political beliefs. At the same time, *American Woman* conceives of sincerity as potentially inhering in a range of dimensions of personhood and personal expression: in speech, in action, in the body, and in writing. Portraying how these dimensions intersect, and sometimes compete with one another, constitutes a significant part of Choi's exploration of what this chapter calls the politics of sincerity and the sincerity of politics.

Jenny is portrayed as someone highly sensitive to the cadences and nuances of speech. Having grown up in California speaking English, she moves with her father to Japan at the age of nine, where, in contrast to his struggles with the language, "she'd seemed to absorb Japanese in her sleep" (161). Returning to live in the United States five years later, she is struck for the first time by the slipperiness of spoken language, its tendency to falsify feeling and emotion as much as it expresses them: "her long absence from English had stripped every English cliché of its comforting chime. Suddenly there were the tepid and fraudulent words: Do unto others, and, If at first you don't succeed, and, Might does not make right" (198). When in her early twenties she begins a relationship with her political science tutor William Weeks, she finds herself frustrated by the artificiality of saying "I love you": "She hates this pro forma exercise; what she really means, what she really feels, needs, craves, is hardly expressed by these words. These words seem like a fence to her, a little white line of pickets that keep things at bay" (227). In order to surmount this white picket fence—the racial and class connotations of US suburban life surely not accidental—Jenny learns to prefer action to speech as a vector of sincere expression. She finds that she is highly effective at carrying out political actions, from her skill at wiring explosives to her inconspicuousness when depositing them. Moreover, the shared quality of her political activities with William contrast with the artificiality of their professions of love: "Every action they had ever done they'd done assiduously together. That had been part of the power of it, that their every movement was in tandem" (74). Jenny's preference for action over speech in both the political and personal spheres is encapsulated by a moment when she returns to her associates after successfully planting a bomb. "Before anyone can say anything, while they're still staring stunned," Choi writes, "she and William walk straight to each other and lock mouths desperately" (226).

While it emphasizes the priority for Jenny of action over speech, this impulsive kiss with William also reminds us that action (and speech) contains a bodily element that is not always under the command of the subject. Jenny is aware of the political significance of the body and considers it at many junctures, as when she thinks about how ideology is inculcated and resisted: "The mind might believe, but the body has trouble. Power has the power to seem natural, and to live in your gut like an ulcer" (198). But throughout *American Woman*, Jenny's own body also becomes a vector of meaning and feeling that escapes her control. This occurs most frequently when her body is racialized by others, as in the scene where Juan, the leader of the fugitive SLA cadre, cites Jenny's race in order to reprove Pauline for her privilege. "'Let's see you accomplish *one fourth* of what Jenny accomplished,'" he chides. "'Let's see you come from a nonwhite-skin background . . .'" Jenny interrupts with a reaction that is both verbal and physical:

> "Oh God," Jenny said. "Don't." The staircase was buckling beneath her. They were still arguing as she crawled upstairs, clutching the banister. Back on her bed, time slowed down to a crawl. Her bed sheets were drenched with sweat but she was shaking from cold. (171)

Commenting on this scene, Deborah Koto Katz observes that "being extolled as a paragon of radicalism solely on the basis of her visible racial difference" produces an instinctive bodily reaction in Jenny.[21] Katz goes on to analyze several similar moments in *American Woman*, reading them as indexing how Jenny's political subjectivity is slowly transformed by the "ugly feelings" that emerge through her body as it undergoes racialization by others, from William to Juan to the media reporting on Pauline's trial. The discovery that others see her race as inseparable from her politics—which to her mind emerged from feelings of powerlessness and frustration as an "average American girl" (350)—leads Jenny to question the reasons she holds the views she does. The place where she learns to work through these questions is on the page, in letters written while underground and later in prison. Jenny's practice of letter writing undergirds *American Woman*'s meditation on the relationship between political sincerity and the phenomenon of writing—its origins, consequences, materiality, and meaning.

Writing is figured in polarizing ways by the male characters with whom Jenny interacts in the novel. For the SLA leader Juan, writing is viewed with suspicion when set next to the immediacies of speech, action, and the body. When the editor and underground operative Rob Frazer first raises the idea of the fugitive cadre members writing a book about their beliefs and experiences, Juan retorts that "'in this country books are such shit'" (37). Though he eventually agrees to the plan, later his position hardens further: "'your stupid-ass book! It's just your way of grabbing our action. Books are for phonies like you who use words when they ought to *do something*'" (206). Under Juan's instructions and against Jenny's counsel, the three cadre members spend most of their time at the farmhouse ignoring the task of writing their book, instead engaging in other pursuits including drinking, arguing, lovemaking, and combat training. On the sole occasion the cadre does attempt to write about their experiences, the results quickly become abstract and impersonal:

> The foundation of their worldview sank swiftly into the past: condemnation of the war required dissection of the Kennedy administration's foreign policy, which demanded criticism of the imperially minded rearrangement of national borders in the wake of the Second World War, which led to a long meditation on the rise of the nation-state. (191)

This substitution of public history for personal experience, and theory for praxis, is reversed in the cadre's only successful spurt of creative endeavor, which results not in the promised book but in a tape, a spoken eulogy for their slain comrades. As the trio congregate around the farmhouse radio to listen to their feverish words broadcast to the nation, Jenny remarks on their seeming lack of appreciation for how those words will sound to others: "It was possible that their own voices were an echo chamber around them, beyond which they grasped nothing" (122). For the cadre, the immediacies of speech, action, and the body serve to crowd out any thoughts of an audience to whom they might communicate.

The editor Rob Frazer, by contrast, is highly audience-aware, largely because for him the audience for writing is always first and foremost a market. He views the tape the cadre sends out as a frustrating waste of precious words, words that could have been converted directly into money: "'If they'd just had the patience to wait, that could have been chapter one of the book. That could have been our *exclusive*'" (180). When Jenny chides him for being interested in the cadre only until "'you have your book and your money,'" Frazer shoots back: "'It's not just about money. Though I seem to remember you're in for a share of it, too'" (125). This is a reminder to Jenny that she too is compromised, and that the imagined purity of her motives cannot be entirely extricated from the requirement to earn if she is to survive. Her fantasy of non-complicity, as Frazer sees it, is hypocritical on both political and personal fronts:

> "Isn't that your thing? Pure heart, pure life. You can't hold down a job in the capitalist system at the same time as you fight for revolution and you can't lie to your lover at the same time as making sure you're perfect soulmates who never power-trip each other! Right?" (49)

As someone who acknowledges his own complicity while still claiming to pursue moral ends, Frazer envisages himself as inhabiting a less self-deceived space: "'At least I'm not deluded about my desires. . . . At least I know that I'm selfless *and* selfish'" (216). Yet Frazer's selfishness trumps his selflessness when Jenny entrusts him with a long letter she has written to William and he fails to deliver it, a failure that underscores his lack of esteem for writing that lacks monetary value.

As the most important male figure in her life, whom she can now reach only through such letters, William's imprisonment serves as the main spur for Jenny's reflections on and through writing. These reflections are informed by the threat of surveillance, which shadows their correspondence and makes self-censorship mandatory and sincerity complicated: "She had to be honest with William while at the same time dropping no clue the prison censors could possibly grasp, and although this meant, basically, lying to William, she still wanted to think that it didn't" (110). The surveillance threat even influences the materiality of the letters themselves, since in order to protect Jenny's identity and whereabouts, both parties must send their letters via a mutual friend, Dana. But while Jenny can receive William's letters in his own hand—even if they still lack "an intangible something, the orthographic equivalent of his hands on her skin" (111)—when Jenny writes to William her letters must be opened and transcribed by Dana before being forwarded on. "And so how must he feel," Jenny wonders of William,

> reading her declarations, already blunted and constrained by their code, and then in Dana's slanting, regular hand. So different from Jenny's own, her pointy insistent block letters, her underlinings and loud exclamations. (111)

This removal of the material sign of Jenny's hand is particularly cruel because of how closely she has been associated with handwriting throughout the text. Frazer initially tracks her down by identifying her handwriting on the sign outside a country mansion where Jenny is hiding out, while we learn that one of her most notable skills as a radical, alongside bomb-making, is inscribing protest placards. Even Jenny's fingerprints—whose appearance on a newspaper in the farmhouse eventually leads to her and Pauline's arrest—are described figuratively as a missive written to the FBI agent who discovers them. "It was a letter to him from this person," we read, "in fingerprint-newsprint, a language" (302).

Writing Collaboratively

Writing is therefore figured in *American Woman* in conflicting ways: as selling, as selling out, and as the site of both the materiality and erasure of the self. It is in Jenny's developing relationship with Pauline, however, that writing takes on a different resonance as a means of sincere communication via intimate collaboration. Their first moment of potential (albeit failed) intimacy occurs when Pauline enters Jenny's room at the farmhouse late at night, looking to show her newspaper clippings marked with Pauline's circlings and underlinings. Although she can read the clippings, Jenny cannot read the gesture, and the verbal response she musters disappoints Pauline for reasons that remain opaque: "Something had not been said that she'd wanted to hear; or something had been said that she hadn't expected; Jenny watched helplessly, as Pauline closed the envelope, carefully pressed flat the small metal brad" (175). Here the actuality of speech fails the promise of writing, but later, during their road trip and then when they are living together in San Francisco in the "serene" days before their arrest, Jenny and Pauline's relationship begins to fulfil that promise (310). It does so via the medium of Jenny's letters to William:

> Lately Jenny gives her letters to Pauline to read over and edit and Pauline pores over them, spreads them on the kitchen table and ponders them, pen in her mouth. The two of them have been laboriously co-composing this particular letter for so long it's become a long letter between them, and they still haven't mailed it. (309)

Pauline has by now become the true addressee of Jenny's writing, which has thereby been transfigured from a signifier of distance to one of intimacy. When they are separated following their arrest, Jenny writes a letter to Pauline from her prison cell, a letter almost fifteen pages long ("I don't have you as my editor now"), and signs it, "*Love*" (347). Just as she is finishing the letter, Jenny learns from her lawyer that Pauline has named her as an accessory to an armed robbery. Despite this betrayal she still sends the letter and continues to fill up notepads in her jail cell, "for Pauline, not herself" (359). Later, "though she knew it was a terrible cliché," Jenny dreams of Pauline continuing to read and edit her writing. In the dream she waits in suspense for Pauline to tell Jenny what Jenny herself has inscribed on the paper: "What had she said: that she loved her? Loathed her? Dreamed of her, even during this moment? That she'd surrendered her whole self somehow, the one thing she'd sworn not to do" (359).

Although Jenny has been established as a figure with a sensitive relation to language, making it realistic for her to view this dream as "a terrible cliché," the passage above still marks a rare moment of metafictional self-reflexivity in Choi's otherwise realist novel. That this moment frames the novel's most direct meditation on the relationship between writer and reader is no coincidence. In Pauline, the figure of the reader is transformed into both a co-writer and someone whose response is necessary for the writer to understand what they have written in the first place. We can see in this the aesthetic and thematic continuity between *American Woman* and the literary New Sincerity of Wallace, Eggers, and Egan, where intention is only realized through recognition, and where the sincerity of the writer can be achieved only in the reader's response. Like her generational contemporaries, Choi figures the relationship between writer and reader as a close and intimate bond with agency on both sides, where writing is not primarily a site of knowledge transfer but of intimate co-construction of meaning, a meaning not identifiable as the property of either party alone. That the intimacy of such writing is always haunted by the possibility of betrayal is made palpable by Pauline's betrayal of Jenny. Yet even this betrayal is interpreted by Jenny as a form of tacit collaboration: "Jenny had to acknowledge that even Pauline's stark betrayal of her had its element of cooperativeness, with Jenny. Jenny had lied, and called herself a captor, a cruel prison-keeper, for the sake of Pauline, and Pauline's response just conformed to that fiction." (356)

In Jenny's long letter to Pauline, which receives no reply, *American Woman* thus thematizes its own risk of failing to reach its addressee, of failing to find the reader who will bring the novel's potential sincerity into being through recognition and intimate engagement. Where Choi's novel moves beyond the examples of literary New Sincerity examined in my previous chapters is through the political context within which these questions of intimacy, address, betrayal, and textual meaning play out. The novel depicts a political underground populated by people who have come to suspect the official narratives about the society in which they live, so that even the meaning of basic sense experience becomes ideologically freighted, open to interrogation and resignification. This is the context in which we find Jenny and Pauline co-writing Jenny's letter to William as a letter between themselves, a context in which they must decide whether the things that surround them in their new life in San Francisco—homemade bread and ratatouille, succulent bottles of wine, "flowers in a vase on the table, a pretty cloth Jenny found at the thrift store"—should be interpreted as "bourgeois things" or "beautiful things" (309). In these late scenes before their arrest, the women have formed a feminist-socialist consciousness-raising group, which aims to challenge the patriarchal dimensions of Left radicalism that the novel has displayed through the characters of William, Frazer, and Juan. The resignification of the domestic as a feminist rather than simply feminine space—"'Our beautiful feminist curtains,' Pauline said. 'They might *look* bourgeois, but they're not'" (292)—is a work-in-progress made symbolically inextricable from the never-sent letter, a work-in-progress abruptly halted by the women's arrest. In these fleeting but heady pages, *American Woman* seeks to inhabit a historical moment in which meaning is being tentatively remade along liberatory lines, marking that moment as one of female collaboration tragically cut short.[22]

If the novel's impulse to remake meaning takes inspiration from 1970s feminism, its relationship to the racial movements of the time is more mixed. Reading Jenny's writing in the novel as "most often the site of humiliation, or of a diminished sense of self," Patricia Chu argues that "Choi leads us to question the twenty-first-century ability of ethnic writing to lead to the emergence of radical visibility and relatedly, to question narrative-generated personhood and humanity as the ground for a viable ethnic politics."[23] While I agree that *American Woman* raises these questions, I would query whether "radical visibility" and "a viable ethnic politics" constitute the aims Choi has in mind. On my reading, Jenny's supposedly "diminished" sense of self in her writing in fact provides an opening onto the possibility of collective being, a possibility inhering in a cross-racial politics shared imaginatively with Pauline and others. This would be a politics "in the voice of feminism," to recall Purdy's essay, but its horizon would also be what he calls "the tradition of democratic socialism, about the division of wealth between capital and labor."[24] Indeed, it is precisely the ongoing division of wealth between capital and labor—and the history of that division in the settler colonization of the United States— that most clearly divides Jenny from Pauline and eventually renders their nascent feminist and socialist politics impossible to achieve. As they cross the Great Plains on their journey west from the farmhouse, Pauline tells Jenny in wonder that she has "never seen anything like" the vast spaces that surround them. "But Jenny knew Pauline had been here before," the passage continues:

> She'd been one of those girls in a calico dress, lace-up shoes, sun-strain pinching her eyes, thin long hair always tangled and wild and not in proper braids. One day, the Crow Indians come along and attack her parents' farmstead, scalp her parents, burn the house to the ground, abduct her thrown over their shoulders, her lace-up boots kicking. And the next thing you know, she's tearing around on a horse, wearing paint, giving the Crows who've adopted her hell . . . Jenny could see it in Pauline's deep eyes, if not in her time-refined features. She might have grown up rich, but where had that money come from? From people who'd gotten here first, that was all, when this land was lawless and even more vast. People who'd stuck it out. Killed enough, grabbed enough. Never looked back. (285)

A few pages earlier, when the women stop for a drink at a roadside bar, a patron asks Jenny "what are you?" before going on to guess "Crow Indian" (278). The man is reprimanded by Pauline—"She's a *person* . . . . She's *Californian*"—but Jenny's subsequent vision on the plains suggests, correctly, that such solidarity between the two women is unlikely to last. Pauline's imbrication with a US imperialism played out in the violent white settlement of the country runs too deep in her racial and class inheritance. It makes her protest against the imperialist war in Vietnam into a stance that can too easily be thrown off when self-interest is once again called for as the capitalist class closes ranks from the mid-1970s onwards.[25]

In recognizing the formidable obstacle to political emancipation provided by US racial capitalism, *American Woman* does not, I would contend, respond by placing its faith in "radical visibility" and "a viable ethnic politics." After all, such visibility and politics were arguably achieved to a significant extent in the late twentieth century.[26] In the case of Japanese Americans like Jenny and her father, such a politics underpinned the Civil Liberties Act of 1988, which resulted in a presidential apology and reparations paid to the surviving victims of Japanese internment.[27] And in the case of Asian Americans more generally, although they make up only about 5 percent of the US population, they account for somewhere between 12 and 18 percent of the student body in Ivy League universities and possess the highest median income of any ethnic group recognized in the census.[28]

With this in mind, Choi's emphasis on Jenny's reluctance to embrace the enthusiastic Asian American support she receives during her trial is significant. Jenny chafes against her "model minority" status (355), and as Patricia Chu herself acknowledges, in *American Woman* "the narrative reward is not Asian American identity."[29] For Jenny, wholly adopting such an identity would risk cutting her off from the less ethnically marked identities she had earlier tried to embrace: anti-imperialist activist, socialist, feminist, "average American girl." Must such an American girl accept the inevitability of racial visibility and ethnic politics, or can she become an "American woman" by helping to bring about an America different from the one in which those developments have become necessary and seemingly inevitable? In prompting its reader, from its title onward, toward asking this question, *American Woman* historicizes the emergence of ethnic identity and diversity politics, a politics that would go on to become a key legacy of this transitional moment in American life. Rather than fully affirm that politics, the novel reflects on alternative political possibilities—feminist, socialist, universalist possibilities—that went unrealized amid the emerging social divisions that would be cynically exploited by the neoliberal counterrevolution.

Unlike *Eat the Document*, to which the next section of this chapter will turn, *American Woman* does not explicitly look ahead to that neoliberal counterrevolution.[30] Nevertheless, in its reflections on the multisided character of writing—as a vector of selling, of selling out, but also of intimacy and shared meaning, both in its moment and across time—Choi's novel does thematize its own status as a written text in and of the neoliberal age. In this context, the meta-question that haunts the novel is whether writing can constitute political action in the present, or whether writing—specifically writing a novel about political action—can only ever be a phony way of "grabbing our action," as Juan puts it when he accuses Frazer of profiting from the revolutionary cause. The final part of *American Woman* addresses this question by introducing a freelance journalist named Anne Casey, who is researching the Hearst saga and becomes intrigued by Jenny Shimada's role within it, even though she is aware that Jenny "isn't the story" (319).[31] Though a minor character in the novel, it is noteworthy that Anne is the figure who brings its many strands together, who sees the wider historical narrative even as she knows that its nuances have little chance of making it into the public domain.

The implied analogy between Choi herself and this implicitly white journalist—an "American woman" with a less historically contested claim to being an "average American girl"—is an interesting move, which seems to demonstrate the author's awareness of, and resistance to, the fact that *American Woman* will be marketed and received as an ethnically authored novel. Choi's more recent fiction has continued to test this boundary between the ethnic text and its unmarked other, while also deepening the experimental gestures of her earlier work.[32] In these later novels, the kinds of questions Jenny asks herself about her own sincerity become questions for Choi's reader to ponder concerning the text, its author, and themselves. If these novels are more obviously reflections on literature—its character, status, and purpose in the present—in *American Woman* the nearest we get to an authorial statement on literary writing comes in Jenny's reflections on the shift in her political methods, from a dependence on violence to a preference for consciousness-raising. "More and more she thought of revolution not as mustered force that might topple The System," Choi writes, "but as a delicate process of changing individual minds, or as the rare chance to try" (295–296).

Acting Responsibly

If *American Woman* is haunted by the question of whether writing can constitute political action, Dana Spiotta's *Eat the Document* conversely wonders whether political action functions like writing, in the sense that its meaning alters in response to different readings, contexts, and acts of appropriation.[33] Taking its title from an obscure bootleg film about a Bob Dylan tour—a film that offers an example of, and metaphor for, the differing ways that cultural texts signify across time—*Eat the Document*'s signature concern is with how processes of appropriation, incorporation, and re-contextualization should affect our understanding of the relationship between intentions and outcomes, in the realms of both politics and art. This concern is foregrounded through a method of historical comparison: while it imagines a similar early 1970s milieu to *American Woman*, Spiotta's novel also moves the story of radical politics forward a quarter century to the late 1990s. The two timelines are treated in nine alternating sections, connected by two activists who go underground in the earlier period and emerge in the later one with new names and identities. In the sections beginning in the 1970s, the focalizing character is Mary Whittaker (later, when she is forced to change her name, Caroline Sherman and Louise Barrot), an anti-war protester who at the age of twenty-two becomes one of the senior figures in a group called SAFE. While initially committed to making protest films, SAFE's modus operandi eventually shifts to planting bombs in the empty summer houses of executives whose corporations are supporting the Vietnam War. One of these bombings goes awry, accidentally killing a housekeeper, and Mary is forced to go into hiding. In the novel's opening scene in a Nebraska hotel room in 1972, Mary reflects on the beginnings of her panicked journey from the East to the West Coast—"a breathless train ride under darkening skies and through increasingly unfamiliar landscape"—as she leaves her old identity behind and heads underground.[34]

The sections of the novel set in 1998–2000 center on a left-wing Seattle bookstore named Prairie Fire. The store is run by Nash, a washed-up former radical who chairs evening meetings for groups of young local anti-corporate protesters.[35] One of the teenage attendees at these meetings is Miranda Diaz, the novel's spokesperson for idealistic beliefs associated with the 1960s New Left. Josh Marshall, another attendee and Miranda's soon-to-be boyfriend, begins the novel as a gifted computer hacker using his skills to undermine corporate websites, and ends it working for a major conglomerate he has attacked, one of the ways the novel highlights how capitalism, as Josh himself will put it, "'revives—reinforces—itself on the blood of its critics and their critique'" (258). While he does not frequent Prairie Fire, a third teenager, the Beach Boys fanatic Jason Barrot, is the locus of the novel's treatment of the roles that popular culture and new technologies play for consumer-savvy millennial youth. Through his first-person journal entries, we learn that Jason is Mary's son, though he knows her only as Louise and initially knows nothing of her past. Taking the reader backward and forward between these two eras, *Eat the Document* draws parallels and contrasts between the defeated survivors of the long 1960s and turn-of-the-century adolescents. The novel thus provides a series of perspectives on the changes that have taken place in the United States over this time span, particularly when it comes to the question of *responsibility*.

In its depiction of both the early 1970s and late 1990s, *Eat the Document* portrays a culture in which matters of responsibility, while always powerfully felt by socially conscious young people, are becoming increasingly confusing and unclear under late-twentieth-century capitalism. A large conglomerate called Allegecom dominates the landscape of 1990s Seattle, investing in numerous markets and projects. Prominent among these projects is the company's plan to create an eco-friendly and "totally-intentional community" (237) on the site of a former women-only commune where the reader has seen Mary hide out in the 1970s, taking part in the kinds of feminist consciousness-raising that also features in *American Woman*. "'Organizations eliminate personal responsibility,'" announces Josh Marshall, the brains behind marketing the new community, in a speech to Allegecom's shareholders. "'That is their purpose. And isn't that what we want? Isn't that a relief?'" (238).

It is not simply the traditions of radical feminism and its conception of the personal as political that are traduced by this credo and the corporate re-appropriations it sanctions. In a typical example of Spiotta's dialectical approach, an implicit negation of Josh's view is provided through the fate of

Henry Quinn, a retired local and the owner of Prairie Fire. Despite having never done military service, Henry suffers from post-traumatic stress disorder and symptoms of exposure to Agent Orange, symptoms that turn out to be temporarily relieved by a drug called Nepenthex.[36] Nepenthex is produced by Allegecom, the company that also manufactured the Agent Orange. The final irony is revealed after Henry's death, when the lymphatic cancer that kills him is linked to his use of Nepenthex. If this sounds knotty and confusing, that is the desired effect: the question is how to find an adequate response amid such a complex network of causes and symptoms. When, after Henry's death, Nash discovers that Nepenthex has acted for Henry as a literal *pharmakon*, both poison and cure, he is prompted to drive to a billboard for the drug. Henry had devoted many of his last painful nights to repeatedly cutting the billboard down as a form of symbolic protest, and Nash has thoughts of doing some damage to it himself in memory of his friend. What he finds on the advertisement, however, is a vinyl overlay with skull and crossbones, and a legend above it in large cutout letters, asking a single question: "WHO IS RESPONSIBLE?" (284)

While it homes in repeatedly on this question, *Eat the Document* is not a novel primarily about corporate or political conspiracy, in the vein of American postmodernist classics like Pynchon's *Gravity's Rainbow* (1973) or DeLillo's *Libra* (1988). Rather, Spiotta's novel outlines this corporate background, with its historical ties to the US invasion of Vietnam, in order to imagine modes of political agency and responsible protest that can occur against it. *Eat the Document* thus combines a postmodernist focus on overarching systems of interpellation and control with a more modernist concern with subjective freedom and the experience of time. In connecting its two eras, the novel foregrounds a particular experience of time, which, following scholars including Peter Brooks and Mark Currie, we can call *the anticipation of retrospection*.[37] Currie argues for the particular salience of this temporal mode—in which we constantly look forward to looking back—in the contemporary era, characterized by an "archive fever" in which moments are being recorded and made available at an accelerating rate for future revisiting.[38] In *Stone Arabia* (2011), the novel that followed *Eat the Document*, Spiotta pushes this logic to an extreme by imagining a musician who constructs his own archive of critical and popular reception without actually releasing the music that is ostensibly being received. In *Eat the Document*, music (as well as film) is likewise a site for engaging questions of time and reception.[39] But in this earlier novel the anticipation of retrospection is also extended to political action in ways that are salutary for considering the politics of sincerity and the sincerity of politics in the New Sincerity text.

In the novel's opening chapter, as she frantically works to commit the details of her new fugitive identity to memory, Mary finds herself lingering in the anticipation of retrospection:

> She imagined in future years there would be time to go over the series of events that led to the one event that inevitably led to the hotel room. It felt like that, a whoosh of history, the somersault of dialectic rather than the firm step of the will. (14)

This feeling of being at the mercy of grand historical forces battles in Mary's mind with the sense that she and her boyfriend Bobby were not innocent of the consequences of their collective's turn from protest filmmaking to protest bombing: "Just in the planning they knew where it would lead. Contingencies are never really contingencies but blueprints. Probabilities become certainties." In the present moment Mary finds herself unwilling or unable to adjudicate on the question of her responsibility for the accidental killing that has sent her underground, even as she anticipates a future moment when "she would explain her intentions to someone, at least to herself" (14). As the novel tracks her subsequent life as Caroline and Louise, we see Mary repeatedly forced to confront the requirement to justify her actions to herself and others. These passages highlight what might be termed the two classic problems that arise when it comes to characterizing individual acts of protest as responsible or not: the means-ends problem and the intention problem.

Early in her fugitive life, Mary tells her new friend Berry that "'we wanted tangible, unequivocal action. . . . I had to meet the enormity of what they were doing with something equal to it'" (188–189). In the later timeline, she offers a similar defense to her son Jason's accusations: "'You can't look at what we did in a vacuum. This immoral war was going on and on. And whatever we did, we thought it would help scare them into ending that war sooner'" (273). Yet elsewhere Mary acknowledges to herself the underlying difficulty with these kinds of claims. If an action is to be justified not by the ethical integrity of its means, but simply by the revolutionary ends it aims to bring about, then that action may nevertheless have drastic and violent effects that make it difficult to distinguish from what it is designed to counter. In an early reflection on the counterculture, she senses just this problem: "Caroline knew she was onto something, she was learning how things get away from people. How gradually they, what? Become the very thing they long to escape" (102).

When Berry and Jason respond with objections to her ends-based argument in the scenes above, Mary switches her justification to the grounds of intention. "'Intentions do matter. They make all the difference . . .'" she tells Berry (189), opining to Jason that "'it doesn't only matter if we succeed with our intentions. It matters what our intentions were'" (273). Yet in her private reflections, Mary likewise recognizes the difficulties with this defense. As analytic philosophers of action have never tired of pointing out, the problem with any appeal to intention lies in the way the outcome of an action retroactively affects our judgment of its motivating intentions. The causal lines operate, in other words, not only from intention to outcome but from outcome to intention, because the anticipation of retrospection ensures that possible outcomes inhabit and shape intentions in advance.[40] The effect is to make problematic the very idea of intention as a valid concept in judging the ethics of action. Painfully aware of this problem, Mary is faced with endless and recurring doubts as to intentions, tactics, outcomes:

> But could she even take a stand? Because the truth of it was she wasn't sure of the tactics they had chosen, or of the consequences. There wasn't moral clarity. The truth was she even doubted the intentions, the motivations. This was tragic, a great, terrible tragedy, to do something so clearly full of consequence, so irreparable, and then to have such foundational doubt. (224)

In a 2006 interview, Spiotta commented that "it's harder than ever to engage the idea of revolutionary violence, even if the intention is only property damage. It's hard to make it legible."[41] Mary's desire in *Eat the Document*—like Jenny's in *American Woman*—is for her acts of protest to be "legible and coherent" (9), to herself and to others. The novel's principal lesson, however, is that the fulfilment of this desire for complete legibility, in the present or in the future, is impossible, because intentions can never be present to themselves, and must always be read retrospectively from the actions and outcomes they subtend.[42] Materially, intentions do not exist in the same way that actions do. And further, any protester realizes this at some level, so that the sincerity of any action is informed by the anticipation of retrospection—by an awareness not only of that action's possible outcomes, but of its semiotic potential, how its meaning is likely to be decided, understood, and appropriated in the future. When it comes to intentions, a certain obscurity thus turns out to be unavoidable. And so what tends to happen, historically and culturally, is that the means of an action, because they seem definitive and present, become confused with the more elusive ends, and are eventually substituted for them.

Mary glimpses all this while underground, when she witnesses how at the tail end of the radical years, the signs associated with a life of countercultural protest—the drugs, the clothes, the language, even the violent acts—start to be understood as the very point of protest:

> These were the days of pale-beneath-the-tan partying, roller skates and halter tops. And harder, meaner drugs. It was as if someone had taken the aura of the counterculture and extracted every decent aspiration. What was left was the easy liberation of sex and drugs. (200)

What is left, in other words, are the outward markers of protest without the spirit that ennobled that protest. Those outward markers have been reinterpreted as the thing itself, have become the material legacy of a time when genuinely progressive collective aspirations were in the air. Yet Mary comes to see that this is less a betrayal than a consequence of earlier confusions; as she asks herself rhetorically, "Was there anything inherently groovy in a drug?" (193). The alienation of drug use from its earlier context, when it was associated positively with an activist outlook, is viscerally brought home by a scene in which Mary is sexually assaulted by a man she shares a joint with while hitchhiking. Mary's struggle to come to terms with her underground insights, and to accept responsibility for the consequences of her own violent actions, becomes the eventual focus of her strand of the novel, culminating in her decision to end her fugitive life and turn herself in. Although she recognizes that this act will signify outside the understanding of the younger generation, and although (perhaps as a result) her final thoughts in the novel are rendered ambiguously, it is significant that what she is ultimately surrendering is not only her freedom but her desire to control meaning: "She was going to turn herself in. And no one would understand. It didn't matter at all" (282).

Meaning Aesthetically

With its dual timeline, whereby the anticipation of retrospection is rendered formally through the novel's proleptic and analeptic structure, *Eat the Document* provokes its reader to make connections between the ethical problems Mary confronts in the 1970s and how her actions come to signify in the culture of the late 1990s. Indeed, as the novel portrays it, when it comes to legitimizing historical acts of protest, the key battleground may not be primarily political or ethical but rather semiotic, a battle to control cultural meaning for the present and for the future. Mary eventually concedes this battle, but in the later timeline, we find that her old boyfriend Bobby (now Nash) has adapted his earlier activism into a political model that attempts to reconcile means and ends, while also addressing the related problems of intention and meaning.

In two separate conversations with Miranda Diaz, Nash makes clear that he now favors a different form of protest, or "test." Initially, conversing on the subject of Native Americans and anarchists, he questions a notion of protest concerned solely with winning: "'The point isn't to win. They'll never win, of course. They just make persuasive and powerful the beauty of their opposition.'" Miranda responds with skepticism: "'Yeah, I guess,' she said. 'But wouldn't it also be great to win? I think you should try to win. Otherwise it is just a gesture. That's not really good enough.'" Pressed further by her accusations—"'You just care about the aesthetics. What about the issues?'"— Nash finally retorts: "'No. What you wear reminds you who you want to be. If you want to be fierce, or scary, or stealth. Those are the issues. They are part of the tactics. They communicate'" (65). Later, in a second conversation, he clarifies his preference for communication over outcome:

> "It is not so much that we do direct action to get a certain result, you know, like pass anti-global-warming legislation," he said. "We do an action for the action itself. Our act is the end, the point.... in our quest for whatever goals we have, we should make sure the tactics themselves are reflective of those goals. We dance in the street and stop traffic not because we want to be on TV to get our message out but because we like to dance in the street. It's the world we want to live in." (142–143)

In conceiving a form of action in which the means and ends equate, Nash shows that he has learned the lesson of his and Mary's earlier life: that the means and ends of any action will always signify beyond the intentions that initiated the action. This is why there is no "pro" to Nash's "test": the test is the thing itself, it performs the world it wants to bring about, it is not *for* anything else, and thus not riven by any intention/action or means/ends split. By emphasizing the form of a process over the content of an outcome, Nash's ultimate wish is to shift the question of justification from its traditional formulation in an ethical or political register to the field of beauty and art: "'Then it approaches beauty of a kind. Then you begin to really be dangerous'" (145).

Nevertheless, this aesthetic solution to the ethical problems of protest—one that anticipates the prefigurative elements of the 2011 Occupy movement—cannot easily solve for once and for all the novel's central question of responsibility. While Mary's story amply bears out the problems with the common maxim "the ends justify the means," in Nash's "test" these polarities are reversed: the means (aesthetic performance, dancing in the street) must justify the reduction in the scope of the likely political ends. Uniting the means and the ends involves, in effect, reducing the ends to the means. According to Nash, it is the altering of consciousness, however briefly, that becomes both the aim and the method, the end and the means: "'The point is for us, the players, and perhaps them, the audience, to feel for one second as if we didn't have AOL Time Warner or Viacom tattooed on our asses'" (144). Unlike Mary's violent protest, the means are not here the potential source of irresponsibility; it is the reduction of the goals in sight that is open to the accusation of quietism and even despair. "Aesthetics and sensibility had replaced substantive and structural politics" complains Jedediah Purdy of the American 1990s; Nash's "test," for all its ingenuity, appears to offer little more than a recapitulation of this trend.[43]

These debates about aesthetics and ethics, intentions and actions, means and ends inevitably raise the question of *Eat the Document*'s own aesthetic form. While Spiotta is clearly depicting "a turn away from a politics of revolutionary collective action to a politics of cultural resistance," her novel is also engaged with the concerns about postmodernism, commodification, and irony articulated by David Foster Wallace in his "E Unibus Pluram" essay from 1993.[44] This much is evident from a conversation between Josh and Miranda that takes place in a large "independent" (but corporate-owned) store, Suburban Guerilla, which sells left-wing propaganda. As they wander the aisles, the couple discuss the commodification of radicalism in contemporary culture, and Josh defends the status quo:

> "This is the purity of capitalism. There is no judgment about content. You have to marvel at its elasticity, its lack of moral need, its honesty. It is the great leveler—all can be and will be commodified. Besides, what's wrong with Emma Goldman being sold at the mall as a cool accessory? It is still Emma Goldman, isn't it?"

Miranda's retort—"'A confused context is the essence of alienation'" (258)—implicitly invokes Mary's earlier observations about the disintegrating counterculture of the 1970s, linking the two women together. But although most readers will intuitively side with the sympathetic idealism of Miranda against the smart cynicism of Josh, the novel again prompts us to ask what kind of response, or responsibility, is required by this state of affairs. When they move to discussing irony, Josh recapitulates Wallace's arguments when he claims that a mode that once had "'the potential to undermine and even to redress the hypocrisy and falseness of the culture,'" has become "'the favorite mode of the new corporate generation.'" "'Even,'" he adds decisively, "'Republicans use irony now.'"[45] Miranda protests that Josh's argument is "'a very shallow reading of things. There is still a lot you can do to upset things'" (259). But her statement is counterpointed by the pack of cards she holds in her hands. The "New Left Series" depicts iconic figures from the radical years; it retails, we are told, at $19.95. Flipping through the deck, Miranda discovers Nash—in his former life as Bobby Desoto—on one of the cards.

Spiotta's inclusion of this scene is consistent with the claim that her fiction "registers among the longest sustained and most aesthetically consistent inquiries into New Sincerity themes and problematics."[46] How do these themes and problematics intersect with the novel's form? Critics agree that *Eat the Document* is typically postmodern in its means, for instance in its employment of narrative techniques—"multiple points of view, unreliable narration, nonlinear storytelling, merging of fact and fiction, and interactions between fictional and real characters"—and its incorporation of discursive modes— "diary entries, dream memories, corporate presentations, and descriptions of fictional documentary footage."[47] Yet there is also agreement that the novel resists certain ends typical of postmodern writing, whether these be "postmodernist irony, self-referentiality and the rejection of any notion of authenticity,"[48] "a postmodern sense of atemporality and generational dislocation,"[49] or a postmodern commitment to the unreadability of signs.[50] The provisional quality of *Eat the Document*'s move beyond postmodernism is described by Pieter Vermeulen as inhering in its *"analog* aesthetic," whereby the novel becomes a "recording device" that aims "to register forms of life and affect that it does not yet understand."[51] Kurt Cavender also emphasizes the provisionality of the novel's post-postmodernism in his claim that Spiotta formalizes the practice of "autocritique"—modeled on the collective self-interrogation practices of radical groups like the Weather Underground—"by splitting (often literally) characters into discrete moments of self-consciousness capable of reflecting on and critiquing their other selves."[52]

The question is whether such practices of self-critique can do more than offer what Cavender calls a "purely negative critical imagination for a new generation of political organization."[53] Certainly negation is prominent in *Eat the Document*, particularly with respect to the characters who feature in its earlier period. The novel's opening half page, for instance, which records Mary's loss of identity, includes no less than seven instances of the prefix "un": unblessed, undoing, unfamiliar, unknown (twice), unnerving, unpleasantly (3). Nash is likewise introduced through negation, via his "Antiology, or study of all things anti. His Counter-Catalog. Compendium of Dissidence. Ana-encyclopedia. The Resist List. His Contradictionary" (36). Even the women-only colony at New Harmon, later the site of Allegecom's "totally-intentional community," is itself presented as the negation of an earlier Native American settlement, and therefore "based on the forgetting of an inconvenient past."[54] Unearthing this past is clearly an aspect of the novel's project, as was the case with *American Woman* and its allusions to settler colonialism. But *Eat the Document* also attempts to look forward, to go beyond negation and its connected assumption—attributed by Wallace to the postmodern ironists—"that etiology and diagnosis pointed toward cure, that a revelation of imprisonment led to freedom."[55] Like many instances of literary New Sincerity analyzed in these pages, Spiotta's novel implicitly encodes the search for a liberated form of life that might be sincerely and collectively affirmed.

The novel's concluding section directly addresses the reader as part of this search. This section is Jason's last journal entry about his love for the Beach Boys, whose music he had earlier associated with his desire to remain frozen in time: "Sometimes I think I am in love with my own youth. I do not want to go forward, I always want to be carelessly lost in this music. I never want to get sick of it, and I never, ever, want to outgrow this or anything" (212). This refusal to look forward finds its counterpoint in his final entry, in his acceptance of growth and change, his realization that part of the joy of both art and life are their openness to repetition that is also alteration: "I might find things in [the Beach Boys records] I never was able to hear before in my younger life. I might become just as enchanted, just as joyously captivated. I could fall in love all over again. All of that could come to pass. It is possible, isn't it?" (289). Jason is here engaging in an anticipation of retrospection that echoes his mother's at the novel's outset, so that *Eat the Document* ends by simultaneously looking backwards and "projecting into a future that it will not show us."[56] Jason's question projects that future as one shared with his reader, a gesture that is repeated in the novel's closing lines:

> My Beach Boys records sit there, an aural time capsule wired directly to my soul. Something in that music will recall not just what happened but all of what I felt, all of what I longed for, all of who I used to be. And that will be something, don't you think? (290).

In the context of the novel's overall trajectory, Jason's closing questions ask his reader whether the complex joys of art, and their intertwining with the rich development of an individual life over time, can provide sufficient consolation for the erosion of a revolutionary collective politics. In placing a bookstore at the center of her depiction of millennial youth resistance—as well as by employing postmodern means to something other than postmodern ends—Spiotta's novel can be read as attempting to sublate these oppositions between art and politics, writing and action. *Eat the Document* thereby echoes the revised conception of revolution offered by the line I quoted earlier from *American Woman*: "More and more she thought of revolution not as mustered force that might topple The System, but as a delicate process of changing individual minds, or as the rare chance to try."[57] In literary New Sincerity, changing minds is a two-way process, wherein a writer develops their aesthetics and politics by anticipating a conversation with their reader. But this anticipation should not go too far: the process must be focused on the means, with responsibility—the keyword of Spiotta's text—lying in a refusal of certainty regarding the ends to which the process leads. This is how Choi and Spiotta address the ambivalent legacies of revolutionary politics for their contemporary moment: not by setting out a concrete vision of a just future, but by exploring the kind of sensibility that has emerged in response to those legacies. In *Eat the Document*, Nash describes the sensibility of the young people he encounters at the bookstore as follows: "everything is both earnest and ironic at the same time with them. Which is either a total dodge or some attempt at a new way to be" (28). In what follows, I conclude this chapter with a novel that more overtly commits to a vision of a just world than either *American Woman* or *Eat the Document*, while maintaining even more blatantly a stance that is both earnest and ironic at the same time.

Being Inauthentically

What does it mean to oppose sincerely a system from which one comparatively benefits?[58] If asked to sketch the subject position for whom this question takes on most force in the American context, we might be tempted to describe a white, straight, cis-gendered, upper-middle-class male in his late twenties, someone who perhaps—at least in the millennial moment of normative neoliberalism—lives in a low-rent Manhattan apartment, works for a large pharmaceuticals company, and finds himself partaking in a series of "romantico-sexual arrangements" with beautiful foreign women.[59] We might, in other words, be describing someone like Dwight Bell Wilmerding, the narrator of *Indecision*, Benjamin Kunkel's first and thus far only novel. Yet despite these markers of ease and privilege (or perhaps because of them), *Indecision*—as its title indicates—opens with Dwight in stasis, unable to decide on questions from the largest to the most basic. Unable to choose between pesto and Nutella to spread on his morning bagel, he buys both. Unable to choose between two guidebooks for a trip to Ecuador, he buys neither. When it comes to choosing whether to go to Ecuador or not, he flips a coin as many times as seems necessary ("I knew a larger sample size would make the stats more accurate" [5]). This method he also uses to decide whether to accept invitations to various events from his friends and family. He outlines the perks of his system thus:

Statistically fair, it also kept my whole easy nature from forcing me to do everyone's bidding; it ensured a certain scarcity of Dwightness on the market; it contributed the prestige of the inscrutable to my otherwise transparent persona; and above all it allowed me to find out in my own good time whether I would actually have liked to do the thing in question. (19)

As we can already sense, Dwight Wilmerding is an easygoing and amusing narrator, given to a philosophical outlook on his lack of direction. Indeed, he has majored in philosophy at college, an education that has convinced him of the significance of self-knowledge—the centrality of the Delphic maxim "know thyself." The problem is that certainty regarding self-knowledge does not fit particularly well with Dwight's actual experience of self, which is of contingency and abstraction rather than essence. "To myself I always seemed totally steeped in my environment, or dyed in local color," he reflects, "and therefore like I might turn out to be anyone at all" (4). This is in sharp contrast to the perceptions held of Dwight by others, who consistently remark on his "apparently remarkable, indestructible Dwightness that was immune to time and place" (3). Like many of his self-analytical flourishes, these early observations by Dwight nod to his reader in a lightly metafictional manner—as with all fictional protagonists, Dwight does indeed emerge steeped in his environment, could turn out to be anyone at all, and inevitably takes on a kind of generality by virtue of his very appearance in a novel. But despite these gestures, the tone of his narration is never overly arch or knowing concerning his status as a literary character. Rather, from the outset of *Indecision*, Dwight appears to be an "honest soul," in Lionel Trilling's Hegelian phrase, one for whom sincere expression is a natural character trait.[60] Yet in the cultural environment in which he finds himself, immersed in "modern—or postmodern life, as it had apparently already been for some time" (18), Dwight wants to partake of "a more strenuous moral experience than 'sincerity'": he wants to become authentic.[61] His guidebook in this search for authenticity is Otto Knittel's *The Uses of Freedom*, the novel's stand-in for Martin Heidegger's *Being and Time*. "Late at night I would look at the words of this very deathocentric book," he tells us. "I read the book at maybe two pages an hour" (18).

In the early pages of *Indecision*, when Dwight associates his indecision with his want of authenticity and puzzles over how to overcome both problems together, there is little hint of any political meaning to his life or experiences. Yet by the end of the novel, our hero has somehow journeyed from his occasionally hapless but mostly routine participation in late capitalist New York society to a heady embrace of democratic socialism in the rainforests of Ecuador. In its account of Dwight's "narrative of important life-changing events" (4), *Indecision* thus offers a comic variation—even a subversion—of one of the most venerable genres in modern prose fiction: the Bildungsroman. Emerging in late Enlightenment Europe—Goethe's *Wilhelm Meister's Apprenticeship* (1795–96) is usually cited as the first major exemplar—the Bildungsroman diverged from earlier literary forms in its central focus on the experiences of a young person. "What makes Wilhelm Meister and his successors representative and interesting," writes Franco Moretti in his classic study of the genre, is "youth as such," the stage of life that represents "modernity's 'essence,' the sign of a world that seeks its meaning in the *future* rather than in the past."[62] This modern world is also a capitalist one, and the classical Bildungsroman offers an optimistic vision of a young person's integration into the bourgeois capitalist order, successfully mediating "the conflict between the ideal of *self-determination* and the equally imperious demands of *socialization*."[63]

For Dwight these staple conventions of the classical Bildungsroman are all out of kilter. Rather than find meaning in the future, he tells us that "I couldn't think of the future until I arrived there" (3). Rather than mediate a conflict between self-determination and socialization, his narrative stresses a comic gap between his experience of self and others' perceptions of his Dwightness. Rather than be reconciled to the capitalist order, by the end of *Indecision* he is committed to promoting an alternative. Given all that has preceded this surprise ending, however, it remains hard to see Dwight as a figure of revolutionary potential. The question of how seriously to take his political conversion would seem to lie at the heart of Kunkel's novel.

This was certainly the key question pondered by reviewers of *Indecision* in the American press. Jay McInerney placed the novel firmly in the Bildungsroman tradition, praised it for delivering "a type of cultural news" closely attuned to "zeitgeist frequencies," and linked Kunkel's ending directly to Wallace's argument in "E Unibus Pluram" for overcoming irony in favor of "single-entendre principles."[64] Joyce Carol Oates similarly wondered whether in the "risky conclusion" to his novel Kunkel was genuinely presenting the decisive awakening of Dwight's political consciousness "without irony."[65] Reviewers were in broad agreement that Dwight's characteristic self-contemplation, buttressed by the self-reflexive aspects of his narrative—the text's elaborate invocation of genre conventions and literary clichés, its lack of storytelling innocence in a genre historically concerned with innocence—offered a humorous spin on the jaded and ironic sensibility of his generation. But there was also agreement that the journey portrayed in *Indecision*—from "the dramatic irony of being self-aware" to "the reconstruction of belief that comes after it"—was intended to represent a wider (actual or hoped for) generational shift.[66] Reading Dwight Wilmerding as "something larger than himself, like the exemplar of a lost generation," reviewers characterized both the content and form of *Indecision* in terms of "the birth of a new earnestness."[67]

This reception for Kunkel's novel confirms, if confirmation were needed, what one scholar has called "a confluence of the genre of the coming-of-age novel and a particularly, or even uniquely, American narrative of national identity."[68] Yet in their rush to proclaim Kunkel's novel as a generational and national allegory, reviewers did not pause long to consider the implicit politics that came with the author's choice of representative protagonist. This despite the aural resonance of "whiteness" in "Dwightness," despite the narrator's regular retrograde comments on the women in his life, and despite the signifiers of class status in the various sites Dwight visits in New York—restaurants, golf clubs, even the psychoanalyst's chair. My point here is not to offer a suspicious reading of Kunkel's novel as an unconscious reinscription of multiple privileges, but to emphasize the extent to which Dwight's author is concerned with drawing attention to privilege, most notably the privilege that comes with having one's life be the subject of a novel.[69] In various essays, reviews, interviews, and public statements, Kunkel has consistently probed this privilege. He has praised the Chilean author Roberto Bolaño, for instance, for keeping the art of the novel "alive and freshly growing" in the face of "modern scepticism" concerning "whose life is worth being represented, or considered representative, in the first place."[70] Conversely, he has criticized exponents of the "misery memoir" for their presumption that their lives should be considered worthy of representation in that genre form. Compared to the Romantics, "who discovered that the self could provide a 'heroic argument,'" the lesson of the contemporary memoir is simply the demobilizing one that "suffering produces meaning. Life is what happens to you, not what you do. Victim and hero are one."[71]

This affirmative mention of Romanticism suggests that Kunkel holds some sympathy with the cultural movement that—as Trilling, Charles Taylor, and many others have argued—propelled the notion of individual authenticity into its key position in the modern world. Nevertheless, *Indecision* is not in agreement with its narrator that his key problem is a deficit of authenticity. Instead, by endowing its "representative kind of idiot"[72] with all the characteristics of the American norm—whiteness, maleness, middle-classness, etc.—and then having him travel to Ecuador, "a terra incognita I knew nothing about" (10), Kunkel's novel stresses that the search for personal authenticity can itself constitute an expression of privilege, one that too easily finds its home on a geopolitical canvas of unquestioned American political and cultural hegemony. The critical point is not simply to uncover the history of American hegemony and imperialist power—an important task in its own right—but to ask whether and how a privileged subject from the "core" of political power can sincerely oppose the power that has constituted their privilege and class position in the first place.

Moving to a higher allegorical level still—and jumping ahead for a moment to *Indecision*'s self-thematizing conclusion—we might say that Kunkel is asking whether publishing a debut novel in New York, the center of contemporary global capitalism and the publishing world, can contribute to the fight against capitalism's manifold injustices, or whether such an act simply constitutes one more demonstration of those injustices. If the problem is, as Wallace argued, that diagnosis has not led to cure, that a revelation of imprisonment has not led to freedom, then what is achieved by one more diagnosis emerging from the complicit heart of power? Like *American Woman* and *Eat the Document*, *Indecision* prompts its reader to consider whether writing and publishing a novel can be a means of political action in the present, a "cure" in Wallace's terms.[73] But Kunkel's novel also wonders more deeply about the autonomy of literature in that present, an era of capitalist realism when, as Purdy suggests, neoliberalism's most visceral critics could turn out to be "more interesting and, in some ways, deeper supporters than the most shameless market-utopian hack."[74]

Kunkel's critical writings emphasize his concern with finding connections between analysis and action, as well as the implications of this mission for literary content and form. Praising Don DeLillo's insights into the affective surfaces of postmodern society, he contends that "DeLillo would be even more the novelist we require if he saw the dilemma of finding a way to *act*, in the world of traffic and TV and motels, half so clearly as he sees this world itself."[75] Lauding Fredric Jameson's ability to capture "the mood and texture of postmodern life," Kunkel similarly notes that "the reader's impression of tremendous intellectual power is accompanied by one of political paralysis."[76] As Emilio Sauri has argued, *Indecision* can be read as a dramatization of Jameson's ideas about postmodernism as the waning of historicity in a seemingly perpetual consumerist present, with many passages from the novel offering comically on-the-nose descriptions of Dwight's historical cluelessness.[77] But Kunkel's focus on the problem of action in the midst of a "windless postmodern stasis" also lends his novel a critical edge.[78]

Dwight's indecision is thus both a literary metaphor and a literal problem stemming from his mode of life. When his girlfriend Vaneetha affectionately describes that mode of life as not only a cliché but "'not even a fresh cliché,'" Dwight can only agree: "I knew she was right. It wasn't very unusual for me to lie awake at night feeling like a scrap of sociology blown into its designated corner of the world." Yet he also points out that "knowing the clichés are clichés doesn't help you escape them. You still have to go on experiencing your experience as if no one else has ever done it" (26). This insight shows Dwight at his most representative: he is exemplary of a generation that have been taught to cultivate self-consciousness, reflexive knowledge, and discursive dexterity as positive traits, but find that their problems are not alleviated but rather exacerbated by self-consciousness, knowledge, and discourse. Despite the postmodern insights Dwight has internalized—which teach him that "everything everybody says" is "in quotes" (54)—he finds that the so-called death of the subject in the postmodern era has not averted the problems of self-understanding and of finding a way to act. Dwight believes that the answer to these problems lies in becoming authentic, in discovering the inner truth of his self. But *Indecision* will suggest that instead of going back to earlier models for answers, Dwight must go forward—he must become post-postmodern, whatever that might entail.

One potential route to post-postmodernism is neurochemical. Almost as soon as Dwight has recounted the basic details of his life, his housemate

Dan, a medical student, diagnoses Dwight's indecision as "'abulia,'" a mental imbalance stemming from a "'protracted civil conflict'" in the brain's "'medial forebrain bundle'" (34). Confirming Dwight's representativeness is the fact that, according to Dan, this condition is "'a complaint for a huge number of ostensibly normal people'" (33). A potential solution has just been discovered, however, in the form of the drug "Abulinix," and this explanation for his problem is immediately seductive to Dwight; as he asks rhetorically, "Doesn't everyone dream of a magic pill?" (31). Of course, Dwight's dream is also the dream of an explanation for his problem that is not simply a re-description of it within the terms of one or another discourse or language game, none of which, at this late stage in history, seem any longer able to claim definitive validity or priority. Before his eureka moment with Abulinix, he had considered numerous possible reasons for his indecision, providing a long bullet-point list that includes:

> ambivalence, laziness, bad faith, good family, suggestibleness (regarding ideas), resistance (regarding events), indiscriminate breast fixation, together with a weakened libido, not having found the right person, not having *been* the right person, sociological sense of one's life (shared with so many others), inconsequence of the self (except to itself),

and so on, ending with a "lack of ground for the individual's action" (32–33), a formulation Dwight draws from Knittel's *The Uses of Freedom*. Political considerations are notably absent from this list, which focuses solely on Dwight's problem at the individual level. Still, a whole gamut of explanation is being run here: candidate descriptions of Dwight's problem are alternately psychoanalytical, ontological, sociological, existential, and stemming from humanist notions of agency and personal authenticity. Later scenes with his father and sister Alice will add further explanations deriving from the realms of religion, anthropology, history, and elsewhere. Each of these descriptions metonymically codifies an entire methodological worldview, and the comedy lies in Dwight's familiarity with all these worldviews, while finding himself unable to ascribe privilege to one. "Only now that I held the panacea in my hand," he tells us with a newfound certainty, "did I recognize abulia as my major basic overriding problem." The answer has finally arrived: "The diagnosis and the cure all at once!" (32).

Deciding Justly

This epiphany initially makes *Indecision* appear as if it might be a "neuronovel" in the vein of Ian McEwan's *Saturday* (2005) or Richard Powers's *The Echo Maker* (2006), which address questions of contemporary identity through the new paradigm of neuroscience.[79] Instead, Dwight's experiences in Ecuador, where he ingests his first dose of Abulinix upon arrival, sends the novel in a very different direction. In a plot twist that gets explained only late in the text, Dwight finds himself journeying into the Amazon rainforest with a Belgian Argentine woman named Brigid. Initially Dwight views their relationship through structures of objectification that serve to fortify the novel's strongly established self/other dichotomy. Waking up on his first morning in Quito, he provides a detailed description of Brigid's appearance and remarks that "she would make a welcome addition to any threesome" (104). Here Brigid is imagined as simply the next in a long line of women in Dwight's life, the proximity of whose bodies, he tells us early on, "tended to really bring home to me the famous other-minds problem" (5). This mode of perceiving otherness (regularly linked in the text to Bildungsroman tropes as well as to philosophical traditions) culminates in a scene when Dwight masturbates in a moment of presumed simultaneity with Brigid, only to discover that he has grossly misunderstood the sounds of crying emerging from her hammock (158–159). This is the low point of their relationship, and it comes after a series of epiphanies undergone by Dwight, which had promised the dawn of a new decisiveness brought on by the Abulinix, have been revealed as inauthentic, each in turn a false dawn.

Epiphany has been, since modernism, the literary trope that has most often served to validate the authentic self-relation of the modern subject.[80] Here such epiphanies offer support to the figure of the imperialist self, the white American heterosexual male whose financial superiority allows him to employ a developing country as the canvas for his project of self-discovery. But in a series of conversations with Brigid, Dwight will begin to recognize that his investment in a paradigm of individuated, self-knowing subjectivity is in fact central to his difficulties, both personal and political. Soon Dwight will take to calling his traveling partner "Bridge," and it is as a bridge, a point of communicative transversal rather than an objectified other, that she will provide Dwight with the key to the potential resolution of the subjectivity/indecision syndrome at the core of the novel.

Brigid constantly challenges Dwight's assumption that self-identity on the one hand, and openness to events and decisions on the other, should be compatible, telling him at one point, "'You thought you were very open to whatever can happen. But the reason you have remained so open is that nothing can enter you. So this is not actually to be *open*. . . . Nothing can happen to you. You are that type'" (175). At another moment, she accuses him of believing in nothing, to which Dwight responds, "'I believe in things, Brigid. I believe in my*self*.'" "'And your self that you believe in,'" she retorts, "'what does *it* believe in?'" (157). Rather than suggesting, therefore, that Dwight has not yet succeeded in establishing his authentic individual identity, as he believes, Brigid consistently presents him as being, in effect, *too much of a self*, too comfortable within his isolating, individuating shell. The implication is that the search for authenticity—linked to this model of selfhood, this imperialist project, and this traditional narrative genre—is doomed to ethical failure. It therefore makes sense that Dwight's culminating moment of decision—his political conversion to "democratic socialism"—appears to have very little to do with self-knowledge, authenticity, or belief.

While Brigid has spent much of their journey through the rainforest patiently explaining the ills of extractive capitalism and its effects on countries like Ecuador, Dwight has shown very little understanding of her message. But then all of a sudden, while he and Brigid are high on a powerful local drug called San Pedro, Dwight joyfully offers to follow her lead and "sign up for justice right now," proving his sincerity by writing down "*Justice!*" in his notebook (202). Kunkel thereby inscribes a moment of conversion into Dwight's narrative by having Dwight mimic the inscription himself; the comic suddenness of this development is underscored when Brigid exclaims, "'What a change from one minute to the next!'" (198), and when Dwight entreats her, "'say it and it's done'" (203). Subsequently, as their sexual awakening progresses in time to Dwight's discovery of his commitment to justice, Brigid tells Dwight of an Eden she imagines in which "'there is no third person, not a him or a her to address. There is only one other so you address the person simply as *you*. You say "you." . . . Only you and I, I and you'" (203). This imagined scenario draws attention to *Indecision*'s new emphasis on the priority of the other as a dialogic companion in the search for truth. And in keeping with this priority, in the remainder of the novel Dwight's conversion experience never hardens into subjective knowledge outside of dialogue, as Brigid continues to correct the many humorous errors he makes about the socialism he has signed up to promote.

Nevertheless, the comic tenor of the scene just described—in which the novel's key themes are brought to resolution only through the drug-fueled mania of two characters in an exoticized outpost of Western (neo-)colonialism—suggests that any such resolving insight on Dwight's part cannot be unquestioningly embraced. Indeed, it is here that the novel most obviously ironizes the sincerity of its message. As they consummate their relationship on the grass of the clearing, Brigid reveals to Dwight that he has been the subject of a plot that has engineered their encounter, "a friendly conspiracy of remarkable women" (214). There are other people in Eden after all, and an improbable twist is situated at the core of the novel's love plot. Meanwhile, with the political-conversion plot also nearing resolution, Dwight's agonized admission that part of his reluctance to "bust a move" on Brigid was because "'I'm afraid of becoming—becoming—a—a—. . . I'm afraid of being a—I'm terrified of becoming a socialist!'" (211) has found its ecstatic post-coital counterpart: "Now that I was a socialist fucking made me joyous, and I wanted to do it again right away" (215). Sex thus appears, for Dwight at least, to be the true path to socialism. As if there weren't already enough indicators of the unlikelihood of Dwight's story of conversion, his friend Dan reiterates it in historical terms: "'Dwight, people don't do this anymore. You don't fly to Latin America, take psychedelic drugs, and find sexual liberation with some suntanned goddess of international socialism. . . . Now is not thirty-five years ago'" (227). Dwight himself is equally aware of the untimeliness of his experience, and in bringing his scene of sexual and social epiphany with Brigid to a close, his comment to the reader is more than a little wry: "Things were maybe getting cheesy. But at least they possessed the dignity of taking place" (217).

Reviewers understandably questioned the seriousness of all of this. While most admitted that Kunkel *seems* sincere in the way he ends the novel, many poured scorn on the abrupt nature of Dwight's conversion, and especially on the content of the "democratic socialism" to which he claims to have been converted.[81] But these critiques of the ending implicitly assume a model of the relationship between selfhood and decision that *Indecision* has done much to question.[82] The reviewers presuppose that Dwight is a sovereign self, capable of decisively adhering to a particular doctrine, of being fundamentally and resolutely altered by the experiences he has undergone. Yet *Indecision*'s conception of change is far more uncertain and provisional, a point underscored by the book's concluding plot twist: the revelation that the Abulinix Dwight thought he had taken was in fact only a placebo.

This twist comes in the final chapter before the novel's epilogue, a chapter that consists almost entirely of a series of emails. Dwight sends missives to his sister, his university class, and his parents, announcing in each one his newfound embrace of socialism (and thereby repeatedly reinscribing his commitment to *"Justice!"*). As the chapter closes, he reads an email from Dan that relays the news about the placebo. Rather than detail his reaction, Dwight instead painstakingly describes his movements to the reader:

> I stood up and looked at [the attendant], a stoop-shouldered student type, thin in the cheeks and lips, but romantic in the eyes and the swept-back hair. "Cuanto?" I asked, and handed him a small sheaf of filthy cotton-soft singles. Then I went out to the street with my change.
>
> Across the street was the empty town square with its sad dry fountain. Brigid had grabbed my hand. She was asking me what the matter was. An old man in a straw hat and dirty suit sat on a bench picking his teeth and watching us with as mild a form of interest as is any interest at all. (225)

Alone among passages in the novel, this narration apes the style of the "dirty realist" fiction practiced by writers such as Raymond Carver and Denis Johnson, in which the numb state of a character is evoked through the description of their surrounding environment, the details of which tend to mirror their inner feelings. The final line of the passage, in particular, seems to take the naturalist tone of such writing to the point of parody, with the man in the "dirty" suit watching "with as mild a form of interest as is any interest at all," the latter phrase a deliberately contorted version of naturalism's stylistic concentration on the world's materiality in order to imply the lack of centrality of the human within it. What there is not, in this passage, is Dwight's usually immediate, reflexive engagement in philosophical speculation and self-analysis. Instead, and once again, it is only in conversation with Brigid that Dwight's inner state becomes identifiable. Here, directly following the passage above, are the final lines of the chapter and the main body of the novel:

I looked at Brigid. "You know what a placebo is?"
"Yes, for a control of the experiment?"
I nodded.
"So? Yes? Dwight, are you all right?"
"I am, actually." I could see in her eyes that she could hear that I was. "I'm fine." (225)

It is only in the eyes of the other, then, that the state of the self can truly be known. But knowledge has here become something other than the sovereign possession of information, just as selfhood must now be conceived dialogically. In order to "know" whether one "is" a socialist, and whether the future can be meaningfully engaged on that basis, the priority of responsive engagement with the other must be maintained. By the end of *Indecision*, dialogue with "Bridge," as well as emails to his friends—something akin to the collaborative writing we saw in *American Woman*—have helped Dwight to identify and clarify his commitment to democratic socialism. But as the epilogue makes clear, on a formal level the crucial and ultimate respondent and collaborator for Dwight must be the reader of his book. While working as a reporter in Bolivia, Dwight keeps his spirits up by writing short emails to Brigid in Argentina. The epilogue itself, however, takes the form of a memoir addressed explicitly to the reader, whose individual response is thematized— via a closing move to second-person present-tense narration—as necessary for the potential sincerity of Dwight's conversion to gain validation.[83]

As the many vexed reviews of the novel indicate, each response to Dwight's culminating decision remains necessarily open-ended, with affirmation only possible, if at all, *in spite of* history, ideology, and literary cliché. Rather than go to lengths to avoid being described as imperialist, patriarchal, and privileged, *Indecision* actually invites that very critique. Like literary New Sincerity more generally, Kunkel's novel offers no conclusive defense against the application of a readerly hermeneutics of suspicion. Dwight's culminating and epiphanic decision—presented, like everything else in the novel, in comic terms—becomes impossible to read as either sincere or insincere, given that it is both inherently provisional and a kind of cliché. Thus the reader is made self-conscious about the undecidability that characterizes Dwight's story and their reading of it, an undecidability that reaches its apotheosis in *Indecision*'s closing lines. These are, appropriately, lines of dialogue spoken not by the self but by the other, in response to the very question that in Western culture usually calls for the most decisive of all decisions. Faced with Dwight's typically spontaneous and shambling request for her hand in marriage, Brigid replies, "'I'd like to. But not now. Maybe not ever. Really I don't know'" (241).

Addressing the genre of twenty-first-century novels about radical politics that have been my subject in this chapter, one critic remarks that they "may be fictions not only of political despair but of epistemological despair as well."[84] While it is too funny and tonally upbeat to count as a novel of political or epistemological despair, *Indecision*—written from the self-conscious heart of what Jameson calls the "epistemologically crippling" perspective of first-world postmodernism—certainly is a novel of political and epistemological uncertainty.[85] Is it possible, *Indecision* asks, for people in certain geopolitical subject positions to sincerely fight for socialism? Can they know what's in their heart when they undertake that fight? Will class interests dominate private intentions in the final analysis? Will the revolution ever come? And are these even relevant concerns for a contemporary American novel to address? On all of these matters, *Indecision* is not sure. But perhaps, at some future moment, its reader will be. Meanwhile, the job of the writer may simply be to affirm faith in the midst of uncertainty; or, as Kunkel has put it, "to write as if your words had the revolutionary power they can never possess."[86]

CONCLUSION: SINCERITY IN COMMON

The Spring 2014 issue of *n+1* that contained Jedediah Purdy's "The Accidental Neoliberal," the essay that opened my last chapter, also included a short story by Benjamin Kunkel, whose novel *Indecision* brought that chapter to a close. At the present time of writing, this story remains the most recent piece Kunkel has published in the New York–based magazine he cofounded with five friends in 2004. It is also the last piece of creative writing to appear by him in any publication. Around the same time the issue appeared, *New York* magazine featured a profile titled "How Benjamin Kunkel Went from Novelist to Marxist Public Intellectual," published to coincide with the appearance of Kunkel's second book.[1] *Utopia or Bust: A Guide to the Present Crisis* appeared from Verso Books as the first in their Jacobin series, a set of titles that "offer short interrogations of politics, economics, and culture from a socialist perspective."[2] The series is a collaboration between Verso—the venerable publishing house of the intellectual Left in Britain, originally inaugurated as New Left Books in 1970—and *Jacobin*, a magazine that launched in 2010 and has since become the unofficial party organ of the Democratic Socialists of America. Kunkel was named a contributing editor at *Jacobin* in 2013, and though he no longer appears as an active presence on the masthead of either *n+1* or *Jacobin*, we can surmise that his migration from the former to the latter (and more recently to the editorial committee of *New Left Review*) indicates a hardening of his socialist convictions over the years since *n+1* was founded and *Indecision* was published.

That moment in the mid-2000s now feels like a long time ago. With the moribund political scene that Purdy describes still prevailing, *n+1* was founded, in Kunkel's words, "to express a sensibility":

> going to college in the 90s, coming of age intellectually in this era of, by then, relatively stale postmodernism, it was easy to feel like there was nothing new under the sun and that you could only recombine things that have already been done. I think *n+1*, particularly the title, expressed hope more than a conviction that something new could be done, that there could be some progress or advance in intellectual life.[3]

Francis Mulhern has described *n+1* as "a micro-culture, a whole way of intellectual life," and has noted the importance to that culture of *Bildung*, "the master-trope of *n+1*."[4] As we saw in Chapter Six, Franco Moretti calls the Bildungsroman the signature genre of a modernity that "seeks its meaning in the *future* rather than in the past."[5] Nevertheless, Mulhern maintains that in the early issues of *n+1*, "the governing feeling is one of belatedness," a sense of uncertainty about the future, or even whether any real future will come to pass.[6] Kunkel's "hope more than a conviction" conveys that uncertainty, as does *Indecision*, a Bildungsroman for an era when growing up in capitalist society has become a newly difficult task.

Yet this sense of belatedness in the tone of *n+1* gave way after 2008, and particularly with the advent of the Occupy movement in 2011, to a new political energy. In "Cultural Revolution," a 2013 essay that offers the nearest thing to a collective historical self-analysis published in the magazine, the editors opine that "things are changing."[7] Proceeding dialectically, they express this change in terms of negation, envisaging the possibilities for solidarity that might emerge as bourgeois intellectuals and cultural producers begin to experience the precarity previously reserved for the working class. In this new context, the demobilizing view of cultural outputs as "just so many types of functionally affirmative, system-stabilizing, content-neutral cultural capital" may finally give way to the possibility of genuine "conviction."[8]

If this cultural shift can be traced in the pages of *n+1*, then the founding of *Jacobin* and many other left-liberal and socialist "little magazines" in the period since the mid-2000s—a trend that continues to the present day with the 2023 launch of the black radical publication *Hammer and Hope*—is an even stronger sign of intellectual revival.[9] Purdy's essay sees in this revival the emergence of a new common purpose: "Where public writing at the turn of the millennium felt monadic and zero-sum, a slow-motion scramble for attention and sponsorship, it now seems less desperately and exclusively that way."[10] Nevertheless, the contradictory positioning of Purdy's essay in the Spring 2014 issue of *n+1*—both "After the New Sincerity" and "Against the Old Sincerity," as I noted in Chapter Six—tells of an uncertain historiography. The ambiguities are both temporal and conceptual: did Purdy's 1999 book *For Common Things* represent an old sincerity (now being rejected) or a new sincerity (now being bypassed)? Is Purdy's "The Accidental Neoliberal" supposed to be *describing* a period "after the New Sincerity" or to be *embodying* that period, written from a contemporary moment in which it is once again possible to be politically sincere? And what of *n+1*'s own relationship to sincerity? The magazine's commitment to sincerity's importance was suggested from the outset by the words that opened and closed its inaugural issue. "We are living in an era of demented self-censorship," its editorial statement began, with Keith Gessen's "Endnotes" to the issue striking a similar note: "It is time to say what you mean. . . . so we've begun by saying, No. Enough."[11] As one scholar has commented, "For *n+1*'s editors, a critical spirit is actually a component of sincerity. In other words, they *believe in doubt*."[12] But perhaps the post-2008 or post-2011 period has allowed a sincerity of doubt to transform into something closer to a sincerity of conviction. Perhaps only now is it becoming possible to say what you mean.

This transformed model of sincerity has been equally observable in American fiction, where the structure of feeling expressed by literary New Sincerity has given way since the 2000s to something different. Although it shares a genre—now widely called autofiction—with *A Heartbreaking Work of Staggering Genius*, Ben Lerner's critically lauded 2014 novel *10.04* is one sign of the distance traveled since Eggers's millennial-era work. *10.04* opens with the narrator telling his reader grandly (and ironically) of his plan to "project myself into several futures simultaneously," to "work my way from irony to sincerity in the sinking city, a would-be Whitman of the vulnerable grid."[13] In one fell swoop, Lerner here pays homage to and parodies the previously regnant literary aesthetic. Born in 1979 and thus more than twenty years younger than the oldest of the writers grouped together in my study, he has inherited literary

New Sincerity as an established tradition, a set of now-hardened themes and tropes that can be repurposed in new ways for a new time.

This post-2008 era is one in which a renewed public awareness of the fragility of capitalism and the fragility of the environment—the sinking city, the vulnerable grid—have combined to make our sense of the future itself fragile, yet simultaneously more malleable than seemed possible under the "End of History" vision that dominated the previous two decades. In place of the isolated individuals that inhabit the novels and stories examined throughout *New Sincerity*, *10.04* takes as its task to envisage future forms of collectivity that might "coconstruct a world in which moments can be something other than the elements of profit" (47). To undertake this task, its narrator imagines addressing "a collective person who didn't yet exist, a still-uninhabited second person plural to whom all the arts, even in their most intimate registers, were nevertheless addressed" (108). This is a rereading and revision of the "you" to whom literary New Sincerity was addressed, a singular reader figured in *Infinite Jest* as an addict in recovery, in *A Heartbreaking Work* as a threatening creditor, in *Look at Me* as a commodified self, and in *American Woman* as a cross-racial and cross-class ally who will, in the end, betray you.

By contrast, the privileged grammatical subject of *10.04* is the second-person plural, the collective "you." The tutelary spirit for this aesthetic, as the opening lines suggest, is Walt Whitman, but a Whitman different from the moody and bombastic inspiration of *A Heartbreaking Work*, a Whitman who is quieter, humbler, more willing to offer the assurance, in *10.04*'s closing line, that "I am with you, and I know how it is" (240). Lerner's novel is itself a kind of Bildungsroman, albeit one where the social order with which the protagonist can reconcile has not yet been constituted. In this respect, too, *10.04* offers a dialectical reckoning with the New Sincerity project, which in this book I have grounded in the early writing of the authors I address, without in most cases going on to track their development into maturity. The implication is that we shouldn't assume that maturity means superiority: as Lerner suggests, maturity is a double-edged sword if it means no more than acquiescing to the political or aesthetic status quo. His treatise *The Hatred of Poetry* privileges youthful sincerity in life and art by arguing that all actual poems fail the idea of the genuine "Poem" in the same way that growing up constitutes "a falling away from the pure potentiality of being human into the vicissitudes of being an actual person in a concrete historical situation."[14] Reviving this "pure potentiality" demands a poetics of virtuality rather than actuality, a poetics aligned in *10.04* with a reader imagined as "transpersonal revolutionary subject" (47).[15] This is a new way to see the core problem faced by New Sincerity writers, which comes down to the fact that sincerity can never be firmly established because the market orientation of the work seems to threaten its purity. But if sincerity could only ever be virtual—could only ever inhere in the *idea* of the work rather than in the work itself—then its lack of instantiation in a particular work is not finally a failure. It is instead an invitation to revolutionary coconstruction, which is in turn the condition of possibility for any future world we might create for others and for ourselves.

The years between the global financial crisis of 2007–08 and Lerner's novel had already seen increased popular politicization in the United States, with the Tea Party protests of 2009–10, Occupy in 2011–12, and the Black Lives Matter protests from 2013 forward. But another decade has passed since Lerner's novel (and Purdy's article), and this period has witnessed still more tribulations. The Sanders presidential campaigns of 2016 and 2020, the popular feminism of the #MeToo movement, the reinvigorated environmental politics of the Green New Deal, the unprecedented street protests following the killing of George Floyd: all these have marked important stages in the Left's upward trajectory. Of course, the Right has also been on the march, with associated names and incidents that hardly need listing here. Compared to the period addressed in this book, the contemporary social situation is one in which the lines of battle have become clearer, and in which the ordinary person's complicity with the system seems less of a pressing concern now that the system is rewarding fewer and fewer citizens while continuing to lay waste to the planet. With today's renewed focus on multiple axes of inequality, the least we can say is that the sincerity of politics is in question in a different way than before, while the politics of sincerity has taken on new meaning. Perhaps sincerity can now name not an interior struggle, shared (at best) with individual readers, but rather a renewed public-spiritedness held in common, or at least held in common among a great many. If this sounds naïve or too hopeful—frustratingly virtual rather than compellingly actual—it is a hope that the present writer wants to affirm. Desperately, perhaps, but nevertheless sincerely.

Notes

Introduction

1. Dave Eggers, *What Is the What: The Autobiography of Valentino Achak Deng: A Novel* (London: Penguin, 2006), 56. Further references in parentheses.

2. Lionel Trilling, *Sincerity and Authenticity* (Oxford: Oxford University Press, 1972), 2.

3. Ibid., 9.

4. Along with Deng's name being excluded from the book's main title and authorship, one critic notes that the copyright of *What Is the What* lies with Eggers, commenting that "it's further odd that for a story that is about dispossession in numerous forms, Deng doesn't legally own the story of his own life and has become a fictional character in someone else's novel." Yogita Goyal, "African Atrocity, American Humanity: Slavery and Its Transnational Afterlives," *Research in African Literatures* 45.3 (2014): 57.

5. Among other accolades, the book was nominated for the National Book Critics Circle Award. The sole exception to the flow of praise was Lee Siegel, whose review of *What Is the What* accused Eggers of "post-colonial arrogance" and "socially acceptable Orientalism." Even Siegel, however, did not place doubt on the *sincerity* of Eggers's approach to his material, instead condemning the author precisely for his "confusion of good intentions with good art." Lee Siegel, "The Niceness Racket," *New Republic* (23 April 2007), https://newrepublic.com/article/62544/the-niceness-racket

6. Elizabeth Twitchell, "Dave Eggers's *What Is the What*: Fictionalizing Trauma in the Era of Misery Lit," *American Literature* 83.3 (2011): 624.

7. Ibid.

8. Ibid. See Jane Elliott, *The Microeconomic Mode: Political Subjectivity in Contemporary Popular Aesthetics* (New York: Columbia University Press, 2018), 141–152; Goyal, "African"; Mitchum Huehls, "Referring to the Human in Contemporary Human Rights Literature," *Modern Fiction Studies* 58.1 (2012): 1–21; Michelle Peek,

"Humanitarian Narrative and Posthumanist Critique: Dave Eggers's *What Is the What*," *Biography* 35.1 (2012), 115–136.

9. Having reached a first peak in 1947, the postwar birthrate reached a second peak in 1957 and then began a long, steep decline until the mid-1970s. James T. Patterson, *Grand Expectations: The United States, 1945–1974* (Oxford: Oxford University Press, 1976), 77. The literary critic most committed to analyzing contemporary American fiction in terms of generations has been Jeffrey Williams; his overview of "Generation Jones" (born 1954–1965) holds similarities to my treatment of the post-boomer generation but differs in important respects. Jeffrey J. Williams, "Generation Jones and Contemporary US Fiction," *American Literary History* 28.1 (2016): 94–122. Nicholas Dames has also written influentially about a "theory generation," albeit he is not specific in defining the beginning and end of that generation, and his review essay addresses a set of novels published more recently than those at the center of my study. Nicholas Dames, "The Theory Generation," *n+1* 14 (2012): 157–169.

10. Daniel T. Rodgers, *Age of Fracture* (Cambridge, MA: Harvard University Press, 2011); George Packer, *The Unwinding: An Inner History of the New America* (New York: Faber & Faber, 2013).

11. On these three developments, see, respectively: François Cusset, *French Theory: How Foucault, Derrida, Deleuze, & Co. Transformed the Intellectual Life of the United States*, trans. Jeff Fort (Minneapolis: University of Minnesota Press, 2008); Andrew Hartman, *A War for the Soul of America: A History of the Culture Wars* (Chicago: University of Chicago Press, 2015); Mark McGurl, *The Program Era: Postwar Fiction and the Rise of Creative Writing* (Cambridge, MA: Harvard University Press, 2009).

12. Ted Striphas, *The Late Age of Print: Everyday Book Culture from Consumerism to Control* (New York: Columbia University Press, 2009).

13. Chuck Klosterman, *The Nineties* (London: Penguin, 2022).

14. "Normative neoliberalism" and "the horizons of political hope..." are from William Davies, "The New Neoliberalism," *New Left Review* 101 (2016): 127. Davies contrasts the normative neoliberalism of the 1989–2008 period with the "combative neoliberalism" of 1979–1989 and the turn to "punitive neoliberalism" after the crisis of 2008. "Capitalist realism" and "capitalism seamlessly occupies..." are from Mark Fisher, *Capitalist Realism: Is There No Alternative?* (Winchester: O Books, 2009), 8.

15. Mark McGurl, *Everything and Less: The Novel in the Age of Amazon* (London: Verso, 2021), 48.

16. On the genre turn, see Paul Crosthwaite, *The Market Logics of Contemporary Fiction* (Cambridge: Cambridge University Press, 2019), 58–62; Andrew Hoberek, "Literary Genre Fiction," in *American Literature in Transition, 2000–2010*, ed. Rachel Greenwald Smith (Cambridge: Cambridge University Press, 2018), 61–75; Jeremy Rosen, "Literary Fiction and the Genres of Genre Fiction," *Post45* (7 August 2018), https://post45.org/2018/08/literary-fiction-and-the-genres-of-genre-fiction/

17. Andrew Hoberek, "The Novel After David Foster Wallace," in *A Companion to David Foster Wallace Studies*, ed. Marshall Boswell and Stephen J. Burn (New York: Palgrave, 2013), 217.

18. Robert B. Pippin, *After the Beautiful: Hegel and the Philosophy of Pictorial Modernism* (Chicago: University of Chicago Press, 2014), 86.

19. Ibid., 87.

20. See Tom LeClair, *The Art of Excess: Mastery in Contemporary American Fiction* (Champaign: University of Illinois Press, 1989).

21. David Foster Wallace, *Consider the Lobster, and Other Essays* (London: Abacus, 2005), 272.

22. It is worth noting here the contrast between Wallace's anti-modernism and the trend in recent literature and art that has been dubbed "metamodernism." James and Seshagiri see twenty-first-century metamodernist novelists—among whom they number J. M. Coetzee, Tom McCarthy, Ian McEwan, Cynthia Ozick, and Zadie Smith—as aiming "to move the novel forward by looking back to the aspirational energies of modernism," notably by privileging "rupture, irony and fragmentation." David James and Urmila Seshagiri, "Metamodernism: Narratives of Continuity and Revolution," *PMLA* 129.1 (2014): 93. For Wallace (at least in his nonfiction), rupture, irony, and fragmentation are not revolutionary strategies but alienating ones, ill-suited to addressing the ills of neoliberal American culture. See also van den Akker and Vermeulen's (to my mind unpersuasive) Jamesonian theorization of metamodernism as a "structure of feeling" that emerges in the 2000s as "the dominant cultural logic of Western capitalist societies," a cultural logic that incorporates "the New Sincerity in literature" among other contemporary art forms. Robin van den Akker and Timotheus Vermeulen, "Periodising the 2000s, or, the Emergence of Metamodernism," in *Metamodernism: Historicity, Affect and Depth After Postmodernism*, ed. Robin van den Akker, Timotheus Vermeulen, and Alison Gibbons (London: Rowman & Littlefield, 2017), 3–4. For a robust critique of this vision of metamodernism, see Martin Paul Eve, "Thomas Pynchon, David Foster Wallace and the Problems of 'Metamodernism,'" *C21 Literature* 1.1 (2012): 7–25.

23. Trilling, *Sincerity*, 7.

24. Ibid., 97.

25. Wallace, in *Conversations with David Foster Wallace*, ed. Stephen J. Burn (Jackson: University Press of Mississippi, 2012), 61. Wallace's artistic model here was not only Dostoevsky but Tolstoy, whose treatise *What Is Art?* was a significant influence. See Matt Prout, "Art or Shit: Value, Sincerity, and the Avant-garde in David Foster Wallace," *Journal of Modern Literature* 45.3 (2022): 81–83.

26. Hoberek, "The Novel," 220. Whitman and Twain are, on Hoberek's account, among the American progenitors of intentional bad form.

27. Without dwelling on the point, I would note that a wish to do away with twentieth-century innovations and return to the heyday of the nineteenth-century novel finds its most prominent contemporary instantiation in the novels of Jonathan

Franzen. Franzen is often included on lists of writers associated with literary New Sincerity, but unlike the writers featured in this book, there is very little formally or conceptually "new" about the sincerity explored in his fiction, and many of the formal tensions that make their work interesting have been preemptively resolved in his. For related critiques of the writer-reader "contract" endorsed by Franzen, see Crosthwaite, *Market*, 182–183, and Rachel Greenwald Smith, *Affect and American Literature in the Age of Neoliberalism* (Cambridge: Cambridge University Press, 2015), 33–37.

28. Twitchell, "Dave," 638.

29. Deborah Brandt, *The Rise of Writing: Redefining Mass Literacy* (Cambridge: Cambridge University Press, 2014), 3.

30. Ibid., 2. "Reading was for learning how to be good—in worship, citizenship, work, and school," Brandt observes. "But writing has always been less *for* good than it is *a* good. While reading has productive value for the reader, writing has surplus value that fuels other enterprises." Ibid., 4–5. Unless otherwise indicated, throughout this book all italics in quoted material are in the original.

31. Ibid., 20.

32. Ibid., 13.

33. Zadie Smith, "Introduction," in *The Burned Children of America*, ed. Marco Cassini and Martina Testa (London: Hamish Hamilton, 2003), xx.

34. Joshua Ferris, *Then We Came to the End* (London: Penguin, 2008), 385.

35. Garrett Stewart, *Dear Reader: The Conscripted Audience in Nineteenth-Century British Fiction* (Baltimore: Johns Hopkins University Press, 1996), 12.

36. Ibid.

37. "We were fractious and overpaid" is the novel's opening sentence. Ferris, *Then*, 3.

38. Amy Rea, "How Serious Is America's Literacy Problem?" *Library Journal* (29 April 2020), https://www.libraryjournal.com/story/How-Serious-Is-Americas-Literacy-Problem

39. Brandt, *Rise*, 3.

40. Trilling, *Sincerity*, 9.

41. William Gaddis, *The Recognitions* (New York: Penguin, 1993), 452.

42. Trilling, *Sincerity*, 2. Further references in parentheses. In support of Trilling's claim about the emergence of a moral discourse of sincerity in the early modern period, see John Martin, "Inventing Sincerity, Refashioning Prudence: The Discovery of the Individual in Renaissance Europe," *American Historical Review* 102 (1997): 1304–1342; and Jane Taylor, "'Why Do You Tear Me from Myself?': Torture, Truth, and the Arts of the Counter-Reformation," in *The Rhetoric of Sincerity*, ed. Ernst van Alphen, Mieke Bal, and Carel Smith (Stanford: Stanford University Press, 2009), 19–43.

43. David Riesman, with Nathan Glazer and Reuel Denney, *The Lonely Crowd: A Study of the Changing American Character* (New Haven: Yale University Press, 1950); C. Wright Mills, *White Collar: The American Middle Classes* (Oxford: Oxford University Press, 1951); Erving Goffman, *The Presentation of Self in Everyday Life* (Edinburgh:

Social Sciences Research Centre, 1956); William H. Whyte, Jr., *The Organization Man* (New York: Simon & Schuster, 1956). For an overview of literary and sociological developments around sincerity and authenticity in this period, see Abigail Cheever, *Real Phonies: Cultures of Authenticity in Post–World War II America* (Athens: University of Georgia Press, 2010).

44. In an influential essay about the period, Jameson calls Trilling's text "an Arnoldian call to reverse the tide of 60s countercultural 'barbarism.'" Fredric Jameson, "Periodizing the 60s," *Social Text* 9/10 (1984): 205.

45. Leon Guilhamet, *The Sincere Ideal: Studies in Eighteenth-Century English Literature* (Montreal: McGill-Queen's University Press, 1974); see also Patricia M. Ball, "Sincerity: The Rise and Fall of a Critical Term," *Modern Language Review* 59 (1964): 1–11; Stanley Cavell, *Must We Mean What We Say?* (New York: Scribner's, 1969); Donald Davie, "On Sincerity: From Wordsworth to Ginsburg," *Encounter* (October 1968): 61–65; David Perkins, *Wordsworth and the Poetry of Sincerity* (Cambridge, MA: Harvard University Press, 1964); Henri Peyre, *Literature and Sincerity* (New Haven: Yale University Press, 1963); Herbert Read, *The Cult of Sincerity* (London: Faber & Faber, 1968); Patricia Meyer Spacks, "In Search of Sincerity," *College English* 29 (1968): 591–602.

46. The opening paragraphs of this section draw on a previously published article: Adam Kelly, "Dialectic of Sincerity: Lionel Trilling and David Foster Wallace," *Post45* (17 October 2014), https://post45.org/2014/10/dialectic-of-sincerity-lionel-trilling-and-david-foster-wallace/; later in this Introduction I also develop material first published in Kelly, "David Foster Wallace and New Sincerity Aesthetics: A Reply to Edward Jackson and Joel Nicholson-Roberts," *Orbit: A Journal of American Literature* 5.2 (2017): 1–32.

47. Amanda Anderson, *The Way We Argue Now: A Study in the Cultures of Theory* (Princeton: Princeton University Press, 2005), 161.

48. Ibid., 187. In later work Anderson will move to calling this proceduralism simply "liberalism," with Trilling remaining her touchstone in literary criticism. See Amanda Anderson, *Bleak Liberalism* (Chicago: University of Chicago Press, 2016).

49. Anderson, *The Way*, 167.

50. Jacques Derrida, "Structure, Sign and Play in the Discourse of the Human Sciences," in *The Structuralist Controversy: The Languages of Criticism and the Sciences of Man*, ed. Richard Macksey and Eugenio Donato (Baltimore: Johns Hopkins University Press, 1970), 247–264.

51. Along with Trilling, who calls Rousseau's writings "one of the decisive cultural events of the modern epoch" (58), see Charles Taylor, *The Ethics of Authenticity* (Cambridge, MA: Harvard University Press, 1991), 27–28; and Bernard Williams, *Truth and Truthfulness: An Essay in Genealogy* (Princeton: Princeton University Press, 2002), 172–191.

52. Jacques Derrida, *Of Grammatology*, trans. Gayatri Chakravorty Spivak (Baltimore: Johns Hopkins University Press, 1976), 141–164.

53. Paul de Man, "Jacques Derrida, *Of Grammatology*," trans. Richard Howard, in de Man, *Critical Writings, 1953–1978*, ed. Lindsay Waters (Minneapolis: University of Minnesota Press, 1989), 215.

54. Ibid.

55. Paul de Man, "The Rhetoric of Blindness: Jacques Derrida's Reading of Rousseau," in *Blindness and Insight: Essays in the Rhetoric of Contemporary Criticism*, 2nd ed. (London: Routledge, 1983), 136.

56. Ibid., 137.

57. For a sympathetic engagement with de Man's reputation after the discovery of his wartime writings, see Jacques Derrida, *Memoires for Paul de Man* (New York: Columbia University Press, 1988). For a polemical condemnation, see David Lehman, *Signs of the Times: Deconstruction and the Fall of Paul de Man* (New York: Poseidon Press, 1991).

58. Williams, *Truth*, 11. The other basic virtue is "Accuracy," with "Accuracy" and "Sincerity" respectively summarized in the formulation "you do the best you can to acquire true beliefs, and what you say reveals what you believe." Ibid.

59. See, for instance: Deborah Forbes, *Sincerity's Shadow: Self-Consciousness in British Romantic and Mid-Twentieth-Century American Poetry* (Cambridge, MA: Harvard University Press, 2004); Elizabeth Markovitz, *The Politics of Sincerity: Plato, Frank Speech, and Democratic Judgment* (University Park: University of Pennsylvania Press, 2008); Tim Milnes and Kerry Sinanan, eds., *Romanticism, Sincerity and Authenticity* (London: Palgrave, 2010); Pam Morris, *Imagining Inclusive Society in Nineteenth-Century Novels: The Code of Sincerity in the Public Sphere* (Baltimore: Johns Hopkins University Press, 2004); Susan Rosenbaum, *Professing Sincerity: Modern Lyric Poetry, Commercial Culture, and the Crisis in Reading* (Charlottesville: University of Virginia Press, 2007); Ernst van Alphen, Mieke Bal, and Carel Smith, eds., *The Rhetoric of Sincerity* (Stanford: Stanford University Press, 2009). This publishing trend would even reach the trade presses with R. Jay Magill, Jr., *Sincerity* (New York: Norton, 2012).

60. Angela Esterhammer, "The Scandal of Sincerity: Wordsworth, Byron, Landon," in Milnes and Sinanan, *Romanticism*, 104–105.

61. Wallace, in David Lipsky, *Although of Course You End Up Becoming Yourself: A Road Trip with David Foster Wallace* (New York: Broadway Books, 2010), 35.

62. David Foster Wallace, "Fictional Futures and the Conspicuously Young," in *Both Flesh and Not* (New York: Little, Brown, 2012), 63. Originally published in 1988 in *Review of Contemporary Fiction*.

63. Ibid.

64. David Foster Wallace, "Greatly Exaggerated," in *A Supposedly Fun Thing I'll Never Do Again* (New York: Little, Brown, 1997), 140, 144. Originally published in 1991 in *Harvard Book Review*.

65. David Foster Wallace, "E Unibus Pluram: Television and U.S. Fiction," in ibid., 81. Originally published in 1993 in *Review of Contemporary Fiction*.

66. Jason Gladstone and Daniel Worden, "Introduction: Postmodernism, Then," *Twentieth Century Literature* 57.3–4 (2011): 291. Repeated in "Introduction," *Postmodern/Postwar—and After: Rethinking American Literature*, ed. Jason Gladstone, Andrew Hoberek, and Daniel Worden (Iowa City: University of Iowa Press, 2016), 1.

67. Ibid.

68. A. O. Scott, "The Panic of Influence," *New York Review of Books* 47 (10 February 2000), https://www.nybooks.com/articles/2000/02/10/the-panic-of-influence/. Other notable treatments of irony in Wallace's fiction include: Marshall Boswell, *Understanding David Foster Wallace* (Columbia: University of South Carolina Press, 2003); Allard den Dulk, "Beyond Endless 'Aesthetic' Irony: A Comparison of the Irony Critique of Søren Kierkegaard and David Foster Wallace's *Infinite Jest*," *Studies in the Novel* 44.3 (2012): 325–345; Mary K. Holland, "'The Art's Heart's Purpose': Braving the Narcissistic Loop of David Foster Wallace's *Infinite Jest*," *Critique* 47.3 (2006): 218–242; Nicoline Timmer, *Do You Feel It Too? The Post-Postmodern Syndrome in American Fiction at the Turn of the Millennium* (Amsterdam: Rodopi, 2010), 146–149.

69. Lee Konstantinou, *Cool Characters: Irony and American Fiction* (Cambridge, MA: Harvard University Press, 2016), 175.

70. Ibid.

71. Ibid., 38.

72. See Dan Sinykin, *Big Fiction: How Conglomeration Changed the Publishing Industry and American Literature* (New York: Columbia University Press, 2023).

73. Susan Sontag, "Notes on Camp," in *Against Interpretation and Other Essays* (New York: Delta, 1966), 276.

74. Raymond Williams, *Marxism and Literature* (Oxford: Oxford University Press, 1977), 132.

75. Anthony Robinson, "A Few Notes from a New Sincerist," *Geneva Convention Archives* (22 July 2005), http://luckyerror.blogspot.com/2005/07/few-notes-from-new-sincerist.html; Jesse Thorn, "A Manifesto for the New Sincerity," *Maximum Fun* (26 March 2006), https://maximumfun.org/news/manifesto-for-new-sincerity/. This latter "manifesto," in which the "awesome" Evel Knievel becomes the movement's avatar, presents cultural New Sincerity as something akin to Sontag's "camp," with its "love of the unnatural: of artifice and exaggeration," and its tendency to "convert the serious into the frivolous." Sontag, *Against*, 275, 276.

76. Ellen Rutten, *Sincerity After Communism: A Cultural History* (New Haven: Yale University Press, 2017), 72.

77. Adam Kelly, "David Foster Wallace and the New Sincerity in American Fiction," in *Consider David Foster Wallace: Critical Essays*, ed. David Hering (Austin: Sideshow Media, 2010), 131.

78. Ibid.

79. Ibid., 146.

80. As this list of possibilities suggests, sincerity can have many opposing terms, including but not limited to irony, authenticity, manipulation, apathy, hypocrisy, and

insincerity. As Bernard Williams notes of Sincerity, "it has to be related, psychologically, socially, and ethically, to some wider range of values. What those values are, however, varies from time to time and culture to culture, and the various versions cannot be discovered by general reflection." Williams, *Truth*, 93.

81. Liesbeth Korthals Altes, "Sincerity, Reliability and Other Ironies—Notes on Dave Eggers' *A Heartbreaking Work of Staggering Genius*," in *Narrative Unreliability in the Twenty-First-Century First-Person Novel*, ed. Elke d'Hoker and Gunther Martens (Berlin: DeGruyter, 2008), 107–128; A. D. Jameson, "What We Talk About When We Talk About the New Sincerity, Part 1," *HtmlGiant* (4 June 2012), https://htmlgiant.com/haut-or-not/what-we-talk-about-when-we-talk-about-the-new-sincerity/; Jonathan D. Fitzgerald, *Not Your Mother's Morals: How the New Sincerity Is Changing Pop Culture for the Better* (Colorado: Bondfire Books, 2012); Ruth Barton Palmer, "The New Sincerity of Neo-Noir," in *International Noir*, ed. Homer B. Pettey and Ruth Barton Palmer (Edinburgh: Edinburgh University Press, 2014), 193–219; Allard den Dulk, *Existentialist Engagement in Wallace, Eggers and Foer: A Philosophical Analysis of Contemporary American Literature* (London: Bloomsbury, 2015), 162–195.

82. Ernst van Alphen and Mieke Bal, "Introduction," in *The Rhetoric of Sincerity*, 16.

83. Rutten, *Sincerity*, 163.

84. We can equally say that (as will be seen most clearly in my reading of Kunkel's *Indecision* in Chapter Six), literary New Sincerity invites a hermeneutics of suspicion in part by applying that hermeneutics to itself. Although I recognize that it would take much space to demonstrate the claim, I would argue that this approach enables literary New Sincerity to transcend the opposition between critique and postcritique that has underpinned so much contemporary debate in literary studies. See, e.g., Elizabeth S. Anker and Rita Felski, eds., *Critique and Postcritique* (Durham: Duke University Press, 2017), and Bruce Robbins, *Criticism and Politics: A Polemical Introduction* (Stanford: Stanford University Press, 2022).

85. Gaddis, *Recognitions*, 497.

86. Ibid., 498.

87. Ibid.

88. C. Wright Mills, *The Power Elite* (New York: Oxford University Press, 2000 [1956]), 348, emphasis added.

89. Ibid.

90. Gaddis, *Recognitions*, 498.

91. Riesman, *Lonely*, 129.

92. Ibid., xxxii, 157; Trilling, *Sincerity*, 66.

93. Goffman, *Presentation*, 10.

94. Riesman, *Lonely*, 194, 196.

95. The literature on neoliberalism is vast. I cite a small number of significant works in what follows, but for a broader discussion relevant to the argument here, see

Alexander Beaumont and Adam Kelly, "Freedom After Neoliberalism," *Open Library of Humanities* 4.2 (2018), https://olh.openlibhums.org/article/id/4519/

96. F. A. Hayek, *The Road to Serfdom: Text and Documents: The Definitive Edition*, ed. Bruce Caldwell (Chicago: University of Chicago Press, 2007), 218.

97. Ibid., 216–217.

98. Corey Robin, *The Reactionary Mind: Conservatism from Edmund Burke to Donald Trump*, 2nd ed. (Oxford: Oxford University Press, 2018), 151.

99. Perhaps the most powerful analysis of the New Right's ethics and politics of constraint is found in Melinda Cooper, *Family Values: Between Neoliberalism and the New Social Conservatism* (New York: Zone Books, 2017).

100. Michel Feher, "Self-Appreciation; or, the Aspirations of Human Capital," trans. Ivan Ascher, *Public Culture* 21.1 (2009): 32. Further references in parentheses.

101. Theodore W. Schultz, "Investment in Human Capital," *American Economic Review* 51.1 (1961): 1–17; Gary S. Becker, *Human Capital: A Theoretical and Empirical Analysis, with Special Reference to Education* (New York: National Bureau of Economic Research, 1964).

102. The idea of "de-proletarianization" was first introduced in Wilhelm Röpke, *The Social Crisis of Our Time* (Chicago: University of Chicago Press, 1950), a founding text of German Ordoliberalism. In its original context it entailed the deliberate dilution of working-class consciousness through the state's cultivation of market-friendly norms of thinking and behavior.

103. Among the most influential critiques of neoliberalism as the extension of economic logic into previously non-economic spheres of existence is Wendy Brown, *Undoing the Demos: Neoliberalism's Stealth Revolution* (New York: Zone Books, 2015).

104. Lest the shift from the free laborer to the human capital paradigm be viewed as no more than an idealist projection—as some Marxist critics have claimed—a compelling account of the pervasive material role of human capital in the lives of the millennial generation (the children of the post-boomers) can be found in Malcolm Harris, *Kids These Days: Human Capital and the Making of Millennials* (New York: Little, Brown, 2017).

105. Feher most closely associates these three critiques with, respectively, Deleuze and Guattari, Foucault, and the Italian autonomists.

106. On the question of whether Foucault was or was not a neoliberal sympathizer, see Daniel Zamora and Michael Behrent, eds., *Foucault and Neoliberalism* (Cambridge: Polity, 2016).

107. It is worth mentioning one other influential account of the rise of neoliberalism that complements Feher's. In *The New Spirit of Capitalism* (1999), Boltanski and Chiapello argue that the 1960s saw the coalescing of two traditions in the critique of capitalism, which they dub the artistic critique and the social critique. The neoliberal transformation of capitalism successfully internalized the artistic critique—which emphasizes "disenchantment and inauthenticity" and "shares its individualism with modernity"—while sidelining the social critique, with its focus on exploitation,

inequality, and collective life. Luc Boltanski and Ève Chiapello, *The New Spirit of Capitalism*, trans. Gregory Elliott (London: Verso, 2018), 38–39. This successful co-optation of the artistic critique provides one explanation for why neoliberalism rather than radicalism won the battle to define the conditions of self-appreciation, in Feher's terms. I will return to the role played by the artist figure in neoliberal ideology in the next section.

108. Feher would eventually articulate his project at book length in *Rated Agency: Investee Politics in a Speculative Age*, trans. Gregory Elliott (New York: Zone Books, 2018). Whatever its merits as political strategy, his argument stands out theoretically in contrast to the recent prevalence of more traditional materialist attempts to re-mobilize the category of economic self-interest for the Left. See, for instance: Vivek Chibber, *The Class Matrix: Social Theory After the Cultural Turn* (Cambridge, MA: Harvard University Press, 2022); Annie McClanahan, "Serious Crises: Rethinking the Neoliberal Subject," *boundary 2* 46.1 (2019): 103–122.

109. Ryan M. Brooks, *Liberalism and American Literature in the Clinton Era* (Cambridge: Cambridge University Press, 2022), 3.

110. Ibid., 4.

111. Lewis Hyde, *The Gift: Imagination and the Erotic Life of Property* (New York: Vintage, 1983), 47. The twenty-fifth anniversary edition in 2007 was retitled *The Gift: Creativity and the Artist in the Modern World*, and David Foster Wallace, Zadie Smith, Jonathan Lethem, and Geoff Dyer were among the writers who wrote blurbs for it. See https://lewishyde.com/the-gift/

112. Ibid., 50.

113. Lee Konstantinou, "Lewis Hyde's Double Economy" *ASAP/Journal* 1.1 (2016): 126–127.

114. Ibid., 134.

115. Sarah Brouillette, *Literature and the Creative Economy* (Stanford: Stanford University Press, 2014), 54.

116. Konstantinou, "Lewis," 128.

117. This is in fact Konstantinou's view: he calls *The Gift* "a palliative for the contemporary author or creative worker," and reads Zadie Smith's *The Autograph Man* (2002) as a logical development of Hyde's account, in that "the artist in Smith's novel becomes not only a model for the liberated creative class worker but is herself changed in return." Ibid., 128, 129. By contrast, I read New Sincerity fiction against the grain of Hyde's account, as a more ambivalent response to the wholly positive picture he paints of the gift.

118. Zadie Smith, *Changing My Mind: Occasional Essays* (London: Hamish Hamilton, 2009), 258.

119. For an overview of how the aesthetic and commercial realms have intersected for artists at prior moments in modern literary history, see Günter Leypoldt, "Professional Countercultures: Network Effects in the Long Nineteenth Century (Weimer, Paris, Grasmere, Boston)," *Symbiosis* 25.1 (2021): 21–49.

120. Martin Hägglund, *Radical Atheism: Derrida and the Time of Life* (Stanford: Stanford University Press, 2008), 37.

121. Ibid.

122. Alongside the neoliberal promotion of the figure of the autonomous artist as ideal worker, there is a broader argument here—taken up more fully in Chapter Two—about the function of the figures of purity and autonomy for neoliberal ideology. On the one hand, the neoliberal subject as human capital is imagined (originally by Becker and Schultz, later in all kinds of self-help discourse) as autonomous in the sense of owning their personal feelings and having responsibility for their personal wellness, and acting in an entrepreneurial fashion so that all the gains of their actions return purely to themselves. On the other hand, the market is imagined (in Hayek's vision) as a spontaneous social aggregator that allows for the pure articulation of "revealed preferences" and the frictionless movement of capital to feed those preferences, with financialization instituting a temporal logic in which the future is imagined as a pure product of the present. Underlying both of these dimensions is a faith in economics as a pure and disinterested science. In Bourdieu's summary, neoliberal ideology imagines that "the economic world is a pure and perfect order, implacably unrolling the logic of its predictable consequences." Pierre Bourdieu, "The Essence of Neoliberalism," trans. Jeremy J. Shapiro, *Le Monde diplomatique* (1998), http://mondediplo.com/1998/12/08bourdieu

123. In this sense, literary New Sincerity works very much in contradiction to the ideological function of sincerity that Ana Schwartz diagnoses in colonial America, where "sincerity is often invoked to circumvent or transcend the discovery of historical entanglement." Schwartz, *Unmoored: The Search for Sincerity in Colonial America* (Chapel Hill: University of North Carolina Press, 2023), 2.

124. I am thinking here of Bourdieu's classic work on the sociology of "cultural capital," for instance in *Distinction: A Social Critique of the Judgement of Taste*, trans. Richard Nice (Cambridge, MA: Harvard University Press, 1984). For an account of how post-boomer writers and thinkers might confront the demobilizing effects of Bourdieusian analysis, see The Editors, "Too Much Sociology," *n+1* 16 (2013): 1–6. I take up *n+1*'s significance as an intellectual response to normative neoliberalism in this book's Conclusion.

125. Linda Hutcheon, *A Poetics of Postmodernism: History, Theory, Fiction* (London: Routledge, 1988), 224.

126. On shifts in US publishing from the midcentury to the present, and their meaning for questions of aesthetic autonomy in contemporary writing, see Crosthwaite, *Market*, 17–29, and Sinykin, *Big Fiction*.

127. Brian McHale, *Postmodernist Fiction* (London: Methuen, 1987).

128. For a more thorough treatment of complicity with relevance to the argument outlined here, see Adam Kelly and Will Norman, "Literature and Complicity: Then and Now," *Comparative Literature Studies* 56.4 (2019): 673–692.

129. David Foster Wallace, *Brief Interviews with Hideous Men: Stories* (Boston: Little, Brown, 1999), 160.

Chapter One

1. Francis Fukuyama, "The End of History?" *National Interest* 16 (Summer 1989): 3. Further references in parentheses.

2. Wallace may have taken the title of *Westward* from the concluding stanza of a 1728 poem by Bishop Berkeley; from an 1861 painting by Emanuel Gottlieb Leutze that hangs in the Capitol Building in Washington, DC; from an advertisement for a farm implement; or, possibly, from all three. See D. T. Max, *Every Love Story Is a Ghost Story: A Life of David Foster Wallace* (New York: Viking, 2012), 91, 314n1. For a consideration of the title in relation to the story, see Philip Coleman, "Consider Berkeley & Co.: Reading 'Westward the Course of Empire Takes Its Way," *Consider David Foster Wallace: Critical Essays*, ed. David Hering (Los Angeles: SSMG Press, 2010), 62–74.

3. David Foster Wallace, *Girl with Curious Hair* (London: Abacus, 1997), 235. Further references in parentheses.

4. The third traveler, the failed actor Tom Sternberg, is identified—in an early allusion to Hegel—with "the Historical Idealists of yore" (254). For him the travelers' destination is "an *idea*, an ever-distant telos his arrival at which will represent the revealed transformation of a present we stomach by looking beyond" (259).

5. Jeffrey Severs—in *David Foster Wallace's Balancing Books: Fictions of Value* (New York: Columbia University Press, 2017), 78—notes the fascist overtones of Steelritter's vision: "The Reunion is a contemporary *Triumph of the Will*." The passage thus offers an early example of Wallace's linking of the triumph of neoliberal capitalism with an incipient fascism, a connection that will become explicit in *Infinite Jest*.

6. In *The Program Era: Postwar Fiction and the Rise of Creative Writing* (Cambridge, MA: Harvard University Press, 2009), Mark McGurl outlines the role of the creative writing program in promoting and instituting modernist values in American fiction. As Kasia Boddy points out, *Westward* shows Wallace to be highly skeptical of claims to autonomy for literary works produced under the aegis of the program: "The story contends that the creative writing class is not a refuge from, but rather an example of, corporate capitalism." Boddy, "A Fiction of Response: *Girl with Curious Hair* in Context," in *A Companion to David Foster Wallace Studies*, ed. Marshall Boswell and Stephen J. Burn (New York: Palgrave, 2013), 29.

7. As Severs notes, the odd name of Wallace's protagonist and author of this story-within-the-story, Mark Nechtr, evokes the German word *knecht*. Severs also highlights earlier references to Hegel in Wallace's *oeuvre*, most notably the misreading by a character in *The Broom of the System* of Hegel's *Phenomenology of Spirit*. Severs, *Balancing*, 86, 54–55.

8. This inversion might also be read as a sped-up dialectic, since Hegel will go on to explain how the positions of lord and bondsman become inverted through the bondsman's discovery of independence through work, while the lord remains dependent on recognition from the bondsman. In one pithy summary, the master–slave dialectic "consists essentially in showing that the truth of the master reveals that he is the slave, and that the slave is revealed to be the master of the master." Jean Hyppolite, *Genesis*

and *Structure of Hegel's* Phenomenology of Spirit, trans. Samuel Cherniak and John Heckman (Evanston: Northwestern University Press, 1974), 172.

9. See Andrew Cole, *The Birth of Theory* (Chicago: University of Chicago Press, 2014), 65–85.

10. The significance of Hegel's dialectic for Fukuyama's vision is worth emphasizing. In *The End of History and the Last Man* (1992), Fukuyama cites the master–slave dialectic as the driving force of history, and thus a force that has been overcome at history's end.

11. "Bodily movements bear meaning as deeds (they have an 'inner' meaning) in the same way that sensible objects like paintings can be said to bear meaning as artworks. In both cases the intention is only 'realized' as the intention it determinately is in the deed or in the work, as that deed or work counts as this or that to a community at a time; before that realization, it is only provisionally and putatively the determinate intention or meaning." Robert B. Pippin, *After the Beautiful: Hegel and the Philosophy of Pictorial Modernism* (Chicago: University of Chicago Press, 2014), 20.

12. Ibid., 21.

13. Ibid., 41.

14. "Hegel was lecturing on art just before the treatment of art began shifting from 'aesthetics' to the 'philosophy of art' (i.e. from the sensible appreciation of beauty to art's interrogation of its own nature and possibility)." In this new era, "the romantic categories, even the whole notion of the beautiful, all seem simply beside the point." Ibid., 8, 48.

15. As Severs observes in *Balancing*, 84: "Honor, kin of honesty, has clear connections to the issue of sincerity."

16. Pippin, *After*, 13. Pippin later provides a clearer definition of the problem of the Absolute: "the account of a possible subject-object identity, how subjects can also be objects." Ibid., 46.

17. David Hering, *David Foster Wallace: Fiction and Form* (New York: Bloomsbury, 2016), 23.

18. Severs, *Balancing*, 83.

19. Hering, *Fiction*, 24.

20. David Foster Wallace, *Infinite Jest* (London: Abacus, 1997), 1022n14. Further references in parentheses.

21. N. Katherine Hayles, "The Illusion of Autonomy and the Fact of Recursivity: Virtual Ecologies, Entertainment, and *Infinite Jest*," *New Literary History* 30.3 (1999): 684. The novel represents its obsession with cycles and loops visually through the "centered, shadowed circles" that separate each of the twenty-eight chapters of *Infinite Jest* from one another. Greg Carlisle, *Elegant Complexity: A Study of David Foster Wallace's* Infinite Jest (Austin: Sideshow Media, 2007), 17. The number twenty-eight can itself approximate a lunar cycle, evoked by the "seven moons orbiting a dead planet."

22. Beyond those contexts enumerated above, the annular pattern is explicitly associated with the ever-present threat of infinite logical regress, as for instance in Joelle

van Dyne's explanation to Don Gately concerning the philosophy of her Union of the Hideously and Improbably Deformed: "U.H.I.D.'d say it's fine to feel inadequate and ashamed because you're not as bright as some others, but that the cycle becomes annular and insidious if you begin to be *ashamed* of the fact that being unbright shames you" (535–536). Annulation arises in more mundane contexts too, for example in a tennis coach's remark that "Michael Pemulis's abilities cancel each other out" (679). Wallace appends an endnote here to observe that the coach "us[es] *s'annuler* instead of the more Québecois *se détruire*" (1052n275).

23. Isaiah Berlin, "Two Concepts of Liberty," *Four Essays on Liberty* (Oxford: Oxford University Press, 1969), 118–172.

24. David Foster Wallace, "'Plain old untrendy troubles and emotions,'" *Guardian* (20 September 2008), https://www.theguardian.com/books/2008/sep/20/fiction

25. The interpretation of Hegel (and Kant) implied in this last quotation aligns with what Alan Patten terms "the conventionalist reading," whereby Hegel is taken to be a spokesperson for the priority of "ethical norms embedded in existing social institutions" over all forms of challenge to those norms. Patten, *Hegel's Idea of Freedom* (Oxford: Oxford University Press, 1999), 8. Another commentator notes a significant strand of scholarship "which sees in Hegel little more than an apologist for the conservative (Prussian) status quo and an advocate of the subordination of the individual to the state." Stephen Houlgate, *An Introduction to Hegel: Freedom, Truth and History* (Oxford: Blackwell, 2005), 181. My argument is that the regressive version of Hegel associated with Schtitt in this passage can be contrasted with the Hegel of "transcendence is absorption," discussed below. In *Infinite Jest*'s annular end of history, the "bad" Hegel thus does battle with the "good" Hegel on the question of whether historical progress will once again become possible.

26. Although this view was unusual in the 1990s, it was not unprecedented. Wallace's analysis was in line, for instance, with maverick military strategist Edward Luttwak; see Luttwak, "Why Fascism Is the Wave of the Future," *London Review of Books* 16.7 (April 1994).

27. "David Foster Wallace: Infinite Jest," *KCRW Bookworm* (11 April 1996), https://www.kcrw.com/news-culture/shows/bookworm/david-foster-wallace-infinite-jest

28. Wallace claimed in an interview that the "Western-industrial" tendency to regard pain as a problem in itself, rather than as a symptom of some deeper problem, could be blamed on the predominance of utilitarianism, "a whole teleology predicated on the idea that the best human life is one that maximizes the pleasure to pain ratio." *Conversations with David Foster Wallace*, ed. Stephen J. Burn (Jackson: University Press of Mississippi, 2012), 23. *Infinite Jest*'s critique of utilitarianism is explored in Marshall Boswell, *Understanding David Foster Wallace* (Columbia: University of South Carolina Press, 2003), 134–136; and Severs, *Balancing*, 103–105.

29. For a reading of "The Entertainment" in terms of emergence theory, see Bradley J. Fest, "The Inverted Nuke in the Garden: Archival Emergence and Anti-Eschatology in David Foster Wallace's *Infinite Jest*," *boundary 2* 39.3 (2012): 125–149.

30. I import the phrase "Higher Power" from the AA strand of *Infinite Jest*—it does not appear in Marathe's rhetoric—in order to underscore the structural similarities the novel draws out among different social spheres of behavior. This literary method—which can be understood as Hegelian in its emphasis on unitary and collective self-understanding (what Hegel calls *Geist*) rather than on the divisions of social class that would underpin a Marxist approach—is perhaps best summed up in the title of a course taught at Enfield Tennis Academy: "The Personal is the Political is the Psychopathological" (307). A Marxist perspective on neoliberal economy will be introduced in Chapter Two as a supplement and partial corrective to Wallace's Hegelianism.

31. This section, and the three that follow, draw on my previously published chapter. Adam Kelly, "Absorbing Art: The Hegelian Project of Infinite Jest," in *Reading David Foster Wallace Between Philosophy and Literature*, ed. Adriano Ardovino, Allard den Dulk, and Pia Masiero (Manchester: Manchester University Press, 2022), 19–47.

32. It is worth noting that my preference for a Hegelian rather than Wittgensteinian reading of Wallace's aesthetics does not deny the well-established influence of Wittgenstein's philosophy on Wallace's fiction. But while I accept Robert Chodat's observation that Wallace's turn away from "the visionless medium of logic and mathematics" led him to the later Wittgenstein, in my view Hegelian thought offers a more fruitful approach to the specific role that aesthetic concerns play in Wallace's fiction. Moreover, the "deep necessity" that Chodat claims Wallace initially sought in analytic logic and math finds an alternative expression in Hegel's science of logic and philosophy of history, as evidenced by the emergence of "The Entertainment" as the logical outcome of the American end of history. Finally, I am arguing that as much as Wittgenstein, Hegel stands as a key communitarian precursor for what Chodat (following John Haugeland) calls Wallace's "socialist phenomenology," his representation of humans as always already existing in a norm-based relation to one another. Robert Chodat, *The Matter of High Words: Naturalism, Normativity, and the Postwar Sage* (Oxford: Oxford University Press, 2017), 246, 244, 259.

33. For a consideration of evidence for all these explanations (he prefers the first one), see Carlisle, *Elegant*, 480–482.

34. When Hal's marijuana habit is first revealed, we learn that his mother and uncle "know nothing about Hal's penchants for high-resin Bob Hope and underground absorption" (51). Later, during the Eschaton scene, Hal's drug use leads to him failing to intervene in the escalating chaos of the game: "Hal, now leaning forward, steeple-fingered, finds himself just about paralyzed with absorption . . . almost incapacitated with absorption" (340). Absorption in drug use is also associated with other characters, most notably Joelle van Dyne, who when we first meet her is embarking on a suicidal binge with crack cocaine: "Her unveiled face in the dirty lit mirror is shocking in the intensity of its absorption" (238). Entertainment (not only "The Entertainment") also plays an absorptive role in the novel, for instance when Hugh Steeply's father dies from overexposure to the TV show *M*A*S*H*. And absorption likewise

characterizes the worst forms of depression, as in the *It* that haunts Kate Gompert, whose "depressed self *It* billows on and coagulates around and wraps in *Its* black folds and absorbs into *Itself*" (695).

35. Severs and Chodat have addressed the role of absorption in Wallace's work, the former focusing on absorption in labor and the latter on absorption in listening and tennis. While I have found their comments illuminating, the thematic approach taken by both critics does not attend to the distinction between *pure/total absorption* and *refractive absorption* that I will argue is crucial to Wallace's aesthetics.

36. Fredric Jameson, *Marxism and Form* (Princeton: Princeton University Press, 1971), 44.

37. Pippin, *After*, 34.

38. Allard den Dulk, *Existentialist Engagement in Wallace, Eggers and Foer: A Philosophical Analysis of Contemporary American Literature* (New York: Bloomsbury, 2015), 194.

39. Pippin, *After*, 29.

40. Burn, *Conversations*, 59.

41. Adam Bristow-Smith, *Growing Up Neoliberal: The Bildungsroman under Neoliberalism* (PhD dissertation: University of York, 2018), 115.

42. Georg Lukács, *The Theory of the Novel* (Cambridge, MA: MIT Press, 1974), 29.

43. Pippin, *After*, 49.

44. Wallace, *Girl*, 259.

45. Hegel writes, for instance, that the aim of Eastern Pantheism is "entire liberation from the finite, the bliss of absorption [*die Seligkeit des Aufgehens*] into everything that is best and most splendid." This aim informs the regime of "symbolic" art, for which the practice of "absorption in something other and external [*diese Versenkung in Anderes und Äußeres*] is the liberation of the inner life from a purely practical interest or from the immediacy of feeling into free theoretical shapes." Of the "classical" art that succeeded symbolic art—and that achieved a perfect sensuous expression of the inner freedom of spirit—Hegel writes that "this absorption in the realm of inwardness [*diese Vertiefung in das Reich der Innerlichkeit*] need not go so far as either to a subjective independence gained by a negative attitude to everything substantial in spirit and stable in nature, or to that absolute reconciliation which constitutes the freedom of truly infinite subjectivity." With the emergence of Christianity, this "realm of inwardness" *does* begin to produce a "negative attitude" to elements of the outer world, and what Hegel calls "romantic" art finds a means to overcome and stabilize this, e.g., "The final achievement of German and Flemish art is its utterly living absorption [*das gänzliche Sicheinleben*] in the world and its daily life." G. W. F. Hegel, *Aesthetics: Lectures on Fine Art*, 2 vols., trans. T. M. Knox (Oxford: Clarendon Press, 1975), 371, 418, 443, 884.

46. E. H. Gombrich, "'The Father of Art History': A Reading of the Lectures on Aesthetics of G. W. F. Hegel (1770–1831)," in E. H. Gombrich, *Tributes: Interpreters of Our Cultural Tradition* (Ithaca: Cornell University Press, 1984), 51–69.

47. Hegel, *Aesthetics*, 30–31.

48. For example, Hegel writes admiringly of the freedom from sin and guilt in Correggio's 1528 statue of Mary Magdalene: "she is unconscious of those times, absorbed only in her present situation [*nur vertieft in ihren jetzigen Zustand*], and this faith, this sensitiveness, this absorption [*Versinken*] seems to be her entire and real character." He writes with similar approbation of the artist who "is united directly with the subject-matter, believes in it, and is identical with it in accordance with his very own self. The result is then that the artist is entirely absorbed in the object [*Dann liegt die Subjektivität gänzlich in dem Objekt*]." Ibid., 868, 604.

49. Michael Fried, *Absorption and Theatricality: Painting and Beholder in the Age of Diderot* (Chicago: University of Chicago Press, 1980), 4.

50. Ibid., 93.

51. Michael Fried. *The Moment of Caravaggio* (Princeton: Princeton University Press, 2010), 2.

52. Robert B. Pippin, "Authenticity in Painting: Remarks on Michael Fried's Art History," *Critical Inquiry* 31 (2005): 578. Although Fried and Pippin mostly ignore it, the rise of capitalism and its paradigm of market exchange is crucial for understanding both the potential inauthenticity of modern activity (done not for itself but for a wage) and modern art (done not for aesthetic but for commercial reasons). On the influence on Diderot of concerns about capitalism, and a critique of Fried's elision of these concerns, see Anthony E. Grudin, "Beholder, Beheld, Beholden: Theatricality and Capitalism in Fried," *Oxford Art Journal* 39.1 (2016): 35–47.

53. Hegel, *Aesthetics*, 619.

54. Fried, *Absorption*, 108.

55. Michael Fried, *Manet's Modernism; or, the Face of Painting in the 1860s* (Chicago: University of Chicago Press, 1996), 405. Apropos this opposition between interrogation and appeal, see Zadie Smith's claim that Wallace's stories "simply don't investigate character; they don't intend to. Instead they're turned outwards, towards us. It's our character that's being investigated." Smith, *Changing My Mind: Occasional Essays* (London: Hamish Hamilton, 2009), 276.

56. Michael Fried, *Art and Objecthood* (Chicago: University of Chicago Press, 1998), 149.

57. Ibid., 153.

58. David Foster Wallace, *A Supposedly Fun Thing I'll Never Do Again* (London: Abacus, 1997), 81.

59. A. O. Scott, "The Panic of Influence," *New York Review of Books* 47 (10 February 2000), https://www.nybooks.com/articles/2000/02/10/the-panic-of-influence/

60. Timothy Aubry, *Reading as Therapy: What Contemporary Fiction Does for Middle-Class Americans* (Iowa City: University of Iowa Press, 2011), 99.

61. Jon Baskin, "Death Is Not the End: David Foster Wallace: His Legacy and His Critics," *The Point* 1 (2009), https://thepointmag.com/criticism/death-is-not-the-end/

62. See here Baskin's recent statement, made in dialogue with my work, that "I take the persistence of irony in Wallace's fiction more straightforwardly [than Kelly],

as a failure—even if a strategically motivated one—to live up to his own ideals." Jon Baskin, "After Analysis: Notes on the New Sincerity from Wallace to Knausgaard," in *David Foster Wallace in Context*, ed. Clare Hayes-Brady (Cambridge: Cambridge University Press, 2022), 124. Baskin's contention that "problems of communication are in the first place problems of the will, as opposed to of the intellect" (ibid., 122) seems to me overly simplistic when it comes to the question of communication through the medium of art.

63. On the theme of failure in Wallace's work, see Clare Hayes-Brady, *The Unspeakable Failures of David Foster Wallace* (London: Bloomsbury, 2016). *Infinite Jest* itself was originally subtitled "A Failed Entertainment."

64. Boswell, *Understanding*, 162.

65. Ibid. While Boswell reads many of the film titles as parodic takes on works of postmodern literature, Hering locates models for these parodies in real art films. Hering, *Fiction*, 104.

66. Mary Shapiro, "The Textually Aware Text: Recursive Self-Consciousness in *Infinite Jest*'s Filmography," *Orbis Litterarum* 75.1 (2020): 26, 27.

67. Hering, *Fiction*, 105. On ekphrasis in the novel, see also Philip Sayers, "Representing Entertainment in *Infinite Jest*," *Studies in the Novel* 44.3 (2012): 346–363.

68. Hegel, *Aesthetics*, 619.

69. Pippin, *After*, 86.

70. Ibid., 87.

71. For an analysis of *The Joke* ("the most hated Incandenza film" [397]) as undecidably avant-garde artwork and hoax, see Matt Prout, "Art or Shit: Value, Sincerity, and the Avant-garde in David Foster Wallace," *Journal of Modern Literature* 45.3 (2022): 77–79.

72. Lee Konstantinou, *Cool Characters: Irony and American Fiction* (Cambridge, MA: Harvard University Press, 2016), 187, 188.

73. Clement Greenberg, "Avant-Garde and Kitsch," in *Pollock and After: The Critical Debate*, 2nd ed., ed. Francis Frascina (London: Routledge, 2000), 49.

74. Ibid., 50.

75. Ibid., 51. This theoretical stance would be reinforced by the work of the Frankfurt School, most notably Theodor W. Adorno in texts like *Philosophy of New Music* (1949) and *Aesthetic Theory* (1970).

76. Clement Greenberg, "Towards a New Laocoon," in *Pollock and After*, 62.

77. Hegel, *Aesthetics*, 38.

78. Pierre Bourdieu, *The Field of Cultural Production: Essays on Art and Literature* (Cambridge: Polity Press, 1993), 115; Stanley Cavell, *Must We Mean What We Say?* (New York: Scribner's, 1969), 185.

79. Wallace's stated views on medium specificity were complicated (Sayers collates some interview quotes on the subject), but his disdain for the "beret-wearing *artistes*" and trend-following "crank-turners" of his time was consistent. Sayers, "Representing," 110–112; Burn, *Conversations*, 28, 30.

80. Simon Schama, *The Power of Art* (London: Bodley Head, 2009), 125.
81. Quoted in ibid., 114.
82. Ibid., 81–82.
83. Indeed, Fried cites Bernini as the epitome of the Baroque theatricality with which Caravaggio's absorptive painting attempted to struggle. Fried, *Moment*, 122.
84. Genevieve Warwick, *Bernini: Art as Theatre* (New Haven: Yale University Press, 2013).
85. Schama, *Power*, 92.
86. Michael Fried, *Why Photography Matters as Art as Never Before* (New Haven: Yale University Press, 2008), 13. The idea that film automatically avoids (rather than attempts to overcome) theatricality is a complicated one, appearing first in "Art and Objecthood" and then developed by Stanley Cavell in *The World Viewed: Reflections of the Ontology of Film* (Cambridge, MA: Harvard University Press, 1973), a work that likely influenced Wallace. On Fried's lack of engagement with film studies, and vice versa, see Daniel Morgan, "Missed Connections," *nonsite.org* (1 November 2017), https://nonsite.org/feature/missed-connections
87. Incandenza's later films are described by Joelle as "narratively anticonfluential but unironic melodrama" (740). The lack of narrative confluence would seem here to clash with the lack of irony, in a way that turns the "emotional thrust" into a cognitive experience that can only be accessed on rewatching.
88. This directly challenges the premises of the canonical treatment of film in the absorption-theatricality tradition; see Cavell's *The World Viewed*, 24: "A screen is a barrier. What does the silver screen screen? It screens me from the world it holds—that is, it makes me invisible."
89. Both quoted in Pippin, "Authenticity," 581, 576.
90. Ibid., 592.
91. Hering, *Fiction*, 86–87.
92. Ibid., 87.
93. Ibid., 94.
94. Here the fact that Wallace needs to imagine his model reader as an "other" is accentuated by Joelle's gender difference from her author. This significant issue—which opens onto the enormous can of worms that is Wallace's presentation of gender norms, femininity, and female sexuality in his fiction—is beyond the scope of the present chapter to consider. I instead take up the proposition that "the subject of the New Sincerity novel is first and foremost a woman" in Chapter Three. For an attempt to grapple with the topic of Wallace and gender, see my chapter "Brief Interviews with Hideous Men" in *The Cambridge Companion to David Foster Wallace*, ed. Ralph Clare (Cambridge: Cambridge University Press, 2018), 82–96.
95. Tom LeClair, "The Prodigious Fiction of Richard Powers, William Vollmann, and David Foster Wallace," *Critique* 38.1 (1996): 34.
96. Boswell, *Understanding*, 143.
97. Aubry, *Reading*, 109.

98. Mary K. Holland, "'The Art's Heart's Purpose': Braving the Narcissistic Loop of David Foster Wallace's *Infinite Jest*," *Critique* 47.3 (2006): 233.

99. Jon Baskin, *Ordinary Unhappiness: The Therapeutic Fiction of David Foster Wallace* (Stanford: Stanford University Press, 2019), 66.

100. Ibid., 72.

101. Severs, *Balancing*, 121.

102. On the "Uncle Charles Principle," see Hugh Kenner, *Joyce's Voices* (Berkeley: University of California Press, 1978), 15–38.

103. Ibid., 16.

104. Andrew Warren, "Modeling Community and Narrative in *Infinite Jest* and *The Pale King*," *Studies in the Novel* 44.4 (2012): 389–408.

105. Ibid., 405.

106. By this light we can also see Joelle van Dyne not only as an ideal reader but also an ideal medium, as modeled not so much by her role in Incandenza's "Infinite Jest" as by her hosting of the radio show "Sixty Minutes More or Less with Madame Psychosis."

107. John Jeremiah Sullivan, "Too Much Information," *GQ* (31 March 2011), https://www.gq.com/story/david-foster-wallace-the-pale-king-john-jeremiah-sullivan

108. William R. Paulson, *The Noise of Culture: Literary Texts in a World of Information* (Ithaca: Cornell University Press, 1988), 83.

109. This may explain why the arch prophet of modernist medium-specificity, Clement Greenberg, saw "literature" (rather than Fried's "theater") as the temptation against which the modern arts must strive. Greenberg, "Towards," 65.

110. Cavell, *Must*, 187.

111. David Lipsky, *Although of Course You End Up Becoming Yourself: A Road Trip with David Foster Wallace* (New York: Broadway Books, 2010), 72.

Chapter Two

1. Dave Eggers, *A Heartbreaking Work of Staggering Genius* (New York: Vintage, 2001), 169. Further references in parentheses.

2. Richard Barbrook and Andy Cameron, "The Californian Ideology," *Science as Culture* 6.1 (1996): 52.

3. Dave Eggers, "Mistakes We Knew We Were Making," in *A Heartbreaking Work of Staggering Genius* (New York: Vintage, 2001), appendix 33.

4. In his later novel *The Circle* (2013), Eggers depicts a social media company in which work exemplifies these ideals, going on to expose the dystopian effects of such a working culture. For a sociological study of the work practices of the dot-com firms, see Andrew Ross, *No-Collar: The Humane Workplace and Its Hidden Costs* (New York: Basic Books, 2003).

5. Quoted in Doug Henwood, *After the New Economy: The Binge . . . And the Hangover That Won't Go Away* (New York: New Press, 2003), 8.

6. Kevin Kelly, *New Rules for the New Economy: 10 Radical Strategies for a Connected World* (London: Fourth Estate, 1998), 1, 2.

7. Ibid., 5.

8. Ibid., 157.

9. Thomas Frank, *One Market Under God: Extreme Capitalism, Market Populism, and the End of Economic Democracy* (London: Secker & Warburg, 2001), 7. Frank is, well, frank in defining the New Economy not as "some novel state of human affairs but the final accomplishment of the long-standing agenda of the nation's richest class." Ibid., 15.

10. Ibid., 9.

11. Quoted in Henwood, *After the New Economy*, 3. Rather comically, "Dornbusch's law" should have warned its author against such hasty pronouncements. The law states: "a crisis takes a much longer time coming than you think, and then it happens much faster than you would have thought." "Interviews: Dr. Rudi Dornbusch," *Frontline* (n.d.), https://www.pbs.org/wgbh/pages/frontline/shows/mexico/interviews/dornbusch.html

12. Joseph Stiglitz, *The Roaring Nineties: A New History of the World's Most Prosperous Decade* (New York: Norton, 2003), 5.

13. Kelly, *New Rules*, 156.

14. Ibid., 159, 160.

15. Rachel Greenwald Smith reads *A Heartbreaking Work* as a text that "mirrors the neoliberal dynamics of agency" and supports "neoliberal emotional norms," in large part by being "so emotionally absorptive that it limits the capacity of the reader to engage with it as a critical agent regardless of the degree to which its formal instruments are exposed." Rachel Greenwald Smith, *Affect and American Literature in the Age of Neoliberalism* (Cambridge: Cambridge University Press, 2015), 79, 89. The contrast between Smith's negative evaluation of the absorption/theatricality dialectic and my more positive assessment in Chapter One should be evident. Elsewhere, Sarah Brouillette criticizes Eggers's texts and paratexts as "profoundly self-justifying," as working "to police the reception of future works and control the way we read Eggers' position in the literary marketplace," as disavowing financial gain only in order "to accrue capital in its other forms." Sarah Brouillette, "Paratextuality and Economic Disavowal in Dave Eggers' *You Shall Know Our Velocity*," *Reconstruction: Studies in Contemporary Culture* 3.2 (2003): paragraphs 1 and 26, http://reconstruction.digitalodu.com/Issues/032/brouillette.htm; As we shall see below, I read the preemptive and controlling dimensions of Eggers's early work as powerfully expressive of financial logics that his texts go on to unsettle. Finally, in a different kind of cultural critique that I will not take up here but that bears upon my interests in subsequent chapters, Mark Greif defines the American hipster circa 2000 as a white male who "aligns himself both with rebel subculture and with the dominant class, and thus opens up a poisonous conduit between the two." Greif goes on to identify the early Eggers as among "the most exemplary hipster artists." Mark Greif, *Against Everything* (London: Verso, 2017), 213, 216.

16. For an account of the relevance of Eggers's entrepreneurship to a reading of his memoir, see Amy Hungerford, "McSweeney's and the School of Life," *Contemporary Literature* 53.4 (2012): 646–680. I will return to the figure of the entrepreneur in my discussion of Helen DeWitt in Chapter Five.

17. Caroline Hamilton, *One Man Zeitgeist: Dave Eggers, Publishing and Publicity* (London: Bloomsbury, 2010), 52.

18. Ibid., 10; Lee Konstantinou, *Cool Characters: Irony and American Fiction* (Cambridge, MA: Harvard University Press, 2016), 198.

19. Wolfgang Funk, *The Literature of Reconstruction: Authentic Fiction in the New Millennium* (London: Bloomsbury, 2015), 137.

20. Nicoline Timmer, *Do You Feel It Too? The Post-Postmodern Syndrome in American Fiction at the Turn of the Millennium* (Amsterdam: Rodopi, 2010), 237.

21. Liesbeth Korthals Altes, *Ethos and Narrative Interpretation: The Negotiation of Values in Fiction* (Lincoln: University of Nebraska Press, 2014), 246.

22. Korthals Altes, *Ethos*, 247.

23. Konstantinou, *Cool Characters*, 198, 174.

24. Ibid., 170.

25. Paul Crosthwaite, *The Market Logics of Contemporary Fiction* (Cambridge: Cambridge University Press, 2019), 75.

26. Ibid.

27. Ibid., 73.

28. Ibid., 58.

29. Eggers, "Mistakes," 34.

30. Annie McClanahan, *Dead Pledges: Debt, Crisis, and Twenty-First-Century Culture* (Stanford: Stanford University Press, 2017), 42.

31. Ibid.

32. Among the most widely noted works, in roughly chronological order, are: Margaret Atwood, *Payback: Debt and the Shadow Side of Wealth* (Toronto: House of Anansi Press, 2008); David Graeber, *Debt: The First 5,000 Years* (New York: Melville House, 2011); Richard Dienst, *The Bonds of Debt: Borrowing Against the Common Good* (London: Verso, 2011); Mauricio Lazzarato, *The Making of the Indebted Man: An Essay on the Neoliberal Condition*, trans. Joshua David Jordan (Los Angeles: Semiotexte, 2012); Fred Moten and Stefano Harney, *The Undercommons: Fugitive Planning and Black Study* (Wivenhoe, NY: Minor Compositions, 2013); Andrew Ross, *Creditocracy and the Case for Debt Refusal* (New York: OR Books, 2013); Miranda Joseph, *Debt to Society: Accounting for Life Under Capitalism* (Minneapolis: University of Minnesota Press, 2014); Wolfgang Streeck, *Buying Time: The Delayed Crisis of Democratic Capitalism*, trans. Patrick Camiller (London: Verso, 2014); Jerome Roos, *Why Not Default? The Political Economy of Sovereign Debt* (Princeton: Princeton University Press, 2019).

33. Robert Brenner, *The Economics of Global Turbulence* (London: Verso, 2006).

34. David Harvey, *The Limits to Capital* (London: Verso, 2006), xxiii. Further references in parentheses. Harvey presents his overaccumulation thesis as identifying the

"deeper problem" that underlies the "surface manifestations" registered by other applications of Marxian theory to the crisis of the 1970s, namely the profit-squeeze explanation, the underconsumption thesis, and the theory of the falling rate of profit (xxiii).

35. Streeck, *Buying Time*, passim.

36. Roos, *Why Not Default?*, 1–2.

37. This development accentuated the financialization of the US economy already begun in the 1970s, since high interest rates, as Greta Krippner writes, "created punishing conditions for productive investment and drew economic activity inexorably toward finance." Rather than vanquishing inflation—an achievement Volcker is usually credited with—"the result was to transfer inflation from the nonfinancial to the financial economy—where it was not visible (or conceptualized) as such." Krippner, *Capitalizing on Crisis: The Political Origins of the Rise of Finance* (Cambridge, MA: Harvard University Press, 2012), 87, 103.

38. Stephen Gill, "Globalization, Market Civilization and Disciplinary Neoliberalism," *Millennium: Journal of International Studies* 24.3 (1995): 399–423. A crucial outcome of the debt crisis in the Global South was that it "helped deliver the coup de grâce to the ambitious third world politics of the 1970s, exemplified by the call for a New International Economic Order, which had been sustained by a global commodity boom." Tim Barker, "Other People's Blood: On Paul Volcker," *n+1* 34 (2019), https://www.nplusonemag.com/issue-34/reviews/other-peoples-blood-2/

39. John Bellamy Foster and Fred Magdoff, *The Great Financial Crisis: Causes and Consequences* (New York: Monthly Review Press, 2009), 46.

40. Colin Crouch, "Privatised Keynesianism: An Unacknowledged Policy Regime," *British Journal of Politics & International Relations* 11.3 (2009): 382–399.

41. McClanahan, *Dead Pledges*, 1.

42. Kelly, *New Rules*, 157.

43. Annie McClanahan, "Investing in the Future: Late Capitalism's End of History," *Journal of Cultural Economy* 6.1 (2013): 83.

44. Lazzarato, *Indebted Man*, 8. Further references in parentheses.

45. Jean-Joseph Goux, "Cash, Check, or Charge?" in *The New Economic Criticism: Studies at the Intersection of Literature and Economics*, ed. Martha Woodmansee and Mark Osteen (London: Routledge, 1999), 122.

46. Lisa Adkins, "Speculative Futures in the Time of Debt," *Sociological Review* 65.3 (2017): 450.

47. Ibid.

48. Ibid., 449.

49. Ibid. On the financial security as the central capitalist form of our moment—replacing Marx's emphasis on the commodity, so that *production* gives way to *prediction*—see Ivan Ascher, *Portfolio Society: On the Capitalist Mode of Prediction* (New York: Zone Books, 2016).

50. Graeber, *Debt*, 362.

51. McClanahan, *Dead Pledges*, 2.

52. Ibid., 14.

53. In this sense Eggers's memoir, a text that follows in the modern tradition established by Rousseau's *Confessions*, can be said to play out the debate between Jacques Derrida and Paul de Man about Rousseau, writing, reading (and sincerity), discussed in the Introduction to this book.

54. Early in Kerouac's 1957 novel, Sal tells his reader that "the only people for me are the mad ones, the ones who are mad to live, mad to talk, mad to be saved, desirous of everything at the same time, the ones who never yawn or say a commonplace thing, but burn, burn, burn like fabulous yellow roman candles exploding like spiders across the stars." As in Eggers's prose, this sentence is restless, immediate, and onrushing while proclaiming the values of restlessness, immediacy, and rushing on. Jack Kerouac, *On the Road* (London: Penguin, 2000), 9.

55. It is no surprise, then, that this is the section of the book most often quoted by critics concerned with explicating Eggers's message and purpose.

56. Friedrich Nietzsche, *On the Genealogy of Morality*, trans. Adrian del Caro, in vol. 8 of *The Complete Works of Friedrich Nietzsche*, ed. Alan D. Schrift and Duncan Large (Stanford: Stanford University Press, 2014), 258. Nietzsche's account of the foundational creditor/debtor relation bears comparison with Hegel's dialectic of lord and bondsman, important to my previous chapter. See, for instance, Philip J. Kain, "Nietzschean Genealogy and Hegelian History in *The Genealogy of Morals*," *Canadian Journal of Philosophy* 26.1 (1996): 123–148.

57. Nietzsche, *Genealogy*, 279.

58. Lazzarato, *Indebted*, 78.

59. Ibid.

60. Benjamin Widiss, *Obscure Invitations: The Persistence of the Author in Twentieth-Century American Literature* (Stanford: Stanford University Press, 2011), 111.

61. In Max Weber's influential account, "religious account-books in which sins, temptations, and progress made in grace were entered or tabulated" were a crucial means by which "Reformed Christians" developed the asceticism that underpinned the emergence of capitalism. Max Weber, *The Protestant Ethic and the Spirit of Capitalism*, trans. Talcott Parsons (New York: Routledge, 1992), 124.

62. Christopher Nealon, "Value, Theory, Crisis," *PMLA* 127.1 (2012): 102. As Donald MacKenzie notes, futures trading fundamentally alters present prices: "You might think that the price of a futures contract on grain would track the price of the underlying physical commodity, but it's actually the other way round: the concentration of buying and selling activity in futures markets means that the price of commodities is often in effect set in those markets, not in the direct buying and selling of the commodities themselves." MacKenzie, "Just How Fast?" *London Review of Books* 41.5 (7 March 2019): 23.

63. Widiss, *Obscure*, 129.

64. McClanahan, "Investing," 89.

65. Dave Eggers, *You Shall Know Our Velocity* (San Francisco: McSweeney's, 2002), 1 (front cover). Further references in parentheses.

66. Karl Marx, *Grundrisse: Foundations of the Critique of Political Economy* (rough draft), trans. Martin Nicolaus (Harmondsworth: Penguin, 1973), 630–631.

67. Ibid., 546.

68. In 2011, a single high-frequency trade took 5-millionths of a second; in 2018, it took 84-billionths of a second. MacKenzie, "Just How Fast?," 23. The speed of thought is more difficult to measure, but it is generally estimated to be much slower than the HFT figure. See Andrew W. Lo, *Adaptive Markets: Financial Evolution at the Speed of Thought* (Princeton: Princeton University Press, 2017).

69. McClanahan, "Investing," 88.

70. Graeber, *Debt*, 364.

71. Even though Eggers's novel was published before American operations concerning "terrorist states" in the Middle East began, it is hard not to think of these developments when we read Will's lament at the effect of his and Hand's seemingly benign and sincere intentions on those they meet on their trip: "Nothing we did ever resembled in any way what we'd envisioned. Maybe we couldn't help but make a mess everywhere we went—" (226).

72. Karl Marx, "The Power of Money," in *Economic and Philosophical Manuscripts of 1844*, trans. Martin Milligan (Moscow: Progress Publishers, 1959), https://www.marxists.org/archive/marx/works/1844/manuscripts/power.htm

73. The way money separates even those in bodily contact is highlighted in a late scene in the novel when Oksana, a Latvian sex worker, lies on top of Will's back to keep him warm. The next morning he thinks: "How much was her lying on top of me worth? You couldn't measure it. You could say it was worth nothing—that it should have been free—or you could say millions and both would make sense. Nothing was quantifiable—or rather, at some point things were so, and numbers could be spoken with confidence, but no longer." But of course the interaction does turn out to be quantifiable, with Will turning over to Oksana all his spare currency. "There is always more for people like you," she tells him contemptuously at the conclusion of their transaction (331).

74. Dave Eggers, *Sacrament*, ed. Francis "Hand" Wisniewski (San Francisco: McSweeney's, 2003), 281–282. In his additional section, Hand also explains that the opening paragraph of the original text, seemingly written by Will from beyond the grave, was in fact a posthumous addition by a ghostwriter: "Will, I suspect, died in an unspeakably horrific way, surrounded by underwater screams. That it was plastered on the cover—written by a ghostwriter, if you'll forgive the dual-sided pun—is a disgrace." Ibid., 259.

75. Ibid., 274.

76. Ibid., 289.

77. Ibid., 287. James Clements identifies the metafictional levels here, noting that "four different types of 'sacrament' are folded into one: the religious sacrament, Will and Hand's acts of charity, Will's text, and Eggers's own offering." James Clements, "Trust Your Makers of Things!: The Metafictional Pact in Dave Eggers's *You Shall Know Our Velocity*," *Critique* 56.2 (2015): 133.

78. Widiss, *Obscure*, 111, 128.

79. John Leonard, "We Are the Fourth World," *New York Times* (10 November 2002), https://www.nytimes.com/2002/11/10/books/we-are-the-fourth-world.html. Sarah Brouillette compares the way Will and Eggers both come into money by selling an image to the public and notes that Jack occupies the motivating role played by Eggers's mother in the earlier book. Brouillette, "Paratextuality," paragraphs 19 and 23. Clements records "several formal markers that also serve to condition readers to approach *Velocity* not as an independent work, but as a continuation of *A Heartbreaking Work*," including the novel's lack of front matter or prefatory material. Clements, "Trust," 128.

80. Konstantinou, *Cool*, 216.

81. Clements, "Trust," 125. Further references in parentheses.

82. Konstantinou, *Cool*, 215.

83. Jacqueline O'Dell, "The Gift Network: Dave Eggers and the Circulation of Second Editions," *New American Notes Online* 11 (July 2017), https://nanocrit.com/issues/issue11/The-Gift-Network-Dave-Eggers-and-the-Circulation-of-Second-Editions

84. Ibid.

85. Ibid.

86. McClanahan, *Dead Pledges*, 185. Lazzarato explains how this class antagonism developed out of neoliberal ideas and practice. The Ordoliberal school, which did much to shape the postwar German economy, had aimed to "deproletarianize" the workforce by involving them in the capitalist management of society as shareholders rather than wage earners. In the era of high neoliberalism, according to Lazzarato, "deproletarianization has taken a leap forward in terms of discourse ('everyone an owner, everyone an entrepreneur'), but it has been transformed into its opposite in fact, namely because of wage depression and State budget cuts. This is how the debt economy institutes economic and existential precariousness, which is but the new name for the old reality: proletarianization—especially of the middle class and the class of workers in those new fields of what was once called, before the bubble burst, the 'new economy.'" Lazzarato, *Indebted*, 93. I take up these ideas about class restructuring under neoliberalism more concertedly in Chapter Five.

87. Allard den Dulk thus misreads *Velocity* when he argues that its moral message is that Will should escape his "problematic attitude of hyperreflexive irony" and instead embrace "trust in and surrender to the outer world that is embodied in the attitude of sincerity." Allard den Dulk, *Existentialist Engagement in Wallace, Eggers and Foer: A Philosophical Analysis of Contemporary American Literature* (London: Bloomsbury, 2015), 185, 187. Den Dulk regards this embrace of sincere presentness as a grand Kierkegaardian leap, but it's not clear where the difficulty would lie for Will in disregarding the structuring economic and political (not to speak of racial and gender) conditions that lead to his privilege as a white, middle-class, American man. Since this "sincere"

disregard of privilege seems to be less the exception than the norm, surely irony is in this case the more honest existential state?

88. Widiss, *Obscure*, 128. It is worth recalling here Nietzsche's passage on the meaning of the crucifixion story in terms of the creditor-debtor relation. In his reading, the concepts of guilt and duty turn back on both the creditor (God) and the debtor (humanity) in a spiraling manner, "until all of a sudden we stand before the paradoxical and horrifying way out in which tortured humankind found a temporary relief, that stroke of genius of *Christianity*: God sacrificing himself for man's debt, none other than God paying himself back, God as the only one able to redeem man from what, to man himself, has become irredeemable—the creditor sacrificing himself for his debtor, out of *love* (would you believe it?) out of love for his debtor!" Nietzsche, *Genealogy*, 280.

89. Crosthwaite, *Market*, 17.

90. Crosthwaite explains beautifully the ambivalent attraction of the efficient markets hypothesis for contemporary novelists. Ibid., 129–186. On the market as source of truth in official neoliberal doctrine (though not for neoliberals themselves), see Philip Mirowski, *Never Let a Serious Crisis Go to Waste* (London: Verso, 2013), 68–83.

91. McClanahan, "Investing," 79.

92. Christopher Grobe, *The Art of Confession: The Performance of Self from Robert Lowell to Reality TV* (New York: New York University Press, 2017), 220.

93. According to Harvey, the phrase "American Century," coined in 1941 by Henry R. Luce, marks a temporal transposition of a fundamentally spatial idea of power: "Luce, an isolationist, considered that history had conferred global leadership on the United States and that this role, though thrust upon it by history, had to be actively embraced. The power conferred was global and universal rather than territorially specific, so Luce preferred to talk of an American century rather than an empire." David Harvey, *The New Imperialism* (New York: Oxford University Press, 2003), 50.

94. Karl Marx, *Capital: A Critique of Political Economy*, vol. 3, ed. Friedrich Engels (New York: International Publishers, 1894), 175, https://www.marxists.org/archive/marx/works/download/pdf/Capital-Volume-III.pdf

95. Bernard Stiegler, *For a New Critique of Political Economy*, trans. Daniel Ross (Cambridge: Polity Press, 2010), 5.

Chapter Three

1. Jennifer Egan, *The Invisible Circus* (New York: Anchor Books, 2007), 67. Further references in parentheses.

2. Alexandra Schwartz, "Jennifer Egan's Travels Through Time," *New Yorker* (17 October 2017), https://www.newyorker.com/magazine/2017/10/16/jennifer-egans-travels-through-time. The contrast between IBM and Apple—implied in Egan's comparison of IBM to Barry's company—is highlighted by Jeffrey Williams as an important marker of generational transition for the post-boomers he calls Generation Jones:

"They evince a shift in style, from a useful if blocky product to a sleek, high-design one, but more deeply they represent the transformation of jobs: IBM was a quintessential postwar success, a large company offering stable, often lifelong employment, and good benefits. Apple pioneered the move to flexible, just-in-time labor and off-shore production." Jeffrey J. Williams, "Generation Jones and Contemporary US Fiction," *American Literary History* 28.1 (2016): 101–102.

3. Charlie Reilly, "An Interview with Jennifer Egan," *Contemporary Literature* 50.3 (2009): 455. Gitlin's work on media is likewise central to Wallace's "E Unibus Pluram."

4. Todd Gitlin, *The Whole World Is Watching: Mass Media in the Making and Unmaking of the New Left* (Berkeley: University of California Press, 2003), xiv.

5. Ibid.

6. See Fredric Jameson, *Postmodernism, or, the Cultural Logic of Late Capitalism* (London: Verso, 1991).

7. Even following the runaway critical and commercial success of her fourth novel, *A Visit from the Goon Squad* (2010), and the publication of her fifth, *Manhattan Beach* (2017), Egan was still describing *Look at Me* as her "most ambitious in my opinion. I have not topped it." Allan Vorda, "Habit of Mind: An Interview with Jennifer Egan," *Rain Taxi* (Winter 2017/2018), raintaxi.com/habit-of-mind-an-interview-with-jennifer-egan/

8. Reilly, "An Interview," 443.

9. Ibid., 444.

10. Brian McHale, *Postmodernist Fiction* (London: Methuen, 1987).

11. Daniel Defoe, *Robinson Crusoe, or the Life and Strange Surprizing Adventures of Robinson Crusoe*, ed. W. R. Owens (London: Pickering and Chatto, 2008), 55.

12. Michael McKeon, *The Origins of the English Novel 1600–1740* (London: Radius, 1988), 120.

13. Maximillian E. Novak, "Sincerity, Delusion, and Character in the Fiction of Defoe and the 'Sincerity Crisis' of His Time," in *Augustan Studies*, ed. Douglas Lane Patey and Timothy Keegan (Newark: University of Delaware Press, 1985), 123.

14. Ian Watt, *The Rise of the Novel: Studies in Defoe, Richardson and Fielding* (London: Chatto & Windus, 1957).

15. Lennard J. Davis, *Factual Fictions: The Origins of the English Novel*, 2nd ed. (Philadelphia: University of Pennsylvania Press, 1996), 156. Further references in parentheses.

16. Catherine Gallagher, "The Rise of Fictionality," in *The Novel, Volume 1: History, Geography, and Culture*, ed. Franco Moretti (Princeton: Princeton University Press, 2006), 337. Further references in parentheses.

17. Pam Morris, *Imagining Inclusive Society in Nineteenth-Century Novels: The Code of Sincerity in the Public Sphere* (Baltimore: Johns Hopkins University Press, 2004).

18. Ibid., 15. "Rather than universal human nature as the grounding of sociability," Morris clarifies, "the concept of sincerity propagates an ideology of human interiority that is mutual to all but individual to each." Ibid., 21.

19. Ibid., 23.

20. Tim Milnes and Kerry Sinanan, "Introduction," in *Romanticism, Sincerity and Authenticity*, ed. Tim Milnes and Kerry Sinanan (London: Palgrave, 2010), 9.

21. George Eliot, from an unsigned 1856 review of John Ruskin's *Modern Painters*, in *Ruskin: The Critical Heritage*, ed. J. L. Bradley (London: Routledge, 1984), 180.

22. Garrett Stewart, *Dear Reader: The Conscripted Audience in Nineteenth-Century British Fiction* (Baltimore: Johns Hopkins University Press, 1996), 27.

23. Ibid., 12.

24. Ibid., 14, 33.

25. Brian McHale, *Constructing Postmodernism* (London: Routledge, 1992), 96.

26. Ibid., 89, 94.

27. In this section and later in the chapter, I draw on a previously published article: Adam Kelly, "Jennifer Egan, New Sincerity, and the Genre Turn in Contemporary Fiction," *Contemporary Women's Writing* 15.2 (2021): 151–170. This and later sections also develop material first published in Kelly, "Beginning with Postmodernism," *Twentieth-Century Literature* 57.3–4 (2011): 391–422.

28. Charlotte Swenson is the narrator of one of *Look at Me*'s two main plot strands, which emerge together in the opening chapter, separate thereafter, and are reunited at the conclusion. Both plots center on a character named Charlotte, and the novel's twenty chapters alternate, roughly speaking, between the story of one Charlotte and the other. They also alternate between a first- and third-person narrative perspective, with the third-person narrative focused on a teenaged girl named Charlotte Hauser and on various people in her life, including her uncle Moose Metcalf and her older lover Michael West, the alias of an Arabic would-be terrorist named Z or Aziz.

29. Jennifer Egan, *Look at Me* (London: Picador, 2003), 256–257. Further references in parentheses.

30. Watt, *Rise*, 14.

31. David Foster Wallace, *Girl with Curious Hair* (London: Abacus, 1997), 330. The numerous similarities between *Look at Me* and *Westward*—the central Illinois setting, the importance of a car journey, the apocalyptic ending filmed as an advertisement, the dialogue with postmodern predecessors—suggest that Wallace's early New Sincerity novella was a direct influence on Egan's second novel, just as "E Unibus Pluram" likely influenced the treatment of irony in her first. Egan would go on to write an acknowledged parody of Wallace's *Brief Interviews with Hideous Men* (1999) in a chapter of *A Visit from the Goon Squad* (2010), while one critic has suggested that the character of Moose in *Look at Me* is directly modeled on Wallace. Michael Szalay, "The Author as Executive Producer," in *Neoliberalism and Contemporary Literary Culture*, ed. Mitchum Huehls and Rachel Greenwald Smith (Baltimore: Johns Hopkins University Press, 2017), 258.

32. Davis, *Factual*, 33.

33. Watt, *Rise*, 12, 13.

34. Ibid., 34.

35. Gallagher, "Rise," 341. See also Gallagher's *Nobody's Story*, in which she connects the rise of fictionality in the eighteenth century to the prominence of female authorship (and also links the latter to figures of debt, the theme of my previous chapter). Catherine Gallagher, *Nobody's Story: The Vanishing Acts of Women Writers in the Marketplace, 1670–1820* (Oxford: Clarendon Press, 1994), xviii.

36. Pankaj Mishra, "Modernity's Undoing," *London Review of Books* 33.7 (31 March 2011): 27.

37. Ibid.

38. For an analysis of revisionist accounts of postmodernism—what I have dubbed "the new postmodernist studies"—see the earlier article version of the present chapter, "Beginning with Postmodernism," in *Twentieth-Century Literature* cited above. It is worth noting that Egan, in an interview following the publication of *Look at Me*, registered anxiety about the gender dynamics of her literary inheritance: "I'm not sure exactly what tradition I'm part of. I hate about myself the fact that I tend to model myself consciously after male writers." Egan in Laura Miller, "Face Value," *Salon* (15 November 2001), https://www.salon.com/2001/11/14/egan_2/

39. The parallels between *The Real Charlotte* and *Look at Me* are many: both explore the relations between the haves and have-nots in their respective societies; both are dark social satires in which class and gender play determining roles for the female protagonists; both involve love plots in which the two female principals have romantic attachments to the same man; both focus on questions of identity, authenticity, and deceit with regard to the main character, the question of who the real Charlotte might be. The gothic uncanny in *The Real Charlotte* (which, despite the pen name of one of its authors, was written by two women) is usually read as concerned with the coming collapse of the Anglo-Irish aristocracy at the end of the nineteenth century. In a similar way, the gothic sensibility of *Look at Me* can be related to what Egan has described as "being buoyed up on the exalted fat times of the '90s and feeling that somehow it was going to come crashing down." Quoted in Miller, "Face Value." One aspect of this "crashing down" is the novel's inclusion of a plotline concerning a planned Arab terrorist bombing of the World Trade Center. The fact that *Look at Me* was published one week after September 11, 2001, only adds to its uncanny quality.

40. Once again Jameson's *Postmodernism* is the ur-text here, but see also Edward Soja, *Postmodern Geographies: The Reassertion of Space in Critical Social Theory* (London: Verso, 1989), and Brian Jarvis, *Postmodern Cartographies: The Geographical Imagination in Contemporary American Culture* (New York: St. Martin's, 1998).

41. Enda Duffy, *The Speed Handbook: Velocity, Pleasure, Modernism* (Durham: Duke University Press, 2009).

42. This layering of representations, a recognizably postmodern gesture, is repeated regularly throughout the novel, as for example when Charlotte describes "watching *The Making of the Making of*, a documentary about how documentaries were made about the making of Hollywood features" (78).

43. Don DeLillo, *White Noise* (London: Picador, 1985), 12–13.

44. Jameson, *Postmodernism*, 16–21.

45. John Barth, *Lost in the Funhouse* (New York: Anchor Books, 1988), 72.

46. Ibid., 72, 97.

47. See Barth's postmodernist manifesto "The Literature of Exhaustion," in *The Friday Book: Essays and Other Nonfiction* (Baltimore: Johns Hopkins University Press, 1984), 62–76.

48. As Mark McGurl has shown, one important embodiment of the institution for contemporary American letters is the creative writing program itself, and specific anxieties about its effects are not absent from *Look at Me*. Indeed, if Irene, the cultural studies academic, embodies the importation of the ideas and language of Theory into the contemporary novel, then Thomas stands for the acknowledgment of the effects of the writing program. When Charlotte innocently asks why, in discussing her life story in her presence, Irene and Thomas constantly refer to "her" and not "you," Thomas remarks that it is a "habit from creative writing class" (254). His language, in this scene and elsewhere, is dominated by the rhetoric of the program: "I'm saying *find* the drama, *find* the beauty, *find* the tension and give it to us" (255).

49. Walpole coined the term in his preface to the second edition of *The Castle of Otranto* (an edition that also saw the novel subtitled "A Gothic Story"). E. J. Clery, *Women's Gothic: From Clara Reeve to Mary Shelley* (Tavistock: Northcote, 2000), 3.

50. Moers defined "Female Gothic" in two alternative ways: as "the work that women writers have done in the literary mode that, since the eighteenth century, we have called the Gothic," and as "a novel in which the central figure is a young woman who is simultaneously persecuted victim and courageous heroine." Ellen Moers, *Literary Women* (London: Women's Press, 1986), 91.

51. Angela Wright, *Gothic Fiction: A Reader's Guide to Essential Criticism* (Basingstoke: Palgrave, 2007), 135.

52. See Benjamin A. Brabon and Stéphanie Genz, ed., *Postfeminist Gothic: Critical Interventions in Contemporary Culture* (Basingstoke: Palgrave, 2007).

53. On the novel's sensitivity to the global dimensions of neoliberalism, see Stephanie Lambert, "'The Real Dark Side, Baby': New Sincerity and Neoliberal Aesthetics in David Foster Wallace and Jennifer Egan," *Critique* 61.4 (2019): 391–411.

54. While Dr. Fabermann and Dr. Miller are the two medical surgeons who feature in the novel, the publicist Victoria Knight is later described as "a surgeon of reality" (194), indicating the malleability of the real at the hands of powerful people in Charlotte's world.

55. Catherine Spooner, "Virtual Gothic Women," in *Women and the Gothic: An Edinburgh Companion*, ed. Avril Horner and Sue Zlosnik (Edinburgh: Edinburgh University Press, 2016), 199.

56. Ibid.

57. Paula A. Treichler, Lisa Cartwright, and Constance Penley, "Introduction: Paradoxes of Visibility," in *The Visible Woman: Imaging Technologies, Gender, and*

Science, ed. Paula A. Treichler, Lisa Cartwright, and Constance Penley (New York: New York University Press, 1998), 7.

58. Ibid., 3.

59. Ibid., 4.

60. Griselda Pollock, "The Visual," in *A Concise Companion to Feminist Theory*, ed. Mary Eagleton (Oxford: Blackwell, 2003), 177.

61. John Berger, "Ways of Seeing," in *The Feminism and Visual Culture Reader*, 2nd ed., ed. Amelia Jones (London: Routledge, 2010), 49.

62. Ibid., 50, 52.

63. These passages about Charlotte's engagement with signs are likely inspired by Naomi Klein's *No Logo*, published in December 1999. The opening paragraph of Klein's text reads as follows:

> If I squint, tilt my head, and shut my left eye, all I can see out the window is 1932, straight down to the lake. Brown warehouses, oatmeal-colored smokestacks, faded signs painted on brick walls advertising long-discontinued brands: "Lovely," "Gaywear." This is the old industrial Toronto of garment factories, furriers and wholesale wedding dresses. So far, no one has come up with a way to make a profit out of taking a wrecking ball to these boxes of brick, and in this little eight- or nine-block radius, the modern city has been layered haphazardly on top of the old.

Naomi Klein, *No Logo: No Space, No Choice, No Jobs* (London: Flamingo, 2000), xiii.

64. Perhaps equally significant, from the point of view of overcoming postmodernism, is the resonance of the quoted passage with a famous one from early in Pynchon's *The Crying of Lot 49* (1966), when Oedipa Maas looks down on the houses of San Narciso and thinks "of the time she'd opened a transistor radio to replace a battery and seen her first printed circuit." This circuit speaks to Oedipa of "a hieroglyphic sense of concealed meaning, of an intent to communicate. . . . a revelation also trembled just past the threshold of her understanding." Thomas Pynchon, *The Crying of Lot 49* (London: Vintage, 1996), 14, 15.

65. Rosalind Gill, "Postfeminist Media Culture: Elements of a Sensibility," *European Journal of Cultural Studies* 10.2 (2007): 164.

66. Ibid., 154.

67. The three examples Banet-Weiser cites as embodying these subject positions are, respectively: Jennifer Ringley, who in 1996 became the first web-based lifecaster through her JenniCam website; Natalie Dylan, who in 2008 attempted to sell her virginity on the online auction site eBay; and Tila Tequila, who *Time* magazine described in 2006 as "something entirely new, a celebrity created not by a studio or a network but fan by fan, click by click, from the ground up on MySpace." Sarah Banet-Weiser, "Branding the Postfeminist Self: The Labor of Femininity," in *AuthenticTM: The Politics of Ambivalence in a Brand Culture* (New York: New York University Press, 2012), 51–52.

68. By the conclusion of *Look at Me*, even the formerly plain Irene has become a postfeminist icon: "As the first 'new new journalist,' Irene Maitlock is something of a legend.... She looks so different, thanks to her much chronicled makeover; without a name, I wouldn't have recognized her" (415). "A makeover paradigm constitutes postfeminist media culture," notes Gill, "Postfeminist," 156.

69. Nancy Armstrong, *Desire and Domestic Fiction: A Political History of the Novel* (New York: Oxford University Press, 1987), 8.

70. We might even say: is first and foremost a female model. As Irene informs Charlotte, "a model's position as a purely physical object—a media object, if you will—... is in a sense just a more exaggerated version of everyone's position in a visually based, media-driven culture" (74). In a newspaper article that fed into the creation of *Look at Me*, Egan commented on the specific importance of the female model to 1990s American culture: "Certainly models are this decade's contribution to our already crowded celebrity pantheon. They are what rock stars were to the 70's and visual artists were to the 80's." Jennifer Egan, "James Is a Girl," *New York Times* (4 February 1996), https://www.nytimes.com/1996/02/04/magazine/james-is-a-girl.html

71. Gill, "Postfeminist," 150.

72. Sarah Brouillette, "The Talented Ms. Calloway," *Los Angeles Review of Books* (10 December 2020), https://lareviewofbooks.org/article/the-talented-ms-calloway/; the quote from Duffy and Hund is also drawn from this article.

73. Szalay, "The Author," 256. Further references in parentheses.

74. See the discussion of the genre turn in the Introduction to this book. Scholars almost all mention 2006's *The Keep* as a participant in the turn to genre, and Egan often appears as one of the few (sometimes the only) female contributor to this literary development in its initial phase.

75. In another important reading, Lee Konstantinou argues that the televisual inspiration identified by Szalay is "incidental" to the most original contribution of *Goon Squad*, which is its lack of squeamishness about commodification and reification: "What is genuinely new in Egan's art is not some especially perverse, preemptive determination to sell out, but the absence of any sort of scandal—any pretense to shame—around rituals of selling out in the first place. It is the *anxiety* of reification that has (almost) disappeared from her prose, and the prose of many of her contemporaries." Konstantinou, *Cool Characters: Irony and American Fiction* (Cambridge, MA: Harvard University Press, 2016), 268, 261. The difference from *Look at Me*, where commodification and reification are central anxieties, should be clear; this difference is also captured in the two novels' respective engagement with social media, where preemptive worries in *Look at Me* about the effects of new media on gender, society, and literary narrative are replaced by "reimagining the form of the novel as a sort of Facebook wall" in *Goon Squad*. Ibid., 260. Konstantinou argues that *Goon Squad*'s sanguine attitude toward branding marks it out as a "postironic" work, and thus I would contend that the New Sincerity of Egan's earlier *Look at Me* should be read *against* this notion of postirony. For more on this distinction, see my conclusion to Chapter Four.

76. Gill, "Postfeminist," 159.

77. "Now," Charlotte observes in the final pages with horror and awe, "a team of 3-D modelers and animators creates my likeness and superimposes her onto my balcony, my sectional couch, my kitchen, my bedroom. From the little I've seen, they're miraculously good: That delivery scene at the hospital? Even I believed it!" (414–415).

78. Sarah Banet-Weiser, quoted in "Postfeminism, Popular Feminism and Neoliberal Feminism? Sarah Banet-Weiser, Rosalind Gill and Catherine Rottenberg in Conversation," *Feminist Theory* 20.4 (2019): 12.

Chapter Four

1. Colson Whitehead, *Sag Harbor* (New York: Anchor Books, 2010), 17. Further references in parentheses.

2. W. E. B. Du Bois, *The Souls of Black Folk*, in *The Oxford W. E. B. Du Bois Reader*, ed. Eric J. Sundquist (Oxford: Oxford University Press, 1996), 102.

3. Samantha Cracknell, "Colson Whitehead," *Aesthetica* (n.d.), https://aestheticamagazine.com/colson-whitehead/

4. Du Bois, *Souls*, 126.

5. Adolph Reed, Jr., *W. E. B. Du Bois and American Political Thought: Fabianism and the Color Line* (Oxford: Oxford University Press, 1997), 127.

6. Ibid., 129.

7. Ibid., 130.

8. Ibid. Reed is thinking particularly here of the work of Henry Louis Gates, Jr., whose influential notion of black "signifyin(g)" I invoke below.

9. Kenneth W. Warren, *What Was African American Literature?* (Cambridge, MA: Harvard University Press, 2011), 108, 139.

10. Ibid., 146.

11. On racial identity, see Walter Benn Michaels, *The Trouble with Diversity: How We Learned to Love Identity and Ignore Inequality* (New York: Henry Holt, 2006); on "black exceptionalism" see Cedric G. Johnson, "The Panthers Can't Save Us Now: Anti-Policing Struggles and the Limits of Black Power," *Catalyst* 1.1 (2017): 57–85; on "the black American narrative" see Charles Johnson, "The End of the Black American Narrative," *American Scholar* (Summer 2008).

12. Reed, *W. E. B. Du Bois*, 176. For a debate on the "class-first" positions set out by Reed, Michaels, and Cedric Johnson, see David Roediger, *Class, Race, and Marxism* (London: Verso, 2017), 11–19, 43–44; and the rejoinder by Johnson, "The Wages of Roediger: Why Three Decades of Whiteness Studies Has Not Produced the Left We Need," *nonsite* 29 (9 September 2019), https://nonsite.org/the-wages-of-roediger-why-three-decades-of-whiteness-studies-has-not-produced-the-left-we-need/

13. The final sentences of *Sag Harbor* do address the reader in the vein of much literary New Sincerity, but in a mood less of urgent appeal than of nostalgic musing: "Isn't it funny? The way the mind works?" (329). Second-person address is employed more consistently throughout *The Colossus of New York* (2003), an essayistic series of

prose poems that opens as follows: "I'm here because I was born here and thus ruined for anywhere else, but I don't know about you." Colson Whitehead, *The Colossus of New York* (New York: Anchor Books, 2004), 3.

14. See Jesse Cohn, "Old Afflictions: Colson Whitehead's *Apex Hides the Hurt* and the 'Post-Soul Condition,'" *Journal of the Midwest Modern Language Association* 42.1 (2009): 15–24; Cameron Leader-Picone, "Post-Black Stories: Colson Whitehead's *Sag Harbor* and Racial Individualism," *Contemporary Literature* 56.3 (2015): 421–449; Ramón Saldívar, "The Second Elevation of the Novel: Race, Form, and the Postrace Aesthetic in Contemporary Narrative," *Narrative* 21.1 (2013): 1–18. Arguably more important than which "post" one prefers is the fact that the Civil Rights era and the Black Arts Movement mark the origin point for understanding soul, blackness, and race in all these uses of the prefix.

15. Trey Ellis, "The New Black Aesthetic," *Callaloo* 38 (1989): 233–243. Reed accuses Ellis's manifesto of "conflat[ing] class and a racialized notion of culture," while Warren spotlights it as a telling moment in the "black petit bourgeois" accession to neoliberal values. Reed, *W. E. B. Du Bois*, 165; Warren, *What Was*, 121. For Whitehead's connection to Ellis, see Derek C. Maus, *Understanding Colson Whitehead* (Columbia: University of South Carolina Press, 2014), 13–14; and Leader-Picone, "Post-Black," 422.

16. Rolland Murray, "Not Being and Blackness: Percival Everett and the Uncanny Forms of Racial Incorporation," *American Literary History* 29.4 (2017): 726.

17. Ibid., 727.

18. For a reading of *Sag Harbor* along these lines, see Richard Schur, "The Crisis of Authenticity in Contemporary African American Literature," in *Contemporary African American Literature: The Living Canon*, ed. Lovalerie King and Shirley Moody-Turner (Bloomington: Indiana University Press, 2013), 239, 248–249.

19. For "racial individualism," see Leader-Picone, "Post-Black." In a headline *New York Times* review, Touré hailed the novel's focus on "successful and ambitious post-black families" who possess "tremendous class advantages" and live free of the psychological burdens of race or class. Touré, "Visible Young Man," *New York Times* (1 May 2009), http://www.nytimes.com/2009/05/03/books/review/Toure-t.html. Comparing *Sag Harbor* favorably to Whitehead's *The Underground Railroad* (2016), Thomas Chatterton Williams praised the earlier novel for its attempt to remove "the contemporary black American experience ... entirely from the realm of extremes." Williams, "Fried Fish," *London Review of Books* 38.22 (17 November 2016): 21.

20. Michaels chastises Touré's review on these grounds, "as if the crucial thing about rich black people is that they offer new ways of performing race rather than the old way of embodying class." Walter Benn Michaels, "Real Toads," in *The Imaginary and Its Worlds: American Studies After the Transnational Turn*, ed. Laura Bieger, Ramón Saldívar, and Johannes Voelz (Hanover: Dartmouth College Press, 2013), 185. Warren's choice of novel to exemplify the neoliberal sensibility in twenty-first-century black fiction, meanwhile, is Michael Thomas's *Man Gone Down* (2007), but,

as one critic notes, it "could easily be the wealthy community depicted in *Sag Harbor*." Warren, *What Was*, 128–136; Leader-Picone, "Post-Black," 424.

21. Marlon Lieber, "(Post-Black) *Bildungsroman* or (Black Bourgeois) Novel of Manners? The Logic of Reproduction in Colson Whitehead's *Sag Harbor*," in *Power Relations in Black Lives: Reading African American Literature and Culture with Bourdieu and Elias*, ed. Christa Buschendorf (Bielefeld: transcript Verlag, 2018), 119.

22. Touré, "Visible." Leader-Picone's critique of Warren's position, for instance, rests on this question: "Warren misses the importance of irony and satire . . . throughout contemporary African American literature's treatment of race and group identity." Leader-Picone, "Post-Black," 431.

23. Laura Miller, "Colson Whitehead's Alternate New York," *Salon* (12 January 1999), https://www.salon1999.com/books/feature/1999/01/cov_12featureb.html

24. Saldívar, "Second," 8.

25. Henry Louis Gates, Jr., *The Signifying Monkey: A Theory of African-American Literary Criticism* (Oxford: Oxford University Press, 1989), 110.

26. Ibid., 111.

27. Toni Morrison, *Beloved* (London: Picador, 1992), 3. Alexander Manshel, "Colson Whitehead's History of the United States," *MELUS* 45.4 (2020): 30.

28. Colson Whitehead, *The Intuitionist* (New York: Anchor Books, 2000), 239. Further references in parentheses. Elevators figure occasionally in *Invisible Man*—as when the narrator is "uplifted" vertically to the battle royal in the opening chapter. More intriguingly, in his introduction to the 1981 reprint edition, Ellison recounts working on *Invisible Man* in a suite on the eighth floor of a Fifth Avenue building, "the highest elevation upon which the novel unfolded," and recalls that "it was only the elevator operators who questioned my presence in such an affluent building." Ralph Ellison, *Invisible Man* (New York: Vintage, 1995), viii. Richard Wright's autobiography *Black Boy* (1945), another canonical African American work, features a scene in which a black elevator operator allows a white passenger to kick him for money, a scene on which Whitehead signifies by splitting it in two: Lila Mae's only black elevator inspector colleague Pompey is kicked on the behind by his white superior before receiving a promotion; and her father Marvin is dismissed from the elevator he operates when it is boarded by a white inspector.

29. As one critic observes, *The Intuitionist* is "a passing novel in both form and content." As well as turning on Lila Mae's discovery that James Fulton, the founder and theorist of Intuitionism, had a black mother and was thus passing as white, the novel itself initially passes as "a dystopic naturalist novel" (in the vein of Wright) before being revealed as "a realist novel with characters of psychological depth" (in the vein of Ellison). Michele Elam, "Passing in the Post-Race Era: Danzy Senna, Philip Roth, and Colson Whitehead," *African American Review* 41.4 (2007): 762–763.

30. Gates, *Signifying*, 131. For a reading of *The Intuitionist* as signifying on Frederick Douglass's slave narrative, see Tim Libretti, "'Verticality Is Such a Risky Enterprise': Class Epistemologies and the Critique of Upward Mobility in Colson Whitehead's *The*

Intuitionist," in *Class and Culture in Crime Fiction: Essays on Works in English Since the 1970s*, ed. Julie H. Kim (Jefferson, NC: McFarland, 2014), 206–209.

31. Stephen F. Soitos, *The Blues Detective: A Study of African American Detective Fiction* (Amherst: University of Massachusetts Press, 1996), 3.

32. For Pynchon, see Alison Russell, "Recalibrating the Past: Colson Whitehead's *The Intuitionist*," *Critique* 49.1 (2007): 49; for Coover, see Spencer Morrison, "Elevator Fiction: Robert Coover, Colson Whitehead, and the Sense of Infrastructure," *Arizona Quarterly* 73.3 (2017): 101–125. The prophecy in Fulton's *Theoretical Elevators* of a return to prelapsarian pure communication recalls Peter Stillman's Tower of Babel vision in Auster's *City of Glass* (1985), while a conversation between Jack Gladney and his son in DeLillo's *White Noise* (1985) is alluded to in a "slow debate about the rain: it's not about the rain at all, but the fragility of what we know" (64). It is no coincidence that *City of Glass*, *White Noise*, and Pynchon's *The Crying of Lot 49* (along with Ishmael Reed's *Mumbo Jumbo*) can all be defined as anti-detective novels: by signifying on these texts, *The Intuitionist* is revising the paradigmatic genre of American postmodernist fiction. Moreover, when we consider the structuring role of race in the work of these white writers, Whitehead's allusions to their fiction takes on multiple layers in a manner typical of the literary act of signifying. As Alexander Manshel points out, Toni Morrison's *Playing in the Dark* (which originated as a set of lectures that Whitehead likely attended while at Harvard) was instrumental in identifying race as the absent presence in canonical American literature. Manshel, "Colson Whitehead's," 30–31.

33. For Whitehead's comments on Reed, see Derek C. Maus, ed., *Conversations with Colson Whitehead* (Jackson: University Press of Mississippi, 2019), 17, 42, 73.

34. Ishmael Reed, "Neo-HooDoo Manifesto," in *Conjure: Selected Poems 1963–1970*. Quoted in Neil Schmitz, "Neo-HooDoo: The Experimental Fiction of Ishmael Reed," *Twentieth Century Literature* 20.2 (1974): 126.

35. Ibid., 136.

36. Elam, "Passing," 762. For accounts of the novel's conflicting signals as to its historical setting, see Manshel, "Colson Whitehead's," 25–26; and Daniel Grausam, "The Multitemporal Contemporary: Colson Whitehead's Presents," *Literature and the Global Contemporary*, ed. Sarah Brouillette, Matthia Nilges, and Emilio Sauri (London: Palgrave, 2017), 121–122.

37. Russell, "Recalibrating," 59.

38. Gates calls *Mumbo Jumbo* "the great black intertext," a novel that provides "both a definition of Afro-American culture and its deflation" by reveling in "the sheer plurality of signification." Gates, *Signifying*, 223, 220, 234.

39. Nicholas Donofrio, "Multiculturalism, Inc.: Regulating and Deregulating the Culture Industries with Ishmael Reed," *American Literary History* 29.1 (2017): 102.

40. Quoted in Robert E. Weems, Jr., *Business in Black and White: American Presidents and Black Entrepreneurs in the Twentieth Century* (New York: New York University Press, 2009), 115.

41. Donofrio, "Multiculturalism," 112, 118.

42. Ibid., 112, 114.

43. Ibid., 124. Donofrio makes clear that critiques of Reed along these lines were made by Black Arts Movement activists at the time, noting Amiri Baraka's inclusion of Reed among a list of "conservatives, capitulationists, and outright compradors." Quoted in ibid., 101–102.

44. This term, which names the ways in which the historical development of capitalism has depended not only on the exploitation of wage workers but on the expropriation of non-white peoples from the eras of colonization and chattel slavery to the present, was introduced to Americanist criticism by Cedric J. Robinson in his 1983 book *Black Marxism: The Making of the Black Radical Tradition* (Chapel Hill: University of North Carolina Press, 2000).

45. Donofrio, "Multiculturalism," 111; Madhu Dubey, *Signs and Cities: Black Literary Postmodernism* (Chicago: University of Chicago Press, 2003), 240. *The Intuitionist* is clearly responsive to the insight that "historically people of color have been casualties of technologically enabled systems of oppression, from colonial expansion, to the racial sciences of craniology and phrenology, to surveillance and information gathering." Alicia H. Hines, Alondra Nelson, and Thuy Linh N. Tu, "Introduction: Hidden Circuits," in *Technicolor: Race, Technology, and Everyday Life*, ed. Alicia H. Hines, Alondra Nelson, and Thuy Linh N. Tu (New York: New York University Press, 2001), 3.

46. Jeffrey Allen Tucker, "'Verticality Is Such a Risky Enterprise': The Literary and Paraliterary Antecedents of Colson Whitehead's *The Intuitionist*," *Novel: A Forum on Fiction* 43.1 (2010): 149.

47. Kevin K. Gaines, *Uplifting the Race: Black Leadership, Politics, and Culture in the Twentieth Century* (Chapel Hill: University of North Carolina Press, 1996), xiv.

48. Ibid., xv, 2.

49. Ibid., 6.

50. Ibid., xxi.

51. Lila Mae's Intuitionist method of elevator inspection, which in the opening scene involves her leaning against "the dorsal wall of the elevator" so that she can "concentrate on the vibrations massaging her back," clearly owes something to her early experience of learning to read with her father using an elevator manual, when "she felt the words in his chest against her back" (5, 119).

52. Darlene Clark Hine, "Rape and the Inner Lives of Black Women in the Middle West," *Signs* 14.4 (1989): 912.

53. Gaines, *Uplifting*, 5.

54. Lauren Berlant, "Intuitionists: History and the Affective Event," *American Literary History* 20.4 (2008): 852; Libretti, "Verticality," 203.

55. Linda Selzer, "Instruments More Perfect Than Bodies: Romancing Uplift in Colson Whitehead's *The Intuitionist*," *African American Review* 43.4 (2009): 682.

56. Russell, "Recalibrating," 50.

57. Luc Boltanski and Eve Chiapello, *The New Spirit of Capitalism*, trans. Gregory Elliott, reprint ed. (London: Verso, 2018), 312.

58. This is a tension that informs Mark McGurl's category of "high cultural pluralism," where the individual ethnic voice is understood to speak for their social subgroup through the medium of a modernist-inflected high style transmitted by one of the key engines of uplift, the university. Whitehead's first novel casts his work as much in the vein of "technomodernism" as high cultural pluralism, thereby emphasizing even more his non-marginal relation to twentieth-century aesthetics. See Mark McGurl, *The Program Era: Postwar Fiction and the Rise of Creative Writing* (Cambridge, MA: Harvard University Press, 2009). In the next chapter I will address McGurl's third main category, "lower-middle-class modernism," in my readings of George Saunders and Helen DeWitt.

59. Maria Bose, "Allegories of 'Postracial' Capitalism: Colson Whitehead and the Materials of Twenty-First-Century Black Cultural Authorship," *Critique* 60.4 (2019): 421.

60. Some critics describe Lila Mae as working class, while usually not being specific as to whether they are referring to her upbringing or her status as an elevator inspector. Dubey, *Signs*, 239. Others acknowledge Whitehead's presentation of elevator inspection as "a profession that demands a rigorous combination of academic and practical preparation along the lines of law or medicine," with Lila Mae's approach involving the "professionalization of intuition." Maus, *Understanding*, 21; Berlant, "Intuitionists," 846.

61. By 1970, 50 percent of black male college graduates and 60 percent of black female college graduates were public sector employees. As a historian of the period observes, "No institution played a greater role than government in breaking the grip of poverty and creating a Black middle class." Thomas J. Sugrue, *Sweet Land of Liberty: The Forgotten Struggle for Civil Rights in the North* (New York: Random House, 2008), 505.

62. Whitehead quoted in Laura Miller, "Going Up," *Salon* (12 January 1999), https://www.salon.com/1999/01/12/cov_si_12int/

63. Colson Whitehead, *Apex Hides the Hurt* (New York: Anchor Books, 2007), 34–35. Further references in parentheses.

64. Zora Neale Hurston, *Their Eyes Were Watching God*, introduction by Zadie Smith (London: Virago, 2007), 44. Further references in parentheses.

65. Describing Hurston's "soulfulness," Zadie Smith calls the novel's depiction of black culture "natural and organic and beautiful as the sunrise." Ibid., xxiv.

66. Gates, *Signifying*, 191. Further references in parentheses.

67. Here I mean "colonization" to signal not only the imagery of the passage, analyzed above, but also the neoliberal project to achieve, in Foucault's formulation, "the extension of economic analysis into a previously unexplored domain" so as to give "a strictly economic interpretation of a whole domain previously thought to be non-economic." Michel Foucault, *The Birth of Biopolitics: Lectures at the Collège de France, 1978–79*, ed. Michel Senellart, trans. Graham Burchell (Basingstoke: Palgrave, 2008), 219.

68. On the commodification of cool, see Thomas Frank, *The Conquest of Cool: Business Culture, Counterculture, and the Rise of Hip Consumerism* (Chicago: University of Chicago Press, 1997); and Alan Liu, *The Laws of Cool: Knowledge Work and the Culture of Information* (Chicago: University of Chicago Press, 2004).

69. The next three paragraphs, and parts of the following section of the chapter, draw on a previously published article: Adam Kelly, "Freedom to Struggle: The Ironies of Colson Whitehead," *Open Library of Humanities* 4.2 (2018), 1–35.

70. Warren, *What Was*, 117.

71. This term was central to Wilson's subsequent book *The Truly Disadvantaged: The Inner City, the Underclass, and Public Policy* (1987), a text that Bill Clinton carried around on the 1992 presidential campaign trail. On the influence of underclass ideology on American public life, see Touré F. Reed, *Toward Freedom: The Case Against Race Reductionism* (London: Verso, 2020), 133–139.

72. Quoted in Daniel T. Rodgers, *Age of Fracture* (Cambridge, MA: Harvard University Press, 2011), 124.

73. Gaines argues that "African Americans have, with an almost religious fervor, regarded education as the key to liberation." *Uplifting*, 1.

74. Stephanie Li, for instance, remarks that "Whitehead's protagonist easily enters and succeeds in white-dominated institutions" and that "his conspicuous evasion of racial markers suggests that he prefers not to have a racial identity at all." Li, *Signifying Without Specifying: Racial Discourse in the Age of Obama* (New Brunswick: Rutgers University Press, 2012), 74, 73.

75. Gary Becker, *Human Capital: A Theoretical and Empirical Analysis, with Special Reference to Education* (New York: National Bureau of Economic Research, 1964).

76. Theodore W. Schultz, "Investment in Human Capital," *American Economic Review* 51.1 (1961): 2.

77. John Patrick Leary, *Keywords: The New Language of Capitalism* (Chicago: Haymarket Books, 2018), ebook, n.p.

78. The work of white economist James Smith and black sociologist Glenn Loury has been crucial to the comparative study of racial outcomes through the measurement of human capital. See James P. Smith, "Race and Human Capital," *American Economic Review* 74.4 (1984): 685–698; and Glenn C. Loury, "A Dynamic Theory of Racial Income Differences," in *Women, Minorities and Employment Discrimination*, ed. Patricia Wallace (New York: Lexington Books, 1977), 153–186. See also the more recent work of black Harvard economist Roland Frye, and Lester Spence's critique of Frye in *Knocking the Hustle: Against the Neoliberal Turn in Black Politics* (New York: Punctum Books, 2015), 90–96.

79. Julian Gill-Peterson, "The Value of the Future: The Child as Human Capital and the Neoliberal Labor of Race," *Women's Studies Quarterly* 43.1–2 (2015): 188.

80. Ibid., 186. The key text here is Becker's early work *The Economics of Discrimination* (1957), which exemplifies the neoliberal (and neoclassical) vision of capitalism as a system based on abstract market exchange.

81. Ibid., 187. See also Eduardo Bonilla-Silva, *Racism Without Racists: Color-Blind Racism and the Persistence of Racial Inequality in the United States* (New York: Rowman & Littlefield, 2003). This perspective is absent from Walter Benn Michaels's influential critiques of diversity, which explicitly rely on taking the claims in Becker's *The Economics of Discrimination* at face value. See, e.g., Michaels, *The Beauty of a Social Problem: Photography, Autonomy, Economy* (Chicago: University of Chicago Press, 2015), 25–26.

82. Leary, *Keywords*, n.p.

83. Schultz, "Investment," 2.

84. Richard H. King, *Civil Rights and the Idea of Freedom*, 2nd ed. (Athens: University of Georgia Press, 1996), xviii.

85. Ibid., 16.

86. Ibid., xi.

87. For a much fuller account of this conservative takeover, which involved both the enthusiastic recuperation of "freedom" by the Right and its relative abandonment by the Left, see Kelly, "Freedom," 5–10.

88. Paul Gilroy, "'After the Love Has Gone': Bio-Politics and Etho-Poetics in the Black Public Sphere," *Public Culture* 7.1 (1994): 55.

89. Colson Whitehead, *John Henry Days* (London: Fourth Estate, 2001), 231.

90. Operation Enduring Freedom in Afghanistan and President Bush's repeated claim that "the advance of human freedom . . . now depends on us" are just two examples of the ubiquity of freedom rhetoric in the government's response. George W. Bush, "A Nation Challenged: President Bush's Address on Terrorism Before a Joint Meeting of Congress," *New York Times* (21 September 2001), http://www.nytimes.com/2001/09/21/us/nation-challenged-president-bush-s-address-terrorism-before-joint-meeting.html

91. Winthrop's 1645 "Little Speech On Liberty" is "often cited as the *locus classicus* of two fundamental meanings of freedom or liberty." King, *Civil*, 16.

92. Christopher Leise, "With Names, No Coincidence: Colson Whitehead's Postracial Puritan Allegory," *African American Review* 47.2–3 (2014): 286.

93. On the ambivalences that attend this realization among artists of the 1960s and afterwards, see Michael North, *Novelty: A History of the New* (Chicago: University of Chicago Press, 2013), 172–201.

94. See Lauren Berlant, *Cruel Optimism* (Durham: Duke University Press, 2011).

95. Cohn, "Old Afflictions," 17.

96. Gates, *Signifying*, 6.

97. Li, *Signifying*, 69; Murray, "Not Being," 727.

98. Morrison, *Beloved*, epigraph.

99. Nature, as we have seen in the passage about the nomenclature's interior territory, is markedly inorganic in *Apex*, but this does not diminish its marketing power. "*Nature* was a strong brand name," notes the protagonist. "Slap *Nature* on a package, you were golden" (153). Similarly, skepticism about sincerity doesn't prevent its

exploitation for capitalist ends, as when we read about "that contemporary brand of establishment, the kind that dressed itself in rustic sincerity but adhered to the rapacious philosophy of the multinational" (39).

100. Barack Obama, *Dreams from My Father: A Story of Race and Inheritance* (Edinburgh: Canongate, 2008), 294.

101. Quoted in Anna Laffrey, "Obama Remembers Toni Morrison as a 'National Treasure,'" *CNN* (6 August 2009), https://edition.cnn.com/2019/08/06/politics/barack-obama-remembers-toni-morrison/index.html. The admiration was mutual: in her letter endorsing Obama for the 2008 Democratic nomination, Morrison praised his "creative imagination which coupled with brilliance equals wisdom," and described him as "someone with courage instead of mere ambition." Tom McGeveran, "Toni Morrison's Letter to Barack Obama," *Observer* (28 January 2008), https://observer.com/2008/01/toni-morrisons-letter-to-barack-obama/

102. Zadie Smith, *Changing My Mind: Occasional Essays* (London: Hamish Hamilton, 2009), 142. Further references in parentheses.

103. Lee Konstantinou, "Barack Obama's Postironic Bildungsroman," in *Barack Obama's Literary Legacy: Readings of* Dreams from My Father, ed. Richard Purcell and Henry Veggian (New York: Palgrave, 2016), 126.

104. Ibid., 133.

105. Ibid., 122.

106. Adolph Reed, Jr. *Class Notes: Posing as Politics and Other Thoughts on the American Scene* (New York: New Press, 2000), 13.

107. Reed, *Toward*, 49.

108. Ibid., 141.

109. Smith, *Changing*, 137. Smith offers this moral as a critique of Polonius's advice to Laertes to be true to one's singular self (and thus as an implicit critique of Lionel Trilling's conception of sincerity, which centers Polonius's speech). Oddly, later in the essay Smith seems to suggest that underneath his multi-voicedness, Obama is *really* black, with his sincerity becoming more palpable to Smith when she sees him "let down his guard a little" by emitting a "culturally, casually black construction" on the television show *60 Minutes*. Ibid., 139–140.

110. Reed, *Toward*, 145.

111. Keeanga-Yamahtta Taylor, *From #BlackLivesMatter to Black Liberation* (Chicago: Haymarket, 2016), 15. Further references in parentheses.

112. Henry Louis Gates, Jr., "Introduction," in Steven J. Niven, *Barack Obama: A Pocket Biography of our 44th President* (Oxford: Oxford University Press), 2.

113. Li, *Signifying*, 99.

114. Whitehead made this skepticism evident in a tongue-in-cheek editorial published on the first anniversary of Obama's election, in which he describes racism as a "branding problem." "One year ago today, we officially became a postracial society," the piece begins. "Fifty-three percent of the voters opted for the candidate who would be the first president of African descent, and in doing so eradicated racism forever."

Colson Whitehead, "The Year of Living Postracially," *New York Times* (3 November 2009), https://www.nytimes.com/2009/11/04/opinion/04whitehead.html

115. Konstantinou, "Barack," 128.

116. Ibid.

117. Ibid., 130; Lee Konstantinou, "Four Faces of Postirony," in *Metamodernism: Historicity, Affect and Depth After Postmodernism*, ed. Robin van den Akker, Alison Gibbons, and Timotheus Vermeulen (London: Rowman & Littlefield, 2017), 96.

118. Maus, *Conversations*, 58.

119. Konstantinou, "Barack," 127.

120. See Henry Giroux, "Reading Hurricane Katrina: Race, Class, and the Biopolitics of Disposability," *College Literature* 33.3 (2006): 171–196.

121. Franco Moretti's *The Way of the World: The Bildungsroman in European Culture* (London: Verso, 1987) is the canonical statement of this argument. I will return to the genre of the Bildungsroman in Chapter Six.

Chapter Five

1. Helen DeWitt, *Lightning Rods* (New York: New Directions, 2011), 23. Further references in parentheses.

2. I intend a contrast here with James C. Scott's influential book *Seeing Like a State* (New Haven: Yale University Press, 1998).

3. Mark McGurl, *The Program Era: Postwar Fiction and the Rise of Creative Writing* (Cambridge, MA: Harvard University Press, 2009), 285. "We blush when we are unable to answer the teacher's question, and blushing embarrasses us further," McGurl explains. "We try to act cool in the cafeteria and, doing so self-consciously, act goofy." Ibid.

4. Ibid., 284.

5. Pamela Fox, *Class Fictions: Shame and Resistance in the British Working-Class Novel, 1890–1945* (Durham: Duke University Press, 1994), 13.

6. McGurl, *Program*, 64.

7. Ibid., 67.

8. Ibid., 294.

9. George Saunders, *Pastoralia* (London: Bloomsbury, 2000), 1. Further references in parentheses.

10. David Huebert, "Biopolitical Dystopias, Bureaucratic Carnivores, Synthetic Primitives: 'Pastoralia' as Human Zoo," in *George Saunders: Critical Essays*, ed. Philip Coleman and Steve Gronert Ellerhoff (Basingstoke: Palgrave, 2017), 106. The ban on speaking English in the cave is another way in which sincerity is discouraged: the narrator must communicate to Janet and the customers only through grunts and actions. While the narrator sticks rigidly to this alienating proscription, Janet does not, meaning that she "occupies the position of Foucauldian madman in the oppressive linguistic system of the theme park." Clare Hayes-Brady, "Horning In: Language, Subordination and Freedom in the Short Fiction of George Saunders," in *George Saunders: Critical Essays*, 29.

11. Louis Althusser, *Lenin and Philosophy and Other Essays*, trans. Ben Brewster (New York: Monthly Review Press, 2001), 109.

12. Guy Standing, *The Precariat: The New Dangerous Class* (London: Bloomsbury, 2011).

13. Kathleen M. Millar, "Toward a Critical Politics of Precarity," *Sociology Compass* 11.6 (2017): 2.

14. See Lauren Berlant, *Cruel Optimism* (Durham: Duke University Press, 2011); Isabel Lorey, *State of Insecurity: Government of the Precarious* (London: Verso, 2015).

15. Wendy Brown, *Undoing the Demos: Neoliberalism's Stealth Revolution* (New York: Zone Books, 2015), 84.

16. Michel Feher, "Self-Appreciation; or, the Aspirations of Human Capital," *Public Culture* 21.1 (2009): 34.

17. Ibid., 26.

18. William Callison, "Movements of Counter-Speculation: A Conversation with Michel Feher," *Los Angeles Review of Books* (12 July 2019), https://lareviewofbooks.org/article/movements-of-counter-speculation-a-conversation-with-michel-feher/

19. Feher, "Self-Appreciation," 32.

20. Michel Foucault, *The Birth of Biopolitics: Lectures at the Collège de France, 1978–79*, ed. Michel Senellart, trans. Graham Burchell (Basingstoke: Palgrave, 2008), 77–191.

21. Brown, *Undoing*, 38. See also Philip Mirowski's claim that "human capital obliterates labor" and that "once a neoliberal worldview takes hold, it ruthlessly empties all Marxist categories of their cogency, and it literally becomes impossible to think like a Marxist." Mirowski, "Hell Is Truth Seen Too Late," *boundary 2* 46:1 (2019): 14, 13. These claims that labor/class "disappears as a category" under neoliberalism have been controversial among critics on the Left who want to hold to a more classically Marxist vision under neoliberal conditions. For a sharp critique of the scholarship on neoliberal subjectivity, which sees it as no more than a projection of the worldview of a declining professional managerial class, see Annie McClanahan, "Serious Crises: Rethinking the Neoliberal Subject," *boundary 2* 46.1 (2019): 103–132.

22. Jane Elliott, "Suffering Agency: Imagining Neoliberal Personhood in North America and Britain," *Social Text* 31.2 (2013): 84.

23. "The social entity designated by the term 'lower middle class,'" McGurl writes, "is bereft of class consciousness in the sense of communal solidarity, but constitutively possessed of and by 'class awareness'—the measurement of oneself and one's social surround in terms of various markers of status." McGurl, *Program*, 65. The "Pastoralia" narrator, constrained by his terrible working conditions, demonstrates neither class consciousness nor class awareness. Another character in the story, however—Marty, who runs the theme park's shop for employees—demonstrates a comically hyperbolic level of class awareness in the advice he gives to his son about interacting with "big-wigs" at his boarding school (12). Interestingly, when cutting down "Pastoralia" for publication in *The New Yorker*, Saunders excised the sections involving Marty, suggesting their peripheral quality set next to the narrator's story.

24. David P. Rando, "George Saunders and the Postmodern Working Class," *Contemporary Literature* 53.3 (2012): 456.

25. Ibid., 456–457.

26. Ibid., 437.

27. George Saunders, *The Braindead Megaphone: Essays* (New York: Riverhead Books, 2007), 10. Further references in parentheses.

28. Saunders offers a particularly amplified version of what Hannah Sullivan identifies as a widespread belief among contemporary writers that "heavy and intensive revision has become an indicator of authorial integrity and the difficulty and seriousness of the revised artwork." Sullivan traces the origins of this belief to literary modernism, which "had to overcome the nineteenth-century preference for writing that was, or at least seemed to be, spontaneous." Hannah Sullivan, *The Work of Revision* (Cambridge, MA: Harvard University Press, 2013), 2, 3.

29. Kasia Boddy, for instance, traces direct connections between two Carver and two Saunders stories. Boddy, "'A Job to Do': George Saunders on, and at, Work," in *George Saunders: Critical Essays*, 7–8.

30. McGurl, *Program*, 403.

31. "I'd always loved Hemingway and all through grad school had been doing some version of a Hemingway imitation. If I got tired of that, I did a Carver imitation, then a Babel imitation. Sometimes I did Babel, if Babel had lived in Texas. Sometimes I did Carver, if Carver had worked (as I had) in the oil fields of Sumatra. Sometimes I did Hemingway, if Hemingway had lived in Syracuse, which always ended up sounding, to me, like Carver." George Saunders, "*CivilWarLand in Bad Decline*: Preface," *Paris Review* blog (7 January 2013), https://www.theparisreview.org/blog/2013/01/07/civilwarland-in-bad-decline-preface/

32. Saunders, *Braindead*, 176.

33. Tim Groenland observes that Carver "highlighted his habits of meticulous revision, noting that while his first drafts constituted the 'scaffolding' of a story, 'the real work comes later, after I've done three or four drafts.'" Groenland, *The Art of Editing: Raymond Carver and David Foster Wallace* (London: Bloomsbury, 2019), 94.

34. "About," *George Saunders* (n.d.), https://georgesaundersbooks.com/about-george-saunders

35. Ibid. Saunders repeats this quotation from Eagleton in his *CivilWarLand* preface, op. cit., and discussed below.

36. McGurl, *Program*, 375–376.

37. Ibid., 295, 377.

38. Saunders, "*CivilWarLand*." Further citations in this paragraph are from this source.

39. The following pages develop the reading of "The Falls" first published in Adam Kelly, "Language Between Lyricism and Corporatism: George Saunders's New Sincerity," in *George Saunders: Critical Essays*, 41–58. Reproduced with the permission of Palgrave Macmillan.

40. Modernist subjectivity has most often been conceived in terms of anxiety rather than confidence. Nevertheless, this is an anxiety linked to the presumed depth and unique interiority of the subject, very different to the anxious subject of literary New Sincerity, whose interiority is threatened by generic cultural narratives and evacuated of singular self-expression. Fredric Jameson's discussion of Munch's *The Scream*—"a canonical expression of the great modernist thematics of alienation, anomie, solitude, social fragmentation, and isolation, a virtually programmatic emblem of what used to be called the age of anxiety"—remains a touchstone for describing the earlier mode of being and expression. Jameson, *Postmodernism, or, The Cultural Logic of Late Capitalism* (London: Verso, 1991), 11.

41. The allegory of an author wanting to save his own two girls from "falling" into a lower-class stratum (having, in this case, tragically failed to "miss the boat") is hard to miss, once one knows the background to the story's creation.

42. As Pamela Fox shows, Lynd's original theorization of shame stems from her reading of the class dynamics of nineteenth-century England, where Lynd saw the overcoming of shame as crucial for moving beyond *both* the individualist mantras of the liberal bourgeoisie *and* the collectivist rigidities of the working class. The failure of this project can leave one feeling marooned with a lower-middle-class identity, an identity of which, as McGurl observes, "nobody is proud." Fox, *Class*, 14–17; McGurl, *Program*, 65.

43. Joseph Schumpeter, *Imperialism and Social Classes: Two Essays* (Cleveland: Meridian Books, 1955), 118–119. As a critique this is not very convincing, given that Marx's treatment of the standpoint of individual capitalists is very much subordinate to his claims about how the capitalist system *as a whole* renews itself through the extraction and reinvestment of surplus value. From the standpoint of the system, it scarcely matters which capitalist is winning and which is losing. But one can certainly see why, for those who want to reaffirm the capitalist as a heroic figure, Schumpeter's reassertion of a place for individual agency within a systemic understanding of capitalism has proven attractive.

44. Corey Robin, *The Reactionary Mind: Conservatism from Edmund Burke to Donald Trump*, 2nd ed. (Oxford: Oxford University Press, 2018), 154.

45. Schumpeter, *Imperialism*, 120.

46. Ibid., 122, 123.

47. Ibid., 121, 123.

48. Ibid., 123, 121.

49. Joseph Schumpeter, *Capitalism, Socialism and Democracy* (London: Taylor & Francis, 2013), 138.

50. Ibid., 132.

51. DeWitt, *Lightning Rods*, 11, 146. Further references in parentheses.

52. Sianne Ngai, "Theory of the Gimmick," *Critical Inquiry* 43 (2017): 497.

53. Ibid.

54. Brown, *Undoing*, 9.

55. David Flusfeder, "Introduction," in Helen DeWitt, *Lightning Rods* (High Wycombe: And Other Stories, 2012), ix.

56. Ngai, "Theory," 502, 503.

57. Dieter Plehwe, "Schumpeter Revival? How Neoliberals Revised the Image of the Entrepreneur," *Nine Lives of Neoliberalism*, ed. Dieter Plehwe, Quinn Slobodian, and Philip Mirowski (London: Verso, 2020), 125.

58. Herbert Giersch, "The Role of Entrepreneurship in the 1980s," *Kiel Discussion Papers* 88 (1982): 5.

59. Jasper Bernes, "Character, Genre, Labor: The Office Novel After Deindustrialization," *Post45* (10 January 2019), http://post45.org/2019/01/character-genre-labor-the-office-novel-after-deindustrialization/

60. McGurl, *Program*, 685.

61. Ngai, "Theory," 504.

62. Mark Fisher, *Capitalist Realism: Is There No Alternative?* (Winchester: O Books, 2009), 8.

63. Arthur Miller, *Death of a Salesman* (London: Penguin, 2000), 77.

64. Ibid.

65. See Helge Normann Nilsen, "From *Honors at Dawn* to *Death of a Salesman*: Marxism and the Early Plays of Arthur Miller," *English Studies* 75 (1994): 146–156.

66. Miller, *Death*, 111.

67. Bernes, "Character."

68. Lee Konstantinou, "Hurricane Helen," *Los Angeles Review of Books* (21 November 2011), https://lareviewofbooks.org/article/hurricane-helen

69. Flusfeder calls *Lightning Rods* "a very American comedy, finding a sort of wonder in the way that American can-do Protestantism manages to overcome any shame or inhibition to produce and market a commodity." "Introduction," ix.

70. Miller, *Death*, 111.

71. Bernes, "Character."

72. Morten Høi Jensen, "Bookforum Talks to Helen DeWitt," *Bookforum* (22 September 2011), https://www.bookforum.com/interviews/-8389

73. Ibid.

74. Helen DeWitt, "Oblivion," *Paperpools* blog post (15 September 2008), http://paperpools.blogspot.com/2008/09/oblivion.html

75. David Foster Wallace, "'Plain Old Untrendy Troubles and Emotions,'" *Guardian* (20 September 2008), https://www.theguardian.com/books/2008/sep/20/fiction; further citations in this paragraph are from this source.

76. Helen DeWitt, "Iterated Polarisation Games," *Paperpools* blog post (21 September 2008), http://paperpools.blogspot.com/2008/09/iterated-polarisation-games.html; further citations in this paragraph are from this source.

77. Christian Lorentzen, "Publishing *Can Break Your Heart*," *Vulture* (*New York*) (11 July 2016), https://www.vulture.com/2016/07/helen-dewitt-last-samurai-new-edition.html

78. Helen DeWitt, "Laugh and the World Laughs with You . . . ," *Paperpools* blog post (2 March 2013), http://paperpools.blogspot.com/2013/03/laugh-and-world-laughs-with-you.html

79. "What he didn't realize is that a genius is different from other people," Joe thinks early in *Lightning Rods*. "A genius doesn't waste time like other people. . . . In fact the only time a genius wastes time is when he tries to follow the rules and act like ordinary people" (10). While this reads as satirical in context, DeWitt has elsewhere commented that "if you want to write a work of genius it is necessary to take risks. He said: Your sanity is more important than writing a work of genius. I thought: Nobody who thinks that will ever write a work of genius." Lee Konstantinou, "It's Good to Be Pragmatic: An Interview with Helen DeWitt," *Los Angeles Review of Books* (21 November 2011), https://lareviewofbooks.org/article/its-good-to-be-pragmatic-an-interview-with-helen-dewitt/

80. Helen DeWitt, *Some Trick: Thirteen Stories* (New York: New Directions, 2018), 25.

81. Ibid., 25–26.

82. Peter Bernstein, *Against the Gods: The Remarkable Story of Risk* (Hoboken: John Wiley, 1996), 1.

83. Ibid., 2.

84. Ibid., 3.

85. George Saunders, "'What I Regret Most in My Life Are Failures of Kindness,'" *Ladders* (20 May 2018), https://www.theladders.com/career-advice/george-saunders-to-syracuses-class-of-2013-accomplishment-is-unreliable

86. Ibid.

87. Boddy, "'A Job,'" 8.

88. Matthew Derby, "Between the Poles of Biting and Earnest: An Interview with George Saunders," *Columbia* 35 (2001): 88.

89. Ibid., 92.

90. Ibid., 89.

91. Boddy, "'A Job,'" 10.

92. Saunders, *Braindead*, 13.

93. "George Saunders: Tenth of December, Part Two," *KCRW Bookworm* (February 21, 2013), http://www.kcrw.com/news-culture/shows/bookworm/george-saunders-tenth-of-december-part-two

94. Ibid.

95. Ibid.

96. Boddy, "'A Job,'" 10–11.

97. As Saunders himself observes, "your stories can end up being smarter than you are, which, in my case, is a tremendous benefit." Derby, "Between," 90.

98. Daniel Hartley, "Style as Structure of Feeling: Emergent Forms of Life in the Theory of Raymond Williams and George Saunders' *Tenth of December*," in *Emergent Forms of Life in Anglophone Literature: Conceptual Frameworks and Critical Analyses*,

ed. Michael Basseler, Daniel Hartley, Ansgar Nünning, and Elizabeth Kovach (Trier: Wissenschaftlicher Verlag Trier, 2015), 171–172.

99. Ibid., 175.

100. Ibid., 180.

101. George Saunders, "Informal Remarks from the David Foster Wallace Memorial Service in New York on October 23, 2008," in *The Legacy of David Foster Wallace*, ed. Samuel Cohen and Lee Konstantinou (Iowa City: University of Iowa Press, 2012), 53.

102. Jurrit Daalder, "Cruel Inventions: George Saunders's Literary Darkenfloxx™," in *George Saunders: Critical Essays*, 175. Further references in parentheses.

103. Boddy, "'A Job,'" 8.

104. David Foster Wallace, *Oblivion* (London: Abacus, 2004), 282.

105. Zadie Smith, "Introduction," in *The Burned Children of America*, ed. Marco Cassini and Martina Testa (London: Hamish Hamilton, 2003), xx.

Chapter Six

1. *n+1* 19 (Spring 2014), cover, table of contents; Jedediah Purdy, "The Accidental Neoliberal: Against the Old Sincerity," *n+1* 19 (Spring 2014), https://nplusonemag.com/issue-19/politics/the-accidental-neoliberal/; Jedediah Purdy, "Politics: Memorandum: The Accidental Neoliberal," *n+1* 19 (Spring 2014): 15. Further references in parentheses will be to the print essay.

2. For considerations of these works as expressions of New Sincerity, see, respectively: Warren Buckland, "Wes Anderson: A 'Smart' Director of the New Sincerity?" *New Review of Film and Television Studies* 10.1 (2012): 1–5; Nate Jones, "I'm Terrified to Rewatch *Eternal Sunshine of the Spotless Mind*," *Vulture* (*New York*) (19 August 2020), https://www.vulture.com/2020/08/eternal-sunshine-is-a-perfect-00s-time-capsule.html; Peter Schulte, "How the New Sincerity Can Make Caring Cool Again," *Kindling* (27 September 2020), https://kindling.xyz/futures/new-sincerity/; Jonathan D. Fitzgerald, "Sincerity, Not Irony, Is Our Age's Ethos," *Atlantic* (20 November 2012), https://www.theatlantic.com/entertainment/archive/2012/11/sincerity-not-irony-is-our-ages-ethos/265466/; Siân Adiseshiah, "Spectatorship and the New (Critical) Sincerity: The Case of Forced Entertainment's *Tomorrow's Parties*," *Journal of Contemporary Drama in English* 4.1 (2016): 180–195; Alena Smith, *The New Sincerity* (New York: Dramatists Play, 2015); A. D. Jameson, "What We Talk About When We Talk About the New Sincerity, Part 1," *HtmlGiant* (4 June 2012), http://htmlgiant.com/haut-or-not/what-we-talk-about-when-we-talk-about-the-new-sincerity/; Kelefa Sanneh, "Mr. Sincerity Tries a New Trick," *New York Times* (16 January 2005), https://www.nytimes.com/2005/01/16/arts/music/mr-sincerity-tries-a-new-trick.html; R. Jay Magill, Jr., *Sincerity* (New York: Norton, 2012), 206.

3. Lucas Thompson, "*Nathan for You* and the New Sincerity Aesthetic," *New Review of Film and Television Studies* 18.4 (2020): 433.

4. See, for instance: Coover, *The Public Burning* (1977); DeLillo, *Great Jones Street* (1973); Didion, *Democracy* (1984); Doctorow, *The Book of Daniel* (1971); Gaines, *The*

Autobiography of Miss Jane Pittman (1971); Morrison, *Paradise* (1997); Oates, *Black Girl/White Girl* (2006); Piercy, *Vida* (1980); Pynchon, *Inherent Vice* (2009); Reed, *The Last Days of Louisiana Red* (1974); Roth, *American Pastoral* (1997).

5. F. A. Hayek, *The Road to Serfdom: Text and Documents: The Definitive Edition*, ed. Bruce Caldwell (Chicago: University of Chicago Press, 2007), 216–217.

6. Mark West, "The Contemporary Sixties Novel: Post-Postmodernism and Historiographic Metafiction," in *21st-Century US Historical Fiction: Contemporary Responses to the Past*, ed. Ruth Maxey (London: Palgrave, 2020), 210. West offers a useful list of novels about the radical years across recent decades. Ibid., 225.

7. Jonathan Lethem, *The Fortress of Solitude* (London: Faber, 2004).

8. Dana Spiotta, *Eat the Document* (New York: Scribner, 2007), 274.

9. Thomas Frank, *The Conquest of Cool: Business Culture, Counterculture, and the Rise of Hip Consumerism* (Chicago: University of Chicago Press, 1997).

10. Richard Barbrook and Andy Cameron, "The Californian Ideology," *Science as Culture* 6.1 (1996): 44–72. See also Fred Turner, *From Counterculture to Cyberculture: Stewart Brand, the Whole Earth Network, and the Rise of Digital Utopianism* (Chicago: University of Chicago Press, 2006).

11. Luc Boltanski and Ève Chiapello, *The New Spirit of Capitalism*, trans. Gregory Elliott (London: Verso, 2018), 38–39.

12. David Harvey, *A Brief History of Neoliberalism* (Oxford: Oxford University Press, 2005), 41.

13. Walter Benn Michaels, *The Shape of the Signifier: 1967 to the End of History* (Princeton: Princeton University Press, 2004); Sean McCann and Michael Szalay, "Do You Believe in Magic? Literary Thinking After the New Left," *Yale Journal of Criticism* 18.2 (2005): 435–468.

14. Studies in this revisionist vein include: Michael W. Clune, *American Literature and the Free Market, 1945–2000* (Cambridge: Cambridge University Press, 2010); Nicholas Donofrio, "Multiculturalism, Inc.: Regulating and Deregulating the Culture Industries with Ishmael Reed," *American Literary History* 29.1 (2017): 100–128; Lee Konstantinou, *Cool Characters: Irony and American Fiction* (Cambridge, MA: Harvard University Press, 2016), especially chapter 3; Bryan M. Santin, *Postwar American Fiction and the Rise of Modern Conservatism* (Cambridge: Cambridge University Press, 2021); Casey Shoop, "Thomas Pynchon, Postmodernism, and the Rise of the New Right in California," *Contemporary Literature* 53.1 (2012): 51–86; Daniel Worden, *Neoliberal Nonfictions: The Documentary Aesthetic from Joan Didion to Jay-Z* (Charlottesville: University of Virginia Press, 2020).

15. See Michel Feher, "Self-Appreciation, or, the Aspirations of Human Capital," trans. Ivan Ascher, *Public Culture* 21.2 (2009): 21–41; Nancy Fraser, "Feminism, Capitalism and the Cunning of History," *New Left Review* 56 (2009): 97–117; Philip Mirowski and Dieter Plehwe, eds., *The Road from Mont Pelerin: The Making of the Neoliberal Thought Collective* (Cambridge, MA: Harvard University Press, 2009); Slavoj Žižek, *First as Tragedy, Then as Farce* (London: Verso, 2009).

16. David Hancock, *The Countercultural Logic of Neoliberalism* (London: Routledge, 2019); Mitchell Dean and Daniel Zamora, *The Last Man Takes LSD: Foucault and the End of the Revolution* (London: Verso, 2021).

17. Mitchum Huehls and Rachel Greenwald Smith, "Four Phases of Neoliberalism and Literature: An Introduction," in *Neoliberalism and Contemporary Literary Culture*, ed. Mitchum Huehls and Rachel Greenwald Smith (Baltimore: Johns Hopkins University Press, 2017), 9. See also Mitchum Huehls, *After Critique: Twenty-First-Century Fiction in a Neoliberal Age* (Oxford: Oxford University Press, 2016).

18. Two recent accounts of the Hearst episode that differ markedly in their conclusions on these questions are Jeffrey Toobin, *American Heiress: The Wild Saga of the Kidnapping, Crimes and Trial of Patty Hearst* (New York: Doubleday, 2016), and Brad Schreiber, *Revolution's End: The Patty Hearst Kidnapping, Mind Control, and the Secret History of Donald DeFreeze and the SLA* (New York: Skyhorse, 2016). Hearst's own (ghostwritten) account can be found in Patricia Campbell Hearst, with Alvin Moscow, *Every Secret Thing* (New York: Doubleday, 1981).

19. Margaret Scanlan, who identifies real-life analogues for most of Choi's characters, notes that Wendy Yoshimura was using the name "Joan Shimata" when she met Hearst. Margaret Scanlan, "Domestic Terror: 1970s Radicalism in Philip Roth's *American Pastoral* and Susan Choi's *American Woman*," *Journal of European Studies* 40.3 (2010): 269. For a detailed account of Yoshimura's story, see Grace I. Yeh, "Wendy Yoshimura and the Politics of Hugging in the 1970s," *Journal of Asian American Studies* 13.2 (2010): 191–218.

20. Susan Choi, *American Woman* (New York: HarperCollins, 2003), 67. Further references in parentheses.

21. Deborah Koto Katz, "Listen to Your Body: Ugly Feelings and the Post-Political Japanese Subject of Susan Choi's *American Woman*," *Lit: Literature Interpretation Theory* 23.4 (2012): 326.

22. It is worth noting that the year in which Jenny and Pauline live together and develop their feminism is an invention of Choi's. In reality, Patty Hearst and Wendy Yoshimura moved into their San Francisco apartment on September 9, 1975, and were arrested nine days later. Scanlan, "Domestic," 265.

23. Patricia E. Chu, "The Trials of the Ethnic Novel: Susan Choi's *American Woman* and the Post-Affirmative Action Era," *American Literary History* 23.3 (2011): 543.

24. Purdy, "Accidental," 15.

25. On the profound connections between US settler colonialism and US imperialist wars abroad, see Aziz Rana, *The Two Faces of American Freedom* (Cambridge, MA: Harvard University Press, 2014); and Nikhil Pal Singh, *Race and America's Long War* (Berkeley: University of California Press, 2019).

26. Colleen Lye offers the following summary: "Much of what has gone on in the name of Asian American politics outside the academy has continued to be defined by national civil rights objectives: equality of protection under the law, in the workplace and on the street. After the ebbing of the Asian American movement, the 1980s and

1990s saw the growth of Asian American organizations at the national level and in regions beyond the West Coast, spurred by the phenomena of the glass ceiling and anti-Asian violence." Colleen Lye, "The Literary Case of Wen Ho Lee," *Journal of Asian American Studies* 14.2 (2011): 249.

27. Yeh, "Wendy Yoshimura," 198.

28. Carolyn Chen, "Asians: Too Smart for Their Own Good?" *New York Times* (19 December 2012), https://www.nytimes.com/2012/12/20/opinion/asians-too-smart-for-their-own-good.html

29. Chu, "Trials," 540.

30. Alongside its realism, what one critic calls "its almost obsessive focus on space" may partly account for the novel's unwillingness to gesture forward in time. Penny Vlagopolous, "The Beginning of History and Politics: Susan Choi's *American Woman* and the Shadow of U.S. Imperialism," *Studies in American Fiction* 37.1 (2010): 129. As part of this focus on space, the prominence *American Woman* grants to the natural environment means that it could be said to voice "an ecological politics"—to cite the third arm of Purdy's "politics of structure"—in ways I have not had room to explore here.

31. Introducing Anne researching in the "Mid-Manhattan Library" (313), Choi recalls the site of Daniel Isaacson's narration in the first major American novel about New Left radicalism: Doctorow's *The Book of Daniel* (1971).

32. For an account of the experimentalism of Choi's fifth novel, *Trust Exercise* (2019), as well its resistance to categorization as an Asian American text, see Ellen Song, "Trust Exercise: The Form of Race in the American Post-Identity Novel," *American Literary History* 35.2 (2023): 795–817.

33. This section, and the next, draw on a previously published chapter: Adam Kelly, "'Who Is Responsible?' Revisiting the Radical Years in Dana Spiotta's *Eat the Document*," in *"Forever Young"? The Changing Images of America*, ed. Philip Coleman and Stephen Matterson (Heidelberg: Universitätsverlag Winter, 2012), 219–230.

34. Spiotta, *Eat*, 4. Further references in parentheses.

35. Nash is revealed late in the novel to be the present incarnation of Bobby Desoto, Mary's boyfriend and fellow member of the SAFE collective in the 1970s, though the reader may have guessed the connection earlier on.

36. The name alludes to nepenthe, the drug of forgetfulness given to Helen by the Egyptian queen Polidamma in the fourth book of Homer's *Odyssey*.

37. In an influential study, Brooks identified this temporality—in which the present is experienced in view of its future as a remembered past—"as our chief tool in making sense of narrative, the master trope of its strange logic." Peter Brooks, *Reading for the Plot: Design and Intention in Narrative* (Cambridge, MA: Harvard University Press, 1984), 23.

38. Moreover, with archive fever—a concept Currie borrows from Jacques Derrida—"the cause-and-effect sequence of an event and its recording as news is reversed in a highly developed media capitalist society: the event is recorded not because

it happens, but it happens because it is recorded." Mark Currie, *About Time: Narrative, Fiction and the Philosophy of Time* (Edinburgh: Edinburgh University Press, 2007), 11. This again recalls Egan's *Invisible Circus*, in which events and experiences in the 1960s are inextricably intertwined with, and shaped by, their own mediation.

39. David Hering, "Play It Again: Reading the Contemporary Through Music in Jennifer Egan's *A Visit from the Goon Squad* and Dana Spiotta's *Eat the Document*," *Contemporary Women's Writing* 15.2 (2021): 244–259.

40. The most famous proof of this idea in analytic philosophy is found in Kavka's toxin puzzle. An individual is offered a large financial reward, payable tomorrow morning, if they intend today to drink a toxin tomorrow afternoon, a toxin that will make them painfully sick for a day but will not threaten their life. The conundrum is that, once the money has been paid, there is no longer any incentive to drink the toxin, and so the question is whether, given this foreknowledge, one can genuinely *intend* to drink it. This difficulty of separating intentions and actions led Donald Davidson (before Kavka) to form his famous "syncategorematic" account, which states that "intention" looks like a noun but does not conform to the functions of a noun: "The expression 'the intention with which James went to church' has the outward form of a description, but in fact is syncategorematic and cannot be taken to refer to an entity, state, disposition, or event." Donald Davidson, *Essays on Actions and Events* (Oxford: Oxford University Press, 2001), 8.

41. Liza Johnson, "An Interview with Dana Spiotta," *The Believer* 39 (1 November 2006), https://www.thebeliever.net/an-interview-with-dana-spiotta/

42. In Chapter One I framed a similar insight in more Hegelian terms, whereby "the intention is only 'realized' as the intention it determinately is *in* the deed or in the work, *as* that deed or work counts as this or that *to* a community at a time." Robert B. Pippin, *After the Beautiful: Hegel and the Philosophy of Pictorial Modernism* (Chicago: University of Chicago Press, 2014), 20. As we saw then, and as also bears upon *Eat the Document*, a Hegelian framing grants a special status to the artwork as the model for what a realized intention looks like, "as the achievement of a speculative identity of inner and outer." Ibid., 21.

43. Purdy, "Accidental," 16.

44. Kurt Cavender, "Autocritique in the Contemporary Weather Underground Novel," *Post45* (8 February 2017), n.p. Spiotta has regularly cited Wallace as one of her favorite authors. See, e.g., Angela Meyer, "Dana Spiotta—Interview" (6 July 2008), https://literaryminded.com.au/2008/07/06/dana-spiotta-interview/

45. The difference, of course, is that Wallace wants to resist this situation whereas Josh, as Miranda observes, "revel[s] in it" (258). Notably, Josh also genders the turn to sincerity that Miranda embodies: "So that leaves the earnest stance you love to use—so tedious, so . . . shrill and feminine" (259).

46. Aaron Colton, "Dana Spiotta and the Novel After Authenticity," *Arizona Quarterly* 75.4 (2019): 32.

47. Aliki Varvogli, "Radical Motherhood: Narcissism and Empathy in Russell Banks's *The Darling* and Dana Spiotta's *Eat the Document*," *Journal of American Studies* 44.4 (2010): 660; Cavender, "Autocritique."

48. Varvogli, "Radical," 660.

49. Hering, "Play," 4.

50. Michael Szalay, "The Incorporation Artist," *Los Angeles Review of Books* (10 July 2012), https://lareviewofbooks.org/article/the-incorporation-artist/

51. Pieter Vermeulen, *Contemporary Literature and the End of the Novel: Creature, Affect, Form* (New York: Palgrave, 2015), 18.

52. Cavender, "Autocritique."

53. Ibid.

54. Hering, "Play," 20.

55. David Foster Wallace, *A Supposedly Fun Thing I'll Never Do Again* (London: Abacus, 1997), 67.

56. West, "Contemporary," 217.

57. Choi, *American*, 295–296.

58. This section, and the next, draw on a previously published chapter: Adam Kelly, "From Syndrome to Sincerity: Benjamin Kunkel's Indecision," in *Diseases and Disorders in Contemporary Fiction: The Syndrome Syndrome*, ed. Timothy Lustig and James Peacock (London: Routledge, 2013), 53–66.

59. Benjamin Kunkel, *Indecision* (New York: Random House, 2005), 64. Further references in parentheses.

60. Lionel Trilling, *Sincerity and Authenticity* (Oxford: Oxford University Press, 1972), 26.

61. Ibid., 11.

62. Franco Moretti, *The Way of the World: The Bildungsroman in European Culture*, 2nd ed. (London: Verso, 2000), 4, 5.

63. Ibid., 15.

64. Jay McInerney, "*Indecision:* Getting It Together," *New York Times* (28 August 2005), http://www.nytimes.com/2005/08/28/books/review/28MCINER.html

65. Joyce Carol Oates, "Dangling Men," *New York Review of Books* 52.17 (3 November 2005): 40.

66. Michael Agger, "Wilmerding Shrugged: The Political Ambitions of Benjamin Kunkel's *Indecision*," *Slate* (3 October 2005), http://www.slate.com/id/2127382

67. Scott Tobias, "*Indecision*," *A. V. Club* (October 2005), http://www.avclub.com/articles/benjamin-kunkel-indecision,4276

68. Kenneth Millard, *Coming of Age in Contemporary American Fiction* (Edinburgh: Edinburgh University Press, 2007), 5.

69. Given that Kunkel is Jewish American, his decision to render Dwight Wilmerding as almost fully WASP (his father is described in the novel as "half-Jewish") should be understood as a deliberate decision to draw a protagonist as close as possible to the American "norm," a norm reviewers implicitly affirmed rather than interrogated.

70. Benjamin Kunkel, "In the Sonora," *London Review of Books* 29.17 (6 September 2007), http://www.lrb.co.uk/v29/n17/benjamin-kunkel/in-the-sonora

71. Benjamin Kunkel, "Misery Loves a Memoir," *New York Times* (16 July 2006), http://www.nytimes.com/2006/07/16/books/review/16kunkel.html

72. A. O. Scott, "Among the Believers," *New York Times* (11 September 2005), http://www.nytimes.com/2005/09/11/magazine/11BELIEVERS.html

73. Like Spiotta, Kunkel has regularly stated his admiration for Wallace; in an obituary in *n+1* following the latter's suicide, he writes, "The temptation is to say: *Wallace changed my life.* For me it feels more accurate to say: *He helped make it possible.*" Benjamin Kunkel, "DFW 1962–2008," *n+1* (27 April 2011; originally published 16 September 2008), https://nplusonemag.com/online-only/online-only/dfw-1962-2008/

74. Purdy, "Accidental," 17. An editorial essay in *n+1*, likely co-written by Kunkel as the magazine's co-founder and senior editor at the time, puts the worry like this: "More and more the social purpose and, therefore, deep content of all culture has seemed one identical substance: the content is capital, and its purpose is to reproduce capitalism." The Editors, "Cultural Revolution," *n+1* 16 (2013): 13.

75. Benjamin Kunkel, "The Unreal World," *Village Voice* (13 February 2001), https://www.villagevoice.com/the-unreal-world/

76. Benjamin Kunkel, "Into the Big Tent," *London Review of Books* 32.8 (22 April 2010): 12, 16. In his 2014 essay collection *Utopia or Bust*, the Jameson essay is retitled "The Cultural Logic of Neoliberalism," indicating not only Kunkel's wish to replace a broadly cultural periodization of the post-1960s period with a more economic one, but also his view that while Jameson's work may be diagnostic of postmodernism, it is symptomatic of neoliberalism.

77. Emilio Sauri, "Mapping Postmodernism and After," *Postmodern, Postwar—and After: Rethinking American Literature*, ed. Jason Gladstone, Andrew Hoberek, and Daniel Worden (Iowa City: University of Iowa Press, 2016), 111–123.

78. Kunkel, "Into," 14.

79. See the essay by Kunkel's *n+1* co-founder, Marco Roth, "The Rise of the Neuronovel," *n+1* 8 (2009): 139–151.

80. Charles Baxter, "Against Epiphanies," *Burning Down the House: Essays on Fiction*, 2nd ed. (St. Paul: Graywolf Press, 2008), 41–62.

81. For critiques of the plausibility of Dwight's conversion, see Mark Lotto, "A Hero for Our Time," *Nation* (24 October 2005), http://www.thenation.com/article/hero-our-time; Michiko Kakutani, "Who's Afraid of Holden Caulfield?" *New York Times* (23 August 2005), http://www.nytimes.com/2005/08/23/books/23kaku.html; Agger, "Wilmerding."

82. That the relationship between selfhood and decision will be a central theme of the book is suggested as early as its title pages: on three of the flyleaves, the central "i" of the title is italicized—"Inde*c*ision." What is the "i" in the middle of this word, the typesetting seems to ask—what does it mean for the "I" to be "in-decision"?

83. "So that—or this—is the book I have now written.... I'm trying to complete the book by tomorrow" (235); "But I don't mean to bring you down as a reader.... Don't

imagine, though, that I have no wish to be a better and more erudite spokesman for things. I do!" (237)

84. Arthur Redding, "Darlings of the Weather Underground: Political Desire and Fictions of Radical Women," *Minnesota Review* 90 (2018): 81.

85. Fredric Jameson, "Third-World Literature in the Era of Multinational Capitalism," *Social Text* 15 (1986): 85.

86. Benjamin Kunkel, "Dangerous Characters," *New York Times* (11 September 2005), http://www.nytimes.com/2005/09/11/books/review/11kunkel.html

Conclusion

1. David Wallace-Wells, "How Benjamin Kunkel Went from Novelist to Marxist Public Intellectual," *Vulture (New York)* (11 March 2014), https://www.vulture.com/2014/03/benjamin-kunkel-marxist-novel-utopia-or-bust.html

2. Jacobin series, Verso Books, https://www.versobooks.com/collections/jacobin

3. Anon., "Austinist Interviews Benjamin Kunkel," *Austinist* (9 May 2006), http://austinist.com/2006/05/09/austinist_interviews_benjamin_kunkel.php (accessed 21 October 2019). The interview is no longer available at this link; readers may contact me for a copy of the text.

4. Francis Mulhern, "A Party of Latecomers," *New Left Review* 93 (2015): 70, 89.

5. Franco Moretti, *The Way of the World: The Bildungsroman in European Culture*, 2nd ed. (London: Verso, 2000), 5.

6. Mulhern, "Party," 89. Mulhern quotes founding editor Marco Roth's quip, "if I'm late to the party, I can start a party of latecomers," a remark that recalls Jennifer Egan's depiction in *The Invisible Circus* of Phoebe's lateness to the party of the 1960s. In the case of *n+1*, as Mulhern observes, the belatedness concerns not only the 1960s but the whole post-60s critical milieu of postmodernism, multiculturalism, and Theory.

7. The Editors, "Cultural Revolution," *n+1* 16 (2013): 13.

8. Ibid., 15.

9. In another of these magazines, *The Point*, Jon Baskin points out the irony of this revival in magazine writing arriving "after the end of history, after the end of long form, and after the end of print." Baskin, "Tired of Winning," *The Point* 16 (23 April 2018), https://thepointmag.com/politics/tired-of-winning/

10. Jedediah Purdy, "The Accidental Neoliberal," *n+1* 19 (Spring 2014): 22.

11. "Editorial Statement," *n+1* 1 (2004): 3; Keith Gessen, "Endnotes," *n+1* 1 (2004): 182.

12. Audrey Farley, "New Sincerity and the Legacy of Psychoanalysis: Benjamin Kunkel's *Indecision* (2005) and Heidi Julavits's *The Uses of Enchantment* (2006)," *Critique* 59.3 (2018): 280.

13. Ben Lerner, *10.04* (London: Granta, 2014), 2. Further references in parentheses.

14. Ben Lerner, *The Hatred of Poetry* (London: Fitzcarraldo, 2017), 17–18.

15. For a compelling reading of Lerner's poetics of virtuality, see Daniel Katz, "'I did not walk here all the way from prose': Ben Lerner's Virtual Poetics," *Textual Practice* 31.2 (2017): 315–337.

Index

absorption, 58–67, 69–70, 74–75, 311–12n34, 312n35, 312n45, 313n48, 317n15; reflective absorption, 76; refractive absorption 77, 82–83, 86
"Accidental Neoliberal, The" (Purdy), 247–49, 253–54, 264, 274, 282, 291–93, 348n30
Adkins, Lisa, 101
Adorno, Theodor W., 314n75
Aesthetics: Lectures on Fine Art (Hegel), 63, 65, 70, 312n45, 313n48
African American literature/art, 40, 169–74, 177, 181–82, 184–89, 198, 203–7. *See also* double consciousness, signifying
Against the Gods: The Remarkable Story of Risk (Bernstein), 241
Age of Amazon, 6, 36
age of fracture, 4–5
Altes, Liesbeth Korthals, 22
American Economic Association, 191
American Indian movement, 250
American Woman (Choi), 41–42, 250, 256–67, 268, 271, 276–78, 282, 289, 294, 347n19–348n32
Anderson, Amanda, 301n48; *The Way We Argue Now*, 15–16, 18

Anderson, Wes, 249
Andre, Carl, 66
anticipation of retrospection, 269–273, 277
Apex Hides the Hurt (Whitehead), 10, 33, 37, 40, 171, 173, 184–98, 201, 203, 204, 206–7, 246, 337–38n99
Arendt, Hannah, 194, 196
Armstrong, Nancy, 40; *Desire and Domestic Fiction*, 161
Arrighi, Giovanni: *The Long Twentieth Century*, 125
Asian American identity, 264–66
Asian American movement, 250, 347–48n26
Austen, Jane, 14, 83
Auster, Paul, 146, 175; *City of Glass*, 149, 333n32
authenticity, 1–2, 14–16, 25, 26, 28, 37, 65, 75, 80, 139, 172, 201, 279, 282–86
autofiction, 293
avant-garde, 69–70

Babel, Isaac, 220, 341n31
Bakhtin, Mikhail, 18, 174
Ballard, J. G., 146, 149; *Concrete Island*, 147; *Crash*, 147

Balzac, Honoré de, 138
Banet-Weiser, Sarah, 160–61, 164–65, 328n67
Bangorian Controversy, 136
Barbrook, Richard, 88, 252
Barthelme, Donald, 221; "The School," 221
Barthes, Roland, 18
Barth, John, 45, 146, 149, 150; "Lost in the Funhouse," 45, 150; *Lost in the Funhouse*, 139
Baskin, Jon, 79–81, 313–14n62, 352n9
Baudrillard, Jean, 149, 156
Beach Boys, 268, 277
Becker, Gary, 26, 29, 191–92, 229, 307n122; *The Economics of Discrimination*, 336n80, 337n81
Beckett, Samuel, 150
Believer, The (magazine), 93
Benjamin, Walter: "The Author as Producer," 162
Bentham, Jeremy, 213
Berger, John: *Ways of Seeing*, 154
Berkeley, George, 308n2
Berlant, Lauren, 215
Berlin, Isaiah, 58; "Two Concepts of Liberty," 54–55
Berlin Wall: fall of, 5, 43, 247
Bernes, Jasper, 234, 236
Bernini, Gianlorenzo, 71–77, 315n83; *David*, 72; *The Ecstasy of St. Teresa*, 71–77
Bernstein, Peter: *Against the Gods: The Remarkable Story of Risk*, 241
Bildungsroman, 39, 62, 129, 133, 163–64, 172, 203–4, 206–7, 280, 285, 292, 294
Black Arts Movement, 331n14
Black Lives Matter, 196, 202, 295
blackness, 168, 170, 172, 201, 205, 331n14
Black Power, 169, 172, 250
Boddy, Kasia, 242–43, 245, 308n6, 341n29
Bolaño, Roberto, 281
Boltanski, Luc, 252–54, 305–6n107

boomer generation, 250
Borges, Jorge Luis, 146
Boswell, Marshall, 68, 314n65
Bourdieu, Pierre, 35, 70, 255, 307n122, 307n124
branding, 20, 36, 40, 159–60, 163, 195, 201, 203, 206, 329n75, 338n114
Brandt, Deborah: *The Rise of Writing*, 10–11, 300n30
Brautigan, Richard, 131
Brenner, Robert, 97
Bretton Woods Accord, 96–97
Brief Interviews with Hideous Men (Wallace), 33, 244, 325n31
Bright Eyes, 249
Brooks, Peter, 269, 348n37
Brooks, Ryan M.: *Liberalism and American Literature in the Clinton Era*, 31–32
Broom of the System, The (Wallace), 18, 44, 52, 308n7
Brouillette, Sarah, 121, 317n15, 322n79
Brown, Wendy, 216, 218, 232, 305n103
Buchanan, James, 26
Burroughs, William S., 146, 149, 150
Bush, George W., 337n90
Byron, Lord, 18, 23, 79

"Californian Ideology, The" (Barbrook and Cameron), 88, 252
Calvino, Italo, 146
Cameron, Andy, 88, 252
Camus, Albert, 59
Capital (Marx), 125
capitalism, 5, 10, 26, 36, 40, 41, 44, 45–46, 50, 70, 82, 89–91, 97–99, 108–9, 118, 126, 136, 161, 178, 181, 188, 195, 211, 215, 219, 221, 233, 235, 238–43, 247–48, 253, 255, 264–65, 268, 280, 282, 286, 292, 305–6n107, 313n52, 320n61, 322n86, 351n74; black, 176–77, 183; entrepreneur in, 229–32, 342n43; and

feudalism, 31, 49, 56; fragility of, 294; and gift economy, 32–34; liberal, 28, 30–31, 43, 90, 96, 139; neoliberal, 34, 39, 119, 151, 183, 216, 243, 253, 308n5, 336n80; platform, 164; racial, 40, 170, 173, 179, 182, 265; speed of, 112–17. *See also* debt, capitalist realism, fictitious capital, financialization, human capital, neoliberalism

capitalist realism, 5, 41, 194, 235, 242, 247, 282, 298n14

Caravaggio, 315n83

Carnegie, Dale, 23–24; *How to Win Friends and Influence People*, 23–25

Carter, Angela, 146

Carter, Jimmy, 256

Carver, Raymond, 211, 221–23, 288, 341n31, 341n33

Catcher in the Rye (Salinger), 15

Cavell, Stanley, 70, 87; *The World Viewed*, 315n86, 315n88

Cavender, Kurt, 276

Chandler, Raymond, 175

Chardin, Jean Siméon, 64

Chiapello, Ève, 252–54, 305–6n107

Chicago School, 191, 217, 229

Chodat, Robert, 311n32, 312n35

Choi, Susan, 5; *American Woman*, 41–42, 250, 256–67, 268, 271, 276–78, 282, 289, 294, 347n19–348n32; *Trust Exercise*, 6, 348n32

Christianity, 108–110, 312n45, 320n61, 323n88. *See also* religion

Chu, Patricia, 264–65

Civil Liberties Act, 265

Civil Rights, 169, 173, 193–94, 196, 202, 250–51

CivilWarLand in Bad Decline (Saunders), 222–23, 226

class consciousness, 41, 172, 187, 205, 207, 214–19, 225, 244, 245, 305n102, 340n23. *See also*

de-proletarianization, professional-managerial class, underclass, working class

Clements, James, 121–22, 321n77, 322n79

Clinton, Bill 336n71

Coetzee, J. M., 299n22

Cohn, Jesse, 198

Cold War, 117; end of, 5, 43

Collins, Jim, 23

Coleman, Philip, 308n2

colonialism, 97, 185–87, 191, 287, 297, 334n44, 334n45. *See also* imperialism, settler colonialism

Confessions (Rousseau), 16–17, 320n53

Constant, Benjamin, 55

Coover, Robert, 175, 250

Correggio, Antonio de, 313n48

counterculture, 132, 250, 252, 271, 275

Courbet, Gustave, 64

creative writing program, 5, 45–46, 219, 308n6, 327n48

Crosthwaite, Paul, 93–95, 124, 323n90

culture wars, 5

cummings, e e, 150, 226

Currie, Mark, 269, 348–49n38

Daalder, Jurrit, 244–45

Dames, Nicholas: "Theory Generation," 298n9

David, Jacques-Louis, 64

Davidson, Donald, 349n40

Davies, William, 298n14

Davis, Lennard J.: *Factual Fictions*, 136–37, 161

debt, 34, 39, 48, 90, 95–102, 104–110, 118, 120–27. *See also* capitalism, fictitious capital, financialization

deconstruction, 16–18

Defoe, Daniel, 135–37, 151; *Robinson Crusoe*, 39, 135–37; *The Sincerity of the Dissenters Vindicated*, 136

DeLillo, Don, 145–46, 149, 150, 156, 175, 250, 283; *Libra*, 269; *Underworld*, 156; *White Noise*, 149, 333n32
Deleuze, Gilles, 305n105
de Man, Paul, 16–18, 320n53
Democratic Socialists of America, 291
den Dulk, Allard, 22, 61, 322–23n87
de-proletarianization, 29, 305n102, 322n86. *See also* class consciousness
Derrida, Jacques, 16–18, 34, 320n53, 348–49n38; *Of Grammatology*, 16; "Structure, Sign and Play in the Discourse of the Human Sciences," 16
Descartes, René, 80
DeWitt, Helen, 4, 200, 211, 238–42, 255, 318n16, 335n58, 344n79; *The Last Samurai*, 237; *Lightning Rods*, 33, 41, 208–9, 211, 229–238, 240, 245, 342n51–343n72, 344n79; *Some Trick*, 238, 240–41
Dickens, Charles, 138, 140, 142
Didion, Joan, 250
Diderot, Denis, 64–65, 75
dissemblance, 179–80
Doctorow, E. L., 250; *The Book of Daniel*, 348n31
Donofrio, Nicholas, 176–77, 334n43
Dornbusch, Rudi, 91; Dornbusch's law, 317n11
Dostoevsky, Fyodor, 8, 138, 299n25
dot-com bubble, 91
double consciousness, 40, 167–70, 172, 175, 179, 186–87, 200, 204–6, 244
Douglass, Frederick, 188, 332–33n30
Dreams from My Father (Obama), 199–201, 203–4
Dred Scott v. Sanford, 178
Du Bois, W. E. B., 40, 167–171, 175, 179, 186, 187, 189, 205; "Of Our Spiritual Strivings," 168–69; *The Souls of Black Folk*, 169, 172

Duffy, Brooke Erin, 162
Dyer, Geoff, 306n111
Dylan, Bob, 267
Dylan, Natalie, 328n67

Eagleton, Terry, 221, 243
Eat the Document (Spiotta), 42, 250–52, 266, 267–78, 282, 348n33–350n56
Eco, Umberto, 146
Egan, Jennifer, 20, 39–40, 130, 132, 134–35, 145–46, 162–64, 171–72, 179, 203–4, 206, 224, 262, 324n7, 325n31, 326n38, 326n39, 329n70; *The Candy House*, 6; *The Invisible Circus*, 39, 128–34, 155, 163–64, 251, 348–49n38, 352n6; *The Keep*, 9, 134–35, 146, 163, 329n74; *Look at Me*, 9–10, 33, 37, 39, 133–35, 139–66, 180, 244, 246, 255, 294, 324n7, 325n27–330n78; *Manhattan Beach*, 164, 324n7; *A Visit from the Goon Squad*, 145, 163–64, 324n7, 325n31, 329n75
Eggers, Dave, 3, 10, 20, 38–39, 92–96, 98, 121–27, 134, 162, 171–72, 179, 203, 206, 224, 244, 248, 249, 262, 317n15; *The Circle*, 316n4; *A Heartbreaking Work of Staggering Genius*, 3, 9, 33, 39, 88–96, 102–11, 113, 120–27, 130, 166, 248, 255, 293, 294, 317n15–318n29, 320n53, 320n54, 322n79; *How We Are Hungry*, 3; "Mistakes We Knew We Were Making," 88, 103, 122; *Sacrament*, 120, 122; *What Is the What*, 1–4, 10–11, 297n4, 297n5; *You Shall Know Your Own Velocity*, 3, 37, 39, 92, 95, 102, 111–22, 246, 321n71–322n79
Eliot, George, 138, 140
Eliot, T. S., 8
Elliott, Jane, 218
Ellis, Bret Easton, 146; *American Psycho*, 159

Ellis, Trey, 171, 198; "The New Black Aesthetic," 171, 177, 188
Ellison, Ralph, 332n29; *Invisible Man*, 174, 332n28
Emerson, Ralph Waldo, 168, 243
"End of History, The" (Fukuyama), 5, 37–38, 43–44, 53, 90, 91
End of History, 44–47, 53, 58, 64, 92, 121, 294
Enlightenment, 280
epiphany: as literary trope, 285
Esterhammer, Angela, 18
"E Unibus Pluram" (Wallace), 19, 23, 36, 67, 130, 198, 274–76, 280, 324n3, 325n31
Esu-Elegbara, 198
Eugenides, Jeffrey, 204; *Middlesex*, 251
Eve, Martin Paul, 299n22

"Falls, The" (Saunders), 41, 219, 223–29, 245
Fanon, Frantz, 194
fascism, 38, 56–58, 81, 86, 308n5
Feher, Michael, 28–32, 216, 253, 305n105, 305–6n107, 306n108
feminism, 31, 39, 42, 134, 153–54, 161, 164, 248, 250, 263–66, 268, 295, 347n22. *See also* postfeminism
Ferris, Joshua: *Then We Came to the End*, 11–13
Feuerbach, Ludwig, 131
fictionality, 86, 136–39, 149–50
fictitious capital, 97–98, 110, 117
Fielding, Henry, 151; *Joseph Andrews*, 137
financialization, 93–102, 109–10, 112, 117–18, 122, 125–26, 307n122, 319n37–319n49. *See also* capitalism, debt, neoliberalism
Fisher, Mark, 298n14
Fitzgerald, Jonathan D., 22
Flaubert, Gustave, 138, 141
Floyd, George, 295
Flusfeder, David, 233, 343n69

For Common Things: Irony, Trust, and Commitment in America Today (Purdy), 247–50, 253–54, 293
Fortress of Solitude, The (Lethem), 251–52
Foucault, Michel, 16, 28–31, 100, 158, 160, 213, 217, 229, 305n105; *The Birth of Biopolitics*, 28, 335n67
Fox, Pamela, 342n42
Frankfurt School, 98, 314n75
Frank, Thomas, 317n9; *The Conquest of Cool*, 252
Franzen, Jonathan, 203–4, 299–300n27
Fraser, Nancy, 253
freedom, 27, 37, 38, 40, 47, 54–58, 63, 82, 173, 188, 192–96, 199, 202, 252–53
Freud, Sigmund, 30, 124
Friedman, Milton, 26, 229
Fried, Michael, 64–66, 69–71, 74, 76, 77, 80, 313n52, 315n83, 315n86, 316n109; *Absorption and Theatricality*, 64; "Art and Objecthood," 66
Fugitive Slave Law, 178
Fukuyama, Francis, 5, 43–45, 47, 49, 52–53, 241; 43–45, 309n10; "The End of History," 5, 37–38, 43–44, 53, 90, 91
Futurism, 116

Gabor, Dennis, 59
Gadamer, Hans-Georg, 18
Gaddis, William, 26; *The Recognitions*, 13–15, 23–25
Gaines, Ernest J., 250
Gaines, Kevin K., 179–80
Gallagher, Catherine, 137–38; *Nobody's Story*, 326n35; "The Rise of Fictionality," 137–38
Gates, Henry Louis Jr., 174–76, 181, 186–87, 198, 202, 205, 330n8, 333n38; *The Signifying Monkey*, 186
Gay Liberation, 250
Geist (spirit), 63, 311n30

genre fiction / genre turn, 6, 8–9, 68, 86, 134, 141–43, 149, 162–64, 298n16, 329n74. *See also* modern novel, realism
Géricault, Théodore, 64
German Idealism, 50, 65
Gessen, Keith: "Endnotes," 293
ghostwriting, 3, 10–11, 20, 84, 140, 143, 147, 149, 163, 321n74
Gide, André, 8
Giersch, Herbert, 233
gift, 32–35, 121–22
Gift, The (Hyde), 32–33, 306n111, 306n117
Gildon, Charles, 137; *An Epistle to Daniel Defoe*, 136
Gill, Rosalind, 160–61, 164, 329n68
Gilroy, Paul, 194
Girl with Curious Hair (Wallace), 5, 44
Gitlin, Todd, 324n3; *The Whole World Is Watching*, 132
Gladstone, Jason, 19
Goffman, Erving, 15, 26; *The Presentation of Self in Everyday Life*, 25
gothic literature, 132, 134, 144, 146, 150–55, 326n29, 327n50
Goux, Jean-Joseph, 101
Graeber, David: *Debt: The First 5,000 Years*, 101–2, 118
Gravity's Rainbow (Pynchon), 39, 139, 269
Great Society, 96
Greenberg, Clement, 74, 316n109; "Avant-Garde and Kitsch," 69–70
Green, Henry, 220
Green New Deal, 295
Greif, Mark, 317n15
Greuze, Jean-Baptiste, 64
Groenland, Tim, 341n33
Grundrisse (Marx), 116–17
Guattari, Félix, 305n105
Guilhamet, Leon, 15

Habermas, Jürgen, 16
Hägglund, Martin, 34
Hamilton, Caroline, 92
Hamlet (Shakespeare), 13, 60, 80
Hammer and Hope (magazine), 292
Hammett, Dashiel, 175
Hartley, Daniel, 243–44
Harvey, David, 97–98, 100, 118, 254; *A Brief History of Neoliberalism*, 253; *The Limits to Capital*, 97–98, *The New Imperialism*, 323n93
Hatred of Poetry, The (Lerner), 294–95
Haugeland, John, 311n32
Hawkes, John, 159
Hayek, Friedrich von, 26–28, 229, 250–51, 307n122; *The Road to Serfdom*, 27
Hayes-Brady, Clare, 314n63, 339n10
Hayles, N. Katherine, 53
Heartbreaking Work of Staggering Genius, A (Eggers), 3, 9, 33, 39, 88–96, 102–11, 113, 120–27, 130, 166, 248, 255, 293, 294, 317n15–318n29, 320n53, 322n79
Hearst, Patty, 131, 256, 347n19, 347n22
Hearst, William Randolph, 256
Hegel, G. W. F., 7, 14, 43–44, 49–50, 52, 54, 55, 59–61, 62–63, 65, 68, 70, 74, 75, 77, 95, 168, 206, 308n4, 308n7, 309n10, 309n14, 310n25, 311n32, 312n45; 313n48; *Aesthetics: Lectures on Fine Art*, 63, 65, 70, 312n45, 313n48; *The Phenomenology of Spirit*, 48–49, 308n7, 308–9n8, 320n56
Hegelian, 7, 38, 42, 49–50, 52, 56, 58, 62, 68, 95, 206, 244, 279, 311n30, 311n32, 349n42
Heidegger, Martin, 18; *Being and Time*, 279
Hemingway, Ernest, 220–22, 341n31
Hering, David, 51, 68, 76–77, 314n65
Heston, Charlton, 85
Heti, Sheila, 6

Hine, Darlene Clark: dissemblance, 179
Hoadly, Benjamin (Bishop of Bangor), 136
Hobbes, Thomas, 59
Hoberek, Andrew, 7, 9, 299n26
Holland, Mary K., 79
How to Win Friends and Influence People (Carnegie), 23–25
Huehls, Mitchum, 254
human capital, 28–32, 35, 40, 41, 62, 81–82, 160, 173, 182, 187, 191–92, 204, 207, 216, 218, 229, 255, 305n104, 307n122, 336n78. *See also* capitalism, capitalist realism, neoliberalism
Hund, Emily, 162
Hurston, Zora Neale, 199; *Their Eyes Were Watching God*, 40, 184–88
Husserl, Edmund, 18
Hutcheon, Linda, 35–36
Hyde, Lewis, 34; *The Gift*, 32–33, 306n111, 306n117

identity politics, 6, 41, 170, 190, 205, 253–54, 265
imperialism, 97, 112, 118–19, 125, 250, 265, 282, 285–86, 289. *See also* colonialism, settler colonialism
Indecision (Kunkel), 37, 42, 246, 250, 278–90, 291–92, 304n84, 350n58–352n86
Infinite Jest (Wallace), 9–10, 38, 52–87, 166, 244, 246, 294, 308n5, 309n20–312n35, 313n58–316n106
International Monetary Fund (IMF), 99
Intuitionist, The (Whitehead), 9, 40, 171, 173, 174–84, 194–95, 199, 204, 206, 332n23–335n62
Invisible Circus, The (Egan), 39, 128–34, 155, 163–64, 251, 348–49n38, 352n6
Invisible Man (Ellison), 174, 332n28
irony, 19–20, 22–23, 67, 88–89, 91, 130–31, 141, 164, 173, 181–82, 184, 188, 197–99, 299n22, 313–14n62, 325n31, 332n22; narrative irony, 180–81, 187, 240; postirony, 20, 36, 93–94, 203–4, 206, 329n75; postmodern irony, 5, 19, 22, 171, 248, 274–76; and sincerity, 19, 22, 40, 61, 89, 92, 103, 127, 139, 164, 166, 170, 173, 174, 204–5, 248, 278, 280–81, 287, 293, 322–23n87; unironic, 73, 78, 127, 130, 133, 165, 245, 315n87. *See also* sincerity, New Sincerity

Jacobin (magazine), 291–92
James, David, 299n22
Jameson, A. D., 22
Jameson, Fredric, 61, 101, 106, 132, 149, 156, 283, 290, 301n44, 342n40, 351n76
James, William, 168
Jane Eyre (Brontë), 11–12, 139
Jim Crow, 170
Jobs, Steve, 129–30
John Henry Days (Whitehead), 171, 183, 195
Johnson, Cedric G., 170
Johnson, Charles, 170
Johnson, Denis, 288
Johnson, James Weldon: *Autobiography of an Ex-Colored Man*, 175
Johnny Tremain (Forbes), 220
Joseph Andrews (Fielding), 137
Joyce, James, 8, 83
Judd, Donald, 66

Kant, Immanuel, 50, 65, 310n25; *Critique of Judgment*, 50
Katz, Deborah Koto, 258
Kaufman, Charlie, 249
Kavka, Gregory S., 349n40
Keep, The (Egan), 9, 134–35, 146, 163, 329n74
Kelly, Kevin, 90–91, 99–100; *New Rules for the New Economy*, 90
Kennedy, John F., 195

Kenner, Hugh, 83
"Kenyon Commencement Address" (Wallace), 55–56. See also *This is Water* (Wallace)
Kerouac, Jack: *On the Road*, 15, 104, 320n54
Keynes, John Maynard, 96
Kierkegaard, Soren, 59, 322n87
King, Martin Luther Jr., 194, 199
King, Richard H., 193–94
Klein, Naomi: *No Logo*, 328n63
Knievel, Evel, 303n75
Konstantinou, Lee, 20, 31–34, 69, 92–95, 121, 201, 203–4, 206, 237, 306n117, 329n75
Krippner, Greta, 319n37
Kunkel, Benjamin, 4–5, 281–83, 290, 291–92, 350n69, 351n73, 351n74; *Indecision*, 37, 42, 246, 250, 278–92, 304n84; *Utopia or Bust: A Guide to the Present Crisis*, 291, 351n76

Lacan, Jacques, 18; mirror stage, 157–58
Lasky, Dorothea, 249
Lazzarato, Mauricio, 100–1, 106, 108–9, 322n86
Larsen, Nella: *Passing*, 175
Leise, Christopher, 195
Lerner, Ben, 6; *10.04*, 293–95; *The Hatred of Poetry*, 294–95
Lethem, Jonathan, 204, 306n111; *The Fortress of Solitude*, 251–52
Leutze, Emanuel Gottlieb, 308n2
Lewis, Michael: *Moneyball*, 240
liberalism, 7, 13–18, 26, 28–30, 35, 41, 43–44, 55, 58, 80, 82, 90, 95, 139, 189, 194, 216–17, 243–44, 255, 292, 301n48, 342n42. See also neoliberalism
Lightning Rods (DeWitt), 33, 41, 208–9, 211, 229–238, 240, 245, 342n51–343n72, 344n79
Lin, Tao, 249

Li, Stephanie, 198, 203, 336n74
Locke, John, 55
Look at Me (Egan), 9–10, 33, 37, 39, 133–35, 139–66, 180, 244, 246, 255, 294, 324n7, 325n27–330n78
Lord, Jack, 47–49
Lorey, Isabel, 215
"Lost in the Funhouse" (Barth), 45, 150
Lost in the Funhouse (Barth), 139
Louis, Morris, 66
Loury, Glenn, 336n78
Lowell, Robert, 125
Luce, Henry R., 323n93
Lukács, Georg: *Theory of the Novel*, 62
Luttwak, Edward N., 310n26
Lye, Colleen, 347–48n26
Lynd, Helen Merrell, 210, 229, 342n42

MacKenzie, Donald, 320n62
Macpherson, C. B., 216
Manet, Édouard, 64–66
Manhattan Beach (Egan), 164, 324n7
"Manifesto for the New Sincerity, A" (Thorn), 21
Manshel, Alexander, 333n32
Marx, Karl, 30–31, 43, 55, 90, 95, 97, 100, 117, 218, 230, 342n43; *Capital*, 125; *Economic and Philosophical Manuscripts of 1844*, 119; *Grundrisse*, 116–17
Marxism, 32, 35, 42, 70, 194, 215, 217, 243, 255, 291, 305n104, 311n30, 340n21; crisis theory, 97–99, 116–17, 125, 318–19n34
*M*A*S*H* (television series), 311–12n34
Matlock (television series), 149, 163
McCaffery, Larry, 19
McCann, Sean, 253–54
McCarthy, Tom, 299n22
McClanahan, Annie, 99, 102, 110, 118, 125; *Dead Pledges*, 95
McEwan, Ian, 299n22; *Saturday*, 285

McGurl, Mark, 6, 221–22, 308n6, 327n48, 335n58, 339n3, 340n23, 342n42; *The Program Era,* 210
McHale, Brian, 36, 135
McInerney, Jay, 280
McKeon, Michael, 135
#MeToo movement, 295
Menzel, Adolph, 76
metamodernism, 299n22
Michaels, Walter Benn, 170, 205, 253–54, 331–32n20, 337n81
Michelangelo, 71
Miller, Arthur: *Death of a Salesman,* 235–36
Mill, John Stuart, 55
Mills, C. Wright, 15, 24–26; *The Power Elite,* 24–25
minimalism, 5, 46, 66, 210–11, 220–23
Mirowski, Philip, 340n21
Mises, Ludwig von, 233
"Mistakes We Knew We Were Making" (Eggers) 88, 103, 122
Modern Family (television series), 249
modernism, 8–9, 13, 15, 36, 37, 46, 64, 66, 70, 74, 86–87, 112, 116, 139, 195, 225–26, 285, 308n6, 316n109, 335n58, 341n28, 342n40
modernity, 40, 50, 116, 173, 177l, 253, 280, 292, 305n107
modern novel, 7–13, 39–40, 62, 69, 77, 83–87, 134–39, 161, 282; realist novel, 138–45, 164. *See also* genre fiction / genre turn, realism
Moers, Ellen, 151, 327n50
Molière, 14
Moretti, Franco, 280, 292
Morris, Pam, 138
Morris, Robert, 66
Morrison, Toni, 174, 199–200, 202–3, 250, 338n101; *Beloved,* 174; *The Bluest Eye,* 174; *Jazz,* 174; *Playing in the Dark,* 333n32; *Song of Solomon,* 200

Moshfegh, Ottessa, 6
Moviegoer, The (Percy), 15
Mulhern, Francis, 292, 352n6
Mumbo Jumbo (Reed), 175–77, 333n38
Murray, Rolland, 171–72, 198

Nabokov, Vladimir, 146
Nathan for You (reality television show), 249
neoliberalism, 28–31, 41, 81–82, 238, 304–5n95; age of, 4, 10, 34–39, 112, 125, 249; and class, 171–73, 183, 192, 201–2, 205, 207, 211, 214–19, 222–23, 237, 322n86, 340n21; combative, 198n14; problem of critique, 35–36, 252–55, 282, 305n106, 305–6n107, 351n76; culture/ideology of, 10–11, 20, 36, 40, 47–52, 126, 133, 163–64, 196, 211, 232, 235, 251, 299n22, 305n103, 307n22, 323n90, 335n67, 336n80; economy of, 35, 39, 92–102, 110, 117, 122–27, 151, 170, 214–15; and entrepreneur (of the self), 19, 31, 41, 100, 110, 124, 126, 182, 192, 209, 219, 229–38; and fascism, 31, 56–57, 81, 308n5; and gender, 154, 160–61, 166, 236; neoliberals, 26–27, 30, 176, 217, 229, 233, 250, 323n90; neoliberal sincerity, 7, 11, 27, 41, 211, 237, 250–51; and subjectivity, 33, 35, 41, 61–62, 69, 100, 127, 160, 162, 187, 205–6, 209, 211, 216–19, 240; neoliberal turn, 15, 28, 32, 44, 129, 177, 266; New Sincerity, complicity with, 33–36, 92, 163, 240–46, 254–55; normative neoliberalism, 5–7, 9, 31, 37, 42, 84, 86, 248, 253, 255, 278, 298n14, 307n124; ontological, 254; and race, 171–73, 181–83, 188–92, 199–207, 331n15; punitive, 298n14; as term, 252. *See also* debt, capitalism, capitalist realism, End of History, financialization, human capital, liberalism, New Economy

"New Black Aesthetic, The" (Ellis), 171, 177, 188
New Deal, 26
New Economy, 38–39, 90–92, 95, 99–100, 102, 129, 317n9, 322n86
New Left, 28, 30, 41, 132, 250, 253, 268, 275, 291, 348n31
New Left Review (magazine), 291
New Right, 28, 253, 305n99
New Sincerity, 4–13, 17–23, 31–42, 50–52, 94–96, 102, 121, 126–27, 130, 133–35, 161–64, 172, 179, 206–7, 211, 224–25, 244–46, 247–49, 262–63, 276, 293–95, 306n117, 307n123, 342n40; as aesthetic, 7–8, 21, 23, 38, 44, 86, 92, 127, 145, 244, 249, 255, 293–94; branding and, 40, 162–63, 206; class and, 40–42, 170–71, 207, 225, 244–45; complicity and, 7, 9, 35–37, 40–41, 211, 242, 255, 295; dialectic of, 18, 32, 34–37, 95, 127, 294, 304n84; ethos of, 6, 23, 36–37, 126; formal characteristics of, 6–13, 21–23, 33–34, 52, 133, 139, 163–64, 299–300n27; gender and, 39–40, 42, 161, 164, 315n94; and hermeneutics of suspicion, 289, 304n84; other uses of, 21–23, 92–93, 247–49, 275, 293, 299n22, 303n75, 345n2; and politics, 37–38, 41–42, 246, 249, 255, 263, 270; and postirony, 20, 206, 329n75; and postmodernism, 5–6, 8, 19, 22, 36; race and, 40, 42, 170–71; as sensibility, 6, 21; as structure of feeling, 21, 293; as term, 36, 293; writer-reader relationship in, 8, 11–13, 17, 34–35, 37–39, 51–52, 80, 85–87, 124, 162, 166, 206, 262, 277–78, 294, 330–31n13. See also irony, second-person narration/address, sincerity
Ngai, Sianne, 231–233, 235

Nietzsche, Friedrich, 100–1, 108, 320n56, 323n88; *On the Genealogy of Morality*, 100
Nixon, Richard M., 96–97, 177; Nixon shock, 97, 99, 118
9/11 attacks, 21, 92, 195, 326n39
n+1 (magazine), 247, 291–93, 307n124, 351n74
Noland, Kenneth, 66
Novak, Maximillian, 135–36

Oates, Joyce Carol, 250, 280–81
Obama, Barack, 40, 173, 199–204, 338n101, 338n109, 338n114; *Dreams from My Father*, 199–201, 203–4
Oblivion (Wallace), 245–46
Occupy movement, 274, 292
"Octet" (Wallace), 37, 77
O'Dell, Jacqueline, 122
Office, The (television series), 249
Olitski, Jules, 66
On the Genealogy of Morality (Nietzsche), 100
On the Road (Kerouac), 15, 104, 320n54
Operation Enduring Freedom, 337n90
Ordoliberalism, 217, 305n102, 322n86
Ozick, Cynthia, 299n22

Pains of Being Pure at Heart, The, 249
Pale King, The (Wallace), 52, 251
Palmer, Ruth Barton, 22
"Pastoralia" (Saunders), 211–19, 221, 339n10, 340n23
Pastoralia (Saunders), 41, 211, 218, 223, 228
Patten, Allan, 310n25
Paulson, William, 86
Phenomenology of Spirit, The (Hegel), 48–49, 308n7, 308–9n8, 320n56
Piercy, Marge, 250
Pippin, Robert B., 7, 49–50, 61–62, 68, 76, 77, 309n11, 309n16, 313n52, 349n42

Point, The (magazine), 352n9
post-boomer generation, 4–5, 7, 11, 20, 23, 31–33, 129, 131, 203, 250–52, 298n9, 305n104, 307n124, 323–24n2
postfeminism, 151, 160–61, 164, 329n68. *See also* feminism
postmodernism, 22, 66–68, 70, 80, 87, 101, 106, 132–33, 140, 145–51, 155–59, 163, 198, 219, 253, 274–77, 279, 283, 290, 292, 352n6; new postmodernist studies, 326n38; postmodern irony, 5, 19, 22; postmodernist fiction, 5–6, 8, 36–37, 39, 44, 46, 64, 135, 139–40, 146, 159, 174–76, 221, 269, 328n64, 333n32
Postone, Moishe, 235
poststructuralism, 16, 19, 23, 34, 79–80
Poulet, Georges, 18
Pound, Ezra, 150
Power Elite, The (Mills), 24
Powers, Richard: *The Echo Maker*, 285
precariousness/precarity, 12, 41, 209, 213, 215–16, 219, 223, 229, 292, 322n86
Presentation of Self in Everyday Life, The (Goffman), 25
proceduralism, 15–16
professional-managerial class, 35, 40, 170, 187–88, 199, 205, 207, 255, 340n21. *See also* class consciousness, underclass, working class
Program Era, The (McGurl), 210
Prout, Matt, 299n25, 314n71
Purdy, Jedediah, 41, 255; "The Accidental Neoliberal," 247–49, 253–54, 264, 274, 282, 291–93, 295, 348n30; *For Common Things: Irony, Trust, and Commitment in America Today*, 247–48, 250, 253–54, 293
Pynchon, Thomas, 145–46, 149, 175, 250; *The Crying of Lot 49*, 328n64, 333n32; *Gravity's Rainbow*, 139, 269

racial uplift, 40, 173, 175, 179–80, 182, 190, 205, 335n58
racism, 178–80, 192, 201, 338–39n114
Radcliffe, Ann, 151
RAND Corporation, 43
Rando, David P., 218–19
Rawls, John, 16
Reagan, Ronald, 5, 90, 95, 168, 195
realism, 9, 11, 39, 46, 66, 76, 94, 95, 106–9, 130, 133–46, 149, 151, 164, 262, 288. *See also* modern novel
Real World, The (television program), 105–7, 126
Recognitions, The (Gaddis), 13–15, 23–25
Reconstruction, 169, 179, 195, 205
Reed, Adolph Jr., 169–72, 201, 204–5, 254, 330n8
Reed, Ishmael, 146, 174–77, 183, 250; *Mumbo Jumbo*, 174–77, 333n32, 333n38
Reed, Touré, 201, 336n71
Reeve, Clara, 151
religion, 81, 85–86, 108–10, 120, 124, 136, 138, 156, 193–94, 320n61, 321n77. *See also* Christianity
Revolutionary Road (Yates), 15
Reynolds, Sir Joshua, 71
Richardson, Samuel, 151
Riesman, David, 15, 26; *The Lonely Crowd*, 25–26
Ringley, Jennifer, 328n67
"Rise of Fictionality, The" (Gallagher), 137–38
Rise of Writing, The (Brandt), 10, 300n30
Road to Serfdom, The (Hayek), 27
Robeson, Paul, 195
Robinson, Anthony, 21
Robinson, Cedric J., 334n44
Robinson Crusoe (Defoe), 39, 135–37
romance, 136, 143, 151
Romanticism, 18, 65, 70, 75–76, 150, 281–82, 312n45

Röpke, Wilhelm: de-proletarianization, idea of, 305n102
Ross, Martin, 146
Roth, Marco, 352n6
Roth, Philip, 250
Rousseau, Jean-Jacques, 14, 16–17, 55, 59, 65, 75, 301n51, 320n53; *Confessions*, 16–17, 320n53
Russell, Alison, 181
Rutten, Ellen: *Sincerity after Communism*, 21–23

Sacrament (Eggers), 120, 122. See also *You Shall Know Our Velocity* (Eggers)
Sag Harbor (Whitehead), 40, 167–73, 180, 204, 330n13–332n22
Sanders, Bernie, 295
Sartre, Jean-Paul, 14
Saunders, George, 10, 37, 41, 200, 211, 219–23, 229, 242–46, 255, 335n58, 341n28, 341n31; "The Braindead Megaphone," 219–220, 242–43; *CivilWarLand in Bad Decline*, 222–23, 226; "Escape from Spiderhead," 246; "The Falls," 41, 219, 223–29, 245; "Pastoralia," 211–19, 221, 339n10, 340n23; *Pastoralia*, 41, 211, 218, 223, 228; "Sea Oak," 218–19; *Tenth of December*, 6; "Thank You, Esther Forbes," 220–21
Sauri, Emilio, 283
Sayers, Philip, 314n79
Scanlan, Margaret, 347n19
Schama, Simon, 71–72, 74
Schelling, Friedrich Wilhelm Joseph, 65
"School, The" (Barthelme), 221
Scream, The (Munch), 342n40
Schultz, Theodore, 29, 191–92, 307n122
Schumpeter, Joseph, 229–30, 233, 237, 342n43
Schwartz, Ana, 307n123
"Sea Oak" (Saunders), 218–19

second-person narration/address, 2–3, 9–12, 17, 35, 51, 85–86, 102–4, 123–24, 126, 166, 255, 277, 289, 330–31n13; "dear reader" trope, 138–39. See also New Sincerity
Seshagiri, Urmila, 299n22
settler colonialism, 264, 276, 307n123, 347n25. See also colonialism, imperialism
Severs, Jeffrey, 51, 82, 308n5, 308n7, 309n15, 312n35
Sexton, Anne, 125
Shakar, Alex, 20
shame, 41, 179, 208–11, 218–19, 225, 227–29, 231, 233–38, 240, 246, 310n22, 342n42, 343n69; and guilt, 210, 218–19
Shapiro, Mary, 68
Shelley, Mary, 151; *Frankenstein*, 153
Siegel, Lee, 297n5
signifying, 40, 171, 174, 176, 179, 181, 187–88, 198, 201, 203, 330n8, 332–33n30, 333n32, 333n38. See also African American literature/art
sincerity, 2–3, 7, 13–28, 36, 42, 60, 65, 67, 78–82, 94–96, 115, 126–27, 130, 133, 142, 144–45, 148, 150, 151, 154–56, 159–61, 164–66, 210, 211, 228, 236–37, 260, 295, 300n42, 307n123, 320n53, 338n109, 339n19; aesthetic/artistic/ authorial sincerity, 7–13, 25–26, 33–34, 38–40, 50–52, 68–71, 77, 84–87, 91, 119–22, 172, 182, 199, 220, 249, 261–63, 266, 295, 297n5; as brand, 20, 162; definition of, 2, 8, 13, 27, 35, 206, 225; exploitation of, 211–19, 337–38n99; and irony, 19, 22, 40, 61, 89, 92, 103, 127, 139, 164, 166, 170, 173, 174, 204–5, 248, 278, 280–81, 287, 293, 322–23n87; neoliberal, 7, 11, 27, 41, 211, 237, 250–51; and the novel, 134–39, 145; of Barack Obama, 199–204; opposing terms, 303–4n80; political sincerity, 41–42,

246–50, 254–59, 270, 272, 278, 282, 286–90, 293, 295; sincerity crisis, 58–62, 135–36; sincerity studies, 18. *See also* authenticity, irony, New Sincerity
Sincerity after Communism (Rutten), 21–23
Sincerity and Authenticity (Trilling), 7, 8, 13–15
slavery, 186, 191–92, 194–96, 334n44
Smith, Adam, 216
Smith, James P., 336n78
Smith, Rachel Greenwald, 254, 317–18n15
Smith, Tony, 66
Smith, Zadie, 11, 33, 38, 200–1, 204, 299n22, 306n111, 313n55, 335n65, 338n109; *The Autograph Man*, 306n117
Smollett, Tobias, 151
Soitos, Stephen, 175
Somerville, Edith, 146
Some Trick (DeWitt), 238, 240–41
Sontag, Susan, 21, 303n75
Sopranos, The (television series), 163
Souls of Black Folk, The (Du Bois), 167–69, 172
Spiotta, Dana, 5, 349n44, 351n73; *Eat the Document*, 42, 250–52, 266, 267–78, 282, 348n33–350n56; *Stone Arabia*, 6, 269–70
Star Trek (television series), 117
Stein, Gertrude, 220
Stella, Frank, 66
Stendhal, 138, 140–41
Sterne, Laurence, 151
Stewart, Garrett, 11–12, 138–39
Stiegler, Bernard, 125
Stiglitz, Joseph E., 91
Stone Arabia (Spiotta), 6, 269–70
Streeck, Wolfgang, 100; *Buying Time*, 98–99

Students for a Democratic Society (SDS), 132
Sullivan, Hannah, 341n28
Sullivan, John Jeremiah, 86
Symbionese Liberation Army (SLA), 131, 256, 259
Szalay, Michael, 162–64, 253–54, 325n31, 329n75

Taylor, Charles, 282
Taylor, Keeanga-Yamahtta, 202
Tea Party protests, 295
Tequila, Tila, 328n67
10.04 (Lerner), 293–95
Teresa of Ávila, 71, 73
theatricality, 64–80, 315n83, 315n88, 317n15. *See also* absorption
Their Eyes Were Watching God (Hurston), 40, 184–88
Then We Came to the End (Ferris), 11–13
Theory, 15–18
Theory of the Novel, The (Lukács), 62
This Is Water (Wallace), 238–39. *See also* "Kenyon Commencement Address"
Thoreau, Henry David, 24
Thorn, Jesse: "A Manifesto for the New Sincerity" 21
Tocqueville, Alexis de, 55
Tolstoy, Leo, 8, 138, 140; *What Is Art?*, 299n25
Touré, 331n19, 331–32n20
Trilling, Lionel, 2, 16, 18, 20, 25–28, 35, 37, 61, 80, 138–39, 144, 225, 279, 282, 301n44, 301n48, 338n109; *The Liberal Imagination*, 15; *Sincerity and Authenticity*, 7, 8, 13–15
Trust Exercise (Choi), 6, 348n32
Truth and Truthfulness (Williams), 18, 302n58
Turgenev, Ivan, 138
Twain, Mark, 299n26
Twitchell, Elizabeth, 3–4, 10

"Two Concepts of Liberty" (Berlin), 54–55

underclass, 168, 189, 205, 336n71. *See also* working class
Underground Railroad, The (Whitehead), 331n19
Unsolved Mysteries (television series), 163
Utopia or Bust: A Guide to the Present Crisis (Kunkel), 291, 351n76

Van den Akker, Robin, 299n22
Vermeulen, Pieter, 276
Vermeulen, Timotheus, 299n22
Verso: Jacobin series, 291; New Left Books, 291
Vietnam War, 96, 250, 256, 265, 267, 269
Village Voice (newspaper), 183–84, 201
Visible Woman, The (Treichler, Cartwright, and Penley), 153–54
visibility, 154, 165; and gender, 39, 150–54, 161, 164–65; of labor, 189; of debt, 95; and race, 192, 258, 264–65
Visit from the Goon Squad, A (Egan), 145, 163–64, 324n7, 325n31, 329n75
Volcker, Paul, 99, 319n37; Volcker shock, 99, 118
Vonnegut, Kurt, 121

Walker, Alice: *The Color Purple*, 174
Wallace, David Foster, 5–6, 8, 18–23, 33, 38–39, 41, 44, 52, 57–59, 61, 65–67, 69, 71, 74–78, 80–84, 86–87, 92, 95, 134, 162, 171–72, 179, 203, 206, 211, 224, 238–42, 244, 249, 262, 282, 299n22, 299n25, 306n111, 308n2–308n7, 310n26, 310n28, 311n30, 311n32, 312n35, 313n55, 313–14n62, 314n79, 315n86, 315n94, 349n44, 349n45, 351n73; *Brief Interviews with Hideous Men*, 33, 244, 325n31; *The Broom of the System*, 18, 44, 52, 308n7; "Kenyon Commencement Address," 55–56; "E Unibus Pluram," 19, 23, 36, 67, 130, 198, 274–76, 280, 324n3, 325n31; *Girl with Curious Hair*, 5, 44; "Good Old Neon," 77; *Infinite Jest*, 9–10, 38, 52–64, 67–87, 166, 244, 246, 294, 308n5, 309n20–312n35, 313n58–316n106; *Oblivion*, 245–46; "Octet," 37, 77; *The Pale King*, 52, 251; *This Is Water*, 238–39; *Westward the Course of Empire Takes Its Way*, 5, 9, 38, 44–52, 53, 56, 58, 63, 65, 67, 78, 84–85, 141, 150, 166, 241, 244, 255, 308n2–309n19, 325n31
Wallace, Naomi, 243
Walpole, Horace, 151, 327n49
Warren, Andrew, 84
Warren, Kenneth W., 170–71, 205, 331–32n20, 332n22; *What Was African American Literature?*, 170, 189, 331n15
Warwick, Genevieve: *Bernini: Art as Theatre*, 71–72
Washington, Booker T., 169
Washington Consensus, 5, 99, 118
Watt, Ian, 136, 141, 144, 161
Weather Underground, 278
Weber, Max, 62, 320n61
West, Mark, 346n6
Westward the Course of Empires Takes Its Way (Wallace), 5, 9, 38, 44–52, 53, 56, 58, 63, 65, 67, 78, 84–85, 141, 150, 166, 241, 244, 255, 308n2–309n19, 325n31
Wharton, Edith, 141
What Is the What (Eggers), 1–4, 10–11, 297n4, 297n5
What Was African American Literature? (Warren), 170, 189, 331n15
Whitehead, Colson, 40, 169–73, 175, 181–84, 194, 198–207, 224, 244, 255, 333n32, 335n58, 336n74, 338–39n114; *Apex Hides the Hurt*, 10, 33, 37, 40,

171, 173, 184–98, 201, 203, 204, 206–7, 246, 337–38n99; *The Colossus of New York*, 330–31n13; *The Intuitionist*, 9, 40, 171, 173, 174–84, 194–95, 199, 204, 206, 332n23–335n62; *John Henry Days*, 171, 183, 195; *Sag Harbor*, 40, 167–73, 180, 204, 330n13–332n22; *The Underground Railroad*, 331n19

whiteness, 42, 168, 186, 281–82

Whitman, Walt, 125, 293–94, 299n26

Whole World Is Watching, The (Gitlin), 132

Whyte, William, 15

Widiss, Benjamin, 108–9, 120, 124

Williams, Bernard: *Truth and Truthfulness*, 18, 302n58, 303–4n80

Williams, Jeffrey J.: "Generation Jones," 298n9, 323–24n2

Williams, Raymond, 21

Williams, Thomas Chatterton, 331n19

Wilson, William Julius, 189–90; *The Declining Significance of Race*, 189; *The Truly Disadvantaged*, 336n71

Winterson, Jeannette, 146

Winthrop, John, 195; "Little Speech on Liberty," 337n91

Wired (magazine), 88–90, 129

Wittgenstein, Ludwig, 18, 311n32

Wolff, Tobias, 221

Worden, Daniel, 19

Wordsworth, William, 14, 18, 23, 79

working class, 40–42, 98, 180, 183, 188–89, 192, 207, 210–11, 215–19, 222–23, 292, 305n102, 335n60, 340n23, 342n42. *See also* class consciousness, professional-managerial class, underclass

World Bank, 99

World War II, 96, 164

Wright, Richard, 332n29; *Black Boy*, 332n28

Yoruba mythology: Signifying Monkey, 198

Yoshimura, Wendy, 256, 347n19, 347n22

You Shall Know Your Own Velocity (Eggers), 3, 37, 39, 92, 95, 102, 111–22, 246, 321n71–322n79. *See also Sacrament* (Eggers)

Yu, Charles, 6